The Recursive Frontier

SUNY series in Multiethnic Literatures

Mary Jo Bona, editor

The Recursive Frontier

Race, Space, and the
Literary Imagination of Los Angeles

MICHAEL DOCHERTY

Aerial view of the swollen Los Angeles River partly showing Elysian Park and the Bullring railroad, Los Angeles, 1938. Photographer unknown. Public Domain. From the collections of the University of Southern California Libraries and the California Historical Society. Digitally reproduced by the USC Digital Library.

Published by State University of New York Press, Albany

© 2024 State University of New York

All rights reserved

Printed in the United States of America

No part of this book may be used or reproduced in any manner whatsoever without written permission. No part of this book may be stored in a retrieval system or transmitted in any form or by any means including electronic, electrostatic, magnetic tape, mechanical, photocopying, recording, or otherwise without the prior permission in writing of the publisher.

For information, contact State University of New York Press, Albany, NY
www.sunypress.edu

Library of Congress Cataloging-in-Publication Data

Name: Docherty, Michael, 1988– author.
Title: The recursive frontier : race, space, and the literary imagination of Los Angeles / Michael Docherty.
Description: Albany, NY : State University of New York Press, [2024]. | Series: SUNY series in multiethnic literatures | Includes bibliographical references and index
Identifiers: LCCN 2023029849 | ISBN 9781438497112 (hardcover : alk. paper) | ISBN 9781438497136 (ebook) | ISBN 9781438497129 (pbk. : alk. paper)
Subjects: LCSH: American literature—California—Los Angeles—History and criticism. | Los Angeles (Calif.)—In literature. | Borderlands in literature. | Race in literature. | Ethnic groups in literature. | American literature—20th century—History and criticism.
Classification: LCC PS285.L7 D63 2024 | DDC 810.9/979494—dc23/eng/20231016
LC record available at https://lccn.loc.gov/2023029849

10 9 8 7 6 5 4 3 2 1

In loving memory of
Margaret Riches
1949–2023
and
Ina Docherty
1930–2022

Contents

List of Illustrations		ix
Acknowledgments		xi
Introduction: "Metaphor that Becomes Epical"		1
1.	Dancing on the Edge: McCoy, Fante, and Desperate Moves on the Ballroom Frontier	47
2.	Pioneering the Office: White-Collar Rewilding with Chandler and Cain	89
3.	Wilderness Works: Making Race and Class in the Industrial Cities of Fante, Yamamoto, and Himes	133
4.	Ephemeral Accommodations: Hughes, Fenton, and the Architecture of Postwar Masculine Crisis	185
Epilogue: "Steaming Remnants of the Fire"		229
Notes		251
Bibliography		301
Index		325

Illustrations

Figure 1.1	Philip Evergood, *Dance Marathon* (1934).	52
Figure 1.2	Floyd Davis, detail from illustration for "Helen, Thy Beauty Is to Me—" (1941).	65
Figure 1.3	Rudolph Valentino, "How Do You Dance?" (1922).	67
Figure 1.4	Floyd Davis, detail from illustration for "Helen, Thy Beauty Is to Me—" (1941).	69
Figure 2.1	The James Oviatt Building (c. 1930).	123
Figure 3.1	Canneries at San Pedro (1928).	139
Figure 3.2	Oilfields and orange groves north of Huntington Beach (c. 1920).	156
Figure 4.1	La Vista Terrace, Westlake (c. 1925).	192

Acknowledgments

I am extremely grateful to Victoria Fante-Cohen and Jim Fante for their kind permission to quote from unpublished works by their father, John Fante. I am likewise grateful to the Blanton Museum of Art for permission to reproduce Philip Evergood's painting *Dance Marathon*. The research that resulted in this book was supported by a University of Kent Vice Chancellor's Research Scholarship, a British Association for American Studies Postgraduate Travel Award, and a US-UK Fulbright Commission Postgraduate Award. Sections of chapter 2 previously appeared in substantially different form in *Crime Fiction Studies* and the *European Journal of American Culture*.

University presses, especially those affiliated with public institutions, are the lifeblood of scholarship; their future is our future. I am honored that this book has found a home at SUNY Press, a publisher responsible for so much work I've admired over so many years. I could not have asked for a better editor with whom to collaborate on this project than Rebecca Colesworthy, whose patience, forbearance, wisdom, insight, and humor are matchless. To Rebecca are due thanks greater than I can express for shepherding this project into the world, and its author through much anxiety in the process. I am likewise extremely grateful to Mary Jo Bona in her capacity as editor of the Multiethnic Literatures series, to Diane Ganeles, Aimee Harrison, James Harbeck, and John Britch, and to everyone else at the press whose labor has made this book a reality. My further thanks go to the readers who peer reviewed my manuscript and assured the press of whatever modest merit it may have—for feedback that improved the book hugely, yes, but also for simply being willing to undertake what is, by nature, a mostly thankless and unrecognized act of professional service.

Like many writers on LA before me, I am an outsider to the city. In 2018, however, I was privileged to spend some months living and working there, conducting research for this book and, equally importantly, getting to know a place I had previously only experienced in the pages of books and on cinema screens. On that trip and others subsequently, I became at least something more than a tourist, even if I could never claim to have become a local. One day, I hope. While I trust that my outsider status does not disqualify me from writing about LA's history and culture, I simply could not have done so without some first-hand sense of the texture and rhythm of life in the greatest city in the world. I am therefore hugely thankful to everyone in Los Angeles who, whether professionally or personally, welcomed me to their pretty town. They include the staff of the English Department at California State University, Long Beach, where I was graciously hosted as a visiting researcher—especially Steve Cooper, who opened his office and his home to me, enthusiastically encouraged my efforts, gave freely and inspirationally of his unparalleled expertise, and has become an invaluable mentor. Alicia Amatangelo and Janette Baisley helped Southern California feel like home, the short rib burrito from Kogi Taqueria sustained me, and the barmen at Musso and Frank made me a gimlet that would make Philip Marlowe's eyes widen.

This book began life as my PhD thesis, conducted at the University of Kent. At Kent I acquired colleagues, peers, and mentors who encouraged, enriched, challenged, and championed me with unwavering enthusiasm and care. Through times of celebration and commiseration, and against a backdrop of disciplinary and institutional crisis, I was humbled to find that many of these colleagues had become friends. I wish to extend particular gratitude to my primary and secondary PhD supervisors, respectively Will Norman and Peter Stanfield, whose contributions to shaping my doctorate, this book, and my wider intellectual development can scarcely be estimated. I also wish to thank Kent colleagues past and present including Ellie Armon Azoulay, Haifa Mahabir, Claire Taylor, Ben Marsh, Erik Mathisen, John Wills, Stuart Barker, David Stirrup, Ariane Mildenberg, Jak Allen, Jack Dice, and Mike Collins. The latter stages of this project proved more tortuous than I had expected, in large part because the task of revising the book's manuscript coincided with a time when, having moved to Austria to take up a job at the University of Innsbruck, I was finding adjustment to life in my new environment a considerable challenge. For that reason among many others, I am profoundly grateful for the support, camaraderie, and tolerance of current and former Innsbruck colleagues, including Sandra Tausel, Johannes Vith, Eva-Maria Müller, Christian Quendler, Cornelia Klecker, Sascha Pöhlmann, Matthias Mösch, Sabine Sanoll, Hilde Wolfmeyer, and Sonja Bahn.

This project would likewise have been impossible to complete without the facilities, resources, and knowledge offered warmly and generously by the staff of numerous research libraries, including the University of Kent's Templeman Library, the British Library, the Wohl Library at the Institute for Historical Research, the Tate Library, Los Angeles Public Library, Santa Monica Public Library, Loyola Marymount University Library, the Academy of Motion Picture Arts and Sciences' Margaret Herrick Library, and especially the Special Collections department of UCLA's Charles E. Young Research Library.

Beyond the institutions where I've conducted work on this book, colleagues in the broader academic world have offered insights, reassurance, and good humor of inestimable worth in the many years of this project's gestation. They include Monica Manolescu, Gloria Fisk, Francisco Robles, Tyler Tennant, Ignacio López-Calvo, Alex Pavey, Diarmuid Hester, Noreen Masud, Matt Mullins, and the late Richard King. I will inevitably fail to name all the friends outside academia who have provided invaluable strength and support in ways large and small, but foremost among their number are Adam Robinson, David Todd, Dorothy Heydecker, Amy Page, Sarah Waldron, Aveek Bhattacharya, Simon Edmunds, Chris Evans, Malcolm Povey, and Simon Barker.

Finally, I extend every gratitude possible to all my family for their enduring support, love, and trust—especially in the precarious years since I embarked on a foolhardy path into academia. Particular mention must go to Liz Riches, Julie Fleck, Jenny Mauger, Jon Garry, Pierre Mauger, Pascale Mauger, and my grandmother, the late and much-missed Ina Docherty. I save the last word for my parents, Terry Docherty and Margaret Riches. One of my very earliest memories is of my father singing me to sleep with a song that I mention briefly in this book's introduction—Jimmie Rodgers's "Waiting for a Train." Dad's renditions of Rodgers's magic words about hopping boxcars across the Texas plains were my first encounters with the myth and mystery of the American West, starting a journey that eventually led to these pages. My mother, meanwhile, did more than anyone in my life to fill me with a love of literature. Mum died unexpectedly in August 2023 and it is a source of great sadness that, after she introduced so many books to me, I am unable to introduce her to mine. Three weeks before her death, however, I was able to show her its cover design, and the look of proud excitement she gave me then sustains me still. I will always be indescribably grateful that someone so close to me understood exactly why one might want to spend a life inside fiction.

Introduction

"Metaphor that Becomes Epical"

> You can't write a story about LA that doesn't turn around in the middle or get lost. . . . Art is supposed to uphold standards of organization and structure but you can't have those things in Southern California—people have tried.
>
> —Eve Babitz, "Slow Days"

On a hot June night in 2018 I stood in darkness at the end of Hermosa Beach pier, two beers into conversation with my friend and mentor Professor Stephen Cooper. I was living in Culver City on a Fulbright fellowship, which Steve had persuaded the Department of English at Cal State Long Beach to support. Most days I caught the bus from the McDonald's at Venice and Overland and rode it up to UCLA, where I was conducting archival research that would inform this book. The bulk of that archival work lay among the papers of the Italian American author and screenwriter John Fante, whose biography Steve wrote and whose ornery presence stalks these pages perhaps more stubbornly than any other author. As I listened to Steve relate a story of one of Fante's many misadventures, I let my gaze fall on the glittering black water below us and was struck by a sudden surge of awareness that this, terrifyingly vast and miraculously near, was the Pacific Ocean.

Somehow, I hadn't until that moment noticed it for what it was—the same Pacific Ocean that laps ominously beneath the feet of the desperate dancers in Horace McCoy's *They Shoot Horses, Don't They?* (1935); the same Pacific Ocean where Arturo Bandini nearly drowns in Fante's

Ask the Dust (1939). Turning around, I looked back toward land, to the distant flickering of city lights. I realized that I stood at last in a place from which a journey to Los Angeles, to the city that symbolizes, in its continent's end location and its paradigmatic urban mass, the terminus of the United States' historical westward expansion, had become an *eastward* one. I realized too, with awe, that to stand in this place was finally to make real the curious remark of Raymond Chandler's that had been my point of departure on the journey that led ultimately to this book.

Chandler once wrote in a letter to Hamish Hamilton that plays were inferior to novels because only the latter could induce the "feeling of the country beyond the hill."[1] When I first encountered that claim, more than a decade ago now, in my final year as an undergraduate, it seemed a strikingly peculiar definition of fiction's aims to arise in the mind of someone who wrote of and at the western limit of the American landmass, and whose works are so suffused with a sense of that place. When a national mythohistory equates forward movement—*American* movement—with westward movement, I wondered what it meant to ascribe to fiction both an ability and an imperative to disclose the "country beyond the hill." I wondered, too, what it meant to make such an ascription in and of a place where, unless one turns around, turns east, turns *back*, there are no more hills for a country to be beyond. Chandler's spatial metaphor for fiction's power and purpose prompted me to reflect on how fictional representations of Los Angeles respond to the city's unique sociogeographic location. If fiction seeks the country beyond the hill, I began to wonder, how are LA fictions' attempts to do so inflected by their subject's lack of the same? This book constitutes some answers to that question.

It seeks those answers by reading fiction through the defining mythohistorical concept of the United States' westward continental march: the frontier. I argue here that from their age's popular theories, histories, imaginings, and fading memories of the frontier, fictions depicting Los Angeles between the onset of the Great Depression and the early 1950s derive a conceptual framework with which to figure and understand the multiethnic spaces of urban modernity. I do so by analyzing certain spaces that recur throughout those fictions—dancehalls, offices, industrial facilities, and homes. Parsing the ways in which characters of varying social positions occupy and move through these recurrent spaces, I show how sociocultural recuperations and revisions of the frontier suffuse the literature of this place and period. What I term "frontier dynamics" can thereby be understood as one of the major ideological discourses underpinning the mid-century literary imagination of Los Angeles, at once reflecting, compounding, and troubling its status as a city with a unique place in American myths of triumphal western conquest. To identify these frontier dynamics in this body of literature is to enable a new interpretation of its contributions to discourses on the American post-frontier condition. Against prevailing critical narratives of recent decades, I propose that mid-century LA fiction figures violent criminality, brutal ethnic divisions, and rampant social inequalities not as the tragic consequences of America's inability to function without a frontier, but as the (no less tragic) consequences of the frontier's persistence.

This book's arguments thus actualize and locate themselves at intersections between two contexts—the place the frontier occupies in the American imagination, and the place Los Angeles occupies in the American imagination. The remainder of this introduction accordingly seeks to articulate those contexts, suggesting how a reappraisal of the relationship between them constitutes the basis of a compelling new way to navigate the iconic cityscapes of LA's mid-century fiction.

Locating the Frontier

Turner's Shadow

To rehearse Frederick Jackson Turner's contributions to American historical discourse is to recite a creed. From the 1890s to the 1920s, Turner promulgated a theory of American history that conceptualized the nation's western frontier, articulated the processes by which it had advanced across the continent, and claimed that those processes "explain[ed] American development."[2] The frontier, Turner held, propagated and demanded a people defined by individualism, willingness to undertake physical exertion in hazardous conditions, belief in democratic ideals flecked with a suspicion of intrusive institutional authority, and above all an insatiable urge for perpetual movement.

Turner was not the first to tell the American story in a manner that ascribed singular significance to the frontier. Turner's frontierism was anticipated, to name just a few examples, in J. Hector St. John de Crèvecœur's belief that the American natural environment had given birth to a "new man," in the folk legends that arose around Daniel Boone and Davy Crockett, and in James Fenimore Cooper's Leatherstocking tales.³ Turner himself acknowledged debts to Francis Grund, who had theorized in the 1830s that Americans were driven by an inherent "expansive power" to conquer wilderness in restless westward motion.⁴ *The Winning of the West* (1889–1896), Theodore Roosevelt's four-volume frontier history, also partially predated Turner's.⁵ Even as the 1893 World's Columbian Exposition hosted the American Historical Association meeting at which Turner first advanced his frontier thesis, just beyond its boundaries spectators flocked to see "Buffalo Bill" Cody's Wild West. By this point, Cody's enterprise had already been a successful traveling attraction for ten years—its popularity and longevity suggestive of a culture that needed little convincing by an academic historian that its story was that of the frontier.⁶

Nevertheless, throughout this book I bring specifically Turnerian theorizations of the frontier to bear upon mid-twentieth-century fictions because it was Turner's influence that determined how the frontier would be understood in the sociocultural discourses to which I see those texts responding. "Within half a decade" of its initial 1893 expression, William Cronon writes, "Turner's thesis had gained wide national attention and was being promoted by a number of leading intellectuals."⁷ The 1910 award of the chairmanship of the AHA recognized Turner's status as his era's professional narrator of nationhood, as did the Pulitzer Prize awarded to his career-summative 1921 collection *The Frontier in American History*.⁸ By 1951, Walter Prescott Webb could look back upon Turner's career and lionize him as no less than "the thinker who could view the whole scene and the whole dramatic experience [of America] and tell what was its meaning."⁹ Webb was, along with Frederick Paxson, one of the most prominent of the post-Turner historians whose embrace of frontierism lent it disciplinary dominance in academia during the period on which this book focuses.¹⁰ Turnerism's rapid acceptance as academic orthodoxy in turn helped to entrench the significance of the frontier in popular conceptions of history and national identity. Turnerian thought, John Pettegrew writes, "penetrated modern US . . . consciousness": its reach extended from the nation's intellectual elites to its middle classes, from the rhetoric of politicians to the themes of cinema—and, as this book contends, to the fiction of mid-century Los Angeles.¹¹ In Kerwin Lee Klein's words, "by 1930 [Turner's] narrative dominated American history as no other tale ever has."¹²

What made Turner's account so compelling—and distinguished it from earlier frontier discourses like those of Grund or Crèvecœur—was that in declaring the frontier to have defined American socioeconomic, political, and psychological development he also declared it dead. Turner famously cites an 1891 Census Office bulletin, which reported that "isolated bodies of settlement" had "broken into" all of the nation's hitherto unsettled territory, on which basis "there could hardly be said to be a frontier line" in America.[13] That casual declaration of the frontier's disappearance, Turner writes, "closed the first period in American history."[14] Situating a case for the frontier's overwhelming significance within an announcement of its closure, writes Cronon, "framed [Turner's] argument prophetically," rendering it a statement about the future as well as the past.[15] The precise meaning of Turner's "prophecy," however, remained stubbornly ambiguous within his own work.

At times, Turner's predictions for the post-frontier era were pessimistic. The frontier had ingrained "energies of expansion" in Americans, and the loss of a "field for [the] exercise" of those energies had created conditions of ominous social unrest.[16] "In the remoter West," wrote Turner, "the restless, rushing wave of settlement has broken with a shock against the arid plains. The free lands are gone, the continent is crossed, and all this push and energy is turning into channels of agitation. Failures in one area can no longer be made good by taking up land on a new frontier; the conditions of a settled society are being reached with suddenness and with confusion."[17] Even as he asserted the finality of the frontier's demise and made grim forecasts on that basis, however, Turner also held that "traces" of "frontier characteristics" remained detectable in places that had long been settled.[18] Even the West itself, the now-exhausted space of the frontier's expression, was fundamentally "a form of society, rather than area."[19] As Pettegrew notes, Turner's writings in fact locate "many examples of the pioneer spirit in modern urban culture."[20] Thus, in some formulations, Turner's "suggestion that Americans inherited the acquired characteristic[s]" of frontier existence was a claim that "the expansive character of American life" could be maintained in the frontier's absence.[21] Elsewhere in his work, though, it was a warning that cultural and economic entropy were inevitable in a frontierless world where essential national characteristics had been rendered inexpressible.

By locating this fundamental inconclusiveness within an otherwise authoritative declaration of the frontier's end, Turner subjected the meaning of that declaration to immediate and intractable public contest. In Philip Fisher's phrase, Turner drew "lines in the sand" that instigated and set the terms of a multivocal, decades-long, culture-spanning discourse about the fate of the post-frontier United States.[22] Some participants in that discourse would affirm Turner's belief in the frontier as the source of American greatness, while others would claim that the frontier condition had in fact inhibited America's social and cultural maturity. Some believed, for better or worse, that the frontier was lost forever, others in the possibility of its transmutation from geographic to metaphorical spaces. Some wished for "new frontiers"; others hoped to avoid them.

The poles of this debate can be neatly encapsulated in a comparison between statements made by two Turnerian historians—Webb and E. Douglas Branch—at opposite ends of the period on which this book focuses. In 1930, Branch wrote that "'Westward' is not accurate as a direction" but rather "finds its greater meaning as a transitional phase in American life," echoing Turner's conception of the West less as any one swathe of land than as a social phenomenon.[23] If the frontier is understood as a "transitional phase," it is repeatable, perhaps inevitably so. If the frontier is a mode of thought, a way of understanding the world, it holds the potential to outlive the geographic circumstances with which it was originally associated. Webb, by contrast, averred in 1951 that the frontier's role in American development resided in its very singularity as a set of social and physical circumstances; no "new frontier" could reproduce the effects of something that definitionally had "no plural."[24] As a result, American society had become irretrievably "homesick" for and thus paralyzed by its pioneer past.[25]

Mid-century Los Angeles fictions exhibit, I will suggest, these countervailing Branchian and Webbian impulses simultaneously. These fictions make frontiers through characters who live in perpetual states of transition, manifesting the possibilities of what it might mean to "live westwardly" in modern urban America—but in doing so they reflect the frontier past's stubborn discursive persistence as a way of structuring American life. Such fictions thereby become legible as vital contributions to a national post-Turner conversation about the endurance or otherwise of frontier characteristics. In order to recognize them as such, however, we must first understand something of the places where that conversation occurred and the shapes that it took.

One school of post-Turnerian thought found an early manifesto in Frank Norris's 1902 essay "The Frontier Gone at Last." Norris concurred with Turner's belief in the frontier's cultural significance but saw cause for optimism in its closure. He wrote that American frontier expansion had emblematized a period of global history in which nations had defined themselves by territorial supremacy. Perhaps, Norris mused, if the passing of the frontier heralded an age bereft of space over which to compete, nationalist ideologies of spatial and commercial conquest could be supplanted with a "new patriotism" of transnational brotherhood that transcended nation state boundaries and rivalries.[26] Exploring the contested multiethnic spaces of fictional Los Angeles in this book, however, I find few equivalent possibilities. Indeed, my readings of Los Angeles's mid-century fiction, especially in chapters 1 and 3, identify frontier ideology's mythologizing of territorially aggressive ethnonationalism as its most persistent and insidious legacy.

Norris's proposal represented a challenge to the views of many Americans, who had the previous year signaled their desire to preserve frontier values by sending a performative frontiersman to the White House. In Theodore Roosevelt, the United States elected an embodiment of widespread contemporary "antimodernist" calls for the preservation of the nation's remaining wilderness and a return to the values that had supposedly been inculcated there. The antimodernists of the late nineteenth and early twentieth centuries echoed Turner's fears about the condition of "settled society" in a belief that, absent the frontier's nation-defining call to heroic, masculinist individualism, America was becoming "overcivilized," denuded of virility and vitality.[27] Such beliefs underscore my readings of visions of white masculinity in chapters 2 and 4 of this book.

Waldo Frank was more confident than the Rooseveltian antimodernists that frontier values would continue to define modern America despite the loss of their geographic proving grounds, but shared Norris's diagnosis of their influence as malign. In *Our America* (1919), Frank attributed a litany of ills in the American character to the nation's frontier youth. Locating the most sinister implication of the Turnerian frontiersman's compulsion to place himself "under influences destructive to many of the gains of civilization," Frank averred that "the pioneer must do violence to himself."[28] For Frank, battle with the wilderness had been an act of psychological self-harm on the part of early American society. The precarity of the frontier engendered a rigid, survival-oriented pragmatism, resulting in an atrophying of the imaginative faculties, a privileging of the material over the intellectual, and a defensive hostility to the alien. As "the legs of the pioneer [became] the brains of the philosopher," America's cultural growth was stunted.[29] Frank was not original in proposing that that rough-and-ready frontier life had precluded the refinement of national character: Turner himself had noted (disapprovingly) how common it was to identify "dishonesty, ignorance, and boorishness as fundamental Western traits."[30] Frank's fear, though, was that precisely because the defining quality of the frontier-derived American mind was a reflexive conservatism, it was capable of enduring far beyond the now-extinct conditions in which it developed.[31] A Frankian notion that the danger of the post-frontier era was not in the dissipation of frontier values but in their insidious endurance, and in the damaging limitations placed upon a society unable to escape the totalizing rigidity of a frontierist worldview, is one this book frequently identifies in its fictional subjects.

The onset of the Great Depression appeared to corroborate Turner's fears for the fate of a people divested of spaces in which to expend their "energies of expansion," and thus invested fresh urgency in the popular contestation of the frontier's legacy and the nation's post-frontier condition. There is no clearer indication of the frontier question's prominence in this period than the fact that Franklin Roosevelt and Herbert Hoover explicitly debated the possibility of "new frontiers" in society, science, and industry while campaigning for the presidency in 1932.[32] In so doing, they built directly upon intellectual groundwork laid two years earlier by *Individualism: Old and New*, John Dewey's "faithful application of the frontier thesis" to the social challenges of the day.[33] Dewey accorded with Frank in critiquing the frontiersman's incapability of thinking "beyond . . . the immediate tasks in which he was engaged," but retained Turnerian praise for the frontier's inculcation of an individualist "character that . . . was strong and hardy, often picturesque . . . sometimes heroic"—and which had on the whole served the nation well.[34]

Dewey was preoccupied with determining how the best frontier traits could be adapted for a new era, and the worst attenuated. At a time of socioeconomic crisis, Dewey remarked, "it is no longer a physical wilderness that has to be wrestled with. Our problems grow out of social conditions: they concern human relations rather than . . . physical nature."[35] This "unsubdued social frontier," unlike its geographic predecessor, could not be conquered by lone individuals. It could only be mastered, suggested Dewey, by directing the pioneering instinct, "through controlled use of all the resources of the science and technology," into "scientific frontiers."[36] The "new individualism" had to reconcile itself somehow to collective enterprises. Dewey, Roosevelt, and Hoover, moreover, all addressed what Webb termed the tension between "the closing frontier and the expanding production of the machine," asking whether modern capitalism was dangerously incompatible with America's now-frustrated frontier spirit, or could in fact become its new vehicle.[37] Such tensions between the rugged individual and the collective imperatives of post-frontier capitalist modernity, wherein the latter ironically becomes a social frontier to be assailed, are present in many of the fictional texts this book explores.

Dewey's *Individualism: Old and New* appeared a year after the first English edition of Max Weber's *The Protestant Ethic and the Spirit of Capitalism*. Weber's theories are broader in world-historical scope than Turner's, but have much in common with them—and with those of Frank and Dewey, both of whom interpreted frontier character as a particularly materialistic strain of Puritanism. A laboring culture of "struggle against one's environment—the kind of practical, here and now struggle that paid off in material rewards," as William H. Whyte would later describe Weber's ethic, also defines Turner's frontier.[38] Webb almost synthesizes the two in describing frontier existence as "The Religion of Work."[39] Both the frontier as conceived by Turner and the Protestant ethic as described by Weber, moreover, share the paradoxical position of having fueled capitalistic growth only to be threatened by their own creation, as forces of industrial modernity foreclose upon a "dream of individual success."[40] Weber never mentions Turner or the frontier by name. Nevertheless, the American publication of *The Protestant Ethic* is another signifier of a culture grappling in the 1930s to resolve its veneration of idealized individualistic labor with the demise of the conditions by which such labor was engendered.[41] Turnerian questions were prominent in the public mind, even when not expressed in Turnerian terms.

Popular culture likewise contested the fate of post-frontier America in the decades of Turnerism's greatest influence. Peter Stanfield notes that the minor studio B-Westerns of the 1930s constructed themselves on narrative grounds "wholly inapplicable" to the "frontier myth"—often set in "a geographical West in which the frontier ha[d] long since gone" and dealing less with "historical imperatives of the winning of the West" than with "intrigue between labor and capital."[42] (Again, Depression-era anxieties about industrial modernity are palpable.) Robert Sklar meanwhile holds that the Western's 1930s decline as an A-picture genre represented the cultural completion of Turner's frontier foreclosure.[43] Thus the frontier could be powerfully present even in its absences: both the Western's fall from favor with major studios and its reconfiguration in B-films as a way of mediating a "tension between old and new worlds" constituted a social reckoning with Turner's declaration.[44] In music, Jimmie Rodgers responded similarly to the negotiation between old and new demanded by the frontier's end. His "railroad bum" travels not west but east, from "Frisco" to "Dixie": if his journey across the "wide open spaces" of the southwestern US enacts a yearning for the past, for a time when one's ability to move through the West was not circumscribed by an officious brakeman, it also feels the limits of Dewey's old individualism—the bleak absence of a "helping hand."[45] Later came Hank Williams. The name of his backing band—the Drifting Cowboys—declared debts to frontier iconography, but maintained ambiguity as to whether "drifting" acknowledged a world that had lost direction or asserted that there yet existed space in which to roam.

Crucially, as Webb himself would note, the frontier's enduring impact on American life in the first half of the twentieth century derived not merely from its historicity as an empirical phenomenon but from its packaging into a potent cultural narrative. Historians themselves were partly responsible, having "made [Americans] conscious of the frontier": if the frontier persisted in the American mind, it was impossible to tell if it did so because that mind possessed a genuine "frontier character" or simply because the frontier had become "a slogan with good sales quality."[46] Webb recognized that Turner's thesis about the frontier's significance had become self-fulfilling. Even if the frontier had not defined the American past to the extent that Turner had claimed, by the 1930s the sheer weight of intellectual, political, economic, literary, and popular cultural discourse about the frontier that appeared in Turner's wake ensured that the *idea* that it had defined the American past in turn defined the American present. In that vein Carey McWilliams, beginning to establish himself as one of Southern California's leading public intellectuals, used a weary 1931 essay to bemoan an America with frontiers on the brain. McWilliams wrote that "the final extension of the frontier to the Pacific" had not quelled but boosted the industry of frontier "myth-making" (as McWilliams categorized all discourse that amplified Turner's belief in the frontier's nation-defining force).[47] The "dolorous mood" of Turner's declaration of frontier closure, McWilliams wrote, had engendered "an inordinate modern-day enthusiasm for the frontier and frontiersman" throughout American culture.[48]

McWilliams looked askance at his era's popular romantic fascination with Old West iconography. Mocking the notion that the frontier survived "in the movie daring of Tom Mix or Douglas Fairbanks" or was psychologically reborn "whenever [Americans] see a pair of chaps," McWilliams was skeptical of what he saw as quasi-superstitious contemporary beliefs in the frontier's conceptual persistence, "hover[ing] above and around us like a disembodied spirit."[49] American culture after Turner, argued McWilliams, found it impossible not to see the frontier everywhere it looked. He was correct, but his observation provides precisely the rationale for seeking the frontier in fictional texts written in the period of Turnerism's greatest influence, a period when diverse cultural spheres, from the highbrow to the popular, gave enduring conceptual life to times and spaces that Turner had declared gone for good. What I locate in Los Angeles's mid-century fiction is precisely that which McWilliams derides, a sense of a frontier that has "seeped inward and survives today as a subjective force," suffusing texts made in and by a world over which Turner's shadow loomed inescapably.[50]

McWilliams, moreover, neglected to note that the frontier's enshrinement at the heart of American culture in the decades following its demise was the work not only of "enthusiasts" but also of the various flavors of frontier refusenik—men like himself, like Frank, like Norris. In the very act of critiquing the Turnerian conception of the frontier's historical significance, the desirability or viability of replacing it with "new frontiers," and/or the cultural "enthusiasm" for the frontier maintained in other quarters, voices like McWilliams's own contributed to the frontier's overwhelming presence in the thought of early to mid-twentieth-century America. It is just such a role that I often find this book's fictional subjects occupying. Their visions of a culture that continues to structure itself upon frontier logic, constantly privileging social values that vouchsafe the possibility of "new frontiers" in modern urban space, are frequently critical. In offering such criticism, however, the texts themselves become locations of the frontier's reconstitution. I read such fictions simultaneously as reflections of, interrogations of, and contributions to the frontier thesis as the defining American cultural narrative of the first half of the twentieth century, texts that intervene in and add to an insistent national conversation about what Fisher terms "the single most important historical idea ever proposed by an American intellectual."[51]

Turnerism's legacies reach beyond the period of this book's investigation, but I depart at a point when frontierism's thoroughgoing acceptance as empirical historical reality became subject to increasing qualification. Webb's 1951 *The Great Frontier*, in constituting arguably the last significant work of emphatically Turnerian history while simultaneously commenting self-reflexively on historians' own role in rendering the frontier central to American consciousness, represented a turning point. The previous year,

Henry Nash Smith had already begun more comprehensively emphasizing the notion that the frontier's greatest historical significance was as a *myth*—a task that would later be taken up magisterially by Richard Slotkin.[52] In the 1980s, the New Western Historians "moved decisively to confront the frontier myth and . . . suggest the possibility of imagining a West that operates autonomously" from it.[53] As Cronon writes, their revisionist critique that Turnerian history is "geographically inaccurate, culturally biased, and potentially racist, leaving too little room for nonwhite ethnic minorities" (and women) is justified.[54] I myself make no claims for the facticity or validity of Turner's model, and I hope that the character of my interpretation of it throughout this book makes clear that I am alive to its problematic lacunae. I deploy Turnerian ideas about the frontier and the American West from a critically historicist perspective, in order to demonstrate and engage with their essential contextual bearing upon the fictions that this book explores.

Similarly, Turnerian and post-Turnerian discourse lightly invokes monolithic notions of American identity, spirit, or character that would make any responsible twenty-first-century scholar wary. When I employ such terms, as I do particularly frequently within this introduction, I do so exclusively within the context of adumbrating historical and historiographical beliefs that such things existed and could be defined, rather than to profess such beliefs myself. It is on the same critical basis that I engage with the central Turnerian dichotomy of "savagery" versus "civilization." This dichotomy and its phraseology are, of course, loaded with an especially problematic set of accrued cultural meanings—even by the standards of nineteenth-century frontier history and whether encountered in their original Turnerian setting or in the twentieth-century literary contexts to which I apply them. Throughout this book, therefore, I always frame instances of "savagery" and "civilization" in quotation marks, to emphasize continually that these terms are invoked with reference to Turnerian thought and with the aim of interrogating rather than reproducing their harmful legacies and implications.

What Does a Frontier Look Like?

Immediately after establishing his central argument with the Census Office's straightforwardly statistical method of determining a frontier, Turner contradicts himself. "The term," he writes, "is an elastic one, and . . . does not need sharp definition."[55] This book, however, requires a more precise sense of what a frontier actually *is*, if it is then to perform its task of identifying frontier conditions in fiction—especially when its subjects describe what are ostensibly non-frontier settings. Despite Turner's airy dismissal of definitions, it is possible to build one by parsing his works.

Turner's frontier lies at the "hither edge of free land," which hardy individuals—"frontiersmen" or "pioneers"—drive into "continuous recession" through the westward advance of American settlement.[56] It is a sociospatial liminality, both its location and the conditions it manifests existing between opposed states of wilderness and settlement, or "savagery and civilization."[57] In describing it as both "a continually advancing frontier *line*, and a new development for that *area*," Turner establishes the spatial complexity of his frontier.[58] It is at once a dividing line between settled and unsettled *and* a discrete-but-permeable area of intermediate space that separates the two. In this sense the frontier's spatial liminality is also temporal: because its existence as the space between settled and unsettled is transitory, part of a process of moving itself forward through progressive geographic conquest, the frontier exists only as a momentary present. This spatiotemporal axis is an "article of American faith," Klein writes: "history runs from East to West."[59]

Turner's metaphor for the frontier of "the outer edge of the wave" apprehends this. As the successive waves of an incoming tide wash higher up a shore, what was once the furthest limit of a previous wave's advance is absorbed into the main body of water. Thus, as the frontier moves westward, former "outer edges" are successively absorbed into settled American "civilization": Michael Steiner describes this as the frontier's "self-destroying process."[60] The frontier's progression is therefore simultaneously cyclical and linear. The tide as an integral whole represents the linear progression of westerly expansion over time, but that overarching process is in fact made up of countless smaller cycles (waves) by which successive unsettled spaces gradually become settled. Such a space is only a frontier while its social qualities manifest both "savagery" (yet-to-be-fully-conquered) and "civilization" (yet-to-fully-conquer) before being occluded by the eventual triumph of the latter. As that triumph is enacted in a given area, the frontier is deferred into the future and into the West, "beginning over again" in "perennial rebirth."[61] Thus Turner's wave illustrates how the frontier's liminality is multiply (if unidirectionally) mobile: its spatial, temporal, and social axes operate in concert. The macro-process of "crossing a continent . . . winning a wilderness" and the micro-process of "developing at each area of this progress out of the primitive . . . conditions of the frontier . . . the complexity of city life" are mutually propelling and inextricable.

These are the spatial and temporal characteristics by which I define frontierlike conditions in the fictions this book addresses. A frontier must exist as a liminality between areas or states figured as settled or "civilized" and those where social regulation breaks down entirely. Moreover, it must be not an inert buffer but rather a mobile space of constant negotiation between the two. This transitive quality may thus render the frontiers I seek temporally liminal—fleeting states, moments that cannot hold. By the same token, however, because the temporal dimension of Turner's frontiers is cyclical, the frontiers I find may be fleeting but repeating, momentary liminalities rendered a constant (even inescapable) state through recursion.[62]

Turner's "free land" is always in some way hostile and does not yield itself up readily—it must be fought for. Turner figures westward movement as "conquest"; land is "won" or "wrested" from its wilderness state, from itself.[63] The frontier demands that its ingressors express themselves in "aggressive courage, in domination, in directness of action, in destructiveness."[64] The frontier condition is therefore defined by conflict: only after it has been won through physical and mental battle by individuals representing "civilization" can the frontier progress further west. Historiographers have debated Turner's conception of the form this conflict takes. As Cronon states, there is a widespread belief that in framing the frontier as a battle between man and "free land" Turner "ignored [the] Indians" whom Americans encountered there.[65] On this basis Slotkin asserts that Turner "marginalizes the role of violence in the development of the Frontier," in contrast to Theodore Roosevelt, for whom "the history of the Indian wars (which are, for him, fundamentally wars of racial superiority) *is* the history of the West."[66] In Slotkin's formulation, Turner rejects "the mystique of privileged violence," while Roosevelt glorifies it: between the two exists a "hunter/farmer dichotomy," with Roosevelt winning the West by "deeds of the sword," Turner through agrarian triumph.[67] Klein writes similarly that Turner "deflected attention from interethnic conflict by imagining the defining American moment as an encounter with pristine nature rather than a collision of cultural worlds."[68] In doing so, he "conflat[ed] Indian and Hispano peoples with wilderness and free lands," and therein "legitimated Euro-American imperialism."[69] For Pettegrew, likewise, Turner both "downplayed violent frontier traits" by framing them as positive and "concealed frontier warfare by portraying Native America as a built-in part of the environment," thereby "conflat[ing] Native Americans with the wilderness."[70]

This criticism of Turner, however, itself conceals the extent to which Turner *does* center human violence. When Turner identifies Andrew Jackson as a frontier archetype he does so substantially on the basis of Jackson's role as a brutal scourge of Native Americans.[71] He names "hostile Indians and the stubborn wilderness" as coequally obstructive and resistant to those who pushed the frontier westward.[72] Above all, he states explicitly that each phase in the frontier's advance "was won by a series of Indian wars."[73] Slotkin is undeniably correct that Turner devotes more attention to the "yeoman farmer" than to the "wilderness hunter or Indian fighter," but Turner is incontrovertibly clear that the efforts of the former depended on those of the latter.[74] As Cronon notes, the Turnerian claim that land unsettled by Americans was "free" was never a claim that the land was "free of *inhabitants*"—only that it had yet to be circumscribed by any property right recognized in American law.[75] Turner does not, in fact, "obscure the historical role of violence" (to borrow Slotkin's characterization) when he elides conflict with Native Americans and conflict with wilderness.[76] Violent encounters with Native Americans do not contradict Turner's sense of the frontier experience as an encounter with "free land" because, as Klein and Pettegrew themselves suggest, the supposed "wildness" of indigenous peoples is, for Turner, merely a symptomatic constituent element of the frontier's defining environmental hostility. Indeed, racial violence is embedded fundamentally in Turner's model precisely because he does not regard Native Americans as ontologically distinct from the wilderness conditions whose conquest frontier expansion effects.

This characteristic of Turnerism is essential to my model of how frontier characteristics might manifest themselves in the spaces of modern, urban fiction, because it obviates any suggestion that frontier conflict must be between human beings and the natural environment, or that a frontiersmanlike figure must be the only human presence in a frontier-like space (which would of course preclude any identification of frontier conditions in depictions of urban modernity). On either the Rooseveltian or Turnerian frontier, the type of conflict with an inhospitable "environment" that an ingressor finds is often human conflict, conducted usually on racial lines. On this basis I justify attributing frontier characteristics to spaces where characters compete with each other through various forms of aggression to assert their sociospatial supremacy, especially where those conflicts are defined by race, ethnicity, or similar power dynamics that frame one party as the representative of hegemonic power ("civilized") and the other as marginal ("savage").

The spaces I examine need not, however, manifest explicit violence between humans to suggest frontierist qualities of conflict and contestation—as Slotkin suggests, Turner *does* often figure the frontier as a conquest of surroundings rather than of people. Thus, while every space I identify as frontierlike must manifest some quality of spatial contest, that contest is as likely to be with the space's own material or social qualities as with a directly hostile human presence. As Ray Allen Billington and Martin Ridge note, the "backbreaking labor" of farmers was, for Turner, among the ultimate frontier conquests.[77] My framing of spaces as fictional frontiers frequently deploys the notion present in Turner's emphasis on the agrarian frontier that labor itself may in its physical and psychological challenges constitute the perpetually mobile conflict between environment and individual by which the frontier is defined. As Webb writes, "all the high words the frontier man used to describe himself and to express his egoistic ideal, meant *work* of one sort of another. Courage, initiative, aggressiveness, and industry, can be best expressed in action, movement; that is, in work."[78] Within this book's context of fictions produced under and depicting organized industrial capitalism, moreover, such work might manifest human conflict (at either interpersonal or structural, class-based, race-based, or gender-based levels) instead of or *as well as* an arduous physical challenge.

In any case, for Turner and his adherents, the labor of advancing through and subduing the wilderness is always an expression of individualism. The frontier both requires and makes individualists. In doing so, however, it creates the defining paradox of Turnerism—the recurrence of which in LA's mid-twentieth-century fiction I identify as one of the clearest ways in which that fiction reveals its frontierist commitments. In quelling the frontier, Turner's frontiersmen act *for* "civilization" but are never *of* it, setting themselves apart physically and socially and therein demonstrating a liminal character concomitant with that of the frontiers they seek out—hence the antimodernist concern with "overcivilization." An individualist desire to seek out and test oneself against the wilderness is, for Turner, a rejection of "the complex political, economic, and social customs required in the stratified societies" of the settled East.[79] Pushing the frontier westward is a "civilizing" act, but one carried out in the process of escaping from the creeping restrictions of "civilization" itself.

This is never, though, for Turner, an anarchistic rejection of belief in exceptionalist American democracy. Quite the opposite—it is the embodiment of what he regarded as that democracy's "truest" (Jeffersonian or Jacksonian) forms:

> Western democracy included individual liberty, as well as equality. The frontiersman was impatient of restraints. He knew how to preserve order, even in the absence of legal authority. . . . Society became atomic. There was a reproduction of the primitive idea of the personality of the law, a crime was more an offense against the victim than a violation of the law of the land. Substantial justice, secured in the most direct way, was the ideal of the backwoodsman. He had little patience with finely drawn distinctions or scruples of method. If the thing was one proper to be done, then the most immediate, rough and ready, effective way was the best way.[80]

The frontiersman's conception of democracy as the "belief that those who win the vacant lands are entitled to shape their own government in their own way," a faith in "the freedom of the individual to seek his own" without "restriction upon his individual right to deal with the wilderness," further determines the frontier's identity as a contested space.[81] When two such individuals have competing designs on "vacant lands," conflict is inevitable—either between the two parties as a "rough and ready" way to determine whose will takes precedence in the absence of adjudicatory structures, or with whatever such institutional structure does exist.

On such a basis I seek to identify frontier dynamics in post-frontier urban fictions via figures who express a frontier character. This means not merely that they must be individualists, but that their individualism must manifest in an iconoclastic desire to seek out some form of arduous conflict and/or labor, and also become a source of conflict in itself. Such figures should embody in some way the Turnerian frontiersman's paradoxical attitude to "civilization" and, according to context, perhaps to the American state specifically. I seek characters who in some way reflect the frontier's intrinsic generative contradiction of an aggressive presence within wilderness that results from a rejection of or by normative societal structures ("civilization") but ultimately becomes a self-erasing act of service to the same.

What Does a Frontiersman Look Like?

Frontierism is "deeply ethnocentric" and male-centric, a "(white) national identity centered on men and in the face of an indigenous ethnic other."[82] The centrality of whiteness to Turner's vision is clear in his acknowledgment that the story of the frontier is a story of race war against Native Americans, not to mention his choice of frontier archetypes: Turner is explicit that Jackson's temperamental embodiment of "the tenacious, vehement, personal West" derived in part from his "Scotch-Irish" heritage.[83] As Valerie Babb writes, the figure of the frontiersman has become one of American culture's "standard models of white identity"; he "represents white conquest of the American frontier."[84] In Babb's words, the foundational role of English Puritan settlement in hegemonic narratives of American nationhood renders the very idea of "conquer[ing] a sometimes unforgiving landscape" inextricable from whiteness in American culture.[85] For Richard Dyer, the frontier was not only "the leading edge of the white world" but also, because Native Americans were regarded by their conquerors as "borderless people," both the imposition of a white ideology of spatial division and that ideology's practical enactment.[86]

Turner's frontier archetypes (Jackson, Lincoln, Jefferson, Boone, Crockett) also frame the frontier as a male space, as does sheer weight of textual evidence: crudely but instructively, Turner's collected frontier writings contain nine occurrences of "woman" or "women," against 272 of "man" or "men."[87] While historical social norms dictated that the very first occupants of a frontier in its wildest initial state (the hunters and fighters Roosevelt venerates) *were* typically men, Billington and Ridge write that "the popular picture of a predominantly male social order . . . bears little resemblance to actuality. On virtually all frontiers that had reached the agricultural stage men outnumbered women only in slight degree."[88] Despite Turner's emphasis on agrarianism, however, that misleading "popular picture" is his. Turner does not suggest that women or children were not or could not be present in the wilderness, but in his history male agency is as absolute over women and their destinies as it is over the landscape itself. Indeed, in the gendered imagery of the Turnerian paradigm women are aligned less with the act of frontier conquest than with the conquered landscape itself—"virgin" territory to be "tamed, plowed, or fenced in" by men, solely a resource for the nation's masculinist self-actualization.[89]

As Klein writes, in the era of Turnerism's cultural dominance even critical conceptions of the frontier's legacies "imagined the story's hero as white, middle class, and male."[90] Turner and his ilk "left Euro-American women, Native Americans, Chicanos and Chicanas, African Americans— all the 'others'—outside of the heroic horizon."[91] This does not mean, however, that in seeking frontier conditions in fiction I examine only white male figures. While white men and their various embodiments of, departures from, and anxieties about frontier archetypes do constitute significant portions of my analysis, I am frequently concerned with how these fictional spaces impose the frontier's ideologies of white masculinity upon non-white characters. The fictional worlds I examine construct themselves as frontiers and thus demand that their inhabitants operate therein as frontiersmen. Yet where those characters are not white, they are prevented by the frontier's logics of whiteness from occupying the identity of its mythic protagonist—rendering claims to the fictional frontier claims to whiteness and vice versa.

Women occupy similarly complex and multifaceted roles throughout the reconstitutions of frontier paradigms that this book identifies in fiction. At times, characters who are male and non-white identify white women as the vehicle by which they hope to make their own claims to whiteness through social frontiersmanship—they exhibit a mirror image of Turner's own "tende[ncy] to cast the North American continent in feminine terms," framing white women as territory to be claimed.[92] Such men find that conceiving of other individuals in such terms is as perilous as any act of geographic frontier negotiation, precisely and ironically because the women they encounter resist their own reduction to symbols of sociospatial conquest. At other times, relationships between men and women in the fiction of mid-century LA model the frontiersman's paradoxical relationship with "civilization"—where women are essential to men's performances of heteromasculinity but simultaneously constitute a domesticating presence hostile to masculine individualism. In still further circumstances, women more actively challenge and threaten the bases of male characters' efforts to construct their own identity on frontiersmanlike lines, because they themselves manifest the kinds of frontier characteristics that their male adversaries believe to be their own exclusive inheritance.

Undeniably, the fictional texts I explore locate sociospatial agency principally in an ability to claim the identity of a rugged white male individualist. These texts frequently frame non-white and female characters as contributing to the construction of ideas of frontierist white masculinity that they themselves can never (fully) embody. That they do so is fundamental to my claim that these texts and their worlds internalize the sociospatial logics of frontierism, but relationships in these texts between non-white and female characters and supposed "ideals" of white male frontiersmanship also repeatedly query, complexify, and problematize the latter. In demonstrating the unease and partiality with which frontierist paradigms accommodate figures who wish to make claims on social space but sit outside an assumed ideal of white heteromasculinity, those "outsiders" demonstrate both the power and the limitations of such paradigms. As I suggest in this book's latter sections, the frontier would ultimately exhaust itself as a governing logic within the textual worlds of fictive Los Angeles precisely because it demands and depends upon the social primacy of a particularly narrow vision of white masculinity, a primacy that came under persistent challenge in later twentieth-century LA as it did in the United States at large. The mid-century non-white and female characters I explore throughout this book also challenge that primacy, even if they often find it insurmountable: in so doing they identify flaws in frontier logic's absolute equation of sociospatial agency with the figure of the rugged white male individualist, revealing frontierism's identitarian rigidity to be its weakness as well as its strength.

The conceptual framework I have outlined thus far suggests that the frontier is defined as much by the characteristics of the individuals who seek to occupy, conquer, and expand it—"frontiersmen"—as by its own environmental characteristics. Those frontiersmen may have been defined by the rigid set of parameters of character, race, and gender that I have outlined—somewhat ironically, given that the most essential of those parameters is supposedly individualism—but within those parameters they took many forms. I have already alluded to this in alighting on a historiographical separation of warlike and agrarian frontiersmen, but far more subdivisions of the type exist: "hunter gatherers, trappers, traders . . . merchants, prospectors, miners, scouts, soldiers, laborers, teamsters, drovers, [and] speculators" all occupied the role of frontiersman.[93] Frontiersmanship, as defined by a set of personal traits, is thus a practice that remains consistent regardless of an individual's actual occupation, provided that said occupation is conducted on a frontier and as part of a process of winning a wilderness: it is no more particular to the experience of the fur trader than to that of the cowboy.

That transferability of traits across occupations is simultaneously a transferability across space and time, from the "coon-skinned trappers and leatherclad 'Mountain Men'" of older, more easterly frontiers to the "starry-eyed prospectors and hard-riding cowboys, badmen and vigilantes" of the Far West.[94] Although Turner's focus on the Far West is limited (Webb and then Billington would light out for that territory, taking Turner's theories on their own expansive westward ride), the frontiersman, for Turner, is as visible in late nineteenth-century California as in late seventeenth-century Massachusetts. Turner writes that the frontier's role in "keeping alive the power of resistance to aggression, and developing the stalwart and rugged qualities of the frontiersman" had been consistent "from that day to this," and that the figure of the frontiersman could be located as readily in the "gambling dens" of the lawless Far West as readily as in the "log huts" east of the timber line.[95] Likewise, "the regulators of the Carolinas were the predecessors of the claims associations of Iowa and the vigilance committees of California"; "the Massachusetts frontiersman" and "his western successor" were indistinguishable in the extent to which they "hated the Indians."[96] Between the frontiers of "the Cumberland Gap and . . . the Rockies a century later" there are differences in specific conditions, but for Turner they manifest exactly the same "procession of civilization," demanding the same human traits.[97]

This sense in which the character of the Turnerian frontiersman is broadly transferable across time, place, and specificity of individual experiences speaks to another irony in Turner's conception of that character as being defined by individualism: the Turnerian frontiersman's exceptional identity is vested in his status as an everyman. As Klein writes, Turner wished to "broaden history to include the common man," locating the propulsion of the frontier in the acts of individuals who were remarkable in their character, their bravery, and their determination, yet unremarkable in their social backgrounds, their economic circumstances, or the numbers in which they existed.[98] While Turner emphasizes the importance of the strong-willed individual, his individuals are largely notional and anonymous rather than actual—significant as evidence of a broadly shared "frontier character" rather than in and of themselves. Slotkin suggests Turner's protagonist was "not an individual hero but a kind of Whitmanian hero *en masse*."[99] Even when Turner does associate the progress of the frontier with "Great Men"—Boone, Lincoln, Jackson—he vests their significance less in biographical specificities in and of themselves than in their narrative capacity to symbolize his broader mass of "common men." Thus "Lincoln represents . . . the pioneer folk"; Jackson's war-making matters because through it he "personifie[s] . . . essential Western traits," exemplifying the "ruthless energy of a frontiersman."[100] Such figures are primarily metonymic shorthand for the activities of the mostly undocumented, substantially anonymous people Turner saw as the quotidian heroes of the frontier.

I attend to this sense that the frontiersman becomes an archetype, a symbolic personification of a set of traits and indeed of the frontier itself, as opposed to any single historical circumstance of frontier life, because it is fundamental to my project of identifying fictional denizens of modern, urban LA as frontiersmen. To frame the frontier and "frontiersmen" metaphorically, as a set of narrative effects, affects, qualities, or characteristics that are not subject to hard limitations on the times or places in which they can be perceived is in fact a wholly Turnerian thing to do. When I claim to locate frontiersmanlike figures throughout fictions that do not describe literal frontiers but were written in Turner's cultural shadow, I derive methodological authority from Turner's own persistent suggestion that attitudes rather than a particular geographic emplacement or historical moment define the frontiersman. On this basis I hope to obviate any potential readerly concern that identifications of "frontiersmanship" in modern, urban figures and spaces are superficial or tenuous. If Turner himself uses the figure of the frontiersman primarily as a symbol, a representation of a set of ideas and characteristics, then the figurative, metaphoric quality of the literary frontiersmanship I identify itself affirms the fiction's adherence to—or entrapment within—a Turnerian view of history.

I aim to show how frontier dynamics, absent the physical environments of their original enactment, continue to organize spaces of urban modernity. I will illustrate how fictions of mid-century Los Angeles structure their worlds on frontierist lines, figuring relations between existential conditions coded as "savage" or "civilized," and the points of contact, transition, and contest between those states, in ways that are analogous to spatial, temporal, and social characteristics of Turner's frontier. Spatial conditions of Turner's frontier may find social analogues in mine, and vice versa. When Harold Simonson wrote of Turner's "metaphor that becomes epical" he was referring to the stirring grandeur of Turner's rhetorical techniques, but could have just as easily been describing the frontier thesis itself.[101] Turner's own construction of the frontier as a set of representative, transferable typologies sets a critical-historical precedent for identifying it as a narrative device.

Locating Los Angeles

SPACE AND RACE AT CONTINENT'S LIMIT

Turner's claims that the West "is a form of society, rather than area," that a frontier's transition to a "settled" condition is gradual, and that the traits of the frontiersman are transferable across place and moment affirm the sense that frontierlike qualities are not exclusive to one particular geography or temporality.[102] That "form of society" and those traits are, however, predicated on and defined by constant westward movement. This quality is the inevitable omission from the previous section's attempts to taxonomize characteristics of the frontier that I will locate analogously in the literature of mid-twentieth-century Los Angeles, because its condition of spatial literalism is such that it cannot be analogized adequately. While Turner emphasizes the transferability of frontier qualities, he circumscribes them within a declaration of "frontier closure" that defines western expansion by its singular irreproducibility as a process.

It is partly the location of frontierlike social characteristics *within* frontier-evoking acts of movement (connections between centers with edges, journeys between settled space and unsettled, explorations of space that either reveal it as or render it liminal) from which this book's claims derive a Turnerian specificity. Nevertheless, such movements cannot reproduce the essentially linear, macro-scale, unidirectional quality of Turnerian westward expansion. It is precisely the purpose of this book, however, to argue that the texts it analyzes hold out the possibility (even the inevitability) of the frontier's perpetuation *despite* the impossibility of their containing constant westerly motion. I make that argument partly because it is consistent with the previously discussed prevalence of a contemporaneous "new frontiers" discourse about America's fate in an era of forestalled westward motion, and it renders these fictions legible as participants in that metaphorical discourse. If the fictional texts I explore in this book decouple the frontier from its conceptual dependence on what Fisher calls the "temporary near-emptiness of the American map," they would resolve the stark dichotomy between twentieth-century American culture's insistence on "newness itself" and the Turnerian "party of nostalgia" it rejects, by creatively deriving the latter from the former.[103]

Moreover, though, when this book claims that certain fictions propose the perpetuation of the frontier absent its geographic reality, that claim also resides more specifically in the place occupied by California, and Los Angeles in particular, within post-frontier discourses. The frontier characteristics I have outlined heretofore might well be locatable in any literary text that addresses unstable, contested, in-flux spaces of one kind or another. The significance of locating them in Los Angeles lies in that city's symbolic role within frontier mythohistory and critical traditions engaged therewith. That is to say, part of my purpose here is to challenge LA's identification as a city that archetypally represents the erasure and impossibility of the frontier in the twentieth century, and to refute existing literary critical orthodoxy, which holds that post-Depression LA fiction intervenes in its era's debate about delimited post-frontier states only to declare "new frontiers" impossible.

In 1870, Los Angeles was still a frontier town with a population of less than 6,000. By the time of the 1890 census that provided Turner with confirmation of the frontier's demise, the city's population had swelled to 50,395; it would then double over the next decade, and by 1930 it exceeded 1.2 million.[104] In the context of frontierist history, one might read this transformation in two opposing ways. The speed and scale of such a change is certainly suggestive of the frontier's closure. As the ultimate example of the rapid urbanization of the post-frontier West and the symbolic terminus of America's westward journey, the remaking LA underwent in the forty-year span following Turner's presentation of his thesis might seem to validate its claims. This, as I will expand upon, is the interpretation that prior critics of LA's mid-century fiction have emphasized.

If Branch was right to claim that the frontier was best understood as a way of conceptualizing a "transitional phase" in social development, however, then LA in 1930 was both the product of such a transitional phase and about to enter another one. A frontier outpost had in sixty years become a major modern city, fifth biggest in the nation, but was yet to experience the further explosions in population and physical area, changes in urban fabric and form, greater development as a national and international economic center, and demographic shifts through which it would become the global urban behemoth we recognize today.[105] Los Angeles's twentieth-century growth has been described as a "virtually continuous economic boom," but within that boom distinct phases can be identified, and my period of investigation is one—a transitional phase between metropolis and megalopolis, regional capital and world capital.[106] If frontiers are temporal liminalities between one state of social development and another, then in Los Angeles the 1930s and 1940s were a frontierlike time. Given Turner's argument that frontier characteristics continued to be felt in an area decades after it had stopped being a "true" frontier, the very speed of LA's transformation from frontier town to modern city itself implies the retention of frontier characteristics.

Indeed, the rapidity of LA's early twentieth-century development, fueled by continuing westward migration that had not abated simply because the frontier had gone, might well suggest the possibility of maintaining in urban conditions the frontierlike state of the transitional phase, of growth, expansion, and enduring newness. By the onset of the period on which I focus, that remarkable transition had attracted national and international curiosity, a curiosity compounded by the city's concomitant ascendance, via the nascent film industry, as one of the world's premier exporters of popular culture. Multiple nonfiction accounts of the place and its history appeared, seeking to "explain" LA's conditions to the world beyond. These accounts grappled with the question (still unresolved by twenty-first-century urbanists) of whether those conditions made LA a truly exceptional city or merely the vanguard of broader modern trends, the "harbinger of what [was] to come" elsewhere.[107] They simultaneously evince, too, what Mike Davis memorably schematized in *City of Quartz* (1990) as an enduring LA division between "boosters" and "debunkers."[108] Nevertheless, the welter of nonfiction attempts to "explain" LA in this period all respond to and emphasize the idea that nothing quite like it had been seen before, as encapsulated in a subtitle considered (though eventually discarded) by the German geographer Anton Wagner for *Los Angeles*, his groundbreaking 1935 study of the city. Wagner sought to describe nothing less than the "The Sudden Transformation of a New World Landscape into a Metropolis."[109]

Louis Adamic's *The Truth about Los Angeles* (1927) was scathing about the socioeconomic realities beneath the city's booming image, with Adamic reserving particular derision for its large population of midwestern retirees, while Harry Carr's *Los Angeles: City of Dreams* (1935) was as optimistic as its title suggests. Between those poles sat Morrow Mayo's *Los Angeles* (1933), in which the author's tone is a kind of enthralled distaste, and the Works Progress Administration's *Los Angeles: A Guide to the*

City and Its Environs (1941). John Keyes, professing studious neutrality in the latter's preface, may as well have named Adamic and Carr when he wrote that LA had been both "lashed as a city of sin and cranks" and "strangled" by "unrestrained eulogy."[110] The booster-debunker divide in LA histories of this period itself suggests a city visible simultaneously—like the frontier—as both a place that represented a future with endless possibilities (Carr's "City of Dreams") and a place where the past had gone to die (Adamic's twilight midwesterners). Mayo meanwhile suggested the ambiguous relationship between LA's rapid urban development and its frontier past when he described the proliferation of "theoretical municipalities" where real-estate boosters lit out for "barren pastures, to launch a subdivision where the coyotes howled and tarantulas and centipedes made whoopee."[111] A little later, in *Southern California: An Island on the Land* (1946), the most enduringly impactful history of the area published in the first half of the century, Carey McWilliams's subtitle conveyed his account's emphasis on regional exceptionality, but an island-like decoupling from the American continent at its western limit might suggest in equal measure either post-frontier finality or its evasion. Nonfiction accounts of LA written during the period that this book explores thus suggest a place that manifests the ambiguity of Turner's own conclusions about whether or not "new frontiers" were possible. The city is legible as confirmation either of the frontier's total demise or of its possible perpetuation.

Among all these LA-whisperers, it is the work of the German Wagner that most closely anticipates my own attribution of frontierlike qualities to this period of Los Angeles's history—and again reflects concordances between Turnerism and the Weberian Protestant ethic. Wagner is explicit in claiming that Los Angeles's transformation, though not itself a transgeographic movement but rather the reshaping of a static geography, had been powered by the same spirit of mobility both physical and social that had carried every pioneer across time and space from Plymouth Rock to Point Mugu—"a Puritan drive to activity." For Wagner, "anyone who was mobile and sufficiently courageous to embrace new opportunities migrated westward," and thus those who had made it furthest West embodied that courageous mobility with the most powerful results, namely Los Angeles.[112] Like the fictional texts I examine, Wagner sees LA as a place where frontier motion still happens while, as it were, running on the spot. Tensions between LA-as-exception and LA-as-typifier recur once more: the city's transformation is unprecedented, suggests

Wagner, except that it *is* preceded by the frontier-surmounting tradition it inherits. He captures this paradox of precedence in an evocative claim that the secret of Los Angeles's improbable rise lies in its being a place where "tradition means mobility."[113] Though explicitly Turnerian language is largely absent from Wagner's account, his description of 1930s LA is also about as complete a three-word distillation of frontier ideology as could be imagined.

If frontier mythohistory is ultimately a racial mythohistory, one in which spatial conquest glorifies whiteness, then the invidious historical relationship between whiteness and LA's transformation from frontier town to modern metropolis further compounds its pertinence as a site for the investigation of the frontier's cultural legacies. From the turn-of-the-century antimodernist moment onward, groups like the Native Sons of the Golden West explicitly associated the need to maintain California's "last frontier" identity with a need to police its racial exclusivity. *Los Angeles Times* publisher Harry Chandler infamously dubbed LA America's "white spot" and many early to mid-twentieth-century Angelenos sought to keep it that way, "a racially pure space . . . built for white Americans by white Americans," enthusiastically policed as such with some of the most racially restrictive housing covenants and zoning practices in the nation.[114] Few individuals had a larger direct impact on LA's changing spatiality in the early twentieth century than Abbot Kinney, the developer of Venice, but even as his new city invoked the Mediterranean, Kinney himself "crusaded for Anglo-Saxon racial purity through eugenics."[115] When Carr described the LA as "the end of the trail" for the "Aryan tribes on [their] restless encircling of the earth," the conclusion of the "epic . . . of the Aryan race," he identified precisely how LA's identity as the city that represented the conclusion of the frontiersman's settling of the American continent was bound up in an identity of triumphal whiteness.[116] The idea of LA as a space of whiteness as envisaged by Chandler, Kinney, et al. was the urban extension of the frontier's mythohistoric whiteness, a space that symbolized and had been earned through the white frontiersman's continent-crossing efforts and thus should be the exclusive reward of his racial descendants.

By the 1930s, however, LA's "myth of a white city" had "clashed with [its] increasingly multicultural reality."[117] Carr's image of the "end of the [Aryan] trail" itself suggested that, in betokening the triumph of white frontiersmanship, LA might also represent the start of white decline. When Mayo sought to explain LA's social conditions in 1933, he drew upon the city's history as "the most disreputable of all American frontier towns," a title acquired principally from the frequency with which white supremacy was asserted through lynchings of Mexican and Chinese residents in the name of vigilante justice.[118] That is, Mayo regarded 1930s LA as an inheritor of violent frontier whiteness, which is precisely what I find frequently in its fictions. As this book will detail in various contexts, the very ethnic minorities excluded from LA's literal construction as a space of whiteness were essential to the city's socioeconomic and spatial transformation. Moreover, as my readings of texts that center African Americans, Japanese Americans, Italian Americans, and Filipino Americans will show, the fiction of LA in this period discloses racial and ethnic diversity's challenge to the city's frontierist whiteness as, ironically, one of the essential means by which it could maintain that frontier identity.

White claims to the city's spaces derived their specific local authority from LA's symbolic place in a frontier history that had itself mobilized an ideology of white spatial exclusivity. Just as the city's seemingly boundless growth is legible as either affirmation or termination of frontier conditions, the role within that growth of figures who challenged the city's foundational myths of whiteness likewise invites interpretation as representative of either the city's loss of its frontier inheritance or its perpetuation of the same. Wagner, for example, describes how "Japanese neighborhoods sprang up on the outskirts of the urban agglomeration of Los Angeles" whenever the "common 20- or 30-year restriction against reselling or leasing newly sub-divided city lots to members of an alien race had expired"—upon which it was seldom long before "American inhabitants vacate[d] the area and [were] almost completely replaced by members of an alien race."[119] That is, nonwhite challenges to restrictive housing practices that had been intended to maintain the image of LA as the great prize of white frontier conquest themselves became legible as a kind of inverted frontierism. Instead of frontiersmen pushing ever deeper into the wilderness, moving onward each time a spot grew too "civilized" in their wake, Wagner depicts those people deemed racially pollutant by their white neighbors as encroaching wherever white-imposed spatial governance frayed a little, forcing the self-deemed "civilized" occupants to retreat to a place of greater safety. Precisely such an image of nonwhite figures who resourcefully and ironically retroengineer the spirit of a frontierist endeavor from which they are excluded, by moving not away from but toward the spaces of "civilization" (from which they are also excluded), recurs multiple times in the fictions this book reads.

If the 1930s and 1940s, as both a "transitional phase" in Los Angeles's history and the period of post-frontier discourse's peak national prominence, determine the broad terms of this book's periodization and thus the literary texts I have included in it, there remain to be determined finer and more subjective questions about the precise start and end points of our journey. (The frontiersman, at least, had the left and right hands of a continent as unambiguous parentheses.) The action of the earliest-set text discussed in this book, Hisaye Yamamoto's "Life Among the Oil Fields: A Memoir," though written in the 1970s, takes place in 1929. I make that year a chronological boundary, as the point from which the Great Depression began to imbue the hunt for "new frontiers" with urgency and Los Angeles, not coincidentally, began to become a site and subject of a distinct literary culture. Prior to the 1930s there are simply very few substantial fictional depictions of Los Angeles with which to work, as might be expected given the lateness of LA's development into a significant urban center.

In 1925, a University of Southern California student named Margaret Climie produced a master's thesis on fiction in which the region had been depicted, a remarkable document and the forgotten foundation stone of Southern California literary criticism. Climie's passionate call for critical recognition of "the myriad possibilities Southern California brings to the story-teller" would be proven prescient by the century of literary production that has followed her thesis.[120] Today, however, her project stands principally as a record of the fact that, at the time of its completion, literature considering Los Angeles *as a city* was principally composed of faddish early Hollywood novels and touristic travelogues exploiting easterly hunger for tales of sunshine and palm trees. Climie identifies few texts with reputations that have to any degree survived their era—and those she does tend to be, like Helen Hunt Jackson's *Ramona* (1884) or Paul Harcourt Blades's *Don Sagasto's Daughter* (1911), romantic expressions of nostalgia for "Spanish California." They may be set in what has since been absorbed into greater Los Angeles, but it is not comprehensible as such in the worlds they depict. Climie wrote too early to include Don Ryan's *Angel's Flight* (1927) in her survey, and Mark Lee Luther's *The Boosters* (1924) also seems to have escaped her notice. These two novels, along with Daniel Venegas's Spanish-language *Las Aventuras de Don Chipote* (1928), and Wallace Thurman's *The Blacker the Berry* (1929)—which, in the portions of its narrative set at the University of Southern California, has a partial claim to being the first African American LA novel—signaled growing interest in depicting through fiction just what a peculiar place Los Angeles was becoming. They are remarkable in this period, however, as exceptions. Only in the 1930s would such a trickle of LA fiction become a stream.

That fact was attested to by the 1941 appearance of Edmund Wilson's *Boys in the Back Room: Notes on California Novelists*. It is to Wilson's slight book, rather than to Climie's thesis, that the first critical identification of Los Angeles as a significant site and setting of literary production is most often credited. Wilson approached with much skepticism the possibility of art being produced in what he deemed an "anti-cultural amusement-producing center."[121] Nevertheless, his appraisal of contemporary Californian fiction, however bracingly qualified, was an acknowledgement of and response to the rapid emergence of a vibrant LA literary scene over the preceding decade, centered on the writers who congregated in Stanley Rose's Hollywood Boulevard bookstore and gave Wilson his title.[122] The texts I focus on throughout this book, therefore, emerging principally from the 1930s and 1940s, reflect not just national post-frontier anxieties and Los Angeles's contemporary state of frontierlike social transition, but also the city's emergence as a literary frontier of sorts. This was a place where new ground was being broken by both authors and critics in terms of recognizing its potential qualities as a place in which to write and to set fiction, but still a place widely perceived as a remote outpost of rather low culture, almost as far in esteem as it was in miles from the commanding heights of literary tastemaking on the opposite coast. Wilson, for example, finds F. Scott Fitzgerald's final relocation to Hollywood predictive of a coming shift in America's literary center of gravity, but fears that shift to be a malign one, Fitzgerald's untimely death its clearest signification. He would not be the last public intellectual to worry that Los Angeles was killing American culture.

If sociocultural and literary-historical shifts both regional and national make the arrival of the 1930s a clear and apposite marker from which to begin considering Los Angeles literature as neofrontierist literature, my end point is somewhat looser. The final chapter of this book's main arc focuses on novels of the mid-to-late 1940s, while texts of the early 1950s—John Fante's *Full of Life* (1952); Raymond Chandler's *The Long Goodbye* (1953)—are also occasional presences. By that time, I argue, the frontier-recuperating energies of the 1930s and 1940s were becoming exhausted; I demonstrate this further with concluding observations that project my investigative frameworks forward onto texts of the late 1960s and early 1970s, and I find there that the frontier no longer functions as the imaginative engine of LA fiction. The Depression, LA's rapid growth, and its parallel emergence as a center of literary production all conspire to make periodizable with some degree of precision the invention of a modern, urban, regional fiction in which the specter of the frontier is identifiable as the guiding intellectual compass. The closure of the period in which such fiction flourished, by contrast, is legible only as a gradual postwar fading out, a dissipation occasioned by a changing world.

Selecting texts from across this span of time, I have attempted to construct a corpus that in some way represents the breadth of Los Angeles's literary culture in the 1930s and 1940s. I make that attempt through significant expositions of works by Horace McCoy, John Fante, Raymond Chandler, James M. Cain, Frank Fenton, Dorothy B. Hughes, Chester Himes, and Hisaye Yamamoto. The more broadly inclusive of multiple voices one endeavors to be, however, the greater the anxieties of exclusion become. On the one hand, such an attempt at representativity cannot succeed without the inclusion of works that are paradigmatic of their period, style, or genre. On the other, the representative impulse creates an imperative to acknowledge that Los Angeles literature of this period was more than its best-known examples. I have attempted to balance this tension through a heterogeneous corpus in which some authors or texts are included because they are well known as representatives of the place and period, others precisely because they are not. Fenton, who was hailed by McWilliams as one of only four novelists to "suggest what Southern California is really like" but whose work has been out of print since its initial 1940s printings and has never previously received academic attention, sits alongside titans of the LA canon like Cain and Chandler.[123]

Fante's place within that canon, following his 1980s "rediscovery," remains ambiguous. *Ask the Dust* has become since the 1990s a subject of increasing critical attention, but the most recent authoritative scholarly history of California literature, a capacious 2015 volume edited by Blake Allmendinger, mentions Fante only to acknowledge his otherwise-total omission.[124] Both of these positions inform my treatment of Fante, whom I discuss principally in chapters 1 and 3, but also in passing throughout. I purposely omit any substantial reading of the critically well-trodden *Ask the Dust* while in fact making larger claims for Fante's potential centrality within the LA canon by considering portions of his oeuvre that remain almost entirely untouched by criticism. These include multiple unpublished works that I was fortunate enough to access in Fante's papers at UCLA. Similarly, Nathanael West's *The Day of the Locust* (1939) has been critically overworked: it thus features in this book primarily in the response I offer to criticism that bases large claims about LA fiction upon it. In other cases, however, notably Himes's *If He Hollers Let Him Go* (1945) and Cain's *Double Indemnity* (1936/1943), I *have* referred primarily to a given author's best- or better-known output, to the exclusion of other works.[125] Again, the hope is that a heterogeneity of rationale results in a heterogeneity of corpus that can aspire to some degree of representativity, bringing the canonical into dialogue with the marginal to create a picture of mid-century LA literature, and therein a picture of mid-century LA, which—while inevitably selective—is nuanced and multifaceted in what it reflects.

Such questions operate at the level of genre as well as of individual text or author. For example, the idea of LA as the *noir* or hardboiled literary city is a critical commonplace. I have no wish to rehearse an erroneous narrative that *noir*/hardboiled was the *only* major current in 1930s and 1940s LA fiction, nor to choose a corpus that would suggest that this book's claims for the presence of frontierism of LA literature are peculiar to or exclusively symptomatic of *noir*. I have therefore omitted some fine LA *romans noirs*, most obviously Raoul Whitfield's *Death in a Bowl* (1931), Paul Cain's *Fast One* (1933), and Eric Knight's *You Play the Black and the Red Comes Up* (1938). Equally, however, the prominence of *noir*/hardboiled cannot be ignored, and it is in recognition of this that it is represented herein by canonical masters—Chandler and Cain. Similarly, although the film industry is a presence in some texts this book explores, it may come as some surprise that I am not significantly interested in the "Hollywood novel" as a distinct genre, given its prominence in my period of investigation. That prominence, though, has been widely observed elsewhere, contributing to critical tendencies to reduce LA and its literature to clichés about illusion and superficiality: as Peter Lunenfeld has it, "the old line about Hollywood-the-Industry—scratch the phony tinsel and you'll find real tinsel underneath—has tended to apply to too much writing about Los Angeles-the-Place."[126] Although alive to the distinctive social, cultural, and economic features that made and make LA unique, I am invested in highlighting texts that remind us of how much Los Angeles life has always been lived far beyond the purview of the movie colony. Part of the frontier's power in the texts I examine, moreover, is in its very ability to present itself in and shape itself to the most quotidian circumstances. If, in order to locate it, we had to visit the exceptional imaginative playground of the studio soundstage, within which any scene can be conjured but outside which nothing persists, that would make no case at all for the presence of the frontier as something central to the experience and representation of mid-century LA at large.

In attempting to select texts that collectively represent the LA of the period in question and allow me to engage adequately with the frontier's complex dynamics of white masculinity, I have selected a corpus that suggests a diverse city with a diverse literary culture. It is nevertheless one that also acknowledges that white male figures were as dominant within that literary culture (as authors and implied readers) as white male characters are within the texts that culture produced. Alongside Anglo-American authors like Chandler, Fenton, McCoy, and Cain are the Italian American Fante, African American Himes, and Japanese American Yamamoto. It will not escape the reader's attention that this list includes no Mexican American perspectives. Indeed, no Latinx authors are discussed in the book. This is an unfortunate absence in a work that frequently seeks to suggest how the frontiers that endured in urban modernity were racial/ethnic ones, when Mexican Americans were the most populous and longest-established ethnic minority group in Los Angeles in the period discussed—indeed one whose presence had not always been as a minority, and was only rendered so by the advance of the American frontier it predated. The role of Mexican Americans (and their oppression) in shaping the spatial-racial liminalities of mid-twentieth-century Los Angeles certainly features in this book, but exclusively as the subject of others' viewpoints (often as an ethnic identity against which to self-define; see my discussion of John Fante in chapter 3).

This, though, is not a deliberate or accidental omission on my part but a reflection of the dearth of published fiction by Mexican Americans or members of other Latinx communities in or about Los Angeles during the period this book covers Ignacio López-Calvo has rightly assailed critics who seek to make representative statements about the character of LA's literature while ignoring or underplaying Latinx perspectives.[127] In the bibliography López-Calvo assembles of Latinx LA literature, however, there are in fact no fictions whatsoever in the period explored by this book; a gap extends from Venegas's *Don Chipote*, at the close of the 1920s, to 1963.[128] Similarly, George Sanchez records the diversity of Mexican American cultural activity in Los Angeles during the first half of the twentieth century, but makes no reference to published fiction.[129] The absence of Latinx voices from this book certainly reflects a methodological limitation of treating a place's literary culture (in its written and published manifestations) as a means of examining that place. Nevertheless, that absence speaks in its own way to precisely the kind of sociocultural narrative marginalization of non-white figures that I find characteristic of the frontier's presence throughout this book, and to the acuteness in that regard of the particular chronological period on which I alight.

Most texts discussed were written contemporarily with their setting, identifying them as works not merely describing but produced from the particular sociocultural contexts with which this book engages, but there are occasional exceptions. The most prominent is Yamamoto's "Life Among the Oil Fields," written fifty years after the period in which its action occurs. Significantly, this exception is heavily autobiographical, written by an author who was present in an LA much like the one she describes: in this sense, it is dislocated but not absent from the experiential historical moment it represents. Moreover, its complex temporal context is itself essential to my reading of the text. Similarly, John Fante's *Dreams from Bunker Hill*, referred to briefly, was published in 1982 but is to a large degree an autofictional account of 1930s LA.

Geographically speaking, meanwhile, my definition of "Los Angeles" for the purposes of text selection is consciously broad and flexible, taking in the wider LA metropolitan area (e.g., the technically discrete cities of Santa Monica or Long Beach count as "LA"). I occasionally even allow myself the latitude of referring to "Southern California." While this book is closely engaged with the complexities of LA's sociogeographies, it is also responsive to the powerful symbolic resonances Los Angeles as a whole holds in American culture—those resonances are not cleanly determined by the administrative strictures of municipal boundaries, and thus neither is my definition. I choose, however, to refer to Los Angeles rather than Southern California in my title as the most succinct way to reflect accurately this book's thoroughgoing emphasis on the region's urban core, even if my readings occasionally take me beyond the city limits.

The Closed Frontier of Los Angeles Literary Criticism

This book responds not only to the ambiguities of LA's relationship with frontier mythohistory at mid-century but also to the fact that those ambiguities are often elided in critical discourses about LA and its representations. In the decades-long debate over whether LA's rapid transformation attested that the old frontier was closed for good or that it could be reopened in urban space, the former position has been dominant. John F. Kennedy suggested as much when, accepting the 1960 Democratic Party presidential nomination, he echoed Roosevelt and Hoover's debates by framing himself (per Slotkin) "as a new kind of frontiersman confronting a different sort of wilderness."[130] Speaking in Los Angeles, Kennedy identified his surroundings' symbolic place in the frontier narrative. Alluding to Walt Whitman, he told his audience he stood "facing west on what was once the last frontier," and invoked the continent-crossing spirit of the pioneers as the inspiration for his own policy program. Yet if Kennedy's speech deployed LA's location at the conclusion of the transcontinental journey to suggest frontiersmanship, it did so in explicit refutation of a belief that "that there is no longer an American frontier."[131] That is, Kennedy rhetorically framed his challenge to political orthodoxy as a challenge to a cultural orthodoxy that LA represents the end of the trail. This book makes a consanguine gesture: I challenge orthodoxy about LA and its fictions by showing how those fictions themselves resist a narrative, dominant in literary and cultural criticism, that LA must always represent and be represented as the frontier's symbolic point of closure.

Criticism of Californian fiction often invokes Turner's anxieties about the impact of the frontier's closure on American life and the Depression-era discourses of loss and limitation that retrospectively cast him as Cassandra. What I term the "closed frontier" school holds that Californian visions of the post-frontier 1920s, 1930s, and 1940s are inevitably what Harold Simonson famously called "studies in literary tragedy."[132] Irrespective of where in the West the Census Office actually located the last area to lose its frontier status, it is "the western shoreline" that has, in the words of James Houston, "acquired the symbolic role of Outer Limit and Farthest Edge, where . . . dreams are put to some final test."[133] In that test, failure is assured, as David Fine argues when he states that "where the continent runs out, the dream runs out with it."[134] Meanwhile, for Simonson, "with the closing of the frontier came the end of the American myth."[135] The notion advanced by this critical position, that it is California's location at continent's end that portends tragedy, is bound up in the peculiar and cyclically "self-destroying" mechanism upon which Turnerian frontiers depend.

Cognate with the frontiersman's divided loyalty—his suspicion of the very "civilization" on behalf of which he notionally works—is a further logical paradox: the frontiersman exists both to conquer wilderness and in the same moment to affirm the continuing presence of wilderness yet to be conquered. His purpose depends upon his ability constantly to consume the very thing upon which his purpose depends. Because frontier expansion is ostensibly a dream of wilderness conquest, it dies in the moment of its apparent realization, and thus instead can only be sustained in the continual westward deferral of its own moment of realization. In California such deferral becomes a geographical impossibility; the final victory of continental conquest is its own ultimate defeat. Hence why, runs the familiar critical argument, literary responses to such a place in the post-frontier decades can offer only grim visions of continental eschatology.

The "world-historical significance" of Los Angeles as "a stand-in for capitalism" is regarded in this vein of criticism never as any kind of "new frontier" but always and purely as the antithesis of the region's prior mythic identity as the continent's last wilderness.[136] LA is held to embody Californian literary tragedy more than any other place, because its size, urban complexity, and reliance on human ingenuity to sustain itself embody more starkly than anywhere else both the frontiersman's triumph over the wilderness and the simultaneous realization that his dream of wilderness-yet-to-conquer has died. It is, as William McClung writes, "on the rim of a void and at the terminus of a journey."[137] In one of the earliest texts of "closed frontier" criticism, Joseph Porter noted a conceptual link between the popular image of the frontier West as "a field of constant violence" and the "social conditions and tensions of modern industrial society" endured in Los Angeles by Raymond Chandler's Philip Marlowe, comparing the detective to the gunfighter heroes of the (fictive) Old West.[138] The image of detective-as-frontiersman has since been returned to by other critics (and I offer a new interpretation of it in chapter 2 of this book), but for Porter the analogy exhausts itself because urban California connotes only frontier closure. "The hard-boiled dick has no place to go. The settlements have reached the Pacific terminus and have spilled back on themselves. The detective hero remains dissatisfied, for his rootlessness is static."[139] Meanwhile, David Wyatt evokes a city literally built upon national anxieties about the passing of free land, writing that "the Anglo-American experience of the Los Angeles basin . . . began as one in which the extension of a mental grid over physical space ruled out unmediated natural encounter. The . . . land booms that tried to lure the first large populations confronted the immigrant with whole towns laid out in comforting right angles, lots that were to become nothing more than homes for tumbleweeds."[140] Both natural and human forces are held up, in this school of literary readings, as embodying the essential tragedy of post-frontier, closed-frontier California, and of LA in particular. Wyatt emphasizes the natural. For him, "life in California is an ironic victimization of scale in which some abiding natural fact—the lack of water, the Santa Ana winds—chastens any extension of the will."[141] The frontiersman's belief in his own self-determination is mockingly circumscribed by unconquerable nature.[142]

David Fine also cites the natural forces that are ready to threaten the city at any moment, seizing man's hubristic construct back from the wilderness, reminding him that he has not truly conquered the land.[143] Fine simultaneously emphasizes, however, the extent to which the natural threats that beset Los Angeles can also represent or metaphorize man's ability to bring about his own downfall. Tod Hackett's "The Burning of Los Angeles" in West's *Locust* appears to be a painting of a "natural" force overtaking the city, but is only that—a painting, a metaphor within the larger metaphor for a dream's end that is the novel itself. The betrayer of that dream is not nature's burning but man's.[144] Again, a location at continent's end seemed to offer a particular promise, a dream, a triumphant end to the transcontinental journey, yet it can only disappoint. Houston makes much the same point, referring to the same novel, when he terms it "a book about the underside of the American Dream, what happens when the dream turns sour, and how disappointment runs that much deeper when the place itself has seemed to promise opportunities that have somehow passed us by."[145] John Scaggs places Chandler's detective fiction in the same framework, arguing that Chandler's LA reflects its post-frontier condition by persistently revealing any hope of renewal or reinvention to be false and hollow.[146]

Reading post-frontier Californian fiction as a set of closed-frontier tragedies is, however, flawed on its own terms. Such reading's shortcomings derive from a misreading of frontier history and from the temptation to elide two related but distinctively different myths or dreams associated with California. As the title of Wyatt's *The Fall into Eden* (1986) indicates, in addition to its association with the frontier dream, California has also long been invoked in terms of a paradisiacal myth. "This is the Garden of Eden!" supposedly exclaimed Charles Maclay on first seeing the San Fernando Valley in the 1870s.[147] In the twentieth century, that image underscored the booster pamphlets of the railroad and real-estate speculators who enticed tired midwesterners to a land of sun and orange groves. Indeed, Morrow Mayo confidently predicted that LA would never become "the great vibrant, vital, nerve-center of the Pacific coast" precisely because its benevolent climate cosseted its inhabitants too much, making them disinclined to "go-getterism."[148] Woody Guthrie ironized California's Edenic dream in noting its material conditions, but thereby attested to its currency, when he sang,

> California is a garden of Eden, a paradise to live in or see;
> But believe it or not, you won't find it so hot
> If you ain't got the do-re-mi.[149]

At stake here is the fact that the dream of the frontiersman described by Turner and the dream of an earthly paradise appear aligned but are in fact radically different. If the frontier exists not in the moment that wilderness is conquered but in the possibility of the wilderness that remains unconquered, the Edenic myth is its antithesis: it resides in the idea that reaching continent's end *is* a moment of triumph, a point of reward, a place of blissful rest. This intractable duality has been a defining characteristic of the Californian imaginary ever since the place's first naming, as a fictional locale in the sixteenth-century Spanish romance *Las Sergas de Esplandián*, wherein it is simultaneously a land of "great wealth," close to the terrestrial paradise (Edenic) *and* "hard to penetrate . . . remote, rockbound" (frontierlike).[150] As Porter evocatively puts it, California's status as the Furthest West means that it invites a "dichotomous view of the wilderness as a howling, evil area, and also as the Golden West, a place of renewal and rejuvenation."[151]

These two views both occupy an American myth about transcontinental manifest destiny; they are both about the civilizational rewards that accrue from a successful fight with an unforgiving environment. Only the frontier dream, however, contains the paradox that the reward sought by the frontiersman is the revelation of yet further unforgiving environments.[152] California's location as what Wyatt terms a "place of national or even racial destiny" thus has utterly different meanings for both of these myths, yet extant criticism tends not to grapple sufficiently with the tensions presented by their mutual incompatibility.[153] Wyatt first argues that the problem with John Steinbeck's California, for example, is that its inhabitants possess frontierlike restlessness but the place forces upon them the "difficulty of settled life." A little later, however, he revises the position: those inhabitants do in fact have a "will to settle" but the place forces *upon* them a frontierlike restlessness by sublimating their craving for settled life into an "immaterial domain of belonging."[154] The California of *The Grapes of Wrath* (1939) is, of course, no Eden; Wyatt's reading of its resistance to the Joads' attempts at entry and its refusal to permit more than "a momentary stay against the confusion of moving on" is unarguable. Yet in Turnerian frontier terms, a land that resists attempts at conquest by man, a land across which one must keep moving, is one that reveals the frontier dream to remain alive. Wyatt's "garden lost" becomes equally legible as a frontier found. Similarly, in reading Chandler, Scaggs claims that California in general and Hollywood more specifically embody myths of both "Promised Land" and "new frontier," but a frontier is not a promised land; a place cannot claim one such mythic identity without erasing its own ability to manifest the other.[155] The same might be said of West's burning city, and I will make similar arguments about Chandler's Los Angeles of irrepressible crime and the racially hostile cities of John Fante, Hisaye Yamamoto, and Chester Himes.

When Davis describes "boosters" and "debunkers" competing to define LA's meaning, he does so to support a larger argument that "Los Angeles has always been about the construction/interpretation of the 'city myth,'" and in the context of a larger taxonomy of competing visions of that myth: he sorts variegated claims to the city's identity into "sunshine" and "*noir*" camps.[156] On the one hand stand images of the "promised land," the "Mediterraneanized idyll" of sunshine and orange groves promoted by municipal and corporate interests, but *noir* continually acts as "a transformational grammar turning each charming ingredient of the boosters' arcadia into a sinister equivalent."[157] Edenic myths of LA of course sit within the "sunshine" spectrum. The frontier, by contrast, is a model that, precisely in its own insoluble paradox, ironically resolves Davis's model into a unified understanding of LA's mythic identities and therein suggests its potential as a structure through which to read representations of the city. Frontierism is a mythic structure in which the promise of more "*noir*"—more danger, more hostility, more contested space, more intrigue, more rough justice—is itself the "sunshine" being sought or sold. Exactly as Aldous Huxley defined LA, the frontier is a paradox of "Dreadful Joy."[158]

Curiously, although Davis flirts with the "closed frontier" literary critics in briefly implying the significance of frontier closure discourse to post-Depression LA fiction, the frontier is in fact a striking absence from his magisterial catalog of LA myths, as either a booster vision of endless progress or a *noir* debunking of the same.[159] In tracing the frontier in mid-century LA fiction we detect the presence of an alternative mythic structure for understanding the city's conceptions and constructions of itself, one that sits in dialogue with but outside Davis's looming critical presence.

Frontiers in Fictional Microcosm: Historical and Spatial Methods

The notion of LA as a place defined by its own compulsive self-narrating to the point of being indistinguishable from it is a familiar one. Michael Sorkin's claim that "LA is probably the most mediated town in America, unviewable save through the fictive scrim of its mythologizers" has become one of the hoariest scholarly saws about the place, having been popularized by Davis in *City of Quartz*.[160] Julian Murphet similarly writes of LA's "subsumption of the real by representation."[161] There are, however, dangers in such claims. Casey Shoop remarks that even Davis's attempts to deconstruct how narratives about LA become LA history and vice versa—how they perpetually shift "between the representation of history and the history of representation"—themselves become "prey to the power of these representations."[162] If such a risk can never be fully obviated, I hope at least to ensure that this book engages actively with it by continually emplacing each chapter's readings of LA fictions in the specific historical contexts they describe.

By such historicism I do not intend a claim of the kind that Murphet rightly derides as quests for (and presuppositions of the existence of) a "deeper and iniquitous essence"—the *real* "real"—beneath all the "slippery signification" of represented LA. Such a naive effort would in fact be, as Murphet writes, a "dismissal of the place," when the history of that place is itself bound up in its prominent cultures of self-representation, while attempts to locate "the real" through historical scholarship can never fully be disentangled from subjectivities of scholar and source alike; they are themselves inevitably representations.[163] I remain, however, wary of any attempt to resolve the tension between LA as historical reality and LA as fictive construct in a pleasingly hermetic claim that the city "is already its own best representation."[164] Tensions between even a notional "real" and its "representation" remain inevitable and insoluble, but they are also productive. It is often in those tensions—between the LA described by literary texts and criticism and the LA of historical record—that my primary texts ascribe frontier dynamics to the city they represent, perhaps most prominently in disjunctions I identify in chapter 4 between LA's actual prewar housing stock and its depiction in fiction. Thus, while this is primarily a literary history of LA, I explore the city's social history not as an adjunct to my study of its literature but concomitantly and with equal curiosity. I have, I hope, constructed a literary-historical method that neither abrogates critical responsibility to reckon with the material realities of LA's past—as does the postmodernist feint toward the "fictive scrim," the ahistorical affectation that LA never existed other than as its own representations—nor naively assumes that historical LA can ever be cleanly extricated *from* its representations. Rather, the two produce each other both in the texts I analyze and in my analysis of them.

A co-production between real and representation with exemplary implications for my own methodological approach to the historical and fictive spaces of Los Angeles is made by Emi, a character in Karen Tei Yamashita's 1997 LA novel *Tropic of Orange*, who claims to be "doing that Joan Didion freeway thang" while stuck in heavy traffic.[165] Emi alludes ironically to the miles compulsively covered by Maria, protagonist of Didion's *Play It as It Lays* (1970), for whom an urge to stalk LA's freeways becomes simultaneously a release from and an expression of mental disintegration. Didion's Maria and Yamashita's Emi both manifest the spatial dichotomy that defines LA's representation in so much cultural discourse—one between the freeway as liberator and the freeway as captor, between mobility-as-escape and mobility-as-entrapment. Moreover, though, that Emi experiences that dichotomy *through* Didion suggests the dominance of the very cultural discourse in which she herself is intervening: she experiences mobility-as-meta-entrapment, not only stuck on the freeway but stuck in LA's narrations of itself as a story of being stuck on the freeway.

In such narrations, the ability to compass the city spatially, through automobility, becomes the only way for its inhabitants compass it psychologically, to render its entirety legible to each other and to itself. For Maria, the freeway is the sole source of "the day's rhythm, its precariously imposed momentum."[166] Didion herself averred that the common experience of the "rhythm" of the freeway rendered it the "only secular communion Los Angeles has."[167] Similarly, though Reyner Banham was influenced by Wagner's perspicacious prewar acclamation of LA as a city defined by mobility, he would hail the postwar freeway as the city's great collective and connective experience, both an instrument of and a metaphor for egalitarian social possibility. Ed Dimendberg writes thus: "Mobility, be it swift spatial passage across the freeway network, or upward social mobility, is the great collective fantasy that Banham discerns in Los Angeles. It promises a world in which geographical or social distance can be obliterated and unfettered access to different social classes and milieux becomes possible."[168] The sprawling auto-metropolis can be conceived as a utopian space, then, but the operative word is "fantasy": for all Banham's LA enthusiasm, Dimendberg notes, his vision is also invested in "showing the limits of . . . mobility."[169] He is aware that, as Dean Franco writes, the freeway "connects and divides, simultaneously."[170] Per Davis's model, dystopian or *noir*-ish visions always invert their sunny counterpart, reconfiguring the endless freeway as a symbol of inertia, of a city segregated by asphalt, where the road's ability to collapse space and time between Compton and Brentwood is only an ironic reminder of the social distance it does not bridge but rather passes (and glosses) over.

Figurations of LA as (negatively) a fragmented no-place or (positively) a kaleidoscopic communality are by no means restricted to post-1950s visions of sprawl and freeways; they also dominate my period of investigation. For Robert Fogelson, indeed, no sooner had California joined the Union in 1850 than conterminously social and spatial qualities of "fragmented community" began to define "the growth of Los Angeles."[171] By the 1930s, the paradigm of a distributed LA was already mature. Carr's *City of Dreams* hailed the "cataclysmic decentralization" of a place where "the distances are enormous" as a kind of experimental anti-city.[172] In Fante's *Ask the Dust*, likewise, the LA of car-powered connectivity and possibility is powerfully felt: "I prowled the city with my Ford . . . pausing only long enough to order a hamburger and a cup of coffee. This was the life . . . ever following the white line."[173] So, however, is the twisted contrary: "We were jammed between two cars. She banged into one, and then into the other, her way of letting me know what a fool I had been."[174] In 1946 McWilliams wrote of the "Los Angeles archipelago," a place arranged in "horizontal clusters."[175] The origins of the adage that LA is merely some number of suburbs in search of a city are murky but most attributions predate World War II.

Recent criticism continues to emphasize such archipelagic paradigms as the default way to think about space in LA and its representations. In *The Border and the Line* (2019), Franco describes LA as a lattice of "journey[s] to and from somewhere else."[176] Opening with a disquisition on the shifting diversities one encounters in traversing the length of Wilshire Boulevard, Franco avers that the way to understand sociospatial division in Los Angeles is to "compare the identities of specific neighborhoods," therein to understand the disjunctive borders and connective lines between them.[177] Other recent studies of Los Angeles's cultures that manifest similar impulses include Alex Pavey's unpublished PhD dissertation "Crime, Space and Disorientation in the Literature and Cinema of Los Angeles" (2018) and Genevieve Carpio's *Collisions at the Crossroads: How Place and Mobility Make Race* (2019). In short, this is a city that, conventionally, considers and demands consideration of space on a macro scale.

The frequency with which this macro model of LA space recurs in cultural criticism suggests its enduring value, but while this book follows Franco, Pavey, Carpio, et al. in engaging with LA's spatial structures of social division, it employs a different methodology and sense of scale in doing so. I operate mostly on a micro scale, taking four spaces—the dancehall, the office, the industrial workplace, and the home (with an emphasis on forms of temporary, multi-occupancy housing)—that recur throughout my primary texts, in order to examine LA fiction's representations of space. There are multiple rationales for this approach. The first is a straightforward desire to offer something original, not to dismiss but to offer an alternative to the accepted critical paradigm.

Secondly, this method reflects my frontierist context. To assert that fictions of mid-century LA depict the frontier as an actively enduring conceptual force organizing the city's spaces *despite* the foreclosure of American westerly movement, my frontiers must not be vested in the idea of physical journeys from one location to another. To claim that frontiers can obviate Turner's condition of linearity, I must reject that condition in choosing how and where I identify them. Moreover, as noted, a frontier simultaneously exists between spaces, within spaces, and as a space in itself. In identifying the existence of frontier traits at a miniature scale, I strengthen the claim that the frontier entirely suffuses the mood of this period's LA fiction, detectable in even the tiniest spatial gesture—returning Turner's grand continental mythohistory to the scale of its constituent driver: the individual. When a character in a Fante story claims LA's shabby Bunker Hill as his "most intimate fraction of American earth," he suggests how an act of reinterpretation or revisioning can relocate and restore myths of continental grandeur to the most demotic and quotidian spaces by recognizing that the part contains the whole.[178] This book operates according to and aims to vindicate such a belief. I do not ignore larger-scale divisions; questions of what it means to move from one area of the city to another and references to such movements recur throughout my arguments. They remain, however, secondary to each chapter's exploration of its key space.

Moreover, this spatial scheme better enables me to historicize LA's sociospatial development across the period on which I focus: by focusing on a single institutional construct in each chapter I am able to alight on elements of mid-century LA experience that relate something pertinent of the city's particular sociocultural conditions during this period *and* its participation in broader American social trends. There is something of an attempt here to walk the line between competing conceptions of LA as an exceptional city and as a paradigmatic one. Rather than exploring aspects of LA that would announce themselves as overtly exceptional (e.g., Hollywood), I alight on types of space that are also typical of other urban locations in the US in this historical moment but that developed in unique ways under LA's particular historical circumstances. Those specific local social contexts are typically essential to my frontierist readings of these spaces: again, these spaces (an office, a dancehall, a factory, a hotel room) might exhibit the same spatial characteristics anywhere, but those characteristics take on frontierist connotations when they also take on the social, historical, and mythic contexts of mid-century Los Angeles, the transitional city at continent's end. My method and I agree with the LA journalist and novelist Héctor Tobar, who asserts that "there are a lot of things that are true of Los Angeles that are also true of other American cities . . . but in no other American cities are those truths as evident as they are in Los Angeles."[179]

Finally, in choosing spaces that recur with striking frequency across the fiction, I choose spaces whose prevalence suggests a role in defining experiences of LA during the period in question. There is another gesture of representativity here, to the experiential breadth of daily life. In reading numerous manifestations of a space of leisure (the dancehall), of domesticity (the apartment), of white-collar work (the office), and of blue-collar work (industrial facilities), I demonstrate that the frontier can be apprehended *throughout* the experience of urban modernity. By "representativity" I do not mean that the fictional experiences of the spaces I choose are somehow able to encompass the entirety of experiences of a historical place and moment; quite the opposite, these are spaces that derive frontierlike qualities in large part from imposing sociospatial restrictions on how and by whom they can be entered and experienced. Rather, I suggest that by choosing spaces that signify "work, rest, and play," I can show that frontier dynamics are ever-present in the life of this fictional city.

In chapter 1, I discuss the role of the dancehall in LA fiction of the 1930s and 1940s, principally through readings of McCoy's *They Shoot Horses* and three shorter Fante texts. After establishing the social significance of the dancehall within LA's leisure culture (and that of the United States more broadly) in this period, I present McCoy's novel as a central text of the "closed frontier" school of Californian literary criticism before offering a counter-reading that illustrates how the terms of that critical school misapprehend the essential characteristics of a frontier space. In subsequently discussing the Fante texts, I parse how movement through and occupation of the highly codified and multiply divided space of the dancehall manifests frontier dynamics that are heavily inflected by each story's protagonist's class status and/or ethnicity.

Chapter 2 situates a discussion of the office as a space of canonical LA hardboiled fiction within the context of a century-long culture war over the office as a definitive space of modernity. Reflecting post-frontier concerns about overcivilization, I suggest that Walter Huff, protagonist of Cain's *Double Indemnity*, embodies the frontiersman's identification with the wilderness he notionally exists to conquer, and ultimately sacrifices himself to assert the persistence of its presence. In approaching Chandler's Philip Marlowe, I suggest that although he shares with Huff the frontiersman's subsistence upon the socially "savage" in his professional life, he more fully enacts the frontiersman's paradox of acting on behalf of "civilization" in order to subdue that "savagery." Accordingly, his engagements with the space of the office are conflicted in character, treating it simultaneously as an anti-frontier space of deracinated modernity and as a space that manifests resistive, treacherous frontierlike conditions in itself.

In chapter 3 I turn from the knowledge economy to the industrial economy and from white-collar work to blue. In doing so I also move from the whiteness in which Marlowe and Huff partially vest their claims of frontiersmanlike identity to figures whose relationship with their worlds' frontier logic is defined by their non-whiteness. Principally examining Yamamoto's "Life Among the Oil Fields," Fante's 1936 novel *The Road to Los Angeles*, and Himes's *If He Hollers*, I theorize and historicize the specific stakes of ethnic and racial difference experienced by Japanese American, Italian American, and African American characters as they attempt to navigate a Los Angeles being transformed both socially and spatially by explosive industrial growth. Close analysis of oilfield, cannery, and shipyard spaces informs an interrogation of the role of non-white figures in a culture that continues to organize itself along the lines of the frontier. These texts, in my reading, demand that their protagonists seek social assimilation and acceptance through frontiersmanlike labors, only to reject them for their ethnic inability to manifest the frontiersman's identity.

Chapter 4 considers my frontier model in the immediate aftermath of World War II, engaging again with questions of white masculinity via the figure of the returning veteran as depicted in Dorothy B. Hughes's *In a Lonely Place* (1947) and Fenton's *What Way My Journey Lies* (1946). I situate such men in the context of how residential space and urban form changed in postwar LA, articulating how the fiction figures certain types of accommodation as spaces of lone masculinity and others as spaces of feminized domesticity. For two veterans whose identities have been constructed in wartime on frontiersmanlike lines, anxieties of reintegration in the peacetime world, anxieties about domesticity and feminization, are made manifest in their attitudes to different kinds of living space. While their fates differ, both seem to suggest the exhaustion of frontierlike masculinity as a model for mastering LA.

My concluding observations cast this notion of frontier exhaustion forward to the 1960s and 1970s, positing that while the frontier may have survived its own closure to continue structuring LA fiction into the 1940s, it did finally meet its moment of continent's-end finality in the later decades of the twentieth century. It proved inadequate as an organizing strategy with which to represent a diversifying city that demanded to be on its own diverse terms, a demand that was reflected in a new profusion of representational perspectives in its literary culture.

"Literature of the American West," Allmendinger wrote in 1998, "has never had the literary equivalent of a frontier hypothesis." This, he averred, was one reason why critics continued to dismiss the writing of half a continent as "insignificant" or merely "regionalist."[180] Much determined work in the quarter-century since Allmendinger made that claim, his own among it, has helped to redress such unjust dismissals, but the observation that we lack a literary frontier theory has held true. I hope it may now at last be found, if imperfectly and incompletely constructed, in the pages that follow.

1

Dancing on the Edge

McCoy, Fante, and Desperate Moves on the Ballroom Frontier

"If you are looking for your brother," said the proprietor to me, "go to the dance hall. That is where you always find them."

—Carlos Bulosan, *America Is in the Heart*

This chapter locates frontier dynamics in literary representations of spaces where social dancing took place in 1930s and '40s Los Angeles. The texts explored are three lesser-known works by John Fante—the short stories "To Be a Monstrous Clever Fellow" (c. 1935) and "Helen, Thy Beauty is to Me—" (1941), and a film treatment cowritten with Jack Leonard, *A Letter from the President* (c. 1950), which I set alongside a more familiar LA dancehall fiction, Horace McCoy's *They Shoot Horses, Don't They?* (1935). The events of all four texts, therefore, take place either within or shortly after the 1920-1940 period identified by Russel Nye as when "public dancing in America reached its highest peak of both popularity and profit, and the dancehall became one of the nation's most influential social institutions."[1] As such, they are all memorials to a unique moment in the history of American leisure.

In these texts, the spatial particularities of the dancehall and dancefloor operate to replicate or recall a frontier model of American expansionist progress, and compel disadvantaged or marginalized individuals to participate performatively in this model via the allure of social, romantic, or financial rewards. These processes reproduce and revivify the now-unviable geographic frontier in symbolic internal spaces by means of complex sociospatial codes. By such means the labor of keeping the frontier alive is outsourced to the "others" of an undesirable social underclass—an ironized labor, for here it resides in what are ostensibly leisure activities. In claiming a role for the dancehall in such purposes, I pursue a 1932 assertion by the sociologist Paul Cressey that no other American recreational institution "reveal[ed] with as much clarity as many of the perplexing problems which make difficult the wholesome expression of human nature in the urban setting." For Cressey, the dancehall embodied "the impersonality of the city, the absence of restraints, the loneliness and the individual maladjustment and distraction characteristic of . . . the urban environment."[2] Paralleling Cressey's conception of the dancehall as a hostile landscape that at once liberates and assaults the individual, all four of these texts conceive of its social space as operating on frontier logic.

Although the establishments at the heart of these texts are all "dancehalls," they differ from each other in their social function and the methods by which they commodify dance. In Nye's reckoning, by 1920 there were "at least five types of places for dancing open to the public."[3] Nye distinguishes between dances for adolescents sponsored and supervised by charitable or municipal agencies; club, charity, and society balls; hotels, restaurants, and nightclubs that provided spaces for dancing; taxi-dancehalls (patronized almost exclusively by men who paid "hostesses" for each spin on the dancefloor); and vast, grand "dance palaces," which attracted a large and socially diverse male and female clientele, and were the most popular type of public dancing space in this period.[4] During the 1920s a sixth type of public dance institution came into being. This was the "dance marathon," which differed from the forms identified by Nye in that while it invited the public to pay for dance-based entertainment, the paying public were not themselves the dancers. "Helen" and *President* feature downtown Los Angeles taxi-dancehalls; the dancing of "Clever Fellow" occurs in a typical dance palace in Wilmington or Long Beach; *Horses* is set in a dance marathon held at the end of a pier in Santa Monica.

As all four texts describe commodified dancing entertainment in the same city and at similar times, but diverge in the forms of commercial dance they describe, they depict a set of related-yet-distinct social practices. The result of those distinctions, to adopt Henri Lefebvre's terminology, is the "production" of diverse types of space. In Lefebvre's triadic model of how space is produced, such distinctions of social form are expressed partly in "representations of space" (i.e., in the materiality of the spaces in which the dancing occurs), and partly in "spatial practice" (the social codes that govern access to and usage of those spaces). The dancehall as a social space is only produced, however, when it also acquires what Lefebvre terms the condition of "representational space": that is, when human beings occupy it either in accordance with or resistance to its representations of space (the physical form) and spatial practice (the non-physical form).[5] I am largely concerned with how McCoy's and Fante's texts make meaning through their characters' dancehall experiences—that is, through their iterations of representational space. In order, therefore, to apprehend the distinctive representational spaces that each of these texts inscribe, and therein the nature of their participation in a frontierist discourse, we must also distinguish carefully between the distinctive formal contexts of their respective dancehalls.

Perpetual Motion:
Horace McCoy's *They Shoot Horses, Don't They?*

Closed-frontier literary critics have upheld McCoy's novel as a central piece of evidence in their thesis that post-Depression Californian fictions are inevitably tragic studies in the frustration of continental motion. David Fine writes that in McCoy's novel "the void of the Pacific" beneath the pilings of the pier where the dance marathon takes place "becomes the commanding metaphor for dream's end."[6] In *Horses*, "Dance, traditionally a celebration of life, becomes a rite of death, a *danse macabre*. There are no celebrants and no winners, only an abrupt and crashing halt after 897 hours of futile movement, underscored by the insistent presence of the ocean pounding against the pilings. . . . The image is claustrophobic, reflecting their constant sense of entrapment, the entrapment of the dream itself."[7] Elsewhere, Fine describes the novel as one in which arriving at "the last place on the land" causes "beautiful dreams [to] become violent nightmares."[8] Similarly, Philip Melling writes that McCoy's tragic heroine, Gloria Beatty, has been lured to Los Angeles by a misguided belief that the West still possesses "regenerative properties." Melling joins Fine in grouping *Horses* with Nathanael West's *The Day of the Locust* as Depression-era Los Angeles novels about the "capacity for self-delusion and the worship of false fictions"—the greatest of all such fictions being the notion that "the frontier was still open."[9] Jan Goggans is less explicit in framing the novel as a tragic response to continental finality, but implies as much by linking a setting "over the Pacific" with Gloria's revelation that a "golden dream" of stardom in Hollywood is "destined for death from the start."[10] Likewise William Hare echoes closed-frontier pessimists in asserting that a sense of entrapped motion—McCoy's marathon's "exhausting relentlessness"—betokens the "hopeless plight of civilization."[11] A careful parsing of the space of McCoy's dancehall, however, problematizes readings of *Horses* as a post- or anti-frontier text.

Dance marathons were, in fact, imbued from their inception with echoes of the Turnerian frontiersman's physical determination, his characteristically paradoxical quality of everyman individualism, and even his resistance to governmental strictures. The marathon's beginnings were part of what Carol Martin terms "a larger cultural discourse . . . about breaking records" in the 1920s, of a piece with such esoteric entertainments as "endurance kissing competitions, marathon hand-holding contests, and milk-drinking, egg-eating, and gum-chewing races."[12] Increasingly improbable marathon dancing world records were set, rising from nine to 217 hours within the first six months of 1923.[13] These early marathons were contests of genuinely life-endangering endurance: Martin sees them as both an anti-puritanical reaction to the restrictions on personal freedom imposed by prohibition, and a way for unexceptional, ordinary Americans without particular talents or training to join the ranks of such famed 1920s record-setters as Amelia Earhart and Charles Lindbergh.[14]

Over the course of the 1920s such contests changed markedly, not least in response to moralizing anti-marathon legislation.[15] Competitions remained grueling, but became increasingly orchestrated, theatrical spectacles; participation was for some a professional occupation. In the new-style marathons of the 1930s, "contestants' health and grooming had become part of the spectacle of the event. Time was broken into discrete hourly units of rest and dancing. Actual dancing was not required, just continual motion and some semblance of the dance position."[16]

Although contestants would on command perform set-piece rehearsed dances, Martin emphasizes the extent to which non-dance entertainments came to dominate.[17] These included vaudeville-style comedy routines, wrestling matches, elimination races, weddings between contestants (some real, some confected), presentations by sponsors, and regular interjections from the voluble promoters.[18] Thus, while conventions of dance—music either live or recorded, the boundaries of the dancefloor as competition arena, male-female pairings as "teams"—persisted as the vestigial exoskeleton of the marathon's form, its spatial language (the acts of formally planning space and socially perceiving space that sit across Lefebvre's categories of representations of space and spatial practice) differed from that of other forms of commercial dance. There was a need for a larger audience space, rest areas for participants, and a dancefloor of a shape and size that suited elimination races and afforded the audience good sight-lines. Nevertheless, the fact that many marathon venues were converted from conventional dancehalls (often the result of the economic exigencies of the Depression) suggests the intimacy of dialogue between the two types of space.[19]

The unnamed Santa Monica location of the dance marathon in *Horses* is described by Robert Syverten, the novel's narrator, as an "enormous old building" that had previously been a "public dance hall."[20] Its size suggests that its prior existence was as one of the dance palaces that first began to dominate the social dancing scene in the 1910s: their vast capacities were their principal innovation, rendering obsolete "the smaller neighborhood saloon dance halls" of the late nineteenth century. In 1930, Santa Monica's Chamber of Commerce boasted of "five piers with every resort attraction . . . available," dancehalls included.[21] The grandest of these, the La Monica, was not constructed until 1924, while the oldest, on Pickering (formerly Fraser) Pier, was constructed in 1913 and enlarged in 1920.[22] Thus, while McCoy's fictionalized setting resists attempts to map his pier to an exact historical analogue, there was *no* pier-end dancehall in Santa Monica during the Depression to match Syverten's description of the dancehall as "old."[23]

Syverten describes a hippodrome-like arrangement of space within the hall. "Inside was a dance space for the contestants, thirty feet wide and two hundred feet long, and around this on three sides were loge seats, behind these were the circus seats, the general admission. At the end of the dance space was a raised platform for the orchestra."[24] Although not stated explicitly, it is unlikely that the long, very narrow dancefloor represents the building's original configuration as a "public dance hall"; rather, it seems that floorspace has been cannibalized to accommodate increased seating for the crowd. This is broadly consistent with Philip Evergood's luridly morbid painting of a marathon scene (figure 1.1), which shows several tiers of bleacher-style seating more common to sporting venues than to ballrooms, though his dancefloor appears circular. We do not know quite how large McCoy's hall is beyond its initial description as "enormous," but the Rendezvous Ballroom, which was operating in Los Angeles at the

Figure 1.1. Philip Evergood, *Dance Marathon* (1934). Evergood depicts a dance marathon scene similar to that described by McCoy. *Source*: Blanton Museum of Art, The University of Texas at Austin, Gift of Mari and James A. Michener, 1991.

same time as McCoy's fictional establishment, had a 12,000-square-foot dance floor, permitting 1,500 simultaneous dancing couples; Santa Monica's La Monica ballroom was even larger, with a 15,000-square-foot floor and the capacity to host 5,000 patrons.[25] Even taxi-dancehalls, which were typically smaller, could still accommodate 200–600 people.[26] The large fictional marathon Syverten recalls commences with only 144 couples: we can thus infer that in the process of conversion from a "public dance hall" to a marathon venue the revision of the building's internal organization has been fairly radical.

McCoy's marathon does superficially appear to support a Finean reading as a representation of the tragedy of frontier closure. Syverten repeatedly remarks on feeling the waves beneath his feet, pounding against the pilings of the pier: he is constantly aware that he is past the point of the continent's end, prompting his dance partner Gloria to scoff that he is "hipped on the subject of waves."[27] The dancehall is, for Robert, a space of utter entrapment, the rickety pier's attempt to eke out just a little more "free land" from the continent an apparently vain one. A closer assessment of this dancehall's peculiar spatiality, however, discloses something else. A space rendered "old" after no more than twenty years suggests the conception of the urban realm as provisional and the fixation upon relentlessly supplanting the old with the new that by the 1930s had come to be identified as characteristic of Los Angeles—not least by Anton Wagner, whose *Los Angeles* appeared in the same year as McCoy's novel. Ed Dimendberg notes that much of LA's urban scene in the early 1930s simply "would not have existed" ten years earlier, and would soon be "ineradicably altered" once more by wartime and postwar redevelopment.[28] McCoy is quite right: a dancehall erected in the 1910s *would* already have looked and felt old. Such insistence on constant forward motion, an impulse to reject the stably established in favor of the newly created, is also the governing principle of frontierism. Unlike the conquered continent, however, the "oldness" of the dancehall does not render its space exhausted, irrevocably de-frontierized. The hall's proprietors, alive to the growth of a new social form (the marathon), have reconceived an old space *as* new, proving not the inevitability of spatial exhaustion in post-frontier America but rather the inexhaustible resourcefulness of a frontier mindset to make new space even where none appears to exist—indeed, where the space seems to be an old, occupied one.

The application of a Lefebvrian model explicates this counterintuitive application of frontier dynamics. A change in social form, from ordinary public dancing to the marathon, has wrought a change in the *spatial practice* of the venue—the codes and expectations governing its perception and usage. This change in spatial practice inevitably and simultaneously produces alterations in the other aspects of the Lefebvrian spatial scheme. The physical fabric of the building itself, its representation of space, remains broadly recognizable from its "public dance hall" days, but has undergone significant alterations. These covalent changes in spatial practice and representation of space effect a change in representational space: the hall's experiential reality has changed markedly in the transition from couples dancing for their own entertainment to pairs of partners vying for prize money and the crowd's attention. Indeed, the competitive dynamic of endurance and exhaustion that governs the marathon is such that the marathon hall's representational space changes constantly throughout the event's duration. That sense of perpetual flux evinces Lefebvre's contention that space is not produced statically or with instantaneous stability but rather should be understood as an illimitably contingent process.[29] Not merely in the conversion of public hall to marathon hall but in the dynamics of the marathon itself, a process of spatial production is continually enacted in the triadic contingency of spatial practice, representation of space, and representational space. From that process a new space is constantly emerging, informed by its former condition but distinct from it: such a spatial dynamic is precisely that by which Turner defines the advancing frontier.

This Lefebvrian analysis of the changes in McCoy's converted dancehall extends a possibility that resourceful individuals possessed of Turner's "frontier spirit" (the innovative marathon entrepreneurs and their intrepid, record-seeking contestants) can reopen space once thought closed, in a sociospatial act of frontierist recycling. That marathons did indeed reach their popular peak during the Depression (and were perceived to offer a psychodrama of its desperations, despite having origins in the Roaring Twenties), while mainstream halls suffered, renders such a reading historically compelling.[30] It is thus possible to read the spatiality of McCoy's novel as suggesting not that the Depression corroborated the contemporary impossibility of America's former frontier ambitions, but quite the opposite—that it actively revived them. Only in a return to a climate of privation, adversity, and hardship not seen since the pioneer days were social conditions created in which the "new space" of the dance marathon, in its perfected form as a bizarre multi-event spectator sport, could be produced. The dangerous lengths to which McCoy's contestants push themselves, and the eagerness of the crowds to watch the grisly spectacle, suggest the extent to which the space of the dance marathon endeavors to reproduce the frontier's former function as a societal "safety valve." Where the existence of a frontier had once promised a solution to straitened socioeconomic circumstances in settled areas, a rich country beyond the hill, here audience and contestants conspire to construct out of their own climate of scarcity and precarity a social form built upon the frontierlike principles of perpetual motion and remaking of space.

The suicidal Gloria mocks Robert's belief that "the big break is always tomorrow," but such a belief represents a profoundly frontierist mode of thought.[31] Because the dream of frontier conquest exists only inasmuch as it can be deferred, and in its achievement in fact extinguishes itself, to live constantly in a state of chasing dreams, never quite grasping them, is to render oneself a frontiersman of sorts. This cast of desperate young people are kept in a liminality of privation and precarity wherein they do not die but cannot live comfortably, instead fending off daily challenges from the promoters and each other to survive in the contest. The contestants depend both materially and spiritually upon the marathon (it is their source of food, shelter, and hope of a final prize that never arrives) but are continually on the verge of being destroyed by its conditions: the "non-stop movement" by which they are sustained is also a "punishment" to be endured.[32] Robert's entrapment in the frustrated present of the dancehall thus performs a labor of frontier struggle on behalf and for the recreational privilege of his fellow Americans. Gloria's death wish, which becomes Robert's by extension, comes to seem less a response to the lack of frontier space than a response to the economic trap of the dancehall's performative frontier. The only way not to continue living in this seemingly interminable staging of a frontier between living and dying is to choose the latter.

In its specificity as a social moment, there are limits to the dance marathon as a model of a perpetually self-renewing frontier: marathons themselves may have seemed endlessly cyclical, but Ralph Giordano notes that before McCoy's novel was even published the marathon craze itself had already peaked, subdued by legislative restrictions and a renewed interest in other forms of social dance.[33] Nevertheless, as we turn to John Fante's depictions of those other, more persistent and familiar forms of dance, we find that they retain (and perhaps even amplify) the marathon's inherent staging of liminality and its imposition of exploitative "frontier labor" upon socially disadvantaged protagonists.

Dancing with Class: John Fante's "To Be a Monstrous Clever Fellow"

Critics have yet to recognize the strikingly consistent import with which the dancehall recurs as a setting in John Fante's writing. In addition to the three Fante fictions discussed in this chapter, a dancehall also appears fleetingly in Fante's best-known work, *Ask the Dust*, which joined West's *Locust* and Raymond Chandler's *The Big Sleep* in making 1939 an *annus mirabilis* for LA novels. Whenever Fante writes about a dancehall, it is a space where socially marginal male protagonists acquire and/or expend social capital by participating performatively in a societal mainstream from which they are otherwise excluded. Such participation is always provisional, temporary, and conditional, yet for that it is no less keenly sought. Fante's protagonists' attempts to access the dancehall, traverse its sociospatial boundaries, and claim the right to its spaces revivify LA as a space possessed of the potential to maintain a "frontier" identity by inverting and therein rendering reproducible the kind of frontier experience Turner had declared no longer tenable. The Turnerian frontiersman moved from spaces of "civilization" into those of "savagery," with the frontier a liminal zone between the two. Fante's protagonists continually attempt to move in what appears to be the opposite direction—away from spaces designated both physically and socially as "wilderness," toward a dominant cultural "center" that simultaneously resists the entrance of incomers, demands their submission to its norms, and is policed as such on lines of race and class.

These attempts are manifest in navigations of the sociospatial codes of the dancehall, which is accordingly produced as a model frontier—the liminal, contested zone Fante's protagonists negotiate to claim participation in a certain vision of American cultural life. It serves as a space of cultural contact between the parts of society coded "savage" and "civilized" by the occupants of the latter, extending to denizens of the former the hope of claiming a new, more socially normative identity. Because that possibility proves at best partial and at worst illusory, however, the inverted frontier dynamics of the dancehall are capable of endless recuperation and repetition. Whereas the original pioneer "conquered" each successive frontier until "free land" was exhausted, Fante's characters never "win" the dancehall; its apparent entrée to the social mainstream is always withdrawn or rendered untenable; "civilized" space stubbornly resists the ingress it seems to invite. The dancehall as it appears in these fictions, therefore, offers as it does in McCoy's *Horses* a striking but troubling rejoinder to notions that mid-twentieth-century fictive Californian space must betoken the frontier's tragic closure. Here the frontier has not disappeared but has merely been transmuted, the cultural labor it demands dislocated from physical space into and across liminalities of race and class.

"To Be a Monstrous Clever Fellow" is the story of a young longshoreman's attempt to find romance among the privileged female college students at the local dancehall. The story is undated and its protagonist unnamed, but the performatively intellectual, near-manic voice of its first-person narration strongly, per Stephen Cooper, "prefigures the Arturo Bandini of *The Road to Los Angeles*," which Fante completed in 1936.[34] The story is likely set between 1930 and 1932.[35] Like the Bandini of *The Road*, the protagonist of "Clever Fellow" repeatedly quotes and muses on Friedrich Nietzsche and James Branch Cabell.[36] "Clever Fellow," however, departs from *The Road* and the vast majority of Fante's other early work in that there is no mention of the protagonist's ethnicity among the sources of the social difficulty he faces. Anxieties engendered by Italian American identity do not appear here, as they so commonly do in Fante's quasi-autobiographical fictions.[37] The protagonist's family are Catholic, but nothing Italianate is confirmed.[38] The protagonist's mother's speech contains none of the accented or broken English with which Fante often identifies characters of Italian origin.[39] Moreover, none of the women whom the protagonist and his friend Eddie meet within the dancehall comment on the protagonist's ethnicity, whereas elsewhere in Fante's corpus it is a perpetual bone of contention in his Italian American characters' attempts to build relationships with women.[40] Indeed, without knowledge of Fante's usual fictional concerns, there would be no reason to assume the protagonist of "Clever Fellow" is anything other than accepted as Anglo-American. Indeed, the very absence of ethnic identifiers in the text implies whiteness as an American social default—a "kind of absence" that functions as a "dominant and normative space against which difference is measured"—an idea to which I will return extensively in chapter 3.[41]

Fante frames the dancehall in terms of sociospatial demarcation. "A white wicker fence two feet high surrounded the marble floor," and Eddie and the protagonist must "bore" their way through crowds to reach that fence, physically asserting their right to the dancefloor through an act of spatial penetration.[42] The space presents an immediate social challenge to that ingress because, the protagonist feels, dancehalls are "places where women managed to be the suaver," putting men at an innate disadvantage.

58 | The Recursive Frontier

Ultimately, however, it is the protagonist's small physical size that renders him reluctant to ask for a dance even from a girl he deems beneath his station.[43] The physical capacity to occupy space, with its implications of masculinity and virility, is at stake. In the dancehall as on the frontier, physical weakness places an individual at a direct disadvantage in a process that tests one's powers as a spatial occupier; here, as there, physical fitness is in direct proportion to the ability to occupy the hostile environment.

Having been rejected once, by an "ugly" girl, the protagonist identifies a new prospect, a woman named Nina Gregg. She accepts his request to dance with a rhetorical "why not?"—on the basis that the number commencing is a "keen tune" rather than because of any qualities in her prospective dance partner.[44] In this hall, dancers buy tickets to access the floor on a per-dance basis rather than via a cover charge on entry to the building. That purchased right to access the floor for a period of time is also, it seems, a right to indulge in fantasy: as the protagonist of "Clever Fellow" steps onto the floor with Nina, he acquires temporary, illusory ascendance in a social hierarchy. Nina feels the protagonist looks familiar and wonders if she has seen him previously on the campus of Stanford University. Anxious to succeed in his romantic endeavors, to avoid another rejection, and to make conspicuous use of his autodidactic erudition, the protagonist weaves claims that not only is he "a Stanford man," but one Professor Cabell, a teacher of communism, no less.[45] The deceit succeeds, and the pair share five dances before retiring for malted milks in a "darkened corner of the hall." As his growing confidence rapidly inverts his prior anxieties of inferiority—he "soon grew tired of her stupidity"—the protagonist makes increasingly forward advances to Nina. If he is to be believed, she is similarly passionate, but will not consent to a walk along the beach as, it is implied, she understands what the protagonist intends by such a request. "I won't leave this hall," she insists, expressing her rejection of greater intimacy by invoking the dancehall's spatial bounding of normative social practice.[46]

Despite rebuking him for impropriety, Nina continues to hold the protagonist's hand, until she eventually notices that its physical condition does not suggest an academic's book-bound existence. "Her fingertips moved gently over the calluses, and her hand became tight, as though recoiling from something disgusting. That morning before work I had split the broken blisters open and applied iodine to keep the inner skin from blistering. I could not work with gloves. The splitting left the mounds sharp and jagged, like an animal's paw, so that rubbing my hand across my forearm left white scratch marks."[47] The deceit is revealed. The protagonist's hand reveals him to be a manual laborer, not a professor, and Nina is disgusted, loudly branding him a liar and "nothing but a ditch digger, or a truck driver, or something."[48] She slaps him about the face and disappears into the crowd. A series of navigations within the codified space of the dancehall have been the key to the protagonist's attempt to move himself closer to a desirable "center" of society, but also ultimately his undoing.

Descriptions of the male dancers have thus far been curiously ambiguous. Superficially, their description as "stags" merely denotes in slang the fact that they have arrived unaccompanied, but it also assigns to them the position of a hunted game animal—an identity cognate with the protagonist's sense that he is socially and physically vulnerable to the dancehall's women. Simultaneously, however, the men are described as circling the room waiting to entrap any unescorted woman who should come near.[49] The dancehall's ticket-taker is a "keeper," but the identity of the game he keeps is uncertain: the men are either prey or predator depending on one's social vantage point.[50] This insolubly subjective mutability in the text's application of "savage" and "civilized" images to its protagonists indicates the dancehall's capacity to model the frontier's mediation between the two. In his being revealed as a manual laborer, however, the protagonist's place in that bifurcated structure of bestial/human imagery is finally fixed: his hand is "an animal's paw." In proclaiming himself a Stanford professor and regaling his dance partner with his most erudite phrases, the protagonist has attempted to claim a position as the very epitome of "civilization." When the physical manifestations of his class position align him with the animal, however, he is confronted with the awful truth that the society in which he has attempted to inculcate himself through his dancefloor deception in fact aligns him ineluctably with "savagery." An attempt to cross and conquer a social frontier has collapsed in a humiliating realization that the poles of frontier exchange are, for him, reversed.

The spatial politics of the dancehall and their capacity to generate social illusions articulate this failed frontier crossing. It is Nina who erroneously imagines she has seen the protagonist at Stanford, and on the dancefloor she believes his lies, despite his obviously young age and ludicrous attempts at erudition—"we sons of Leland are proficient with the nether limbs."[51] If the protagonist's physical struggle through the crowd to reach the dancefloor in the center of the room spatializes his attempts to enter rarefied academic (and romantic) society through social deceits, it also affirms that any access he can gain to such spheres is as illusory as the lies he tells to achieve such access. This is because his lies have a hard spatial limit: beyond the floor they begin to fall apart. The spatial practice of the dancefloor appears to be one of extreme possibility, imbued with scope for illusion. In dancing with the protagonist over the course of five songs, Nina has presumably had ample time to become acquainted with his tell-tale, calloused, animal-paw hands, yet while on the floor she does not notice. Upon leaving the floor, however, even a darkened corner of the room cannot hide the protagonist's true identity.

The dancefloor, then, is in "Clever Fellow" produced as a social space that manifests conditions of illusion, fantasy, and rarefaction. Its physical position in the hall and its psychological position as the locus of the protagonist's social aspirations, moreover, suggest that this state of spatially and temporally limited illusion also models an American society into whose core working-class individuals cannot penetrate deeply or for long. In this respect it reconstitutes the dynamics of the frontier because it calls upon such individuals to bridge a gap between perceived "savagery" and perceived "civilization" located within itself. The inconsistent application of the hunting imagery and the protagonist's ultimate discovery and rejection, furthermore, indicate the dancehall's frontierlike status as an environment with the capacity to betray. When such individuals are compelled to participate in its paradigm they are invited to consider themselves representative of the "civilized," only to confront a subsequent disclosure that dancehall spatial practice in fact accords them a "savage" role.

Taxi Drivers: John Fante and Floyd Davis's "Helen, Thy Beauty Is to Me—"

The short story "Helen, Thy Beauty Is To Me—" first appeared in the *Saturday Evening Post* in March 1941.[52] In it, Fante develops and complicates the dancehall-frontier paradigm established by "Clever Fellow" by introducing additional economic and ethnic stakes to the dancehall's spaces. Here we enter a taxi-dancehall in the company of a Filipino migrant laborer named Julio Sal. Although "Helen" and "Clever Fellow" were written only around five years apart, they are divided in their settings by nearly a full decade.[53] Geographically, however, they are almost counterposed upon each other. Julio Sal lives in the same neighborhood and does much the same exhausting dock work as the narrator of "Clever Fellow." Their living circumstances are to some extent comparable, too: the Clever Fellow shares his home with family, Julio with friends, but their domestic lives are similarly cheek by jowl and lacking in privacy. There was already a significant Filipino community in Los Angeles by the early 1930s, when "Clever Fellow" is set.[54] In that story, though, labors (both on the docks and in the dancehall) that in "Helen" are performed by an immigrant of racially liminal status are instead performed by an apparently white American man. Like McCoy's marathon impresarios revisioning the architecture of obsolete halls, Fante reinscribes near-identical spatial parameters with different representations of space, a creative act itself suggestive of a pragmatic post-frontier urge to produce new space in old.

The social and commercial characteristics particular to the taxi-dancehall as a specific subvariety of dance establishment are intrinsic to how Fante develops his dancefloor-frontierist discourse of space, place, race, and capital. The practice of taxi-dancing began in gold-rush San Francisco and persisted for around a century thereafter (with, apparently, a brief revival in 1970s Los Angeles), but experienced its peak of popularity in the 1920s and '30s when, in the words of Lawrence Hong and Robert Duff, it became "one of the most common forms of masculine recreation."[55] A taxi-dancer around this time might undertake seventy to eighty dances per night, charging each customer ten cents per dance, of which the house would take a 50 percent cut.[56]

This pursuit captured the public imagination, evinced by its representation in prominent cultural artifacts of the day such as the 1930 short film *Roseland* (named after the New York ballroom on which it focuses) and an outbreak of artworks entitled *Ten Cents a Dance*: a Rodgers and Hart-penned song that was a big hit for Ruth Etting in 1930, a 1931 film starring Barbara Stanwyck, and a 1933 painting by Reginald Marsh. As Ernest Burgess suggested in his introduction to Paul Cressey's study of taxi-dancing, the general public's image of the taxi-dancehall was largely informed by (often sensationalist) media portrayals rather than by first-hand familiarity.[57] The taxi-dancehall or "closed hall" was popular, but its clientele was largely limited to ethnic minority or otherwise socially marginalized men. As Gregory Mason put it in a 1924 *American Mercury* piece, "the chief *raison d'être* [sic] of the closed hall is to provide amusement for worthy but unattractive men who are unable to compete against the perfumed haberdashers and bank clerks of the palaces."[58] As Giordano confirms, this meant "working class whites, Filipinos, Chinese, Mexicans, Polish, Italians, Greeks, Jews, and college and high-school boys, as well as patrons with physical handicaps"—almost any men "shunned by society," except African Americans, who remained excluded even from taxi-halls.[59] Indeed, taxi-dancehalls, like marathon halls, had often been converted from older, smaller examples of the "conventional" dancehall (and in so doing accepted a less desirable clientele of societal fringe-dwellers) as a direct result of their inability to compete with a newer generation of grand dance palaces.[60] The buildings themselves, like their clients, were the undesirable outcasts of the dancing industry.

If, however, the public fascination with taxi-dancing was disproportionate to actual participation therein, then the moral panic it engendered was equally outsized. Certainly, all forms of public dance attracted scrutiny from moralizers and religious groups throughout its period of greatest popularity, but the taxi-dancehall was singled out for particular indignation, especially with regard to links with vice.[61] In 1933 Jesse Steiner averred in a report for President Hoover's Research Committee on Social Trends that the "problems of control and supervision" presented by taxi-dancing had "not yet been successfully met." Indeed, repeated attempts were made across the country to ban taxi-dancehalls outright: in Chicago they were shut down as part of efforts to "clean up" the city ahead of the 1933 World's Fair.[62] Mason described the case made by "moral crusaders" against the taxi-dancehall as resting on a belief that it was "more frankly commercial, primitive and sordid than either the club or the palace."[63] Indeed, it is this quality of being "more frankly commercial," more brazen in its laying-bare of the transactional mechanics underpinning its entertainments than other forms of dancehall, that seems to have aroused particular moral concern. Taxi-dancing was not merely more sordid *and* more commercial than other forms of dance, it was more sordid *because* it was more commercial. Thus both Steiner and Ella Gardner, in a 1929 report on dancehall regulations for the Children's Bureau of the Department of Labor, refer disapprovingly and in near-identical language to the taxi-halls' "extreme commercialization" of dance.[64] Actual immorality in the taxi-halls was, by contrast, reported by Cressey to have been substantially exaggerated.[65]

If the taxi-dancehall's place in the public imagination in this period initially seems incommensurate with its marginalized clientele, then the pejorative terms in which it was described disclose that its disproportionate prominence in contemporary cultural discourse arose not in spite but because of the socioethnic status of taxi-dancing's patrons. In a 1947 PhD thesis, Clyde Vedder noted that "the first taxi-dance hall of Los Angeles, the 'Red Mill' (1919) was closed because church people opposed the idea of 'our blondes' dancing with Filipinos and Orientals."[66] While Los Angeles's anti-dance legislation remained minimal, Vedder confirms that local police developed an informal code for dancehall management, and Linda España-Maram notes that police in this period frequently raided the taxi-dancehalls popular with the city's Filipinos and Mexicans.[67] Although typically this was ostensibly to break up scuffles between patrons rather than directly on morality or vice grounds, the association between taxi-dancehalls and immigrant populations lay behind much of this supposed social concern. Anxieties about the taxi-halls' commercial frankness coded a deeper anxiety about ethnic others purchasing access to a social institution that in turn promised access to white American women (even if in an illusory or temporary form). This is precisely the kind of access that the immigrant itinerant laboring protagonists of Fante's taxi-dancehall texts—"Helen" and the later *A Letter from the President*—attempt to purchase.

Of all the immigrant groups peopling California's taxi-dancehalls, it was the state's Filipino community that made the taxi-dancehall a particular center of its cultural life. España-Maram asserts that taxi-dancing was "the leisure activity arguably most closely associated with Filipino immigrants of the 1920s and 1930s."[68] In Los Angeles, the Filipino community was made up in 1930 of around 4,000 year-round residents, but swelled considerably on a seasonal basis as workers migrated from job to job.[69] Ninety-four percent of the Filipino immigrant population in Los Angeles was made up of young men, and part of the taxi-dancehall's success was indeed that its provision of commoditized female companionship ameliorated the social effects of that gender disparity.[70] España-Maram, however, accords far greater social significance to the taxi-dancehall as a feature of California Filipino life, identifying it as a "dynamic alternative subculture," with a richer and broader role within a community defined by the patterns of migratory labor than simply providing a simulacrum of female intimacy.[71]

> Earning meagre wages for tedious, hard work often in closely supervised positions, Filipinos . . . create[d] meaning in their lives by developing cultural practices that spoke to the connections between rural and urban experiences. The taxi dance

> halls . . . became significant rendezvous points for calling the community into being . . . along the migration circuit. . . .
>
> In their search for places that afforded them some sense of dignity and relative freedom of expression, Filipino workers flocked to taxi dance halls to tout young brown bodies not as exploited workers but as agents of enjoyment, style, and sensuality.[72]

Fante conveys little of España-Maram's sense of the taxi-dancehall as part of a distinct, proudly Filipino form of social expression. While it is clear in "Helen" that taxi-dancing is a huge part of Filipino social life, Fante's account frames this in terms of variably successful attempts to participate in and assimilate to American culture rather than to generate a new social form.

For precisely that reason, assessments of Fante's clutch of Filipino-centered stories by Filipino and Filipino American critics have not been flattering; in 1948 Manuel Buaken wrote that "Fante has virtually no understanding of the subterranean spiritual life" and dismissed Julio Sal as offensively "stupid, ignorant, and helpless."[73] In 1976 Marcellino Foronda offered similar criticisms, but was more generous in attributing to Fante noble but misguided aims.[74] More recently, Augusto Espiritu has likewise conceded that Fante, along with Carey McWilliams and William Saroyan, "championed the 'Filipino' in various ways," but notes that "their portrayals nonetheless evinced a mixture of caricature, condescension, and sometimes hostility, unable to escape the colonial and racialized image of the Filipino as 'little brown brother.'"[75] Indeed, Fante adopted not merely that image but precisely that description as the unfortunate working title of a planned novel about Filipino migrant labor, which was to have reused "Helen" as its first chapter. Fante abandoned *The Little Brown Brothers* after scathing feedback from Viking, his publisher, on a partial draft: even white readers of the 1940s concluded that Fante's efforts to inhabit the California Filipino experience were insensitive at best.[76] To defend Fante's Filipino writings, moreover, risks replicating the very shortcomings that demand defense, as when Richard Collins argues that these stories almost match Fante's Italian-focused material because they share its "ethnic flavor and passion."[77]

Yet as Pasquale Verdicchio writes, Fante "wants his writing to . . . shake readers out of any comfortable and illusory distance we might assume."[78] He may be incapable of inhabiting Filipino voice or experience, but he succeeds precisely in impressing upon an audience implicitly more economically and spatially privileged than his protagonist that distance itself is so often illusory. In "Helen" it is revealed that constant and immutable physical parameters are inadequate tools with which to measure and map spaces. Rather, Julio Sal's experiential mapping affirms that spaces continually flex to produce new dimensions and meanings that depend upon and change according to the relative social, racial, and financial positions of the individual intending to occupy them. In these unstable occupations of space, as in those of McCoy's marathon contestants, frontier dynamics are an incipient presence. The dancehall is the theatre in which Fante stages those dynamics, the dancefloor the surface upon which he re-contests the problematic logics of the frontier. Such efforts are instructively suggested by the Floyd Davis illustrations that accompanied "Helen" in its original magazine publication. In its original print appearance, it was impossible to read "Helen" without also reading Davis's images, and thus I read them in concert here.

In one image, which in the magazine occupies almost the entire recto of a double-page spread (figure 1.2), we see Julio Sal dancing with Helen, the taxi-dancer of his dreams. In the background, Davis depicts

Figure 1.2. Floyd Davis, detail from illustration for "Helen, Thy Beauty Is to Me—" (1941). Julio Sal dances with Helen at the taxi-dancehall, watched by his envious compatriots. *Source: Saturday Evening Post*, March 1, 1941, 15.

Sal's compatriots, whom Fante describes as watching the dance with envy. "Ten of them strained against the railing, each clutching a fat roll of tickets, ready to rush upon the golden girl the moment Julio's last ticket disappeared inside the glass box."[79] The other Filipinos in the image are drawn as crude racial stereotypes: with their identical attire and "oriental" features they are almost indistinguishable from each other. Curiously, however, Julio Sal, seen in profile, bears scant resemblance to his countrymen. Where their hair is loose, Julio's appears slicked back. His dignified, thoughtful expression contrasts starkly with his counterparts' scowls, laughs, and vacant stares. Unique among the Filipinos as depicted by Davis, Julio's nose is defined and prominent and he seems to have a supratarsal fold (the upper eyelid crease that many people from East Asia typically do not possess).

Thus, while his fellow Filipinos are presented as an unindividuated mass of East Asian grotesques in accordance with the physiognomic conventions of ethnic caricature, Julio Sal appears at least quasi-"European." His complexion is no lighter than that of the other Filipinos, but the radical difference between Julio's features and those of his countrymen recontextualizes the racial connotations of the skin tone he shares with them: on the dancefloor, Julio's overall appearance might more readily be parsed as Latino than as Filipino. Indeed, if this image invokes any racially inflected stereotype of the day, it is that of the "Latin lover" popularized on film two decades earlier by Ramon Novarro and Rudolph Valentino (see figure 1.3). According to Cressey, this is indeed exactly how Filipinos were sometimes perceived in taxi-dancehalls. He quotes a dancer who "didn't even know what a Filipino was. I thought they were movie actors or something," due to their good manners and expensive tastes. "The acceptability of the Filipino, in preference to other Oriental groups, is explained by such factors as his Occidental culture, represented in the Spanish influence in the Philippine Islands; his suave manners, dapper dressing, and politeness; and the romantic Spanish-lover role which it is possible for him to play."[80]

Julio Sal's appearance, however, is inconsistent in Davis's illustrations. At one point in Fante's story, Julio purchases a nine-dollar bottle of champagne at the ballroom's bar, at Helen's request. She has taken Julio into her confidence, counterintuitively, by breaking the dancehall's thin illusion of intimacy, frankly laying bare for him the transactional mechanics that underpin its facsimile of a "real" date by informing him that her preference for expensive drinks is a mercenary one—she receives a percentage commission on what her partners order. As soon as the

Figure 1.3. Rudolph Valentino, "How Do You Dance?" (1922). Compare Floyd Davis's rendering of Julio Sal with Rudolph Valentino's expression, posture, hairstyle, and features as he appeared with Gloria Swanson in a (supposedly self-penned) guide to tango dancing published in the April 1922 issue of the movie fan magazine *Screenland*. The images were taken by Paramount Pictures' in-house still photographer, Donald Keyes. Source: *Screenland*, April 1922, 37. Public domain.

champagne is poured, however, Helen induces Julio to return to the dancefloor with her, as her "favorite number" has just begun. When they take their seats again, after the dance, the champagne has already been cleared away. Despite (or perhaps because of) Helen's earlier openness with him regarding her financially incentivized motivations, Julio suspects that Helen has "tricked him." He protests to the "tall, Kansas-like," implicitly white waiter but receives only a humiliating reminder of the persistent social disadvantages at which he is placed by his ethnicity, and is forced to buy a second bottle to save face.

> "No. You cheat me. Nine dollars, not one drink."
> The waiter leaned across the table and the waiter's thick hand clutched the throat of Julio Sal, pushed back his head.[81]

In depicting Julio's humiliation by the waiter (figure 1.4), Davis discomfortingly renders the story's protagonist as almost simian in appearance, with a flat nose and large upper lip; his arms are contorted and his previously slick hair unkempt as the imposing waiter makes his supposed racial superiority manifest in bluntly physical fashion. Of course, neither the Filipino population at large nor its 1930s Californian diaspora are or were ethnically homogenous, not least given the legacy of centuries of Spanish colonialism. It is accordingly not merely plausible but factual that some Filipinos could (like Davis's dancefloor Julio Sal) be said to "look more Hispanic" than others. The fact, however, that the racial coding of Julio's appearance changes from one illustration to another, while the Filipino bystanders *are* depicted as a homogenous group (and one whose homogeneity is racially pejorative), precludes the attribution of Julio's changing appearance to some appreciation of Filipino ethnic diversity on Davis's part.

Meanwhile, Fante's reference to Julio's "Malay brain" carries troubling implications of racial psycho-anthropology and eugenicist thought, but in the context of the period's Anglo parlance does little to suggest any real particularity of ethnic heritage that might offer a clue as to how Julio's proximity to whiteness, relative to that of his peers, might have been perceived. Contemporary legal wrangles over Filipino legal status, particularly those around interracial marriage (most famously the case of Roldan v. Los Angeles County), hinged on the question of whether Filipinos were members of "the Mongolian race" or "the Malay race," illustrating that "Malay" was in this period deployed as a broad racial category to which

Dancing on the Edge | 69

Figure 1.4. Floyd Davis, detail from illustration for "Helen, Thy Beauty Is to Me—" (1941). The racialization of Julio Sal's appearance shifts to emphasize his humiliation by the white waiter. *Source: Saturday Evening Post*, March 1, 1941, 14.

all Filipino ethnic groupings could be assigned.[82] As Peggy Pascoe suggests, contemporary anti-miscegenation law essentially used "Malay" as a synonym for "Filipino."[83] As early as 1945, ethnologist Herbert Krieger lamented the popular prevalence of "Malay" as an umbrella term for an inaccurate and arbitrary grouping of distinct ethnic groups invented by white colonial powers—the "erroneously so-called Malay race."[84]

A reference to a "Malay brain" might, then, at least suggest that Julio is intended to be presented as "indigenously" Filipino, as opposed to as an individual with largely Spanish ancestry.[85] Later, however, Fante refers to Julio's "Spanish-Malay passion for bright leather," another invidious attribution of character traits to ethnic background, but one that imputes to Julio a more mixed heritage than the initial reference to a "Malay brain" implies, the inconsistency further clouding the question of ethnicity and by extension appearance.[86] We know merely that Julio is from Luzon, of peasant stock, and has some mixture of "Malay" and "Spanish" in his ancestry. Fante does not in fact provide *any* truly distinguishing information about Julio's ethnic identity or its possible implications for his appearance. Julio is essentially offered, problematically, as a generic everyman "California Filipino."

Thus, while one cannot reliably attribute Julio's changing appearance in Davis's images directly to specific cues from Fante's text, both text and images reflect a conception of Filipino ethnicity and appearance as something mutable or indeterminate. Davis allows Julio's appearance to differ from that of his fellows and to shift dramatically from image to image, while Fante subtly modulates a "Malay brain" into a "Spanish-Malay" passion. These details suggest the extent to which Filipinos living in the United States at this time occupied a socially liminal space—ill-understood and difficult to categorize, an uncomfortable anomaly within the totalizing structures of race and rights that existed in America upon their arrival. Just as the "Malay race" controversy placed Filipinos in a uniquely "curious and equivocal" sociolegal position, so did the Philippines' complex constitutional relationship with the United States.[87] Filipinos were "neither citizens nor ordinary aliens," occupying in law a near-literal frontier between citizenship's full participation in American "civilization" and the dangerous otherness of alien status.[88] Filipinos' status as a "mobile labor force"—repeatedly relocating from state to state or region to region for seasonal work—placed them likewise in a sociospatial liminality.[89] They did build communities in cities like Los Angeles, in this respect adhering to expectations of assimilative ethnic incomers, yet these communities were often small, impermanent, and portable, sharing space with those of other ethnicities, expanding and contracting with the laboring seasons.[90] The ambiguous and shifting approaches taken by Fante and Davis to Julio's ethnic appearance articulate the strange social mutability of California Filipinos in the 1930s, even if their vagueness about how Julio looks and where he comes from is simply symptomatic of the same.

Intentionally or not, the apparently protean ethnicity suggested by text and drawings alike interrogates Julio's ability to move within an ethno-social spectrum that is mapped closely to financial exchanges and designations of space. The ethno-visual language of Davis's illustrations can be understood, in concert with Fante's text, as serving to represent the way in which the dancehall's hierarchies of race and capital intersect both with each other and with the precisely demarcated divisions of space that structure the ballroom itself and codify its social forms. Despite all its illusions—of which Julio Sal is at times entirely aware, at others wholly possessed—the dancefloor *is* a socially and even physically transformative space. Fante notes that "five feet, four inches was the height of Julio Sal, but when that Helen's golden head lay on his shoulder, strength and grandeur filled his body."[91] Superficially, it is Helen who confers this transformation upon Julio; she makes him feel in every sense a bigger man. Helen, however, is only accessible via the dancefloor, and by the continual purchase of the ten-cent tickets that promise the bearer another minute with his chosen woman. Indeed, the entire story centers around Julio's misguided belief that Helen is a genuine romantic prospect, a belief that will ultimately reveal itself as unsustainable outside the space of the dancefloor: it is access to this space itself that grants Julio's transformation.

The dancefloor is mapped in five dimensions. The first three are those of space: a "wicker fence" with a railing separates the dance space from the rest of the dancehall; the sole point of ingress and egress is a small gate that opens only between dances. Those who have run out of tickets are ejected from the space at this point (not by force but by convention), while men who have tickets rush in to replace them. This marks the point at which the spatial dimensions of the dancefloor intersect with its fourth dimension, time. Dances last for one minute, and a bell clangs between each, drawing an easily-navigable but unbreakable temporal grid across the space. Time, however, parceled out metonymically into dances, must be paid for: this financial structuring of the space is its fifth dimension. One-minute, one-dance tickets control access to the space; nobody can dance without the wherewithal to keep buying time/ dances. It might be argued that a sixth dimension is a code of mutually understood conventions and expectations: the "rules" determining where one dances, who one dances with, how one obtains a dance, how long it lasts, and so on. Certainly, an understanding of these social conventions is intrinsic to understanding the space, but those conventions do not constitute a separate dimension as much as they suffuse and are suffused by all five former dimensions individually and collectively. As Lefebvre articulates, all space is produced contingently, and all space is social.

The space of the dancefloor is furthermore in all respects a transitory one. It is structured upon:

a. the transitory nature of time, which when demarcated into minutes by tickets and the tolling bell is lent a scarcity value;

b. the transitory nature of space, in that patrons move not only across the floor while dancing but to and from the floor in order to dance (another demarcation which creates a scarcity value inside the boundary fence—the dancefloor can only accommodate so many dancers);

c. the transitory nature of money, in that its transference (from the patron to the ticket clerk or dancer) grants the patron control over space and time, but only to a limited and partial extent. The patron remains subservient to the governing spatial and temporal codes of the space, as dictated by convention and the proprietors.

This state of constant transition effected on interlinked axes of temporal, spatial, and social progress (on the dancefloor manifest as the exchange of money for dances) is one the taxi-dancehall shares with the frontier as schematized in Turner's wave model.

Julio navigates the hall's monetary dimension to access the spatial dimensions of the floor via its temporal dimension, and in doing so appears to grow in stature, apparently literally, "towering over" Helen's golden hair to look out at his watching countrymen. Unless Helen is remarkably short, it seems implausible that Julio, at "five feet, four inches" really "towers" over her. He is tall enough for her to rest her head on his shoulder, but looking again at Davis's image, we note that while Julio is indeed taller than Helen in the image, he certainly does not "tower."[92] Moreover, she does not look up at him adoringly as Gloria Swanson does to Valentino in figure 1.3, but rather down at her feet, as if trying to avoid drawing herself up to her full height. Davis's illustration perhaps gestures to the ways in which Helen, a seasoned professional used to dancing with Filipinos—"all the Filipinos loved Helen"—may be employing subtle physical tricks to support the illusion of dominant masculine stature that her clients wish to purchase along with their dance.[93]

The most profound effect, however, is not physical but a psychic illusion of social transformation. Given the association, in both stereotype and data, between Filipino men and a shortness of stature relative to most American men, it is hard to read the extra height—the "strength and grandeur"—felt by Julio when he dances with Helen as anything other than a feeling of becoming more American.⁹⁴ Buying time and space with an American woman on the dancefloor is an act of buying access to a fleeting, illusory experience of sharing her citizenship. That illusion reveals itself as such when the "dismay" of the Filipinos who have been watching Julio turns instantly to mockery upon the expenditure of his final dance ticket. "The wicker gate opened and he [Julio] was lost in an avalanche of little brown men fighting for the golden girl."⁹⁵ Fante traffics in the crude racist stereotypes of the day—depersonalization ("avalanche"), animalization ("fighting," apparent pack behavior), the description "little brown men" itself. Those pejoratives do, however, affirm that the transformational effect of a move between the space within and without the dancefloor is a racial/ethnic one. Julio may be "lost" among the "avalanche" of his compatriots, but paradoxically he remains distinct enough for his "lostness" to be visible. A dance with Helen renders Julio distinct from "the little brown men."

This illusion of ethnic distinction enables Julio to sustain, for as long (and only as long) as he remains on the dancefloor, an elaborate reverie of marriage to Helen, in which she "fr[ies] his bacon and eggs in a blue-tinted kitchen like in the movie pitch."⁹⁶ The reality, that (quite apart from Helen's feelings on the matter, which go unconsidered in Julio's thinking) any possibility of such a "blissful future" had been foreclosed in California by the definitive extension of anti-miscegenation law to Filipinos in 1933, only occurs to Julio after he leaves the hall.⁹⁷ The "movie pitch" suburban domestic fantasia of the dancehall reverie suggests that Julio's dream of love and marriage with Helen is a dream of claiming or at least approximating American whiteness. That suggestion is affirmed in Julio's regret that he cannot write to Helen in English. He must instead ask his university-educated friend Antonio Repollo to write to Helen on his behalf: tearfully, Julio acknowledges that his failure to attend "American school" when younger was a "big mistake."⁹⁸ Fante connects the possession of literacy with the possibility of possessing Helen through less-than-subtle symbolism: Julio first attempts to write the letter himself, only to sit for half an hour, sweat breaking upon his brow, before the "white and untouched" paper. Just as lack of linguistic proficiency in "American" prevents Julio from making his mark upon one pristine whiteness, his inability to *be* American precludes any intimacy with Helen beyond the paid-for, illusory realm of the dancehall.

It thus becomes clear that Floyd Davis's rendering of Julio Sal as dramatically less "East Asian" in appearance than his watching compatriots reflects the transformation that occurs when he steps through the gate and onto the dancefloor. Here, for ten cents a minute, via the company of a blonde, white American woman, he can buy momentary access to an American identity. Even here he cannot quite ascend the racial hierarchy to the "full whiteness" of Anglo-American personhood, hence his perhaps Hispanic appearance. Nevertheless, as long as one's dance tickets last the possibility is maintained that one can buy a fuller participation in American society, becoming American through a monetary exchange that grants access to a rarefied area of space and time. With his fluent English and University of Washington degree, Repollo appears to have purchased with cultural capital a fuller access to American identity. Yet he too is apparently still working in the canneries with his fellow Filipinos, sleeping in the same cramped, malodorous bunkhouse. Repollo's attempts to access the advantages of American society through education may appear more substantial than Julio Sal's imitation of American courtship at the dancehall, but have in fact been scarcely more successful. Indeed, while Julio's misguided courtship of Helen fails, in actual prewar Los Angeles the dancehall *did* provide Filipinos with social opportunities ordinarily only accessible to Anglo-Americans, such as quasi-romantic interactions with white women and the opportunity to be "served" by white staff (in contrast to the typical racial orientation of their socioeconomic roles).[99] Problematic and limited though Fante's presentation of California Filipino culture is, he apprehends at least some of España-Maram's sense of the taxi-dancehall as a space that was sought by Filipinos because it "afforded them some sense of dignity and relative freedom of expression."[100] In the same gesture, though, he also identifies the dancehall's restriction of such dignity and freedom within spatial, monetary, temporal, and social limits.

In both Fante's text and Davis's drawings, the scene where Julio argues with the waiter illustrates precisely these limits. Despite writing to Helen for three months without reply, Julio's hopes of marriage remain strong. He has doubts, but reassures himself, spending $125 of his carefully-saved $350 in wages on clothes in order to boost his confidence and impress his beloved, and a further $75 on an engagement ring.[101] On returning at last to the dancehall with the intention of proposing to Helen, he is troubled to see that she "had changed in three months," then realizes "she did not remember him." This lack of recognition does not directly crush Julio's resolve but acts upon him with a subtler horror. "Some peculiarity" about Helen's smile "made him suddenly conscious of his race, and he was glad she did not remember Julio Sal."[102] Julio is beginning to realize not only the foolishness and implausibility of his plan but also the fact that the ultimate barrier to any relationship between him and Helen is not the exclusively professional nature of her prior interest in him: rather, it is racial difference. When Helen asks his name, therefore, he adopts the pseudonym "Tony Garcia" (alluding, a la *Cyrano de Bergerac*, to his friend Antonio, the real letter-writer), for fear that she may remember him. It is shortly after this that the pair order champagne and the argument with the waiter ensues, bringing to Julio a fuller realization of the impossibility of transcending the social boundaries of his racial position.

The waiter's response to Julio's protest at the removal of the bottle is not merely the physical intimidation demonstrated in Davis's illustration, but a firm declaration that he doesn't "have to take that kind of talk from a Filipino." This fills Julio with "shame and helplessness"; he feels nauseous and wants to cry.[103] Helen seems alive to Julio's distress and begrudgingly offers to forgo a replacement bottle of champagne, but in the moment of the waiter's humiliation all illusions have been shattered irreparably. After this Julio drinks five bottles of champagne he can ill afford and ultimately gives Helen the ring he had bought for her, saying that he had intended it for another girl, who had died.[104] Helen stops tearing the tickets as the bell continues to clang, now dancing with Julio for free, and ultimately informs him that he can take her home if he wishes. Her body language, and the fact that she implores him to cease buying champagne as it's "for suckers," breaking the commercial code of the dancehall, suggest that these changes in her behavior are motivated not solely by the gift of the ring but by some real feeling, although whether this is more than pity remains uncertain. Regardless, Julio's response is striking: he assents to taking Helen home, tells her he will wait for her downstairs, but then simply leaves, heading straight to the bus station and splitting town on a one-way ticket to Santa Rosa.

Despite Helen's apparent belated receptiveness to Julio (or, rather, to "Tony"), he knows from the instant that the waiter threatens him that his original plan is hopeless. The bar, like the dancefloor, appears to offer a space where he can buy a further simulacrum of a date with an American woman, and also pay for the privilege of being served by a white American man. Liquor is the commodity sold, but the value purchased is a brief illusion that his race does not place him at a social disadvantage. It becomes immediately clear, however, that he is only permitted this illusion provided he obeys the rules of the establishment, which, because his race *does* place him at a social disadvantage, are stacked against him.

The white waiter may be professionally subservient to Julio, but his supposed racial superiority immediately supersedes this when Julio dares to question the codes by which the space operates (i.e., the champagne scam). It thus becomes clear that the dancehall is effectively an operation that exploits Filipino men's social inferiority within a racist society in order to sell them an illusion that such inferiority does not exist, while paradoxically issuing reminders of that inferiority precisely to strongarm patrons into continue purchasing the illusion.[105] These are the mechanics of a protection racket: the party responsible for endangerment sells a (false) promise of safety from itself.

The mocking face of the cigar-chomping barman in the background of Davis's illustration (figure 1.4) emphasizes this. His employment—a service role in an establishment patronized mostly by Filipinos—places him well down the social ladder. Yet, secure in whiteness, he can comfortably laugh at his customer, a "sucker" whose apparent control over the space as patron has been removed by a reminder that such control is in fact subject to strict racial rules. The venue's white staff are empowered to punish any breach of those rules with a humiliating reminder of the customer's insurmountable non-whiteness. Just as the only solution to being ejected from the dancefloor and its promise of glamorous white femininity is to buy more tickets, the only solution to the waiter's reminder that he doesn't have to "take that kind of talk from a Filipino" is to buy another bottle of champagne. As the waiter himself says, Julio's only options are to "take it or leave it."[106]

Thus Davis's two drawings of Julio Sal show the character's changing self-perception; or rather his changing perception of how others perceive him, in two proximate but markedly different moments and spaces. One indicates the temporary, illusory access to racial privilege granted by the dancefloor, as Julio purchases the momentary belief that he could be a racially suitable partner for Helen, while the other shows how fleeting and fragile that belief is: under the waiter's threat, Julio morphs suddenly back into the racial grotesque he fears he may be in Helen's blue eyes. Davis's drawings schematize Julio's anxieties and conflicted feelings about his race, its impacts on his social opportunities, his hopes for overcoming those impacts, and the way those hopes are contingent upon and restricted by his ability to successfully occupy different spaces within the dancehall.

As the evening ends, "Tony" dares to tell Helen that she may know his friend, one Julio Sal. Helen reveals that she has indeed received Julio's letters, declaring him "nuts." "Tony" agrees, almost crying as he does so. What was nuts, it appears, was a belief that the enjoyments sold by the dancehall could be transposed beyond its tight spatial, temporal, and monetary dimensions. Julio looks at the clock above the bar and acknowledges that the dancehall's rigid temporal limits mark the limits of the space in which his hopes can be lived: "It was twelve-thirty. The dream was dead."[107] Julio's ultimate realization is that his race renders even Helen's newfound fondness insufficient to carry his hopes into the "real" space beyond the dancehall's fictive one.

Some knowledge of the social reality of taxi-dancehalls in this period makes this all the more affecting. Cressey affirms that it was in fact not uncommon for white American taxi-dancers to enter into romantic relationships with their Filipino patrons.[108] A 1942 study records that prior to the 1933 intermarriage ban Filipinos were markedly more likely than LA's other ethnic minorities to marry "native-born whites," and that most such brides were taxi-dancers, midwesterners who, like McCoy's protagonists, had arrived in LA seeking Hollywood but had found only dancehall stardom.[109] Cressey writes that dancers typically "first regard[ed] the Filipino as an object of exploitation," but "many before long [came] to take an entirely different attitude."[110] Fante does not make clear if Helen truly undergoes such a transformation regarding Julio over the course of the evening, but she does at least invite him to take her home—kissing his "calloused palm," accepting exactly the physical quality that occasions the Clever Fellow's rejection. Marriage is a legal impossibility for Helen and Julio in 1941; a relationship of some kind, as Helen implies at the last, is not. Indeed, Rhacel Salazar Parreñas has argued that Filipino men and white taxi-dancers formed what constituted a powerfully expedient intersectional alliance against their mutual social marginalization.[111] Such knowledge suggests, discomfortingly, that the frontierist sociospatial codes of Fante's dancehall have not merely extended a vision of fuller participation in American life that ultimately proves unsustainable, but that it proves unsustainable because of Julio's prejudice, not Helen's. Her change of heart comes too late because the cruel logic of the dancehall works, as suggested by Julio's changing appearance in Davis's illustrations, to internalize anti-Filipino sentiment within Julio himself.

The activities that take place in both the taxi-dancehall and the dance marathon ultimately cease to be much about dance at all. In the taxi-dancehall, one does not really pay for the act of dancing, one pays to occupy a rarefied space with a white woman; space, time and social prestige are the true commodities. In the dance marathon, as McCoy's novel accurately describes, there was very little actual dancing; the only requirement to remain in the contest, and thus claim a prize, was simply to keep moving—conservation rather than expenditure of movement was rewarded. Both "Helen" and *Horses* thus present spaces that embody the socioeconomic limitations to which their protagonists are subject. McCoy's main characters, Robert and Gloria, are both white, but in the midst of the Depression they have been forced to divert their Hollywood dreams (his of directorship, hers of stardom) into a marathon dance contest, along with so many desperate and hungry others. That this is their best shot at being picked out for film industry success seems as forlorn a hope as the belief held by Fante's protagonist that his ten-cent dances with Helen hold out a genuine route toward marrying her. In both texts, there is a moment just prior to the conclusion where such improbable dreams seem to unfold at least the tantalizing possibility of coming true. As Helen at last seems to develop some kind of real affection for Julio, in the closing stages of *Horses* Robert has an encounter with Mr. Maxwell, a representative of a company that has (at the behest of Mrs. Layden, a dance marathon connoisseur) sponsored his and Gloria's efforts in the contest. Maxwell seems, on Layden's recommendation, to have an opportunity in the offing for Robert; we do not discover what it is, but Robert certainly interprets the encounter as carrying the possibility of a route into the film world. Much as Julio concludes that Helen's end-of-evening affections will not truly extend the dimensions of the dancehall fantasy to the wider world, Gloria's death ensures that Robert's fleeting glimpse of his dream is likewise only that.

In the taxi-dancehall and the marathon alike, then, participants who exist (ethnically, economically, or both) on the margins of the "civilized" are induced to society to occupy a prized but hazardous territory for a given time, time that is structured in cyclical repetitions, in order to gain either a social or an economic reward dangled tantalizingly just beyond reach. In this respect, both offer conditions for modeling a frontierist vision of American history, one of people either spurning or spurned by more comfortable society who invest themselves instead in making new social forms by occupying and asserting themselves within a particular type of space. The hazards in the marathon are its tests of physical and psychological endurance, whereas in Fante's story they are primarily emotional and social perils: the establishment's tricks and scams that exploit and heighten racial insecurities, the competition presented by one's compatriots for space on the floor and a dance partner, the dangers of letting oneself believe that a dancer's purchased affections are sincere. No Edenic spaces of pure pleasure, Fante's taxi-dancehall and McCoy's marathon hall alike offer moments of ecstatic sociospatial conquest, whether in a dance with Helen or in seeing another couple slump to the floor, but these must be fought for through battle with the environment, and are only fleeting, grasped for a minute before being deferred to the next dance and another frontierist cycle of hazards. Where Turner envisages a cycle of frontier conquest that moves geographically from East to West, occupying successive spaces, the cyclical mechanics of the dancehall enable this symbolic frontiersmanship to be conducted repeatedly upon the same space. The bell rings; we begin again.

The repeatable progress of the marathon does admittedly have limits; there will, eventually, be a last pair of dancers standing—and while one might in theory enter another contest, McCoy's novel stages the end of the marathon as a moment of mortal finality. No such linearity necessarily applies in the taxi-dancehall. One can occupy the privileged space of the dancefloor as many times as one has tickets; closing time will come, but the hall will open again the next night. The crowds vary and the dancers vary, as Julio's brief uncertainty at Helen's changing appearance suggests. The space can thus be reproduced with minor variations near-endlessly. Where Fante departs from a frontier model is in suggesting that an incomer like Julio Sal, an ethnic "other," challenges and recrients some of the goals of frontier conquest, even as his dancehall fixation emblematizes the extent to which he maintains their mechanics. As a Filipino, Julio challenges Turnerian notions that conquest of American space is a) achieved by white Americans and therefore b) essentially a matter of *internal* migration, and moreover that c) the progress of such spatial conquest moves from East to West. Julio responds to the post-Turnerian conundrum about where to go when one can no longer travel west, by traveling from the opposite direction, from an "East" that is, in contravention of Turnerian geography, further west than the West. Moreover, he offers that response in California, so often conceived of as "looking west toward the sea and not back toward the rest of the West."[112]

Julio upends the Fine-McCoy notion that Los Angeles is the western end of the American continent, a place of dreams forestalled by geography, instead presaging later twentieth-century revisions of LA as the furthest reach of the "Far East," a capital of the Pacific rim.[113] As such, while as an immigrant with an uncertain position in society Julio does occupy a social liminality that models Turner's frontier zone, his direction of travel is not away from the established mainstream of society but always toward it. Fante makes this clear when he describes Julio's bunkhouse. By the docks in Wilmington, it is literally as close as one can get to the edge of the continent; Julio has been travelling around California for some time but the impression is as if he has just made it to land. As if to underscore this, we are informed that Julio's nearest neighbors are "five Japanese families"—that is, his place of habitation has more in common with the Pacific or the East than it does with America. Fante goes to great lengths to describe the ephemera of industry and commerce that surround his protagonist: "the fertilizer vats, the tar, the oil, the copra, the bananas and oranges, the bilge, the old rope, the decaying anchovies, the lumber, the rubber, the salt."[114] The emphasis is not merely on the many strong odors among these goods, and their unpleasant combination, but on the fact that Julio lives in the midst of the material upon which American society subsists, as it arrives in raw form and on an industrial scale. As far as the society in which he lives and works is concerned, indeed, Julio is of much the same order as these goods. He is "stored" in the same place, kept far away from the city's more salubrious districts, discrete and discreet.

Every time Julio wishes to travel downtown to the dancehall from the docks where he lives and works, he walks eighteen miles. Based on this measurement and a stated location on Main Street it seems likely that Fante's Angels Ballroom was inspired to some degree by such LA dancehalls as the Hippodrome Dance Palace and Danceland.[115] Thus, every time he wishes to see Helen, Julio must make a challenging expedition from his home beyond the fringes of society, into its locus on Main Street (the Filipino community gravitated to this area, but it was a mixed zone in the heart of the city). This is an arduous journey; it results in his shoes becoming ruined and takes so long that his neighbors are already rising for work by the time he returns.[116]

Julio therefore undertakes a more demanding and extreme (in both its physical parameters and its stakes of social difference) version of the Clever Fellow's "reversed" frontiersman's journey: he toils in manual labor at the edges of society, then repeatedly journeys to its symbolic center. Once there, he undertakes actions (the purchase of fine clothing and Anglo women's company) that enmesh him more fully (but only ever temporarily and superficially) within the white American societal mainstream from which he is excluded. Julio's marginalized status here problematizes the very idea of frontier movement as a model for American development. This is because the very reason that Julio can continue to make his frontiersman's journeys time and again, despite the exhaustion of literal, geographic "frontier" space, is that the social space to which he transfers the frontier dynamic remains resolutely unconquerable. He enjoys the superficial illusion of mastery over his surroundings, only for the world to revert to its prior state with the clang of the bell or the long walk home to the bunkhouse in Wilmington. Julio cannot find a way to navigate toward an accommodation within American society that is more permanent than an evening with Helen or more real than the illusion that he is his smirking waiter's social equal. He thus shows that the frontier's condition of a space that can be claimed and occupied anew can still be found in the endlessly reiterable social space of Los Angeles, but in doing so he lays bare the consequences for an individual "frontiersman" (that is, an immigrant laborer) of a society that maintains frontier labor as its guiding myth.

Citizen Ramirez: John Fante and Jack Leonard's *A Letter from the President*

Striking parallels exist between "Helen" and *A Letter from the President*, a film treatment that Fante cowrote with Jack Leonard around 1950.[117] The tale's protagonist, Chu Chu Ramirez, shares much with Julio Sal, to the extent that it seems reasonable to assume that *President* represents, in part, Fante's attempt to recuperate some of the thematic material from his abandoned *Little Brown Brothers* project. Like Julio, Chu Chu is a migrant laborer in California; like Julio he is characterized (patronizingly) by a guilelessness about his position within American society and the ways in which he is continually exploited by it; like Julio he lives in close quarters with a group of his fellows; like Julio he falls in love with a white American taxi-dancer (though in *President* Chu Chu knows the woman before she enters that profession). Chu Chu, however, is of Mexican rather than Filipino origin, and is in fact an American citizen.[118] Indeed, his most prized possession is a letter from President Truman, written in grateful reply to Chu Chu's own missive informing the White House of his pride at gaining citizenship. For the intensely patriotic Chu Chu, the letter from Truman is his unarguable documentary proof that, whatever inequality and abuse he may face in America as a result of his ethnic origin, he retains equal status and rights within the nation's civic structures. When his claim of citizenship is doubted by Anglo-Americans (as it frequently is), he produces the letter with a triumphant flourish, as a direct assertion of his status.[119]

When Chu Chu finds the cynical, manipulative Nancy Walker in financial trouble, he not only rapidly becomes besotted with her but immediately endeavors to help her—pawning his prized letter to help Nancy pay her rent. Immediately thereafter, however, the pair argue over what Nancy sees as Chu Chu's hopeless naivety about the benevolence of America. She soon forgets about him, but they encounter each other sometime later in Sacramento. Nancy, to Chu Chu's amazement and delight, informs him that they are immediately to go on a date together, though he is aware (echoing Julio's final visit to Helen in the dancehall) that she did not at first remember his name. Nancy is "angry and impatient."[120] They visit several clubs, ducking in and out of each one momentarily, before they find one that suits her. It emerges that she was attempting to find a man with whom she *had* intended to spend the evening, only for him to stand her up. When she sees this man on the dancefloor with another woman, Nancy begins to kiss Chu Chu passionately, having only wanted a "date" with him in order to make her flighty Anglo-American lover jealous. That man is disgusted at the sight of Nancy kissing "a Mexican," and begins to argue with her. Chu Chu affirms that he does not want to cause trouble, but is ignored. When the man lays a hand on Nancy, however, Chu Chu quickly intervenes, grabbing the man's wrist with a grip so firm it sends him first to his knees and then running from the club. At this point, it seems, the cynical motivations that had first driven Nancy's apparent interest in Chu Chu are replaced with something more sincere. "Her face was soft now, glowing with respect for this strong soft-spoken brown man," and she asks him to dance with her.[121]

Here, then, are inversions or modulations of what occurs between Julio and Helen, but their ultimate import remains essentially the same. Chu Chu's triumph over and humiliation of an aggressive Anglo-American man precisely mirrors Julio's subjugation and humiliation by the aggressive Anglo-American waiter. Where that point of confrontation cruelly strips Julio of his illusions that Helen could ever see him as her ethnic and social equal, its reversal in *President* is what causes Nancy to be able to begin considering Chu Chu in such terms. Again, the dancehall manifests spatial demarcations that symbolize shifts in social dynamic. Whereas for Julio the illusory, temporary removal of ethnic difference and disadvantage (and equally illusory romance) is the reward for purchasing access to the dancefloor, in *President* it appears that access to the dancefloor is the reward for proving oneself equal to an American.

As sincere as Nancy's feelings may be at this point, however, they are fleeting: she and Chu Chu continue to see each other, but only in the confines of a café where Nancy works, one that operates rather like a taxi-dancehall. Hostesses drink with customers in exchange for being bought "whiskey," which is in fact only tea, at fifty cents an ounce—but Nancy, increasingly depressed, has begun drinking the real thing.[122] It appears that Chu Chu's dancefloor-derived access to the possibility of romance, itself a proxy for the possibility of equal participation in American society, was ultimately as temporary as Julio's. Nancy informs Julio that she is moving to Los Angeles to become a taxi-dancer, sardonically referring to the occupation as a "respectable job."[123]

Aside from Chu Chu's relationship with Nancy, the plot of *President* concerns a man named Stone and his intensely xenophobic wife, who employ Chu Chu as a laborer on their farm, then pay him with a bad check. Chu Chu, believing in the inviolability and benevolence of American institutions, follows all the correct avenues of civic and legal recourse to obtain his money, and the system works up to a point. Stone must pay Chu Chu, and if he fails to will go to jail.[124] Stone still refuses to pay, however, and thus the day before he is due to be arrested Chu Chu makes a final visit to the Stones' property to plead for his money and attempt to reason with his former employer. Instead, Stone threatens him, demanding he withdraw his complaint, and ultimately pulls a gun on Chu Chu. In the ensuing scuffle, attempting to disarm Stone, Chu Chu accidentally shoots his adversary dead.[125] With the words of Mrs. Stone proclaiming him a murderer ringing in his ears, Chu Chu flees. His faith in American justice remains steadfast, however: he runs all the way to the sheriff's office to turn himself in, only to find that Mrs. Stone has preceded him and convinced the sheriff of her version of events. Chu Chu is jailed and awaits trial.[126] Terrified by this failure of the systems he had placed so much faith in, having done the right thing only to be disbelieved and punished, and now fearing that justice will not prevail in court, Chu Chu escapes and goes on the run. He makes contact with associates, who devise a plan to smuggle him out of the country and back into Mexico. Fante here presents a cruelly ironic reversal of a much more familiar migratory journey, one that Chu Chu himself had once made. An American citizen (but one who has been failed by the American justice system precisely because it did not accept him as *truly* American), he must now travel southward to make an illegal and clandestine border crossing into Mexico.

Chu Chu's affection for Nancy, however, proves his undoing. Having made it as far south as Los Angeles, where he must await a rendezvous for his trip over the border, Chu Chu comes across the taxi-dancehall where Nancy works and is unable to resist stopping to see her. Chu Chu is entirely cognizant that his decision to see Nancy will doom his attempt at escape: he would rather assert his rights and identity as a citizen by facing imperfect justice in America than have those rights and that identity taken from him by being forced into exile by that same justice system's inequities. He finds Nancy on the dancefloor, seizing her from the arms of a Filipino—it is tempting to imagine an intertextual cameo from Julio Sal. As they dance, he explains the situation while plain clothes policemen close in on all sides.

> He glanced around, and he saw them too, the little triumph of their cunning faces, and Chu Chu gave out a great sigh, as if relieved that the chase was over, that he need run no more. He guided her to the band-stand, took a ten dollar bill from his pocket, and gave it to the piano player.
> "Please," he said. "You play 'La Golondrina' three, four times."
> There were four tickets in his hand, and that meant four dances. The band went into La Golondrina, and Chu Chu held the girl very close, whispering, "Is like I always say, Nancy. Everything possible in America. Even for one so beautiful as you to love Chu Chu Ramirez."[127]

President, then, adds in this scene the air of criminal jeopardy to augment what "Helen" says about the dancehall as a space symbolic of ethnically and socially liminal figures' attempts to gain a foothold within (and acceptance by) an Anglo-dominated American society. Again, tickets are desperately purchased and exchanged for time while others wait beyond the boundary to seize their own opportunity. In Chu Chu's case, the meager minutes he can purchase with Nancy on the dancefloor stand in starkly ironic contrast to the years of jail time he will face when apprehended. Having been plunged into this predicament by his failed attempts simply to obtain the honest wage owed him, Chu Chu now spends his last dollars to purchase, like Julio Sal, the temporary illusion of what he had once, naively, believed to be true: namely, that he was a full participant in America. As in "Helen" and "Clever Fellow," the dancefloor's quality of rarefied spatiotemporal demarcation limns the essential bounds of a marginalized protagonist's ability to access a sense of the social center. Here, though, the precarity of such access and the stakes attached to losing it are reified by the presence of the plainclothesmen who are ready to apprehend Chu Chu but seemingly cannot do so until the dance is over.

"La Golondrina" is a Mexican song of farewell and of longing for home, written by Narciso Serradell Sevilla upon being exiled during the second Franco-Mexican war, and Chu Chu demands it just as he believes himself about to be forced into exile.[128] The irony is that Chu Chu's exile is to Mexico itself; his farewell is to America. He now must return to a place that had once been his homeland but in which he is no longer a citizen. To request "La Golondrina" therefore seems in part to betoken Chu Chu sadly acknowledging that he has not been accepted by his adopted home, but it is also a recognition of his new statelessness. The dancefloor again stages an immigrant experience of being forced by a host culture to live in a cruel, narrow, frontierlike liminality, neither permitted to ingress fully into the nation's civic heart nor able to abandon it without personal abjection.

Although Chu Chu's every interaction with Nancy up to and including this point has been purchased with money, proximity to her remains a means to assert the full and equal participation in American citizenry vouchsafed to him by his letter, even after that participation has been proven comprehensively to be as illusory as the dancehall itself. The police just beyond the borders of the dancefloor, by contrast, stand (like the venal Stones and byzantine legal system earlier in the text) as American reality, an unnavigable social/civic landscape that solicits attempts at ingress only to reveal itself as a wilderness, doling out (like McCoy's marathon) punishment in gross asymmetry to its promised rewards via unreliable, deceptive, self-contradicting systems and codes. If the wilderness Chu Chu faces is more explicitly carceral in nature than that in which Julio lives, such a distinction only makes explicit the truth which both men ultimately apprehend. Both are entrapped in a dynamic that enforces full participation in certain aspects of the notional American social compact (punitive "justice" either legal or extralegal—the waiter takes this role in Julio's dancehall—a scarcely less punitive labor market, and helpless consumerism) while strictly limiting participation in other aspects thereof (restorative justice, romance, financial and spatial security, a sense of belonging). The limitation of that participation in the wider world is indicated by the fact that it only achieves fuller realization within the illusive, elusive space of the dancefloor, which embodies the persistent liminality that is Chu Chu and Julio's enforced social role.

Through Julio and Chu Chu, then, we glimpse a society whose ills result not from the tragic closure of the frontier, but quite the opposite: its invidious dynamics continue to structure American space, always to the detriment of those who exist beyond its boundaries and wish to come within. Its poles, however, are strangely reversed. Turner's men of "civilization" strode beyond their societal bounds to claim land from "savagery." Julio (regarded in law, social convention, economic power, and geographic location as residing near the "savage" end of the human spectrum) and Chu Chu (whose citizenship proves that ethnicity, not nationality, is the truest guide to who is deemed "savage") reproduce the frontier dynamic but invert its direction of travel. They set out with hopes of staking a claim, in the dancehall, upon a space of "civilization," as they believe they have been invited to do. "Civilization," however, ultimately retains complete control over the pace and the extent of their progress, the extent to which they are permitted to model that inverted cycle of frontier journeys. The social space of the dancehall compels such inverted frontier labor while simultaneously rejecting the emotional laborers who perform it. By laboring in frontiersmanlike roles, ethnic others like Julio and Chu Chu attest to the contemporary endurance of frontier dynamics within a host society gripped by anxieties of frontier closure. They find, however, that the supposed societal benefits of an open frontier do not accrue to them, evoking in mythic terms the one-sided bargain of Grayson Kirk's 1942 description of Filipino legal status—as a group which "owe[d] allegiance to the United States but [was] not eligible to share in . . . benefits . . . restricted to United States citizens."[129] Something similar characterizes the desperation of McCoy's protagonists in *Horses*; spectators flock to watch a performance of desperation and survival that produces a frontier space for a society that would otherwise lack one. Though Robert and Gloria's social marginality is a matter solely of economic privation, lacking the dimensions of xenophobia and racism that afflict Julio and Chu Chu, they share a fate with Fante's protagonists inasmuch as the rewards of their labor accrue not to themselves but elsewhere in the transactional model that underpins their dancing.

The "outsourced" solutions to the cultural trauma of the end of the frontier that each of these texts propose are in all cases provisional, unsustainable, and time-limited. The tortuous feats demanded of the marathon participants proved too much for the national social conscience to accept, as both regulation and lack of patronage forced them out of existence, just as they are too much to bear for McCoy's characters. Having been revealed as bestial by his class position and thus placed in the "savage" position of the dancehall's social frontier, the Clever Fellow eventually retreats to the notionally safer ground of his home, only for his own mother to confirm there that, yes, he is a "dirty animal."[130] It seems unlikely that he will perform the frontier dance again any time soon. Moreover, the thematic resonances between "Clever Fellow" and "Helen" suggest that Fante's working-class frontier labor has, by 1940, been dislocated another step down the social ladder, to the immigrant population. Julio too abandons his attempts at inverting the frontiersman's journey in the social field when he gives up on Helen, but he is fated to persist in the other dimension of his societally mandated frontier role in that he must continue his arduous labors beyond the edge of "civilized" whiteness (whether on the docks or in the fields). Chu Chu is granted a happier ending, reflecting *President*'s intended cinematic audience and the marketability of propagandistic endorsements of the American way in the immediate postwar years, but even he receives this only because two individuals (Nancy and Mrs. Stone) have dramatic changes of heart at the story's climax. The *system* that endangered Chu Chu's liberty and compelled him to manifest an American social frontier is never reformed.

Fante's reflection of a changing political climate in supplanting the legally ambiguous Julio with the citizen Chu Chu demonstrates that the former dances on an even more hazardous societal edge than he, or Fante, could have known in 1941. Writing in the following year, Kirk noted that the efforts of Filipinos in helping American troops repel the Japanese invasion of the Philippines had seen them dubbed "undesirable heroes."[131] That phrase equally aptly describes Julio Sal, the rejected frontiersman, whose labors heroically offer renewed life to a mythic vision of American identity feared lost, but for which he is never offered an American identity of his own.

2

Pioneering the Office

White-Collar Rewilding with Chandler and Cain

> In answer to my advertisement, a motionless young man one morning, stood upon my office threshold, the door being open, for it was summer. I can see that figure now—pallidly neat, pitiably respectable, incurably forlorn!
>
> —Herman Melville, "Bartleby, the Scrivener"

I advance in this chapter a case that James M. Cain's Walter Huff and Raymond Chandler's Philip Marlowe, two notably hardboiled fictional Angelenos of the 1930s and 1940s, engage suspiciously, subversively, and combatively with the spatial practices of the office. In this period, the office had only relatively recently become the definitive workplace of American modernity. Moreover, the office's transformation of American cultures of work was not merely concurrent with, but to a considerable extent defined, Los Angeles's transformation into a metropolitan center. Not only had "large business development progressed more rapidly [in LA] than perhaps anywhere else in the country between 1900 and 1930," but in a city with a large service economy and little industrial base prior to the twentieth century, that development was disproportionately office-based.[1]

In Los Angeles, growth in "clerical and white-collar positions" throughout the early twentieth century outstripped even the city's simultaneous explosion in industrial employment, profoundly "shap[ing] the local culture."[2] Huff and Marlowe's attitudes to and ways of navigating the offices of 1930s and 1940s LA identify them with a century-long American intellectual tradition that characterized such spaces as destructive to the values of wilderness life—rugged, practical, masculinist individualism.

"Civilized Too Much": Spaces of Intellectual Conflict

The American genesis of what the French academician André Siegfried would dub "l'age administratif" was the rapid formation in the nineteenth century of a "clerking class" of white-collar workers.[3] As late as 1870, there were only 91,000 clerical workers in the United States; by 1910 there were 1,770,000.[4] In the largest cities, ubiquity came sooner: by 1855 clerks were the third-largest occupational group in New York.[5] No sooner had clerks "rise[n] into the lower frequencies of the American imagination" than they became objects of simultaneous mockery and fear.[6] Cloistered, effete, and unmasculine, these men of the new administrative professions appeared at once risible and troubling to an established vision of American masculinity that glorified robust outdoor labor.[7] Writing in *Life Illustrated*, Walt Whitman—"bard of the masculine professions"— was among the first to "establish that clerking was antithetical to manly American democracy."[8] Whitman reserves more derision for clerks than for any of the other social groups he sees on New York's streets, mocking them for the unmanliness of both their sensibilities and their physicality.[9] More significantly, however, the clerks are the only city dwellers on whose work Whitman offers no exposition whatsoever. He admires the work of laborers, is less enthusiastic about shop girls, and has a deep distaste for businessmen, yet even their professional activity at least bears description, whereas that of the clerks is wholly absent. Instead, their unmanly appearance constitutes the entirety of Whitman's account.[10]

The absence of the clerks' labor from Whitman's text embodies a widespread contemporary suspicion of clerking as a form of work that "did not produce anything."[11] To the extent that Whitman describes the clerks, they are not workers at all. Consider likewise Herman Melville's Bartleby. As a figure who is unsettling precisely because he would "prefer not to," Bartleby manifests the contemporary fear that clerking, because it did not seem to result in "an actual product," was a kind of non-work, which prompted a "crisis in the meaning of industriousness" that was also a crisis in the meaning of masculinity.[12] Thus nineteenth-century anti-clerk invective consistently mobilizes unfavorable comparisons with "*real men* who did *real work*" and a belief that office life's defining characteristic was its immutable opposition to masculine wilderness existence.[13] Positions similar to Whitman's recur throughout this period in the pages of the *American Phrenological Journal, American Whig Review, Vermont Watchman and State Journal, New York Star, Putnam's Monthly,* and *Vanity Fair*.[14] In abandoning physical, outdoor labor for the ledger and desk, the new clerking class was perceived to have committed nothing less than socioeconomic self-castration—"selling their manhood for a wage."[15]

As a relatively minor Whitman work participated in the foundational generation of anti-office social critique, his better-known celebrations of the individual within nature simultaneously "provided the immediate literary background" for late nineteenth- and early twentieth-century America's anxious scramble to preserve masculinity and vitality by reengaging with a vanishing wilderness.[16] As Roderick Nash writes, Whitman prefigured anxieties about "the American male . . . suffering from over-civilization' under the conditions of a "disappearing . . . frontier way of life."[17] T. J. Jackson Lears parallels Nash in describing a turn-of-the-century moment that saw "concerns about overcivilization" manifest a strong "antimodern impulse" in American culture.[18] For Lears and Nash alike, this moment of antimodernist panic about "overcivilization" was a response to an increasingly urbanized society defined by the "business values and . . . highly organized . . . economy" that the rise of the office represented.[19]

We thus apprehend, in Whitman's dual roles as archetypal anti-office critic and father of the antimodern moment's embrace of wilderness, the ideological connection between the perceived effects of a loss of frontier life, the demasculinization of the American man, and increasingly ubiquitous clerical work. That connection expresses itself in "On Being Civilized Too Much," an 1897 essay by Henry Childs Merwin. Holding the post-frontier pessimist line that without "closeness to nature . . . mankind could not long exist," Merwin adopts Turnerian rhetoric to posit that man functions optimally in an intermediary condition between "savagery" and "civilization."[20] That is, the ideal man not only descends from frontierlike conditions but must in himself embody frontierlike conditions. Some cultural refinement is societally beneficial, Merwin contends, but it is deleterious in excess: "undue prominence of the intellect" renders individuals "over-sophisticated and effete . . . paralyzed or perverted."[21] Merwin identifies "the close air of the office"—urban, indoor, cloistered—as one of the conditions effecting this paralyzing perversion of frontier-wrought American manhood.[22]

As "the legacy and the myth of . . . agrarian and frontier virtues" went on, in Graham Thompson's words, to suffuse "American masculinist culture throughout the twentieth century," the office continued to be a site where that mythic legacy and its implications for masculinity were contested.[23] As modernity advanced, it was "through office work and . . . increasingly omnipresent white-collar discourse" that American men experienced their growing sense of disconnection from a "pre-urban, pre-civilized, pre-feminized world"—a frontier world—that "lingered in the cultural imagination."[24] The long 1950s brought a particularly high tide in critiques of American corporate or "organization" culture, its prominence in national life, its signature space (the office), and the supposed effects thereof upon the individual and upon society at large. The culture that developed as the office became an ever-more-dominant facet of American life (nonmanual workers began to outnumber their manual counterparts in 1957) was, to its mid-century critics, one of alienation, conformity, stultification, anonymity, and rigidity.[25]

Such critiques of office work permeated the era's fiction and nonfiction. Literary contributions included Sloan Wilson's *The Man in the Gray Flannel Suit* (1955) and Richard Yates's *Revolutionary Road* (1961). A Los Angeles satire of byzantine, enervating office culture likewise constitutes a subplot of Alison Lurie's *The Nowhere City* (published in 1965 but set around 1960), a novel to which this book returns in its conclusion. Nonfiction counterparts included Riesman, Glazer, and Denney's *The Lonely Crowd* (1950), C. Wright Mills's *White Collar* (1951), Kenneth Boulding's *The Organizational Revolution* (1953), William H. Whyte's *The Organization Man* (1956), and Alan Harrington's *Life in the Crystal Palace* (1959). Meanwhile political figures enfolded what Whyte termed a culture of "false collectivization" (group-oriented, conformist, systems-driven) in Cold War rhetoric.[26] Office culture emblematized the anxieties of Arthur Schlesinger Jr.'s exhortation to "give the lonely masses a sense of individual human function" lest they become "traitors to freedom," and Adlai Stevenson's warning of "violent pressures" that would obliterate the individual into "anonymity."[27]

Critiques of the office from the age of the organization man are conspicuous by their ideological proximity to the frontierist, antimodernist, anti-clerking invective of Whitman and Merwin, despite dramatic changes in political, social, and economic context, and in the form of the office itself, over the intervening decades. Whyte admonishes corporate culture's inability to accommodate a philosophy of "survival of the fittest," "struggle against one's environment," and "'rugged' individualism" while, like Turner, pinpointing the turn of the century as the moment at which such a philosophy became "strained by reality."[28] As Nikil Saval puts it, the postwar wave of office criticism maintains its nineteenth-century antecedents' central argument that "the office was destroying the frontier-exploring spirit in man."[29] Nineteenth- and mid-twentieth-century critiques provide contextual poles for the office's century-long rise to cultural omnipresence—two similar panics, one heralding the office's arrival as a social phenomenon and one marking the point at which its saturation of the texture of American life was complete. Where Cain and Chandler emerge as distinctive anti-office critics, however, is partly in the determinedly frontier-oriented methods by which their protagonists greet the office's status as the frontier's symbolic antithesis, but also in the fact that their criticism appears, chronologically, *between* these two historical peaks of anti-office sentiment. They write at a time when the still-developing modern office was enjoying its most concerted and widespread period of boosterism.

Technological advances throughout the nineteenth century had made it easier for businesses to operate on a regional or national level, precipitating growth in the scale of companies, necessitating increasingly complex organizational structures and therefore an "expansion in the range and scope of the office, in the specialization and refinement of its activities."[30] The spatial conditions necessary for the fullest expression of such developments were made possible by steel-framed buildings: large, flexibly divisible floor plates enabled larger groupings and easier supervision of workers. Such architectural advances would be further refined, and accompanied by new technical innovations (lighting, heating, air conditioning). Consequently, by the 1930s, "space planning and design" to optimize "the way business used its office space" had become a "new industry."[31] This new science of office design was a counterpart to the work of Frederick Taylor's school of "scientific management." From the 1890s onwards (though "scientific management" did not acquire its name or widespread public attention until the 1910s), Taylor propagated the principle that the systematized administration of the workers performing a company's nominal function should in fact itself be considered the company's most important work. As businesses became Taylorist meta-companies, their managerial and administrative castes swelled—demanding ever-larger, purpose-built office spaces in which to manage and administrate.[32] There grew an "increasing distinction between those conceptualizing a task and those doing it," the former group abstracted ever further from whatever the enterprise produced or sold—if, indeed, as the service economy grew, it sold anything tangible at all.[33] Taylor had invented what David Graeber would a century later term the "bullshit job."[34]

Though Taylorism had been developed for the industrial shop floor, the ubiquity of its "management ethic"—strict hierarchical strata, hyper-specialization, precise procedural regimentation to ensure efficiency, and close observation of employees—would in the interwar decades "transform the office" and come to define modern corporate America.[35] Even if the 1929 stock market crash foreshadowed later anti-office fears about disastrous entrapment within a megastructure of purely theoretical, paper-bound business, it also suggested that, if anything, Wall Street had retained *too much* frontierlike "Wild West" laissez-faire lawlessness, failing because of an insufficient (rather than overenthusiastic) embrace of Taylorist systems, checks, balances, and regulatory mechanisms. Indeed, although office enthusiasm in the two decades preceding World War II was not universal—consider, for example, King Vidor's film *The Crowd* (1928), or Sinclair Lewis's *Babbitt* (1922)—the period represented the high point of idealism about the new workplace's transformative possibilities for American life. This was the era in which it was most seriously believed that new ways of working could represent not the negation and abandonment of frontier values (per Merwin, Whitman, et al.) but their pragmatic renewal.[36] The bullshit job was once a utopian proposition.

Even as Taylor decried as outmoded the veneration of individualism that had defined frontier ideology, with his maxim that "in the past the man has been first; in the future the system must be first," he argued that technological and economic frontiers accessed through his methods could replace the old geographic ones.[37] In lieu of free land and limitless physical resources America could sustain a spirit of unhindered growth upon incremental but theoretically perpetual scientific advances in production methods, space planning, communication technologies, and management techniques. Simply preserving dwindling natural resources as a solution to post-frontier anxieties was, Taylor suggested, a solution fatally limited by physical finitude, whereas the world of systemic refinements and productivity gains was new each day.[38] Simultaneously, as ever more of the population shifted from manual to nonmanual work—physically undemanding and systematized to maximal, labor-saving efficiency, in clean environments and with sociable hours—more individuals would theoretically have time and energy to pursue personal goals outside work. A famously overoptimistic iteration of such a proposal came from John Maynard Keynes, who, remarking in 1930 on the transformation of the global economy through science and technology, and with it the increasing loss of manual labor to machines, foresaw a fifteen-hour work week, in which individuals could spend more time on "the arts of life" than on "the activities of purpose."[39]

An economy where such work as remained did so only in offices might thereby not strip away frontier-wrought vital individualism but restore and expand it—releasing, to borrow Herbert Marcuse's skeptical gloss on all such beliefs in the liberating powers of technologized control of labor, "individual energy into a yet uncharted realm of freedom."[40] Even Turner hailed technological advancement in office work as a new socioeconomic frontier, providing renewed opportunity and possibility to an America divested of wilderness. It is instructive, though, when so many writers and thinkers located the office's anti-frontier qualities in its attenuation of masculinity, that the possibility Turner found in the office was that of its role in "the rise of women . . . in the business world."[41]

Into this interwar window of office optimism step Chandler's Marlowe and Cain's Huff.[42] Both characters irritate the systems of this world, skeptical of their supposed advantages. They are antagonistic mirror images of both the organization man and his ancestor, Taylor's "trained man."[43] Their navigations and negotiations of various types of office space disclose a skepticism and suspicion of corporate cultures of surveillance, hierarchy, division, and regimentation. They challenge and subvert to their own individual ends the structures and rules governing these spaces, repurposing the offices' intended meanings to redesignate them as frontier zones, contested between occupier and aggressor. In thus wilding the tame they assert the ability and, indeed, necessity of the individual to retain agency when presented with the dehumanizing power of the office. They thereby renew antimodernist skepticisms of earlier decades and anticipate postwar critiques of office-bound regimentation—not least that of Chandler's own *The Long Goodbye* (1953), which, as Sean McCann notes, contains a modish swipe at organization culture in the form of a corporatized detective agency.[44]

The Plot Against the Office: James M. Cain's *Double Indemnity*

In 1942, the psychoanalyst Franz Alexander identified in the delinquency of young American men a malign transfiguration of the spirit of "individualism and adventure" that had defined their "pioneer forefathers." Without a frontier for its "realization," that spirit had become "pathological."[45] Walter Prescott Webb quoted Alexander approvingly, suggesting that criminality was a means by which modern Americans sought to retrieve a time and a place in which "each man was . . . his own law."[46] For Webb and Alexander, modern antisocial behavior denoted simultaneously the "frustration of frontier ideals" and a "retreat" to them: crime's violent mourning of frontier conditions paradoxically revealed their darkly triumphant persistence, even renewal.[47] Cain's Walter Huff offers fictive vindication of Alexander and Webb's theory. Huff's turn to criminality expresses itself not only as a desire to recuperate frontier values of "initiative, bravado, and individual accomplishment," but also as a direct assault upon the anti-frontierist values of the modern white-collar business world and its office-based culture.[48]

There is longstanding critical agreement that James M. Cain's fictions and characters are motivated near-exclusively by some combination of sex and money.[49] Nowhere does this seem more apparent than in *Double Indemnity* (1936/1943), wherein Huff is incited to murder by the erotic promise of Phyllis Nirdlinger and the financial promise of her husband's life insurance policy. Without dismissing the narrative centrality of those imperatives, however, we can locate Huff's suspicious, confrontational engagement with the office as a third essential dynamic at the core of the text. John Irwin has acknowledged that *Double Indemnity* is legible as an anticorporate novel—about "the resentment of having a boss—of not being one's own man and thus not being fully a man"—yet the more specific stakes of Cain's engagement with the cultural, social, and historical particularities of the office remain unexamined.[50]

A cursory reading of the opening scenes of Billy Wilder's Chandler-scripted 1944 film version of Cain's novel (in which the protagonist is renamed "Neff") suggests the scale and significance of this critical lacuna. Here the disclosure of the novel's narrative-framing conceit—that it is its protagonist's confession—is shifted to the start of the narrative, which is then related in flashback. Moreover, the film transforms the confession from a hospital bed dictation into an audio recording made in the offices of General Fidelity, Huff/Neff's insurance firm employer. These directorial decisions make immediately explicit what is latent in the novel: the office is the locus of the protagonist's crisis. Neff's motivations remain opaque in the film's initial, brief, wordless shots of his car speeding through Los Angeles at an unsociable hour (such an activity might have a noble goal). The first hint that Walter is an agent of misdeed is that he must rap on the glass door of his office building to be admitted by the nightwatchman, who notes that he is "working pretty late."⁵¹ *Double Indemnity* first signifies that its world is out of joint by showing a white-collar worker breaking the spatial practice of his office workplace. To seek ingress long after closing time, even as an employee, is to disobey one of the space's basic rules and thus immediately to attract suspicion.

One of the parameters by which the space of the office is produced has been corrupted. Lefebvre writes that, although the physical, mental, and social aspects of space—"the triad of the perceived, the conceived, and the lived"—are "interconnected," they may not always "constitute a coherent whole."⁵² Because the constituent parts of the triad are "not only things but also relations," producing space contingently, to destabilize any one of the three inevitably and immediately renders the whole incoherent, throwing into doubt any and all of a space's commonly accepted meanings and significations.⁵³ Although Neff's transgression is itself minor, the social codes of office life are so clear, commonplace, and rigid that his out-of-hours arrival is conspicuously aberrant to viewer and nightwatchman alike. Indeed, that it so readily serves as a proxy for greater unease is itself an indicator of how widespread understanding of and conformity to the sociospatial terms of the office had become by the 1940s, when almost 23 percent of American urban workers were employed in clerical and related fields.⁵⁴ The film exploits the office's cultural ubiquity to render a seemingly harmless act ominously suggestive of greater social disruption.

Neff enters an up-to-the-minute office space of the day, confronting a balcony/mezzanine giving access to the individual offices of senior staff members and running the perimeter of a large, unbroken space below—precisely the kind of space that advances in steel-framed building technology had made structurally possible. Ranks of desks for administrative and secretarial staff can be surveilled from above. The space is defined by boundaries, segregation, and hierarchy, with the size, position, and individuation of one's space denoting relative primacy within the corporate structure. Occupying Walter's perspective, we peer over the balcony at caretakers emptying wastepaper baskets. The cleaners disposing of "evidence" of the previous day's work echo (for Neff) and foreshadow (for the viewer) the two signature elements of his crime—a deception that is both paper-based (hinging on an insurance policy) and dependent upon a late-night "disposal" (that of Herbert Nirdlinger's body on a railway line). Although Neff's deed remains to be revealed, his reluctance to enter the office, the shot of the caretakers, his out-of-hours entry, and the film's relocation of his confession to the office itself conspire to suggest one thing: to return to the office in *Double Indemnity* is to return to the real scene of the crime.

Walter Huff/Neff embodies a frontierist enmity toward corporate cultures of surveillance, hierarchy, division, and regimentation in his interactions with his employer.[55] Insurance is a notional product, existing entirely in the abstract, in the act of being agreed upon by two parties; even its sole physical manifestation on paper merely signifies that act. Produced by calculations, probabilities, systems, and statistics, insurance is "knowledge work," intrinsically a post-Taylor meta-business. General Fidelity has field agents (if we are to place Huff in a frontiersmanlike role it is telling that he is one), salesmen who must be present in the world in order to sell the product, but that product is "made" in the office; salesmen merely gather the one necessary raw material (customers) that cannot be conjured from a ledger. In insurance, administration *is* manufacturing. Wilder's shot of Neff watching the office caretakers at night suggests this suspicious abstract emptiness—in which both product and waste effluent are paper, the means of production the office itself. Insurance is thus the apotheosis of the kind of nothing-making business against which Whitman and Merwin had counseled, and a prototypical manifestation of the alienatingly abstract "organization" that would trouble postwar office critics. Chandler offers a similar comment on insurance in the first Philip Marlowe novel, 1939's *The Big Sleep*, wherein luckless grifter Harry Jones works for crooked bookie Puss Walgreen, who uses an insurance business as a front but would only "sell you insurance . . . if you tramped on him." Here, the idea that insurance is an empty, purely notional construct is taken to its literal extreme: it does not exist other than as "what it says on the door."[56] Behind that door is only a hollowness where a company should be, the intrinsically abstract characteristics of insurance providing the ultimate corporate absence in which Walgreen can sublimate his real business.

Besides the turning away from the physical world that its nothing-making quality as a business suggests, insurance as a product further embodies anti-frontierist qualities because it manifests a belief that risk is manageable and predictable, and can be mitigated against. (Harry Jones's fate is particularly ironic in this regard—he fails to calculate accurately the risks of his schemes and as a result is poisoned in the very insurance offices where Walgreen supposedly sells the idea that risk *can* be calculated.) Insurance and the frontiersman both venerate risk, but the former does so only to the extent that it profits from danger that does *not* materialize. The development of the insurance industry and the fall of the frontier in fact occupy the very same moment: only by the late 1800s had a "formal insurance market" evolved.[57] The contemporary insurance industry insists both that risk is not what it used to be and that the tools of its diminishment lie no longer in the frontiersman's physical subordination of a threatening world but in the new knowledge economy's powers of predictive regularization.

Regularity is the frontiersman's nemesis. He demands conditions of unpredictable, intractable hazard against which to test himself, conditions that insurance obviates through a claim that, while risk may still exist, it is minimal enough to be profitably insurable and moreover need no longer fall upon lone individuals but can instead be pooled in collective safety. Indeed, by the time Cain wrote *Double Indemnity* an active discourse had developed around "the erosion of personal agency threatened by the large-scale industrialization of insurance."[58] Insurance's regularization of risk, its diminution of individual agency, its increasingly industrial scale, its abstraction, and its deskbound culture, then, all evoke post-frontier anxieties. Huff's criminal plot aims to exploit (and reveal as mistaken) the idea that the world in its current state is predictable, capable of being rationalized into probabilities and premiums, filing cabinets and ledgers. As an institution in which probability ensures that the house always wins, Walter compares insurance to gambling—suggesting that the writing on Puss Walgreen's door may be accurate after all, that insurance is less a front for bookmaking than a euphemism for it. Walter intends to reveal just such a truth with a brutal act of murder that shatters the social boundaries upon which General Fidelity calculates the odds of the world, disrupting the structures on which the insurance business subsists, via a powerful reinjection of unpredictable frontier risk.

Herbert Nirdlinger is thus less the target of a crime than collateral damage in a strike against the anti-frontier values of "regularity" embodied in a culture of contemporary white-collar business. As Walter remarks, "the business I'm in"—the stultifyingly regulated and risk-managed worldview of his employer—is what has driven him "nuts," and it is therefore the business upon which he seeks revenge.[59] Cain derived his novel's central conceit—an insurance agent who uses his expertise in detecting fraudulent claims to carry one out—from a tale he had heard about a printer whose decades spent removing profane typographical errors from newsprint left him unable to resist "watching for chances" to insert one: in Roy Hoopes's words, "dynamite was lurking there in the printer's compulsion."[60] In the insurance office, Huff retains from the "printer's compulsion" a desire to lay dynamite in a seemingly anodyne world of paper.

When Phyllis Nirdlinger suggests to Walter the idea of murdering her husband in a phony swimming pool mishap, he dismisses the plan as flawed.[61] Instead, he proposes staging a railroad "accident," which will maximize the ensuing life insurance payout—the eponymous "double indemnity." Walter's plot ultimately exploits a mistaken institutional assumption that a corporatized, office-bound America occupies an irretrievably post-frontier condition. He explains that insurers

> found out pretty quick, when they began to write accident insurance, that . . . the spots that people think are danger spots, aren't danger spots at all. I mean, people always think a railroad train is a pretty dangerous place to be, or they did anyway, before the novelty wore off, but the figures show not many people get killed, or even hurt, on railroad trains. So on accident policies, they put in a feature that sounds pretty good . . . but it doesn't cost the company much, because it knows he's pretty sure to get there safely.[62]

The early days of rail to which Walter refers have longstanding cultural associations with the latter, trans-Mississippi days of the frontier era. The compassing of the continent by rail brought larger waves of immigration to the Far West and was thus both a phase in frontier history *and* a harbinger of the frontier's end.[63] The railroad made possible the population growth and concomitant economic, industrial, and agricultural development that closed the frontier, but was itself initially defined by frontier conditions.

The train itself, moreover, was deemed, as Huff says, a "dangerous place." In the period when the frontier remained unarguably open and the American railroad network was embryonic, however, trains had in fact been relatively safe. It was only in the 1850s, "as trains speeded up and services became more frequent," that railroad safety became a *cause célèbre*.⁶⁴ The very technological developments that enabled the railroad to destroy the frontier (by webbing the continent with greater efficacy and completeness) were those that lent it the frontier's essential quality of being not merely novel, liminal, and westwardly mobile but also mortally dangerous. Thus, early rail travelers journeyed through frontier lands while embodying the de-frontierizing of those lands, while their means of transport embodied both the frontier's conquest *and* frontier conditions. In levering popular memory of the risky days of early rail travel, then, Huff's plot resonates paradoxically with both pre- and post-frontier worlds.

Accordingly, the most tantalizing aspect of Huff's history of double indemnity policies is the suggestion that the man on street has an unarticulated, instinctual—and empirically illogical—belief in the present-day persistence of frontier-era risk dynamics. This belief is sufficient to convince the insurance purchaser that a double payout for rail accidents is worth an increased premium. The "novelty" of frontier-era rail may have worn off, but its supposed concomitant dangers have left vestigial traces in prospective insurance purchasers' mental calculations. Insurers, occupying the regulated and regulating post-frontier world of the office, operate on no such illogical, instinctual basis. Their calculations are made solely on the dispassionately Taylorized basis of "the figures," which show that modern trains are safe: the intention of the double indemnity policy is actively to exploit customers' supposedly erroneous superstition that the risk profile of rail travel has changed far less since its frontier incarnation than it has. The genius of Huff's plan, therefore, is in effectively reconstructing the risk profile of frontier rail, artificially inflating (to 100 percent) the probability that Herbert Nirdlinger will *seem to* suffer death on the rails (the murder actually happens in a car). Walter and Phyllis do not prove that the insurers were wrong in their assessment of modern rail travel's safety, but they create the appearance of corroborating the insurance consumer's frontier-legacy superstition that trains are fraught with danger.

Through this plan, the conspirators make themselves antimodern, anticorporate agents of the frontier. In murdering Herbert to secure their own futures (or so Walter believes), they corroborate Joan Didion's suggestion that "wagon-train morality"—the frontier-birthed belief that it may be morally admissible to harm or even kill another person to ensure one's own survival—continued to define social relations in the modern

American West.[65] This, though, is a recursive iteration of frontier morality, because it is deployed in securing a future for the frontier itself. The plotters vindicate a societal hunch that the hazards of the frontier have not been suppressed as effectively as the insurers' figures suggest. Reinvesting with danger the great mechanical symbol of America's western expansion, Waler and Phyllis keep the violent, unpredictable frontier symbolically alive. Even the implacably aligned forces of post-frontier anti-individualism, insurance, and the office where it is "made" cannot mitigate against one source of frontier-era danger: the unbound human.

Huff's anticorporate assertions of individualism situate him alongside other Cain characters who comment on Taylorized corporate modernity and its social effects. In *The Postman Always Rings Twice* (1934) Cora Papadikis's desire to improve the shabby California diner-garage she runs with her husband Nick underpins the murder plot: she must lose Nick in order to realize the potential of the business in which her dreams and selfhood are vested. Frank Chambers, the narrator and Cora's co-conspirator, tells Nick early on that his refusal to invest and innovate, manifest in unclear and outdated signage, is damaging the business. The current configuration "don't make me want to stop and get something to eat. It's costing you money, that sign, only you don't know it."[66] This might accordingly appear a "pro-business" murder, carried out partially in the name of organizational improvement and in retribution for Nick's failure to modernize: homicidal Taylorism. Yet even if Cora's violent seizure of the diner contains a hope of improving its business practices, it is made manifest in a direct attack upon the person previously in control of those practices—she is motivated by what Irwin terms an aggrieved subordinate's determination to "beat the boss."[67] In doing so Cora also becomes the boss, but even though she may be a forward-thinking, ideas-driven businesswoman, she discloses to Frank after Nick's death that she is no systematizing Taylorist. Explaining her plans for commercial success, she notes that every other roadside joint is "lousy" because it has been "set up ready-made by the Acme Lunch Room Fixture Company"; all such establishments offer fare "that's the same from Fresno down to the border."[68]

Cain himself suggests something similar in "Paradise," a 1933 essay on Southern California for *The American Mercury*, in which he protests the blandly interchangeable, abstracted sloganeering of a contemporary commercialism that

> never manages to be delightful, produces nothing but an endless succession of Rabbit Fryers, 50c; Eggs, Guaranteed Fresh, 23c

Doz.; Canary Birds, 50c, Also Baby Chix, Just Hatched; Car Mart, All Makes Used Cars, Lowest Prices; Orange Drink, 5c; Eat; Drink Goat Milk for Health, Drive Right In; Pet Cemetery, 300 Yds., Turn to Right; Finest English Walnuts, 15c Lb.; $100 Down Buys This Lot, Improvements Installed, No Assessments; Eat; Scotty Kennels, 100 Yds.; Pure Muscat Grapejuice, 35c Gal., We Deliver; Eat.[69]

What Cora wishes to bring to the marketplace is *not* the repetitious rhythm of corporate standardization but something emphatically individuated and distinct—the same individuation she seeks for herself in disposing of her husband. The eponymous protagonist of *Mildred Pierce* (1941), a Glendale divorcée turned entrepreneur, is of a similar disposition to Cora in this respect—possessed of keen business instincts but no organization woman. Commercially minded as both women are, their approach to business manifests a single-minded individualism counter to their era's embrace of relentless managerial systematization. There is a little of the frontier in them, too. Cora and Mildred, though, are small-businesswomen, where Huff is merely a salaried employee. Where they become bosses of modest concerns, at least temporarily, he is enmeshed in a larger corporate structure over which he has no control. He cannot become the boss, the one figure in the corporate structure whose individuality is permitted to protrude above it. His strategies of self-assertion against the corporate machine are thus limited to the stubborn enmity he embodies toward General Fidelity's cultures of surveillance, hierarchy, division, and regimentation.

Walter's frontiersmanlike allegiances are further revealed in persistent suggestions that the murder plan is not merely a defiance of the odds his employer exists to calculate, but that such defiance is, for him, the act's greatest reward. He yearns to disabuse General Fidelity of its belief that it "know[s] every crooked trick."[70] In order to beat the odds, Walter tells Phyllis, they must "be bold. It's the only way."[71] This approach—individualist to the point of foolhardiness, high-risk, high-reward, deliberately *inflating* hazard to make a subsequent triumph more heroic and thrilling—is both cognate with the frontiersman's credo and entirely antithetical to the values of his employer. As Turner defines it, the frontier must be "at first too strong for the man," who must "accept those conditions or perish": a frontier is not a frontier unless there is a genuine possibility of it conquering—rather than being conquered by—its ingressor.[72] Walter seeks to create for himself an analogous paradigm. Unlike Phyllis, who has a death wish, he *does* wish to triumph over his situation—to complete the plan successfully, escaping alive and enriched—but it is no triumph at all unless achieved from a position of seemingly overwhelming unlikelihood.

Trying to explain the need to "be bold," Walter draws an analogy with gangsters gunning down an enemy in full view of a crowd, suggesting that a seemingly high-risk crime, if committed perfectly, is in fact the one most likely to evade suspicion.[73] His explicatory efforts, though, are conspicuously inadequate, marked by lacunae in their logic: ultimately there is no convincing practical reason given as to why a plan with less "audacity" could not be pursued more safely.[74] Justification for "hitting it for the limit," raising the stakes to extremes, is entirely circular—"that's what I go for. It's all I go for."[75] That such boldness defies rational explanation is precisely its point: the irrational act is the one that defies his employers' conception of a predictable, regularized world. Walter must place himself in the situation of greatest possible danger because its compensation is not only double indemnity but also self-actualizing individuation, distinction from both the predictability embodied by his employer and the equally predictable wrongdoings of lesser crooks—"punk[s] up in San Francisco" pulling "piker job[s]."[76] In a compulsion to assert an exceptional, odds-defying capacity for survival within self-imposed conditions of hazard, which is simultaneously to defy both his employer's probability-based vision of the world and the anti-wilderness values of the workplace where those probabilities are calculated, Walter is wholly frontiersmanlike.

That Walter's murderous project is a frontierist one carried out against the modern corporate edifice and its values is further demonstrated by the identity of his adversary throughout the narrative: Barton Keyes, the company's chief claims administrator. Although Walter's greatest crime is ostensibly murder, the professionalized forces of law enforcement or criminal inquiry are conspicuous by the fact that they are *not* positioned as the main investigators of his misdemeanors. In *Double Indemnity* the police and private detective, the twin loci of justice and crime-solving in hardboiled convention, are both relegated to background roles. The police are seldom mentioned, their investigation largely undisclosed. Inasmuch as it is, it does not appear particularly thorough or effective; if murder were the only crime here, and the police the only investigators, it seems that Walter and Phyllis might have evaded justice. They do not because within the narrative's logic Walter's crime is one committed less against Herbert Nirdlinger than against his own employer. Even when he is not *in* the office, Walter spends much of the novel being surveilled *by* his office (the only private eyes in the novel are agents—synecdoches—of the insurance company). The text's narrative-framing confession is made not to an arresting officer, nor to a judge, but to Keyes. It is the sin against the employer, the breach of trust between staff member and corporate institution, that must be admitted.

In *Double Indemnity*, conventional criminal investigation is to all narrative purposes replaced by General Fidelity's claims assessment process. The internal practices and procedures of an insurance firm are in effect the "crimefighter" in this hardboiled plot. Cain takes the investigatory mechanics of the crime novel away from the offices of the district attorney and private eye, relocating them in the office of the claims administrator. This corroborates the sense that Huff is motivated to murder not only by money or sex but at least as substantially by a desire to challenge the professional arbiters of risk who believe that the world can be organized by predictive systems. That General Fidelity is the entity within the novel most urgently concerned with subduing Walter reflects the fact that it is the entity whose values and integrity he has most assailed.

Thompson writes extensively about the steady development in modern America of a "surveillance culture" centered around the office.[77] Such surveillance could take many forms, from the direct supervision of a manager (facilitated by space planning strategies) to the remote contact successively easier and more intimate by telegram, telephone, and computer, to increasingly intricate and precisely maintained records of work done and not done. Barton Keyes deploys such tools in his role (employee records, claim records, recording devices, the employment of private investigators), but more importantly he himself embodies the office world in which a surveillance culture predominates, the very world that has driven Huff "nuts." Keyes, as his name suggests, unlocks secrets on behalf of the company by simultaneously guarding its own institutional memory. As "a holdover from the old regime" of General Fidelity's founder, he seems embedded in the organization's corporate history, but his name likewise indicates a figure representative of the modern organization's self-conception as a scientized machine in which employees operate in an integrated series of mechanism-like processes. We are told that Keyes approaches his job as "a theorist," whose intricate thinking "make[s] your head ache to be around him," evoking the contemporary Taylorist drive to systematize every aspect of work.[78]

Keyes lives entirely in the world of paperwork: when memos and telegrams flood in following Nirdlinger's death, they all come directly to Keyes, piling up to the point that he is forced to secure them under a weight.[79] When Keyes voices suspicions to Huff about the Nirdlinger case, he claims that "when you've handled a million of them, you know, and you don't even know how you know."[80] This investigator pretends no incredible deductive powers or insights; he does not even understand the fuller depths of his own knowledge. He is in this sense the triumph of the modern, systematized business that so maddens Huff because he is its internalization. Keyes knows what he knows not through native genius but through endless repetition, not by individual ingenuity but by its obviation—via immersion in procedure so complete that aberrations become obvious without thought.

He is exactly Taylor's idea of a "trained man" and thus Walter's psychic as well as procedural nemesis, a figure who embodies the culture of the modern white-collar workplace exactly as Walter embodies a re-frontierizing disruption thereof. Indeed, Keyes's investigation into Walter is impeded by his faith in the system of corporate bureaucracy and recordkeeping: when he is first advised to place Huff under the watch of a private investigator, Keyes responds that, in effect, it is not necessary to do so because Huff is effectively already surveilled by other means, surrounded by a network of data and information that enable risk to be assessed without further human intervention: "All his statements check closely with the facts and with our records, as well as with the dead man's records. I have even checked, without his knowledge, his whereabouts the night of the crime, and find he was at home all night. . . . I point out to you further, his record which has been exceptional in cases of fraud."[81] Revealingly, given Keyes's refusal to deploy an investigator, it is unclear how he comes by Huff's whereabouts on the night of the crime—the one non-record-based piece of information in his surveillance mosaic. This is an office somehow eerily able simply to *know* the movements of its employees, even outside work. Temporarily, though, Huff is able to prove fallible these structures of regiment and control: the picture of Huff's trustworthiness that Keyes's systems present is wildly inaccurate. Moreover, Keyes's confidence in his ability to manifest the modern office's panopticon eye is shown to be misplaced precisely through a spatially transgressive subversion of its culture: Huff learns that there will be no investigator appointed to tail him by violating the sanctity of Keyes's office after hours and accessing memo recordings. Huff simultaneously assails and evades the logic of the office by chaotically ignoring its spatial practice and inverting the purposes of its systems.

Keyes embodies the characteristics about which prophets of the office's deleterious effect on frontierist masculinity had warned. "Big and fat and peevish," a profuse sweater, his form has become a gross reflection of his hypertrophied intellectual existence, evoking anti-clerking invective's fears that deskbound life would ruin the constitution of rugged American manhood.[82] Huff's adversary, then, represents anti-frontierism both because he embodies his employer's risk-managed, rule-based culture of systems and safeguards (and has sacrificed individuality to the collective in doing so), and because he attests physically and in his investigatory activities to the office world's deleterious effects on frontier qualities in a man. (Indeed, his investigation only succeeds when he eventually does admit instinct and permit it to trump the empirical systems that would otherwise place Walter above suspicion.) *Double Indemnity* thus foreshadows the disquiet over increasingly paranoiac working culture and its effect on the individual psyche that would become so prominent in 1950s anti-organization discourse.

Walter believes that Keyes and the office culture he embodies understand the darker vicissitudes of existence and the irrationalities of the human mind far less well than they claim to. He therefore sets out to prove, by his own hand, that unpredictable chaos can still exist in the world, untamable by loss adjusters and claims investigators. He evokes the frontierist/wilderness ethic of what the American (masculine) individual should be, because he believes himself possessed of preternatural ability to enter a situation of danger, risk, and chaos and navigate it successfully by his own ingenuity alone. Unlike his symbolic predecessor, however, he is also the agent, the mobile space, within which those forces of unpredictability are vested: his identity is thus cognate not only with the frontiersman but with the frontier *itself*. Mistakenly, Walter believes that the dangers he unleashes are unpredictable only to others, but not to him. The "savage" forces he unleashes upon the world of the office are, like those of the Turnerian frontier, beyond individual control: Walter is ultimately overwhelmed not by the juggernaut logic of the organization but by the literally and figuratively unmanageable consequences of his own his social boundary-crossing.

Those consequences are manifest in the figure of Phyllis Nirdlinger, whose role in the murder plot and Walter's eventual undoing demonstrates that its sexual and frontierist/anticorporate contexts are not contradictory or, ultimately, even separate. Phyllis's willingness not merely to cuckold but to murder her stuffy businessman husband in order, seemingly, to secure a future with Walter appears to him to affirm the power of his rugged, rule-breaking masculinity. In Phyllis, Walter seems to find not just a co-conspirator in murder but an ally in his attack on office culture—because she affirms the danger-loving, risk-taking vision of frontierist manhood that he seeks to embody and to which the office and insurance are antithetical. Phyllis's flattery of Walter's masculinity aligns her with his frontier values. Walter apparently does not realize, however, that if Phyllis shares with him an adherence to the creed of the frontier, she must be as dangerously unpredictable as he is. Perhaps Walter fails to see this precisely because the association of frontierism with maleness, which Phyllis herself affirms in Walter by flattering his self-perception as an irrepressible force of unregulated, violent instability, makes it impossible for him to consider that a woman might manifest those very values.

In Walter's own destruction, his frontier-reviving project succeeds: if he truly had mastery over the uncertainties he (re)introduces to a world built upon a logic of "orderly expectations," he would experience no *genuine* risk, only the illusion thereof, in fact validating and remaining complicit in the ideology he attempts to subvert. If *he* could predict events, thereby anticipating Phyllis's caprices and thus escaping his fate, he would only prove the triumph of a systematized, predictable world. Walter's death is ultimately the result of a failure to anticipate Phyllis's own manifestation of the kind of risk, hazard, and unpredictability he himself embodied and seeks to reintroduce to the world. Only in dying, therefore, can Walter prove (contrary to the prevailing currents of his age and the fears of a century of anti-office discourse) his own claim that humankind's volatile, irrational individualism cannot be managed out of existence.

Interrogating Space: Raymond Chandler's Detective-Frontiersman

Raymond Chandler once wrote in a letter to a fan that Philip Marlowe had been a claims investigator for an insurance firm prior to establishing himself as a private detective—he flirted with becoming Barton Keyes. Chandler tantalizingly suggests, albeit in a source of dubious canonicity, that Marlowe once endeavored to work within insurance's culture of corporate systematization, but couldn't stick at it, turning ultimately to the private eye's altogether more solitary and self-directed existence.[83] Like Huff, Marlowe expresses antagonism to the spatial practices of the office by means of (and to sustain) frontier values. Chandler's letter invites the curious conclusion that Marlowe's frontier-oriented antipathy toward the office is also like Huff's in that it is a rejection of a culture that was once his own. (A trace of that culture persists, perhaps, in the subconscious of a man who believes he "need[s] a lot of life insurance" despite having no dependents who would benefit by it.[84])

John Scaggs rightly notes that "the identification of the frontier hero as the archetype of the private eye is well established."[85] When critics add "frontiersman" to the detective's catalog of symbolic identities, however, they typically do so only in broad terms, often within larger typologies of white masculine heroism, as when Philip Durham counted "the American frontier hero" among the detective's mythic masks but focused instead on the detective-as-knight.[86] Scaggs and McCann both typify the near-exclusive focus in existing detective-as-frontiersman models on shared cultural values or character traits—rugged individualism, white masculine heroism, the desire to pursue and subdue conflict, the power to bring order through rough justice. McCann identifies "the fading virtues of the open frontier" as an object of Marlovian quest; Scaggs emphasizes comparability in physical strength, moral fortitude, and capacities for violence.[87] Such readings fail to consider fully that the frontier is defined not merely by values but by those values' mobilization within and articulation of highly codified spatial dynamics. Thus Megan Abbott observes that the detective has "forerunners in like-minded navigators of Western space or wilderness" but stops short of exploring precisely how his navigations of space invoke the frontier.[88] Richard Lehan proposes Marlowe as a "frontiersman . . . transformed by the city" without considering the correlative possibilities that such a figure's presence might transform the city's spaces into frontiers.[89]

Lee Horsley exemplifies critical failures to bring a true consideration of the frontier's essential spatiality into the detective-frontiersman analogy when he frames the two figures as both "patrolling the border between civilization and savagery."[90] Here, Horsley slightly misdescribes frontier spatial dynamics. Although the detective's mediation between "civilized" and "savage" is indeed essential to his frontiersmanship, frontiersmanship is avowedly *not* "border patrol," an act that maintains and secures an existing "civilizational" boundary. Quite the opposite, the frontiersman renders that boundary unstably mobile through his perpetual acts of spatial incursion. Ross Macdonald came closest to apprehending this when he identified the detective as embodying the "*restless* man of American democracy."[91] To fully test Philip Marlowe's capacities as a model frontiersman, we must assess how he performs the fundamental action of frontiersmanship—his "restless" movement through space.[92]

The frontiersman and detective are both roles that guarantee unpredictable adventures in uncomfortable environments amid volatile and dangerous people. The private investigator is licensed, he has an honorary sheriff's badge, but operates independently, in trouble with the cops as often as he is in league with them. In the Marlowe novels the enforcement of law does not necessarily mean justice, nor is justice necessarily legal. In this, Marlowe represents justice cut loose from institutional and bureaucratic ties, resituated instead in the principles and instincts of a pragmatic individual. Such characteristics not only resonate with the legacy of Turnerian frontier justice (in which "the personality of law" took precedence over any "organized machinery of justice," privileging "the duel and the blood-feud"), they lend the detective a quality of frontierlike liminality, between regulated institutional order and lawless expediency.[93] Chandler exploits this aspect of the detective's professional identity to have Marlowe perform sociospatial negotiations that are themselves strongly redolent of frontierism.

Narratively as well as professionally, Marlowe's typical task is to pioneer an investigative passage between spaces separated by money, by law, by class, by race—the canyonside mansion and the tumbledown apartment house, the exclusive club and the dank barroom. This gymnastic sociogeographic mobility is suggested in Macdonald's essential observation that the detective's role is as a social "mask" worn by the text in order to "face the dangers of society high and low."[94] Fredric Jameson expands on that theme, writing that

> the various classes have lost touch with each other because each is isolated in its own geographical compartment. . . . Since there is no longer any privileged experience in which the whole of the social structure can be grasped, a figure must be . . . superimposed on the society as a whole, whose routine and life-pattern serve somehow to tie its separate and isolated parts together. . . . Through him we are able to see, to know, the society as a whole, but he does not really stand for any genuine experience of it.[95]

Such ability to maneuver between "society high and low" places Marlowe in a doubly frontiersmanlike role. Not only does it suggest the frontiersman's ironic quality of becoming exceptional precisely because he is an everyman (Chandler wrote that a detective must be "a common man and yet an unusual man"), it also places Marlowe in a position of negotiating between "civilized" and "savage."⁹⁶ Marlowe's navigations between the "civilized" societal surface and its "savage" underbelly, however, in fact serve to reveal that the two exist in threatening proximity to each other—or are even manifest in *the same* place or person. In Chandler, high-society Anglo-Americans provide the locus of masked personal "savagery" at least as frequently as the small-time crooks whose socioeconomic position (and, in several cases, their ethnic identity) would appear to place them outside the respectable mainstream of American life.

As Liahna Babener notes, "virtually every one of Chandler's seven novels pivots on . . . mistaken, disguised, or altered identity."⁹⁷ *Farewell, My Lovely* (1940) charts the failure of Helen Grayle to maintain the suppression of her former identity as low-rent lounge singer Velma Valento. Grayle believes that she has consigned to history every trace of her old life, but it returns in the form of Moose Malloy. His animal name and overwhelming strength (he throws a man "clear across the room" with a crash that could be "heard in Denver") connoting uncontrollable bestiality, Malloy's symbolic import is clear: however "civilized" you believe yourself to have become, a Turnerian "hither edge" of untamable atavism remains closer than you think.⁹⁸ In *The Big Sleep*, Arthur Geiger disguises his identity as pornographer, blackmailer, and homosexual behind his respectable professional status as a bookseller. The camera, that archetypally contemporary instrument with which Geiger produces the pornography that defines his hidden, scandalous identity, is itself hidden inside a totem pole, an object that fetishistically suggests America prior to its urbanization and de-frontierizing by white, western men. A connection between resurgent social wildness and the original "wild" frontier is manifested by their superposition in a single object.

Marlowe's ability to thus locate the "savage" *within* the "civilized" only affirms his allegiance to frontier values. For Turner, although the frontiersman produced a "civilizing" effect upon wilderness, a suspicion and rejection of "civilization" was what drove him westward. Likewise, the Merwinite antimoderns who mourned the frontier's loss feared that society was as vulnerable to an overdevelopment of "civilization" as to "savagery"—indeed that the decadence of "overcivilization" was enacting its own form of "savagery" upon individual character. Marlowe makes a cognate claim when he reveals that lawlessness, duplicity, and vice are equally present in spaces of apparent refinement and less salubrious environs: his investigative ability to navigate between the two collapses the sociospatial distance by which the former affects moral distinction from the latter. In Marlowe's world, as in the frontiersman's, too much "civilization" and too much "savagery" ultimately have the same deleterious impact on the bodily and moral integrity of the individual, hence the continual failure of the former to mask the latter. By revealing not only that acts of depravity are locatable in both Beverley Hills and Bunker Hill but that those acts of depravity are often extensions of each other, ultimately one and the same, Marlowe discloses the frontiersmanlike worldview of someone whose assault on "savagery" and rejection of excessive "civilization" are held in perfect tension. Indeed, it is precisely because he holds that worldview that such connections become possible.

The importance of this connective role to Marlowe's actions runs counter to Stanley Orr's suggestion that the hardboiled detective is "heroically isolated from a world of compromised borders," both "inured to and polarized against the dark places of the metropolis."[99] Quite the opposite: in performing his Jamesonian social role as the locator of and conduit for contiguities between the "civilized" world and the "dark places" from which it pretends a *cordon sanitaire*, Marlowe is both a compromised border and a compromiser of borders, a frontier and a frontiersman. As the figure whose detections of social threats reveal spaces possessed of both insufficiency and excess of "civilization" to be equally likely sources of such threats, Marlowe is frontiersmanlike. As the vehicle for the detections by which those spaces are connected, however, Marlowe himself becomes the space of their connection, and thus also like a frontier—a mobile liminality where a contest between "savage" and "civilized" reveals both forces to be equally inimical to the individual. Not merely Tzvetan Todorov's "vulnerable detective," who becomes "integrated into the universe" when he "loses his immunity," Marlowe is the permeable detective, penetrated by the spaces he penetrates, permitting the universe to become integrated in himself.[100]

Although Marlowe's apprehensions of "savagery" do not map with sociogeographic predictability to where he finds himself in the city, the performance of such acts is, however, mapped to the way he *moves through* spaces—to the repeated, codified formula by which Chandler organizes space and Marlowe's navigation of it. The frontiersman advances the limit of navigable space by interrogating prior understandings of the notional divide between space that is safe, mapped and stable, and space whose properties are not yet known. He claims a right to scope the latter despite having no formal title to it, and even though in many cases it may already be claimed by other occupants. The frontier advances because when the frontiersman moves from known space to unknown, he brings the latter under the control of the knowledge he carries with him from known space. Frontiersmanship, therefore, is not merely a demand to enter certain resistive spaces, it the ability to contest and change their meaning upon entering. In these respects, Marlowe is the frontiersman's exact double.

In Geiger's store, for example, architecture mimetically informs moral character: only a partition door withholds access to a world of murder, treachery, and sexual degeneracy.[101] This membrane appears thin and permeable, but the detective is alone among those who reside on the "civilized" side of the partition in his willingness not only to see that the two spaces are in fact one but to reveal them as such. He demonstrates a frontiersman's refusal to accept the conceptual division (while corrupt cops, supposed defenders of social rectitude, work to protect Geiger's illusion). Likewise, in *The Lady in the Lake* (1943) bodies lie behind shower curtains and beneath sunken piers, and at the minutest level a crucial clue hides in a box of sugar.[102] Even when he is not physically present, it is Marlowe's ability to interrogate the construction of space in an account of a Mexican hotel room in *The Long Goodbye* that enables him to apprehend Cisco Maioranos's true identity as Terry Lennox.[103] This mapping of revelations about people to discovery and redefinition of space on a micro-scale suffuses the Marlowe novels. Marlowe's ability to reconnoiter a physical space, and therein identify and navigate through some flaw in a barrier or boundary, is necessary to reveal all.

Turner creates a vision of exceptionalist American identity built not on notions of unassailability or impregnability but rather on vulnerability, on the constant presence of existential threats to itself. The frontiersman's existence depends simultaneously (and paradoxically) on the endurance of hazards to which he is subject and on the possibility of conquering those hazards. Cain's Walter Huff falls afoul of this truth by failing to recognize that his personal revivification of "savagery" renders his own conquering inevitable. Marlowe, by contrast, operates at a remove, closer to the original frontiersman in that he does not attempt to invert personally the "savage"/"civilized" dichotomy but only to prove its ongoing existence. Where Huff assumes that the office's culture of regimented, bloodless "civilization" has achieved social supremacy and works to subvert and disrupt it, Marlowe's belief that "savagery" is always latent in "civilization" means his project of is one of *revealing* frontierist subversion of rigorous corporate rectitude already present within the office's regulated culture. (Puss Walgreen's insurance company front is once again instructive here.) Marlowe accordingly shares, on the level of professional identity, the frontiersman's quality of existing to root out and subdue danger while his existence is itself dependent on the ongoing presence of such danger.

He is the means by which Los Angeles's social "savagery" is exposed and, in individual cases at least, quelled, but in fact, Marlowe depends upon social transgressors; he needs crime. If no crimes were committed, he would have no crimes to solve. He would no longer subsist as a professional detective or exist as a narrative construct. Jameson apprehends some of this paradox in noting Marlowe's "peculiar" fondness for his gangster foes and describing him as "an *involuntary* explorer of the society."[104] Orr's Todorov-indebted reading of the hardboiled detective as a figure who "'takes blows' in pursuit of boundary maintenance" is thus undeniable, but incomplete. Because the detective inherits a frontiersman's complicity with or dependence upon the very danger he assails, his acts of boundary maintenance (expunging criminality, minimizing danger within society) are simultaneously acts of boundary breakage (excavating criminality, disabusing society of its illusions about its own gentility).[105] Like the frontiersman, Marlowe assails the edges of space and societal structure while depending in existential paradox on the presence of those edges.

Where Marlowe departs from his spiritual forebear to offer a dark dream of inexhaustible frontierism is that his *conceptual* division of space within and without the frontier is not restricted by geographical finitude. Marlowe's ability to find frontiers is determined not by a rigid geographical equation but by what a given space and his ability to occupy it signify at a given moment. His spatial frontier negotiations therefore become endlessly iterable. On the mytho-geographic frontier, space was contested between pioneer and environment, cowboy and Native American. Marlowe's spatial battle is between the other parties to each case and, therein, between different potential epistemic and narrative meanings located in each newly navigated space. The application of the navigational instruments of logic, deduction, and legal principle to successive spaces of criminality partially regulates and "civilizes" such spaces, but simultaneously iterates further contests over the multiplying possibilities of how, why, where, and whodunit.

Such navigations also invoke a Gothic tradition in which spatial, psychic, and narrative processes of revelation-through-permeation are closely mapped to each other, and indeed in which the protagonist's acts of boundary-crossing are internalized and mediated within the self. Eve Kosofsky Sedgwick codifies this Gothic "spatial model" as having "three elements (what's inside, what's outside, and what separates them)" and a "self massively blocked off from something to which it ought normally to have access."[106] Marlowe's spatial navigations both echo and complicate this spatial paradigm. Certainly, his movements through space manifest a similar tripartite structure of inside, outside, and a separation that must somehow be permeated. Moreover, the detective's own occupation of a sociolegal boundary is precisely why he can permeate spatial boundaries and discover in that process new meanings (both the plot-advancing detections made by spatial conquest and the investiture therein of frontier qualities). In this respect, he further occupies Sedgwick's sense of Gothic consciousness as not only a breaking and crossing of boundaries (often from literal prisons) but itself an impossible puzzle of liminality—a "prison which has neither inside nor outside" and therefore "from which there can be no escape."[107] Marlowe's frontierist excavation of "savage" characteristics hiding in superficially "civilized" space, his dredging up of an unsettling, atavistic past, thought buried for good, also recalls Gothic convention's subsistence on the stubborn refusal of the past to stay imprisoned. Marlowe's concordance with the Gothic thereby comes to stand as in itself further evidence of communion with Los Angeles's own "Gothic" prisoner: the suppressed frontier. In Chandler, in Sedgwick's Gothic, and on the frontier alike, the "worst violence" and "most potent magic" both reside in "the breach of the imprisoning wall."[108]

The breaches by which Marlowe is called upon to apprehend violence (and in so doing effect a magical restitution of the frontier), however, typically take the form of incursion into rather than (as in Sedgwick's Gothic) escape from a sanctum. Even when the evidence of misdeed sought is not material, when Marlowe merely is speaking to clients, witnesses, or suspects, it is striking how frequently Chandler's scenes conform to a default spatial format in which Marlowe is mobile, and enters a home or workplace occupied by a subject who remains essentially—and defensively—static. Marlowe does not merely move through space; like the frontiersman he moves, continually, into spaces that are perilous, and that immediately become interrogatively contested. When Marlowe meets General Sternwood in *The Big Sleep*, for example, the latter's greenhouse is figured explicitly as a jungle; Marlowe can scarcely breathe, so inhospitable is the physical space he must occupy in order to begin his case.[109]

Again, Marlowe's project of uncovering the wild, like the frontiersman's, is bound up in his ability to hold his own in certain kinds of hostile space. Orr thus concurs that "the Sternwood mansion becomes a synecdoche for Chandler's California," and recognizes the significance of the westward frontier journey in birthing that "world of breached borders."[110]

For Orr, the Sternwood mansion's literal "urban jungle" is evidence that Chandler's essential context is the political and narrative legacy of high colonial adventure. Chandler, writes Orr, "inherited from [Joseph] Conrad the agonism of the western sojourner striving to retain his "civilization" in a "savage" wilderness."[111] On that basis, Orr claims, "Chandler's response to the triumphalist spirit of Manifest Destiny, which perhaps found its highest expression in the 'California adventure' " (otherwise known as the frontier quest), is to recast the Californian booster myth of "the Anglo-American colony as the savage colonial periphery of late-Victorian adventure."[112] Orr is right that Chandler recasts the apparently urban, modern, California as "savage periphery," but his model fails to capture the ambivalence of Marlowe's place (and the complexity of his directions of travel) within the "savage"/"civilized" dichotomy. The frontiersman provides a more comprehensively effective model for understanding Marlowe's sociospatial negotiations than Orr's colonial adventurer, as can be seen in how Marlowe uses the office.

Though the colonial adventurer's identity as a figure of rugged outdoor masculinity corresponds strongly with ideals of manhood that Merwin et al. feared were being lost in offices, he is also a figure who represents (much less ambiguously than the frontiersman) the *ushering in* and indeed enforcement of modernity upon the "uncivilized" rather than a turning away from it. Marlowe's office engagements, by contrast, reveal a determination less to bring "civilization" to the wilderness than to preserve wilderness in the face of apparent "civilization." The way Marlowe "re-wilds" space in the "civilized" office demonstrates that he descends more directly from the frontiersman—who nominally represents "civilization" yet exists in co-dependent complicity with the wilderness he endeavors to conquer, modernity's own antimodernist—than from the less fraught and self-contradicting colonial adventurer.

Further, the office proves one of the most rewarding territories for Marlowe's frontiersmanship in part because of the sheer density of its spatial production: it is so clearly drawn, demarcated, and codified along conceptual, social, and physical lines (the same highly determined and well-understood array of meanings that announces Walter Neff's late-night call to his workplace as a harbinger of ill-doing). In the office, power relations between unwanted guest, invited or authorized visitor, employees of different standings, and owners/proprietors are mapped upon and made manifest in the system of desks, doors, and partitions that can, depending on their context, denote defensiveness or receptivity, intimidation or invitation. That is to say, the spatial practice of the office expresses itself in an architectural and systemic language by which it is rendered a zone of contested borders.

A near-schematic indicator of Marlowe's power to reiterate frontier conditions by the redesignation of space occurs in *The High Window* (1942). Two key locations in the story, the office of the coin dealer Morningstar and that of the dental technician Teager, occupy "the same relative position" on identical floors of an archetypally modern space of identikit commercial compartments. Their rooms are "cut up differently," but only slightly; they are essentially twins.[113] Both offices are divided by a partition, and in both cases Marlowe, as so often, must pass from one side of the divide to the other by covert means and without regard to the existing ownership of the space. Crucially, however, these otherwise identical incidents involve opposite directions of travel. Marlowe's progress through the frontiers of Teager's space is as one might expect: he enters the outer office with a key obtained from the elevator operator, then proceeds into the back office to make his discovery. In a perfect model of frontier dynamics, as he navigates through successive spaces the jeopardy of his position increases because his claim on the space is increasingly weak. Earlier in the book, however, with Morningstar, Marlowe enters both public-facing outer office and private sanctum freely, by invitation of the occupant. He is in no peril. He in fact only makes a frontierist navigation when he returns to the outer office, pretends to have left, but in fact hides behind the partition to hear an incriminating phone call before actually exiting. At the moment when he chooses to occupy the previously "neutral" space of the outer office, it is no longer a space in which his position is secure; it has been reinvested with jeopardy—re-frontierized—by Marlowe's navigational gesture.

The mirroring of Marlowe's movements in his navigations of the twin spaces of Teager and Morningstar, then, evinces his flexibility in navigating, even generating frontiers: his frontiers do not depend on any single and thus finite construction of spatial movement. In *The Long Goodbye*, Marlowe claims that whether Los Angeles appears "rich and vigorous and full of pride" or "lost and beaten and full of emptiness . . . all depends on where you sit": the meaning of a space is determined by one's position within it. He therein positions himself as a figure empowered through mobility to see both cities at will.[114] In the offices of both Teager and Morningstar, Marlowe proves precisely that creative ability to redesignate meanings of space by changing his position within it. Such redesignatory spatial power allows Marlowe to claim that the frontier never disappeared: it was merely transmuted into different types of space, which the detective both explores and manifests in himself.

Crucially, too, in the Teager and Morningstar navigations the nature of Marlowe's frontierism is specifically articulated by and exploits the particular formal features of the office block—the qualities of repetition and sameness that act to draw the two movements into a structural dialogue with each other. Invoking the Lefebvrian spatial triad we can say that offices are understood as offices on the basis of the type of space they produce: there is a common cultural understanding of the physical, social, and conceptual characteristics that conspire to the definition of "office." There are variations within the paradigm, of course, for example between the Teager/Morningstar-style sole trader in a block of individual office suites and the corporation occupying an entire floor (which I will address in the following section), but both are recognizable via their sociospatial practice as varieties of the same thing, with a common accrued set of (anti-frontierist) cultural meanings. As he shows in the rooms of Teager and Morningstar, Marlowe's navigations exploit and respond to exactly this sense of the office as predictable, formulaic space and cultural symbol, defined and recognizable by its sociospatial codification. The office thus makes the detective's movements legible with especial clarity as a process of revealing frontier qualities in a seemingly post-frontier culture: Marlowe's ability to locate inexhaustible frontiers is not only evidenced within but *generated by* the characteristics of an archetypally modern, urban structure that would ostensibly appear to stand as evidence of a post-frontier condition.

In the office, the abstractly frontierist quality of Marlowe's usual exploratory, revelatory movement into "savage" spaces occurs in a space that is in theory the ideological antithesis of frontier values. The very sociospatial formality of the office, the structures of division and regularization that render Marlowe's frontierist navigations there visible with a peculiar clarity, simultaneously denotes the office's anti-frontierist culture. Thus the office is perhaps unique among Marlowe's recurring investigatory environments because while its culture stands in direct opposition to frontier values, the sociospatial practice of its internal construction invites interpretation as a frontierist topography. In the office, Marlowe's movements do not merely serve to uncover frontier qualities through his marshaling of space; they generate a specific conflict with the directly anti-frontierist values of that space itself. In *The High Window*, moreover, Marlowe's ability reconceptualize an anti-frontierist space as a landscape of frontierist hazard is precisely the means by which he locates lawless social "savagery" hiding in the "civilized" spaces to which it is supposedly antithetical—the offices of a respectable business culture harboring a criminal (Teager) and a criminal's victim (Morningstar).

Although Jameson admits that "the shabby office building, in general, is a fundamental component of the Chandler cityscape," he obscures the specific symbolic implications of Marlowe's territorial conquests over office spaces by arguing that Chandler's "thematics of private and public" enact a "co-ordination of home and office."[115] For Jameson, that "co-ordination" becomes conflation, as when he argues that because Chandler's gangsters are typically confronted in their nominal workplaces (clubs, casinos) these places should be regarded as their homes.[116] In the imprecision of Jameson's spatial categorizations, the crucial frontierist specificity of Marlowe's engagement with offices is lost. Jameson's refusal to acknowledge the particularity of *literal* offices in Chandler occludes the special ideological significance of Chandler's exploratory and revelatory activities therein. The stakes of the office as a symbol of systematized, "overcivilized," post-frontier modernity are such that it can do more perhaps than any of Chandler's other typical environments to demonstrate that Marlowe's interpretations of space are intrinsically frontierist. A weight of frontier-invocative historical and cultural meaning accrues to the office in a way that it simply does not to Art Huck's garage in *The Big Sleep*, Dr. Sonderborg's hospital in *Farewell, My Lovely*, or other Chandlerian workplaces.

Marlowe, of course, is an office dweller himself—puncturing the detective's *noir* glamour, Mike Davis describes him unarguably as a "small businessman"—but a reluctant one.[117] The characteristics of his "official" workplace prove redolent of the frontierist work he carries out in those of other people. In the same letter that reveals Marlowe's past in the insurance industry, Chandler describes Marlowe's office, noting that he "could very easily subscribe to a telephone answering service" but chooses not to: if office culture embodies an anti-frontierist embrace of the technologized systems of modernity, Marlowe refuses that embrace where possible.[118]

While Marlowe cannot entirely escape the theoretically anti-frontierist strictures of office life, his is an ironized office, one that, in reflection of its proprietor, comments self-consciously on the antagonistic relationship between crime and the modern workplace in Chandler's texts. In *The Big Sleep*, Marlowe's office contains "five green filing cases." Three are empty, but Marlowe does not describe them thus. Instead, he says they are "full of California climate."[119] This is on one hand a way to say they have nothing in them, not even California air, which, while still an absence of files and documents, would at least have an in some sense tangible, if invisible, substance. "Climate," by contrast, can only denote the conceptual—the mere generalized *idea* of what the atmospheric conditions are like, rather than any specific physical attributes. By the same token, however, this is a way to say that the office drawers contain a whole world beyond themselves. California's climate, such a dominant facet of popular images of the place, is so pervasive that it has found its way into Marlowe's drawers, a micro-scale spatial division within a spatial division (the inner office), within a spatial division (Marlowe's suite as a whole), within a further spatial division (the building). Here is a statement that Marlowe's office holds things that should not, by rights, be held in an office, nor, by synecdoche, in any of the structures of the tamed urban modernity that the office represents. Even when Marlowe is operating entirely within the hermetically sealed, sterile structures of the urban realm, says the image of a drawerful of "California climate," the natural characteristics of the region will assert themselves.[120]

Marlowe's is a world in which too much of the fierce and capricious strength of California's natural temperament has become locked up inside drawers and offices: he will spend several books discovering that nature where it is secreted and letting it spring dangerously but revivifyingly free from its drawers, before locking it provisionally away again. (The frontiersmanlike formal lot of the serial detective is that danger will and indeed must spring free no sooner than he is able to contain it.) The climate of California has a notoriously double-edged role in the state's history, folklore, and imagery. On the one hand, the "pleasant climate" of a "Land of Sunshine" defined Southern Californian boosterism from its inception and continued to fuel an economy of agriculture, tourism, and property speculation as Chandler was writing.[121] Yet, on the other hand, the California climate is also one of mortal danger and uncontrollability, of "every blighting caprice of Nature," as Morrow Mayo put it in 1933, by which the state is "inundated or burned up" each year before "boom[ing] again."[122] It is the climate of wildfires, mudslides, and the Santa Ana winds that Chandler himself described in one of his finest short stories as making "wives feel the edge of the carving knife and study their husbands' necks."[123]

This environmental duality lies at the root of why California incubates the superficially similar but ultimately contradictory myths of the frontier and the new Eden: its climate can present both conditions near-simultaneously. Walter Huff also suggests that contradiction when he says that "in California February looks like any other month."[124] He ostensibly seems to remark on California's identity as an Edenic land of perpetual summer, but the notion of California as a place where the year never ages, in which winter never comes, also suggests a place where the present may sustain conditions that ought to have slid into the past. Huff finds in the seasonless environment a sense of temporal anomaly and disjunction that reflects his own scheme—one in which the atavism of a bygone frontier is relocated to modern institutions. Cain's rogue insurance agent and the California weather share a common consciousness.

Everywhere the eye falls in Marlowe's conspicuously colorful office it meets a suggestion of the occupant's preoccupation with a deceptive environment: the verdant green filing cases sit beneath a blue sky—the "sky-blue floor" in the picture on Marlowe's calendar. That picture is of the then-famous Dionne quintuplets, whose eyes are described as being "as large as mammoth prunes," again suggesting the supposed mellow fruitfulness of Southern California. Their eyes, however, are "sea-brown," not an image of the Pacific that would please the proprietors of the Los Angeles area's many piers and seaside funfairs, nor those of boat trips to Catalina Island. Meanwhile the "rust-red" carpet evokes the recalcitrant desert upon which the city has been boldly imposed, while the ersatz artificiality of that imposition is attested to by chairs that are not real walnut but rather "near-walnut."[125]

Furthermore, if California climate is what Marlowe has in his office drawers instead of case files, then the nature of the work he conducts from that office implies which of the capricious climate's two faces is the dominant one. In containing California climate the drawers *do* in a sense contain Marlowe's case files because the worst and wildest that (human) nature has to offer is precisely what he seeks out beneath superficially sunny exteriors. Just as the seeming land of balmy sunshine continually betrays its occupants with the savage return of wind, fire, storms, and earthquake, so do the most genteel Californians so often turn out to be the state's most depraved residents. In that respect, Marlowe's drawer full of nothing proves to be nothing but. What at first implies placid emptiness becomes a suggestion that these drawers could contain absolutely anything.

Marlowe's drawers thus attain the condition of "figural stealth" that Julian Murphet identifies as the defining quality of *noir* fiction's assault on booster fantasies of a utopian LA.[126] In suggesting through their own deceptive meaning the unpredictable and often inhospitable climate of Marlowe's business, the office drawers likewise contain (and in another sense fail to contain) Californian booster anxieties. The Edenic myth of sunshine and orange groves may not, after all, have achieved supremacy over its counter-myth; nature-as-aggressor, red in tooth and claw on the perpetual frontier of the American imagination, remains threateningly pregnant in Marlowe's drawers. Chandler locates in a synecdoche for the office (the filing case) a clear opposition to (and moreover a literal attempt to constrain spatially) the frontierist forces of danger, risk, and individualism embodied in the "California climate"—and its metonymic companions, Marlowe's criminal foes. This scene thereby underscores the office as a site that, time and again in Chandler's fiction, proves fertile ground for the reiteration of frontierist contests.

Deracination: Marlowe Meets his Match

When Marlowe attempts to visit a prospective client in *The Lady in the Lake*, the spatial practice of the corporate world resists Marlowe's frontiersmanlike efforts to traverse its office landscape, but does so in an instructive manner, affirming the Turnerian maxim that sometimes the frontier must, by definition, defeat the pioneer.[127] Derace Kingsley is a senior executive at the Gillerlain Perfume Company, which has its offices in a building that is named the Treloar by Chandler, but is analogous in its location and physical characteristics to the historical James Oviatt Building, which opened in 1928 at 617 S. Olive Street (figure 2.1).[128]

Seeking to cement the status of his business, a luxury gentleman's haberdasher, in the minds of well-to-do consumers in Southern California and beyond, James Oviatt took a literal approach, in the form of an extravagant temple to both design and consumerism situated in the most fashionable part of downtown. With its thirteen stories and clock tower, Oviatt's commercial Xanadu rose as high as local ordinance would allow.

Figure 2.1. The James Oviatt Building (c. 1930). A view of downtown Los Angeles, with Olive Street running northeast past Pershing Square and on toward Bunker Hill. On the left, just before the intersection with 6th Street, stands the James Oviatt building: we can imagine Derace Kingsley's expansive office suite on an upper floor. *Source*: Los Angeles Area Chamber of Commerce Collection 1890–1960, University of Southern California Libraries and California Historical Society. Public domain.

It is a popular misconception that the 150-foot limit on building height maintained in Los Angeles between 1911 and 1957 was an anti-earthquake measure; the bigger civic concern, in truth, was one of aesthetics.[129] Oviatt, though, saw no contradiction between height and beauty; indeed, he saw them as equally vital to his project: the building bearing his name was to be an up-to-the-minute monument to the new Art Deco style in its most luxurious form.[130] Thirty tons of René Lalique glasswork accompanied an illuminated glass ceiling and awnings by Ferdinand Chanut and Gaetan Jeannin. Fixtures and fittings were shipped from France at vast expense via the Panama Canal. Bronze statues were studded about the premises and an artificial outdoor palm grove allowed customers to try on their new apparel in natural light.[131] The building was a spectacle, its opening a major regional news event; the *LA Times* marveled that it been "dreamed true" by Oviatt.[132] The lowest three floors and basement were occupied by Oviatt's firm, the building was topped by an opulent penthouse for Oviatt himself, and the intervening floors were rented to numerous businesses as offices.[133] Although the building did not approach the scale of the skyscrapers of New York and Chicago, it was nonetheless its skyward wonder that fixed it in a local cultural imagination and saw it dubbed "the castle in the air."[134]

Oviatt's dream thus serves as instructive reminder that Los Angeles's status as a spreading, horizontal, rather than a concentrated, vertical city—centrifugal rather than centripetal, in Ed Dimendberg's dichotomy—was not yet a foregone conclusion as the city greeted the 1930s.[135] Even though city fathers' concerns with maintaining local aesthetic character and preventing the construction of a Manhattan of the West restricted LA's builders to a more modest scale, Los Angeles could still fetishize vertical modernity with fervor.[136] Much of Jameson's argument as to why Los Angeles requires Marlowe as a sociospatial explorer resides in his belief that Los Angeles' horizontal sprawl does not support anything like the "Parisian apartment house" that could, as in Zola's novels, encompass (bourgeois) society in vertical microcosm.[137] Although Jameson is right about the detective as the city's social glue, Marlowe's presence within a fictionalized Oviatt Building is a strong rejoinder to the case that he was birthed by a dearth of slice-of-life spaces. The multi-use tower stratifies society both vertically (from ground-floor retail to owner-occupied penthouse) and, as Marlowe will discover, on an internal horizontal axis through the spatial demarcations governing access within an individual company's offices.

It is similarly curious that Sean McCann omits the Oviatt/Treloar Building's physical prominence and pertinence to plot from his reading of *The Lady in the Lake*. McCann contrasts the verticality of the extra-urban dam where the novel climaxes with the "confusing horizontality of urban Los Angeles," but this is a novel that begins with its protagonist's incursion into a fictionalization of the second-most-famous tall building in the Los Angeles of its day (after City Hall, a 454-foot restriction-busting behemoth). The Oviatt/Treloar Building serves in the novel's design as a counterweight to the corresponding verticality of its denouement, and thus also to McCann's claim that the dam, by standing against a supposedly horizontal Los Angeles, is an "architectural rendering of the way [Chandler's] novel works to contain dangerous movement."[138] Not only does the Treloar, the dam's mirror image in the book's structure, indicate that verticality is possible in Los Angeles, its role in Marlowe's investigation as a site of urban frontierist spatial practice provides further evidence that Chandler's world is at least as much about the practice of "dangerous movement" as its containment.

Entering the building, Marlowe summarily walks past an arcade of shops; he is characteristically uninterested in public-facing facades other than as concealers of his true target. The "castle in the air" that Marlowe seeks is not a residential fantasia but a corporate one: he proceeds into "a vast black and gold lobby" and then takes the elevator to the seventh floor, where he enters Gillerlain's offices.[139] Marlowe's object is, as ever, something behind closed doors, spatially distanced and concealed: he must thus penetrate to the very center of the building on both horizontal and vertical axes. The premises of Teager and Morningstar participated in modern office culture by being located in a modern office building and thus manifesting its spatial characteristics (the architectural reproductions exploited by Marlowe). As the workplaces of sole traders, though, they also displayed clear connection to older cultural and architectural traditions. The small-scale business in a little suite of partitioned rooms, the inner and outer office, appears in Chandler in its latest guise, with the technological conveniences and characteristic spatial repetition of modernity, but is recognizably in the lineage of what an office meant in a text like "Bartleby." When Marlowe visits Gillerlain, however, he confronts the office of the new corporate America, something closer to the systematized apparatus of deracinated knowledge work that so enervates Walter Huff. If the Teager and Morningstar offices recall Melville and Whitman's suspicion of clerks, Gillerlain foreshadows Wilson and Whyte's fear of the organization. If Dennis Porter is correct that the connection between the private eye and the frontiersman is that they share a "non-organization man's eye," then we might expect to find that connection disclosed in the eye that Marlowe casts across the Gillerlain premises.[140]

There is nothing clandestine or illicit about Marlowe's visit to Gillerlain; he is not hunting for evidence or surveilling a witness—he is, in theory, there to meet somebody who wishes to meet with him. Curiously, though, he has more difficulty in navigating this space than he does in many of those he enters by less legitimate means. What frustrates Marlowe's spatial progress here are the physical and social structures of the early to mid-twentieth-century, post-Taylor American office—its cultures of suspicion, surveillance, technology, recordkeeping, and hierarchy, and the architectural devices that enforce those cultures in space. Having made his way to the seventh floor, Marlowe must first pass through imposing "swinging double plate-glass doors bound in platinum."[141] This unlocked door in a semi-public area is no real physical barrier, but the entrance to this office has been conspicuously designed to have an imposing effect upon the ingressor, whether visitor or employee. It exemplifies what Thompson terms "codes of visibility incorporated into the architecture of office spaces."[142]

Marlowe then enters a reception room, the description of which seems to bespeak contemporary anxieties about self-propagating, self-multiplying office work's abstraction from any physical evidence of a company's actual "production." Although the room features a showcase of examples of Gillerlain's wares, it is at sea in surroundings characterized by an eclectic, even proto-postmodern mélange of "Chinese rugs," "angular but elaborate furniture," and "sharp shiny bits of abstract sculpture."[143] The company's actual products are alienated from the viewer/reader, overwhelmed and decontextualized by an array of other objects that have no logical relationship either to the products themselves or even to each other. The "abstract" nature of the sculptures matters: they exist only as themselves, denying external referents and thus refusing to claim and relate to the context of their environment. Conversely, the perfume showcase and the perfume itself, the only things in the room that actually represent the Gillerlain Company's purpose, are incapable of being described in terms of themselves; they exist only by being metonymized into other things. The showcase becomes an image of a geographical feature, made up of "islands and promontories," while the firm's premier product bears the slogan "*The Champagne of Perfumes*": it can be described only as something else.[144] Even the supposed physical entity that is Gillerlain's product is itself merely an ephemeral mist that disappears visually in an instant and olfactorily within hours. The office's entire physical appearance manifests the abstract and the arbitrary, the decontextualized and anti-referential, while the only verifiably sensate and tangible output of the company's workings must instead latch onto a descriptive context from outside themselves in order to achieve describable form. One can scarcely imagine a more complete metaphor for a contemporary concern not only that office work was becoming increasingly divorced from the tangible production of companies, but that the former had in some sense supplanted the latter. This is an abstract, oblique company, producing only the scent of something "real."

Keeping lookout at the gates of this abstract space, which Marlowe must navigate in order to reach his goal, are the company's secretarial staff. A "neat little blonde" guards the PBX (internal telephone exchange), which in turn forms a technological barrier between the executive in his private office and any assailants who penetrate the sealed corporate world's first lines of defense either physically (via the great platinum doors) or remotely (via an outside line). Even the PBX operator herself is physically protected by the spatial organization of the room, sitting in the "far corner . . . behind a railing and well out of harm's way."[145] What real harm she could come to is unclear; it seems Marlowe is mocking the office's culture of physical demarcations and, as Huff did, its hyper-dogmatism about adherence to operational rules and procedures, which are frustrating his progress through its space. Once again, the office discloses itself as a critical location of Marlowe's frontiersmanlike identity because while the seeming rigidity and overprescription of its physical and social structures denote a culture in complete opposition to frontier values, those same structures present themselves to Marlowe *as* a frontier—a hostile landscape of barriers and hazards.

Accordingly, when Marlowe revisits the office later in the book, he signals to the "fluffy little blonde" his ability to refrontierize the meanings of space by acting out some literal frontiersmanship. Giving her "the gunman's salute, a stiff forefinger pointing at her, the three lower fingers tucked back under it, and the thumb wiggling up and down like a western gun-fighter fanning his hammer," he signals his values' divergence from those of her workplace.[146] The gesture is of course unmistakably phallic, penetrative, but the frontier context from which it derives renders its penetrative implications primarily spatial rather than sexual. The gesture is, moreover, suffused with irony, because it is an acknowledgment to the secretary of mutual recognition from Marlowe's previous visit, and on that visit his usual frontiersmanlike skills in penetrating and subduing hostile space were sorely lacking. Marlowe's salute admits that, when he last visited the office, the integrity of the space was impervious to any of the investigatory ammunition he typically uses (persuasion, subterfuge, dissembling, brute force). If the gunman's salute does contain a sexual implication, it is one of impotence rather than Marlowe's usual penetrative power. Emphasizing its own bathetic failure to be a *real* gun, the salute tells the secretary that Marlowe knows he has thus far been firing blanks. Indeed, on that first entrance Marlowe does not even get as far as persuading the PBX operator to put a call through to the boss, because he is first blocked, physically and interrogatively, by another secretary, Adrienne Fromsett.

In his interaction with her we see how the spatial and social practices of the office intimately inform each other: Marlowe's goal is to pass through a certain door, behind which is Derace Kingsley. Kingsley is a busy and apparently short-tempered man; he is in conference and has no time for visitors, especially those without an appointment. Marlowe admits this is not "anything I could argue about."[147] There is nothing physical stopping him from seeing Kingsley; he could barge past the secretary's desk and through the presumably unlocked door to Kingsley's private office, but the disruption and offense this would cause would defeat the object of his visit. The situation is compounded by the fact that the nature of his business is delicate and personal to Kingsley. Marlowe cannot, in the semi-public space of the reception room, tell a secretary the nature of his call or even his occupation, making his passage through the space even more difficult. Executives are unlikely to wish to see a man they have never heard of, with no appointment, who can only tell the secretary that they have been sent by a "Lieutenant M'Gee."[148] Marlowe is bound not merely by the space's physical characteristics but by the social rules that dictate how those physical characteristics should be used, because his goal is not merely to enter Kingsley's private space but to gain a positive commercial outcome from his entry. As frustrated as Marlowe is by barriers to his ingress, the hostile environment upon which he is testing his frontiersmanship, he knows that to overcome them he must work within the rules of the system by which they were constructed.

Marlowe, it transpires, carries two sets of business cards. One gives no indication that he is a private detective—the "plain card, the one without the tommy gun in the corner"—while the other has "the business on it."[149] When introducing himself to Fromsett and asking to see Kingsley, he presents the former. The latter might speed his ingress, by making clear to Miss Fromsett the private nature and urgency of his visit. The former, meanwhile, constitutes a refusal to disclose the nature of his work or his potential engagement with Kingsley, and thus relegates him to a long wait in the reception room. Marlowe does not know at this stage that Fromsett is well aware of the matter on which Kingsley wishes to engage a detective; he cannot therefore risk the indiscretion of making a secretary aware that her boss requires the services of such a clandestine operative. To do so would be to compromise his relationship with his client before that relationship has even been established.

Again, Marlowe weighs his frustration at reaching a spatial and temporal impasse with the goal he ultimately wishes to achieve through his spatial progress. To show the tommy gun card would have the same effect as barging through the door: it might speed progress in the short term, but it would see his long term-aims founder. This is characteristically Marlovian and likewise typically frontiersmanlike: unless otherwise forced by another party, he moves always with the intention of gaining an advantage, performing a spatial conquest. That he struggles do so in the Gillerlain offices is because something about the space of a modern corporate operation is unreadable: because it conducts its operations largely in a carefully guarded, abstract, conceptual space that does not map easily to its physical one, Marlowe cannot interpret it in order to deconstruct it as he can on Teager and Morningstar's premises. "You can't tell anything about an outfit like that," he remarks as he waits. "They might be making millions, and they might have the sheriff in the back room."[150]

Used to operating in a sociolegal liminality where decisions must often be taken on hunches, trust, the testimonies of others, and personal knowledge, Marlowe's frontier ethics founder in the regimented, procedurally defined space of corporate America. Not only does he have no appointment, but it transpires that Kingsley has never heard of "Lieutenant M'Gee," the individual who has referred Marlowe. Kingsley knows a Sheriff Petersen, who knows M'Gee, who knows Marlowe, but such informal, uncodified networks are inadequate in the world of the office. Marlowe is eventually able to explain these connections to Kingsley, but only *after* gaining access to the private office for a one-to-one audience.[151] Prior to this, with only a referral from somebody nobody has heard of, and no appointment, plus a line of business that he cannot disclose in the semi-public space of the reception room, Marlowe has no way to prove he has any business being there at all. Thus the Gillerlain Company manifests a space that refuses to yield up its meanings to Marlowe; instead it demands that he yield up his. In this combination of inscrutability and paranoia—the institutionalized secrecy and suspicion that Thompson asserts is the office's defining condition—Gillerlain proves itself an environment capable of arresting the progress of the ever-mobile detective-frontiersman. If Marlowe usually succeeds because he has a capacity to divine navigable structure within impenetrable Sedgwickian spaces that appear to lack either inside or outside, here he encounters the opposite problem: a space that refuses to dissolve.

Marlowe, however, understands the social-spatial practices of the office well enough that he also understands the points at which he can disrupt them. When Kingsley, heading out for a haircut having steadfastly refused to entertain his visitor, sees Marlowe waiting and addresses him curtly, Marlowe seizes his momentary window of opportunity. He gets to his feet and gives Kingsley the tommy gun card, silently stating the nature of his business so as not to break the rules of the semi-public space, but pushing their limits by even revealing this symbol of private matters. Whether out of sheer annoyance at being kept waiting or on a hunch that a man of Kingsley's status will have his interest piqued by someone prepared to speak to him without deference, having caught Kingsley's attentions with the card Marlowe launches into some cute wisecracks. Somehow this approach succeeds, and the detective is finally admitted.

There is, however, something wholly unsatisfying here. Kingsley even draws attention to it: "God knows why" he is prepared to give the stranger three minutes of his time in private, he wonders aloud.[152] Chandler spends several pages enumerating the sociospatial barriers that prevent his protagonist from entering a space that, given that its occupier is a potential client who has requested the services of a detective, Marlowe should have a "right" to access (that is, his interests in entering the space are aligned with the interests of the person who owns it). In the Teager and Morningstar episodes, Marlowe is able to navigate through the heavily regulated and demarcated space of an office world *because* he is doing so illicitly or clandestinely—he can navigate the space because he is able and willing to ignore the social codes that govern its normal usage. Here, by contrast, being forced to obey the office's spatial practice stumps him.

He is, in effect, not allowed to make use of his full set of frontiersman's navigational tools, as their impropriety in this "overcivilized" space would preclude his larger purpose. It is less through Marlowe's skills as a sociospatial trailfinder and much more through Kingsley's never-explained whim, his sudden decision to acknowledge and then invite into his private office the man he has been ignoring for much of the afternoon, that Marlowe progresses. This is a space he cannot subvert; he can access it only by the whim of its unchallengeable possessor, the dictator of local spatial practice. That much is emphasized explicitly when, after finally inviting him into the private office, Kingsley lets the door swing to in Marlowe's face before he can enter. The detective has won no free passage through this space or triumph over the environment; he is in most senses still barred from it, save by dint of Kingsley's indulgence for this brief moment. He remains excluded even as he is included.

The frontiersmanlike mechanics of Marlowe's office navigations are more complex and contradictory than those of Huff, who seeks merely to tear down the organization's values through a violent injection of "savagery." Precisely because Marlowe shares with the frontiersman an existential dependence on the social "savagery" he supposedly exists to conquer, his frontierist explorations come under a certain tension. Working to uncover "savagery" in the notionally "civilized" spaces of modern corporate America, he runs the risk of placing himself in the devil's party, not a pro-"civilization" frontiersman but an agent of wilderness itself. It is in this vein that Marcus Klein has noted how, in the early days of the professional detection industry, "to know crime and criminals so well as to be a detective was to be suspect. It takes a thief to catch a thief," ran the logic.[153] As his frustrations in the Gillerlain lobby indicate, Marlowe is indeed opposed to the restrictive, anti-individualist values of post-frontier corporate culture. Ultimately, however, and unlike Walter Huff, Marlowe does not seek to turn over the edifices of "civilization" to lawlessness. He sets out more modestly to prove that those edifices are not quite as hegemonic as they appear, to show that "savage" and "civilized" continue to occupy, as in his own filing cases, as in Teager and Morningstar's offices, and, as *The Lady in the Lake*'s plot will reveal, in Derace Kingsley himself, the same spaces.

In the office Philip Marlowe makes disclosures of individual agency to combat that space's conformist, systematizing effects on society while simultaneously protecting society from a malignant excess of the very same agency. In uncovering personal and social wildness there, Marlowe appears to strike a regulatory blow on behalf anti-frontierist forces, but in the same act proves that the sociospatial regime of modern corporate culture has *not* succeeded in asserting superiority over the individual (both himself and the "savage" element he finds lurking beneath the office's regulated surface). In this way he can preserve in the modern city the state of liminality or transition between the two that was sought by the frontiersman, and the most overtly anti-frontierist space Marlowe encounters becomes the perfect venue for his restaging of frontier contest. Megan Abbott suggests that Marlowe models a frontier identity via a "deep connection to a possibly imagined past," rendering him "increasingly anachronistic" in a "compulsively changing city."[154] Marlowe's use of space in fact reveals that his frontier inheritances are the source of his contemporary relevance, not its undoing. By using frontier principles to negotiate post-frontier spaces he makes a case that those principles remain relevant and necessary precisely as a means of surviving the dominant conditions of "overcivilized" modernity while at the same time querying the extent of that dominance.

Within this paradigm, though, the eventual, never fully explicable ingress that Marlowe manages to make against the odds in the Treloar Building remains disconcerting not least because it stands in marked contrast to another attempt at sociospatial navigation of office space made a few years later and on the opposite American coast in Ralph Ellison's *Invisible Man* (1952). Expelled from university, the protagonist repeatedly seeks audiences with the executives to whom he has been given what he believes to be letters of introduction. Time and again, though, he is summarily rebuffed. The invisible man is never, unlike Marlowe, granted a window of opportunity by the spatial practice of the office. Tellingly, at his most discouraged, he goes to the movies and watches "a picture of frontier life with heroic Indian fighting and struggles against flood, storm, and forest fire, with the outnumbered settlers winning each engagement; an epic of wagon trains rolling ever westward."[155] For the invisible man as for Marlowe, there is an association drawn between frontiersmanship and attempts to move through the modern corporate landscape, but the two men have opposite fates.

Given that the racialization of frontier conquest in both history and myth has rendered the frontiersman's image irrevocably one of whiteness, the invisible man's association of his *failed* office ingress with frontier imagery functions as a salutary reminder that Marlowe's mere whiteness is one of the essential navigational tools by which he is able to perform frontiersmanship—in the sense both of his ability to manifest the frontiersman's image and of the social license he has to enter and occupy space. One wonders how much more difficult Marlowe's attempt to enter Kingsley's office might be without the calling card of whiteness to accompany the one with the tommy gun. Already, in the dancehall, we have apprehended something of how the adoption (or imposition) of a frontiersmanlike social position presents unique challenges to those who cannot perform the racial identity at its core. The frontier's gauntlet of whiteness—never considered by Marlowe or Huff even as they unconsciously maintain it—returns ever more insistently as we move ahead.

3

Wilderness Works

Making Race and Class in the Industrial Cities of Fante, Yamamoto, and Himes

> Industry brings the tyranny of the clock, the pace-setting machine, and the complex and carefully-timed interaction of processes: the measurement of life .. in minutes, and above all a mechanized *regularity* of work which conflicts . . . with all the inclinations of a humanity as yet unconditioned into it.
>
> —Eric Hobsbawm, *Industry and Empire*

The workplace protagonists of the previous chapter were white-collared and white-skinned, and those characteristics invited and enabled their adoption of the frontiersman's mantle. If they complicated the frontier-conquering paradigm by entertaining social "savagery," they did so freely; the liberty to make frontiersmanship on their own terms was itself an expression of the white frontiersman's privileged ambivalence toward his own civilization. Turning to depictions of blue-collar labor, however, we find spaces that compel non-white protagonists to perform a frontiersmanship that is inverted: the dynamic that structured Julio Sal's leisure time proves also to structure rigidly the working day of his fellow ethnically marginalized Angelenos. Non-white characters labor toward the positions of social primacy occupied by whiteness through participation in the industrial economy, but find themselves trapped in sociospatial zones of hazardous liminality. As frontier logic simultaneously demands and rejects performances of whiteness, non-white characters fulfill their era's socially urgent demand to recover the nation's pioneer energies, but find that the benefits of such frontiersmanship do not accrue to them.

Frontiers of Industry

In writings by John Fante, Hisaye Yamamoto, and Chester Himes, we can feel Los Angeles's transformation into a major industrial center through three signature manifestations of that transformation. We can smell it in the stinking halls of a fish cannery, see it in the shadow of an oilfield's foreboding derricks, and hear it in the metallic din of a shipyard. Yet it is not only Los Angeles's industrial development we can detect in these texts. We will also breathe a toxic atmosphere of racial contest, and find it become ever more suffocating as the city readies itself for war both abroad and at home. Beyond their ostensible outputs of canned fish, or oil, or ships, the industrial facilities depicted in these texts disclose a deeper shared purpose: the production of race and its discontents. Those products, moreover, seem in these texts to be limitless in potential: they only ever increase in supply—betraying the culture these industries serve as one with an insatiable demand for the constant production and reproduction of racial division. In this manufacture of racial disharmony, the industrial concerns of Fante, Yamamoto, and Himes thus also reveal a common reliance on a particular set of conceptual machinery: the mechanics of the frontier. In these texts, the ongoing industrial manufacture of racial animus proves a strategy for the continual recuperation of frontier dynamics by and in urban modernity, and vice versa. These industries thus display once more a society in the grip of the cruelly recursive logic that is ontologically intrinsic to the frontier: a demand for frontier conditions—in this case a demand for brutal interethnic conflict—can only be "satisfied," counterintuitively, by perpetuating itself ever further.

Although unpublished until 1985, Fante's *The Road to Los Angeles* was completed in 1936 and is set at the beginning of the same decade, by which point LA was already the largest manufacturing economy on the West Coast.[1] The '30s were the decade in which "large scale farming [and] food processing" developed alongside the manufacture of clothing, automobiles, small machinery, airframes, and ships to transform California's economic makeup.[2] Los Angeles's "fulsome industrial job machine . . . had begun rolling" in the 1920s, but it was in the '30s that it acquired national prominence, with California rising to eighth place in national manufacturing output rankings by the eve of World War II.³ LA's industrial base would then be further transformed as $11 billion in government contracts saw the city take on a tenth of the nation's war production.⁴ Between 1939 and 1945 the number of industrial workers in LA rose by 280 percent, as internal migrants flocked to the city to take advantage of labor shortages.⁵ Many of those newcomers were African Americans, initially optimistic about the emancipatory potential of LA's new industrial opportunities.⁶ Himes's *If He Hollers Let Him Go* (1945) represents, in the form of the navy-contracted Atlas Shipyard and its uneasy partial integration, this phase in the region's industrial and demographic development. Yamamoto's "Life Among the Oil Fields: A Memoir," meanwhile, occupies a more complex temporality, written after both the Himes and Fante texts (in 1979) but set prior to them (in 1929). It also implies a longer view of LA's industrial history, one that reaches back to the last days of the frontier, oil extraction having been the enterprise through which LA first experienced industrialization, in the late nineteenth century.⁷ Simultaneously, however, Yamamoto's spatial and thematic deployment of oil and its extractive apparatus anticipates the racial fractures of World War II. In 1870, before oil was first struck in the Los Angeles basin, California was "still a frontier boasting only one true city," and that city was not Los Angeles but San Francisco. By 1945, Los Angeles was not only California's industrial powerhouse but an essential economic engine for the nation. To read Fante, Yamamoto, and Himes in concert is to read a story of how Los Angeles came of age as an industrial city, but it is also to discover that the city's frontier character remained perturbingly undimmed in the process.⁸

In the early twentieth century, California's changing relationship with industry and its changing relationship with the frontier were in fact two mutually inflecting aspects of the *same* relationship. California's industrial transformation invited those seeking to solve the forbidding conundrum of America's post-frontier socioeconomic identity to assert that a ready answer had been found. If the development of a modern industrial economy on the West Coast embodied the demise of a United States defined by an open geographic frontier, it simultaneously extended the possibility that metaphorical frontiers—of industry, of commerce, of science—could fulfill more sustainably the same role in the nation's psyche. This narrative undergirded exchanges between Franklin Roosevelt and Herbert Hoover on the 1932 presidential campaign trail. In San Francisco on September 23rd, Roosevelt acknowledged that, as Arthur Schlesinger Jr. would later reflect, "the age of expansion had come to an end," capturing Depression-era "intellectual moods" that took economic collapse as corroboration of Turnerian fears about a frontierless nation.[9] A nation that had reached its "last frontier," Roosevelt argued, had to seek further economic development not in the "discovery or exploitation of natural resources, or necessarily producing more goods," but in more effectively "administering the resources and plants already in hand."[10] The conservationist arguments that the antimodernists, wilderness cultists, and Roosevelt's namesake predecessor had made regarding the precious finitude of America's areas of uncapitalized nature were here repurposed with a mechanistic and instrumentalist urgency, in the service of capital itself.

Roosevelt admitted that such ambitions were "soberer, less dramatic" than "climbing into a covered wagon and moving west."[11] Simultaneously, however, he justified the value and intrinsic Americanness of his program by couching it in frontierist language and principles. Arguing for increased governmental intervention in the economy, he anticipated criticism that this would "qualify the freedom" of business by framing his aim as quite the opposite, an enshrinement of liberty.[12] Restraints had to be placed on the "financial Titans" of the industrial-age economy, Roosevelt argued, to protect the "place" and "power" of "every individual," and prevent those individuals from "running a losing race" against oligarchic modernity.[13] A speech that Schlesinger characterizes as an "acceptance of a transformed American destiny" in fact contained a frontier-revanchist rallying cry for the contemporary viability of the essential economic engine of Turner's America—the unfettered individual.[14] Roosevelt, moreover, mindful of his audience, even moderated his acceptance of American material finitude by asserting the persistence of the frontier-mythic identity of "the great West, and of this coast, and of California," as the apotheosis of America's "potentialities of youth . . . change and development." Roosevelt suggested that in an era of global (and particularly trans-Pacific) trade, the rapidly industrializing West Coast might not merely retain its special role in the frontier mythos but develop it further, as the place where "currents of . . . commerce of the whole world meet."[15]

Hoover claimed that his opponent was a defeatist, abandoning the pioneering "spirit which ha[d] made this country," but Roosevelt's speech was ultimately a nuanced attempt to reconcile frontier values to the modern world while preserving them against its assaults. Hoover's counter-proposition, certainly, was alluringly straightforward: he advocated transmuting the frontier from literal spaces into figurative ones, "frontiers of . . . science and of invention."[16] Nevertheless, the two candidates' speeches in fact dispensed only divergent prescriptions for a common diagnosis. Both Hoover and Roosevelt acknowledged the frontier's geographic demise while maintaining that its principles could, in fact, be preserved to sustain American development. Both, moreover, suggested that those values could be located *within* industry, technology, and global commerce. Even if Hoover was straightforwardly bullish about a "road of countless progress" where Roosevelt saw obstacles to the individual in that road, both identified "the symbol of the machine" not with the foreclosure of American ambition but with what Leo Marx would famously identify as a "rhetoric of progress" venerable as the republic itself.[17]

Roosevelt and Hoover attested to the Depression's role in catalyzing a national conversation about conceiving the new spaces of industrial modernity as receptacles into which the frontier could be decanted, extricating the US from malaise in the process. If the literary representations of Los Angeles industry offered by Yamamoto, Fante, and Himes manifest the frontier characteristics so keenly sought in their era's public discourse, however, they simultaneously problematize the bases of that very discourse. In these texts, the new "frontier of industry" embodied by Los Angeles's transformation into an industrial center *does* partially reconstitute the qualities of its geographic forebear. The frontierist dynamic it recuperates, however, is not a gleaming ideal of unlimited individualist possibility but a truer and more troubling history of ethnonationalist spatial contest. Three racially marginalized protagonists—Japanese American, Italian American, and African American—bear witness to and participate in that contest as they strive to navigate industrial space.

Processing Race: John Fante's Canneries

In John Fante's fiction, the fish processing industry is a recurring setting.[18] A cannery adjoins Julio Sal's bunkhouse in "Helen, Thy Beauty is to Me—" and joins a litany of unedifying workplaces in *A Letter from the President*, ironizing Chu Chu Ramirez's misplaced idealism about the United States' socioeconomic promise. Hoover's vision of industry's limitless possibilities for frontierlike progress does not extend to the immigrant laborers who power it: Chu Chu believes he is "going places," but the migratory labor cycle will always bring him back to the "stinking fish cannery."[19]

In unpublished synopses detailing how the novella *1933 Was a Bad Year* (posthumously published in incomplete form in 1985) was to be completed, Italian American schoolboy Dom Molise makes his way from

Colorado to California to pursue a dream of baseball stardom, but finds his hopes dashed and is forced to take a cannery job. Dom's westward journey has broken him. "The world is a huge place, too large, too brutal for his hopes"; Los Angeles itself is "bewildering" and takes three days to traverse.[20] The cannery as the bathetic climax of Dom's journey is representative of his dream's failure, but that failure proves the persistence in Los Angeles of conditions of danger, treachery, disappointment, and struggle: an enduring capacity to defeat the individual attests to the city's retention of recalcitrant frontier characteristics. Moreover, cannery labor is collocated with Dom's awareness of his occupation of a racial borderland: while working at the cannery he must bunk with Filipinos who strongly resemble Julio Sal's compatriots, in a discomforting disclosure that his own whiteness is only partial and conditional.[21] Also among Fante's unpublished manuscripts is a story simply titled "Fish Cannery," which likely dates from the same period as *The Road to Los Angeles*, Fante's most significant treatment of cannery labor.[22]

Fante's recurring protagonist Arturo Bandini is in *The Road* a teenage would-be intellectual alienated from both white America and his own selfhood. Dismissive of his immigrant family and other immigrant populations, he is a *flâneur* of Los Angeles Harbor and the surrounding shabby neighborhoods of Wilmington and San Pedro, the city's southern industrial hinterland (see figure 3.1). The novel recounts Bandini's frustrated attempts to make the world around him accept and respect what he sees as his true identity of race and class: a complete (i.e., fully white) American—and "no ordinary American" at that (as his analogue in "Fish Cannery" puts it), but a great novelist, a Menckenian member of the nation's cultural elite.[23] Turner's sense that the frontiersman was an exceptional everyman is present. Ultimately Arturo will conclude that to achieve this self-actualization he must leave his home in the city's physical and cultural margins and make for LA proper, a spatial center promising greater social opportunities.

In this respect, Bandini reveals an inverse-frontierist kinship with another Fante creation, Julio Sal.[24] Like Julio on his long trudges to the downtown dancehall, Arturo concludes that the kind of social journey he wishes to make (from America's working-class ethnic fringes into its suspicious, resistant establishment) depends upon the enactment of concomitant spatial journeys—from an edge to a center. Like Julio, by reconceiving the physical and social center, rather than its edge, as the recalcitrant, hazardous space to be claimed and conquered, he reimbues

Figure 3.1. Canneries at San Pedro (1928). Small boats lie docked at Fish Harbor on Terminal Island, their catch delivered for processing. Picture a humiliated Arturo Bandini, skulking around the piers and plotting revenge on his co-workers. *Source*: Los Angeles Area Chamber of Commerce Collection 1890–1960, University of Southern California Libraries and California Historical Society. Public domain.

the space where Los Angeles lies with the frontierist quality that the city's very presence appears to deny. To realize that possibility, however, Bandini must first test his social ambitions against the spatial limits of Wilmington. He does so by rejecting a series of menial, manual jobs that are, he believes, beneath his ambitions, unsuited to his intellectual temperament, and deleterious to his desire to transcend ethnicity and class. Like the narrator of "To Be a Monstrous Clever Fellow," Bandini yearns for a rarefied intellectual life and performs its mannerisms while unwillingly enduring employment in manual labor.

Bandini's rejection of physical labor is essential to his imbrication in frontier discourse because it positions him as a figure who believes himself to have moved beyond the kind of muscular masculinity associated with America's wilderness past. Bandini is certainly an individualist, but in no sense a rugged one. He is a walking assertion that the nation has surpassed the values that the frontier had privileged—that the post-wilderness century would be less fixated on ideals of virtuously toiling manliness. That Bandini is nevertheless compelled to engage in physical labor but is repeatedly humiliated when he attempts to do so, though, implies prematurity in what his bearing asserts. His experiences suggest that a man's success, even survival, at least in the city's precarious, working-class fringe, *does* remain dependent on his ability to embody something of frontier masculinity. That much is affirmed when Bandini takes another job, this time in the canning plant of the Soyo Fish Company, the ironic location of many of his efforts to locate himself within America's socioethnic elite.[25]

Meeting the cannery manager, Shorty Naylor, Bandini preposterously claims that he is only taking the job because he is a writer gathering material for a "book on California fisheries."[26] Naylor is indifferent to Bandini's bluster, but expresses concern about hiring an "American" because, in his experience, "Americans can's [sic] stand the pace," quitting "soon as they get a bellyful."[27] For Shorty, Americans have, as the likes of Henry Childs Merwin had feared, become soft and cosseted. Unlike their frontier-bred forebears, they shun hazardous, unpleasant, physically demanding work. Shorty has thus turned to ethnic minorities, Mexicans and Filipinos, for such labor. If the sphere of industry *is* to be America's new frontier, Shorty suggests, the new frontierspeople (many of the cannery's staff are female) are not to be Americans.

This has consequences for Bandini's conception of the cannery as a frontier of racial contest. Italian ethnic status was itself, as Thomas Guglielmo writes, "highly problematical" in this era of American history.[28] Anti-Italianism was "fierce, powerful, and pervasive," but "perceived racial inadequacies aside, [Italians] were still largely accepted as white by the widest variety of people and institutions—naturalization laws and courts, the US census, race science, anti-immigrant racialisms, newspapers, unions, employers, neighbors, realtors, settlement houses, politicians, and political parties."[29] Guglielmo argues, however, that even if Italians were perceived as "white on arrival," they nonetheless suffered "extensive *racial* discrimination" as distinct from "simply 'ethnic' discrimination."[30] To be "Italian" was to manifest a racial identity with both physical and cultural characteristics. Nevertheless, as Italians arrived in Los Angeles in significant numbers around the turn of the twentieth century, Gloria Lothrop notes, they "did not experience the discrimination [they] commonly encountered" on the East Coast because, in the West, "Mexicans, Asians, and Native Americans" bore the brunt of Anglo-American ire.[31]

Lothrop's observation bears out Guglielmo's claim that, whatever their "racial inadequacies," Italians benefited "in resources and rewards" from "their privileged *color* status as whites."[32]

David Roediger, however, contradicts Guglielmo, categorizing Italians among "not-yet-white ethnics"—capable of ascending to whiteness through social and cultural development but *not* necessarily white on arrival. Roediger writes that one could be Italian "without being white," and indeed that Italians were among the groups "historically regarded as non-white, or of debatable racial heritage, by the host American citizenry."[33] The disparity between the analyses offered by Roediger and Guglielmo only serves further to affirm the messy mutability of Italianate racial and ethnic identity in prewar America. In any reading, being Italian was to occupy a racial frontier, a liminal zone between multiple "inferior" racial groups and ever-superior Anglo-whiteness, *close* to the settled social space of racial normativity's privilege but never quite able to possess it, not entirely "savage," but not completely "civilized" either. These ambiguities in the Italian racial position are reflected in the attitudes that Bandini demonstrates toward his own ethnicity prior to entering the cannery.

Bandini curses a shopkeeper as a "Dago fraud," yet also condemns his own Uncle Frank as an "American boor" for his lack of culture.[34] Bandini doesn't just recognize a difference and separation between Italian and American identity; he sees the composition and division of such identities within an individual as unstable and context-dependent. An Italian American can occupy the role of either an Italian or an American in a particular given moment. This does not, however, equate to a capacity for Italian Americans to code-switch at will: contrasting ethnic identifiers for the shopkeeper and Uncle Frank are not self-claimed but deployed (wholly pejoratively) by a third party. These men's ethnic identity flexes not in accordance with their own self-perception but rather in whichever way enables a hostile force to place them at the position of greatest disadvantage. The Italian reputation for dishonesty ("Dago fraud") is contextually appropriate to an accusation that Bandini levels at the shopkeeper; Frank is castigated for his lack of culture, so the Menckenian "Boobus Americanus" is the most appropriate avenue of insult. An Italian American is Italian up to the point that it inflicts a greater humiliation to call them American. Bandini, himself an Italian American, is able and willing to mete out judgment to his fellows as to whether, in a given context, it is their Italianness or their Americanness that renders them most risible. From this ambivalence arises the question of whether or not Bandini does indeed crave thoroughgoing Americanization. Indeed, he tells Naylor that "patriotism is universal," that he "swear[s] allegiance to no flag," for a moment sounding like Frank Norris when he imagined the post-frontier world as a post-national one.[35] The cannery, however, forces Bandini to reveal himself as an anxious nationalist, possessed of mutually inextricable desires to prove himself fully American and to prove himself fully white.

Multiple immigrant groups navigate the hazards of the factory floor in vicious competition with each other, possessed by the vain hope of conquering their own socioethnic liminalities. Transporting boxes of canned mackerel, Bandini is determined not to be outdone by the Mexican Manuel, "a mere peon" who totes ten boxes on his hand truck and whose name suggests a figure defined by the nature of his labor. Despite his inexperience and physical weakness, Bandini attempts twelve boxes; predictably, they (and the cans within them) soon go flying across the factory floor. Embarrassed, Bandini drops to his knees to retrieve the escaped cans while the other truckers, whose progress has been impeded by his accident, gather around. "It was disgusting," Bandini recounts, "with me, a white man, on my knees, picking up cans of fish, while all around me, standing on their feet, were these foreigners."[36] The dual valence of "disgusting" is transparent. Syntactically as well as semantically it denotes both the revolting nature of the task's physical qualities—scrabbling on one's hands and knees to gather cans on a grubby, "wet" and "slippery" factory floor—and Bandini's sense that its dynamics of racial humiliation are equally "disgusting."[37] For Bandini the two "disgusting" aspects of the scene (the physical qualities of the cannery as a space and the psychological injury of his humiliation by others whom he considers his racial inferiors) are indivisible from one another. Bandini's nauseous revulsion over the unpleasant odors and textures of cannery are both literal and a proxy for his horror at being held economically and spatially captive by and in subordination to people he considers his racial inferiors. Notably, though, he contrasts his whiteness not with their color but with their foreignness, suggesting Guglielmo's conception of the Italian position in the racial hierarchy as a site of contest and uncertainty: as an "inferior" form of whiteness, Arturo's racial status is unstable and open to challenge; his citizenship (as American-born) is not.

Roediger writes that immigrants from "white ethnic" groups have historically "equate[d] whiteness with Americanism in order to turn arguments over immigration from the question of who was foreign to the question of who was white."[38] Second-generation Arturo, because he is confident in his citizenship ("I was born . . . under the stars and stripes") but not in his whiteness, is compelled to do the opposite.[39] The same sense inheres in "Fish Cannery": its narrator worries that "a stranger is liable" to think him a Mexican, prompting him to perform his "ecstatic pride in [his] Americanism" in response.[40] He fears that his questionable whiteness will compromise his theoretically unimpeachable nationality. In this respect he echoes the ethnonationalist anxieties of Cora Papadikis in James M. Cain's *The Postman Always Rings Twice*: being married to a Greek "made her feel she wasn't white" despite the fact that she is from Iowa and has "nice white skin." Mere proximity to an imperfect Mediterranean whiteness imperils her own epidermal purity—and thus her Americanness—because it causes others to code her "Mex."[41] For Bandini, who really *is* Mediterranean, the anxiety is all the more intense.

Although Italian American rather than the unqualified American *sine qua non* he repeatedly and loudly claims to be, according to the racial hierarchy of American society at large Bandini *is*, by virtue of his whiteness (however "inferior" a strain of whiteness it may be), notionally "superior" to the Mexicans and Filipinos among whom he works. Within the confines of the canning plant, however, he becomes the non-normative minority, and the inferior of his colleagues in his ability to carry out the work that the environment demands. The image of Bandini surrounded by his Mexican co-workers reflects this duality and discloses the paradoxical stakes of Bandini's broader social status as an Italian American. In that tableau he appears dominated but also physically and visually *central*, at once a center and an edge. Further attesting to the frontierist quality of an Italian American identity, Bandini is rendered marginal to those both within *and* without the American socioethnic establishment. The factory is filled with those whom Bandini considers "uncivilized," and he hopes to prove by contrast with them that he is a genuine American—that is, to show himself as the emblem of "civilization" in a space of "savagery." He finds instead that he is less a frontiersman than a frontier unto himself, unable to exist as anything other than an uneasy contact point *between* the "savage" and "civilized." Simultaneously, however, the fact that this scene of racial abjection results from Bandini's inability to match the Mexicans *physically* suggests that even as he himself embodies frontierlike qualities of precarious liminality, he is unable to claim the masculine robustness upon which survival in this environment depends. The specter of the frontier is multiply present, but Bandini's possession of one set of frontier associations (a location in America's ethnic hierarchy that models the frontier's location at the "hither edge" of wilderness) does not render him able to engage with another (the cannery's demand for a brutal constitutional toughness). He embodies one element of the frontier while being alienated from another.

Despite the cannery's ability to map in physical space the racial centers and edges that structure Bandini's consciousness, however, Bandini's attempts to assert clear racial distance between himself and his fellow employees are compromised by encounters where physical indicators of race in fact prove (as in Floyd Davis's illustrations of Julio Sal) mutable, deceptive, and easy to misread. After an incident in which he is humiliated by his co-workers, Bandini repairs to the employee restroom, where he is joined by one of his Filipino colleagues. Bandini is certain that the Filipino is there to mock him further: he claims that the Filipino watches him "on purpose . . . in such a way that I would know he was watching me and nothing else," that when the Filipino smiles at him it is purely "to let me know he didn't think much of me," and that this smile quickly turns into a sneer. The Filipino's reported speech, however, is nothing but courteous; he asks Bandini how he is feeling and refuses to rise to the increasing racial abuse that Bandini hurls his way. It is in that abuse that Bandini unwittingly dismantles his own attempts to schematize the world as one of stark and immutable racial hierarchies. Bandini first describes his bathroom adversary as a "dark Filipino," but later clarifies that he only noticed the darkness of the man's "nut brown" skin because of its contrast with his white teeth.[42] Bandini tacitly acknowledges here the subjectivity and arbitrariness of the color-based racial hierarchies in which he wishes to ascend, the absurdity of a system he would gladly defend if only it would let him. That which is held to be such an absolute and innate determinant of one's position in and treatment by society is admitted in this moment to be wholly relative and contingent.

Bandini "suddenly [knows] what to say" to the Filipino upon recognizing the darkness of his skin, and addresses him as "nigger." Bandini is delighted by the word's effect. "That hit him. Ah, but he felt that baby. Instantly there was a change, a shift of feelings."[43] Curiously, however, Bandini then modifies the trajectory of his insult. "You're not a nigger at all," he says, "You're a damn Filipino." This apparent correction, a recognition of the man's actual ethnic identity, is a rhetorical sucker punch, followed instantly by the stinging rejoinder that to be a Filipino is in fact "worse" than being "a nigger." Bandini then modulates the insult further, calling the man a "yellow Filipino. A damn oriental foreigner," and asking the man why his ethnicity doesn't make him "uncomfortable . . . around white people." (In so doing Bandini seeks to assert himself as one such white person but in fact betrays his own anxieties about being revealed as less than white by the presence of whiteness—he is galled that the Filipino is apparently unafflicted by comparable racial discomforts.) The man he had identified as notably dark moments before is now "yellow as a canary."[44] Bandini remarks on this mutability: "'Boy!' I said. 'You came close to fooling me. All the time I thought you were a nigger. And here you turn out to be yellow.'"[45] Bandini's attempt at a compound humiliation depends upon an understanding between both men that they are locked in a battle to ascend the ladder of America's socioethnic hierarchy. He first inflicts the blow of "mistaking" the Filipino man for an African American—relegating him from his intermediate racial position as an Asian American. He then changes the stakes with the implication that, in fact, to be "oriental" is *worse* than to be a "nigger." This in itself is a doubled insult, because it robs the Filipino man of what little sense of precedence and security in the racial hierarchy he believed himself to have, while simultaneously erasing the specificity of his ethnicity by placing him carelessly in a generic "oriental" group. As the encounter ends, Bandini rejects his adversary's conciliatory parting offer of a "Filipino cigarette," but once alone desperately gathers up the Filipino's discarded butt and smokes it until it burns his fingertips, before grinding it to "a brown spot" beneath his heel.[46] The conspicuous reference to the butt's color and the compulsion to grind it out of existence constitute an ashamed and self-disgusted admission of racial complicity.

Bandini tries the same trick when he knowingly calls three female Mexican cannery workers "pretty Filipino girls."[47] They, however, realize their ability to inflict the same humiliation of racial misrecognition upon Bandini: "'We're not Filipinos!' she screamed. 'You're the Filipino! Filipino! Filipino!'"[48] Bandini's response is, as it was in the restroom encounter, to invert his original insult, shifting from an insulting misidentification of the women's ethnicity to an attempt to characterize their actual ethnicity as being worse than his original suggestion: "'I beg your pardon!' I yelled. 'Excuse me for making a mistake! I'm awfully sorry! I thought you were Filipinos. But you're not. You're a lot worse! You're Mexicans! You're Greasers! You're Spick sluts! Spick sluts! Spick sluts!'"[49] Bandini takes a manic glee in inflicting the humiliation, just as he had with his Filipino colleague in the employee restroom. In both cases he is explicit that the motivation for his racism is the memory of his own repeated humiliation as a "dago": Arturo's attempts to racially derogate others are always about shoring up his own ethnic status by asserting his difference from his supposed inferiors, claiming a relative whiteness.[50] In Fante's better-known *Ask the Dust* Bandini pursues the same strategy, and justifies it on the same basis, in the abuse he metes out to the Mexican American waitress Camilla Lopez. In both novels, Bandini projects the trauma of racism onto others, claiming the identity of a perpetrator of racial abuse to erase his status as a victim of the same. Bandini's actions reflect the strange racial frontier zone that Guglielmo describes individuals of Italian ancestry as occupying in this period—accepted as white but perhaps not fully accepted as American, uncertain and insecure as to what kind of place in the racial hierarchy an "inferior" whiteness grants and what kind of challenge it might face from non-whiteness. Bandini's analogue in "Fish Cannery" suggests something similar when he admits of Mexican co-workers that he is "jealous because they speak smoother than my father, who was once an Italian peasant": the sense again is of profound fear that the relationship between whiteness and Americanness might not be directly proportionate, that the limited privilege of inferior whiteness is vulnerable to usurpation by members of non-white races.[51]

In repeatedly drawing attention to the arbitrary, mutable quality of physiognomic signifiers, Fante's text emphasizes the extent to which Bandini's ethnic self-conception places him in a state that embodies the paradoxical dynamics of the frontier. As his own insults attest, the ethnic hierarchy Bandini inhabits seems to be flimsy, in a state of constant flux (the frontier's ever-moving, constantly conquered quality), and yet, because he nevertheless cannot overcome or escape its oppression, it is simultaneously unsurpassably rigid (the frontier's enduringly hostile, resistive state). In a later depiction of racial strife on the grubby fringes of mid-century Los Angeles, Walter Mosley's Easy Rawlins will alight on a similar sense that hierarchies of race are unarguable precisely because they lack a consistent internal logic. In *Devil in a Blue Dress* (1990), Rawlins notes of his erstwhile boss Benny Giacomo (another ethnically liminal Italian American) that even though "his skin color was darker than many mulattos I'd known . . . Benny was white and I was a Negro."[52] If Giacomo, despite actual skin tone, is able to assert whiteness in ways his fellow Italian American Bandini is not, that reflects both the racial status of the man upon whom he is asserting it—an African American—and the differential of class and organizational status that exists in the interaction:

Giacomo is a manager, Rawlins an underling. Bandini, too, his physical and verbal attempts to assert racial superiority over his co-workers having failed, hopes a distinction of class will prove firmer ground upon which to show himself their better. Seeking to make an ostentatious display of his intellect, and in so doing explicitly position himself as being above the blue-collar labor he has been striving so hard to prove himself capable of, Bandini abandons work and sits down to write. This, however, only results in fresh humiliation: a co-worker mimics Bandini's writing pose, then produces for all to see a drawing of Bandini as a freckled cow, with the word "writer" scrawled beneath. Bandini's pursuits of racial and class status are of course interrelated, but to acknowledge the full implications of their connection would be to acknowledge that highbrow literary tastes and a voluminous vocabulary, however well they might function as class markers, are never enough in themselves to beat a charge of non-whiteness.

This intractable nexus of race and class reveals Bandini's cannery experience likewise to have two intimately interrelated dimensions. In one respect the cannery produces a frontier because it engages Bandini in a project of contesting and attempting to quell an unstable, perilous liminality. This exists between the co-workers from whose non-white ethnicity he wishes to distance himself and the fully "American" quality that he claims to have but that his "dago" insecurities reveal to be something he cannot securely grasp. Part of that project, however, subsists in his claim to *intellectual* superiority over his co-workers. Roediger charts how white working-class racism has historically precluded the "doubly liberating potential" of solidarity between struggles for class and racial liberation.[53] Bandini finds himself defeated by the cannery precisely because he wishes to decouple himself from *both* of those struggles, which disclose themselves as socially inseparable from each other. He can seek no ethnic solidarity with his co-workers because this would be to admit to the precarity of his whiteness, nor can he conceive of any class solidarity with them, because, in his intellectual pretensions, he does not wish to see himself as working-class. In an immediate local context where ethnic others *are* the working class, moreover, an admission of one status would be an admission of the other. When the Mexicans whom Bandini hoped to humiliate on racial grounds in fact manage to humiliate him for his intellectualism, however, they also emphasize the cannery's second frontierist aspect: this is a space in which survival is determined by the individual's physical strength, constitutional toughness, and ability to withstand trial and hazard. In his related projects of seeking to prove himself unsuited to the drudgery of cannery work on both racial and class grounds, Bandini thus reveals his workplace to be doubly imbued with frontier characteristics. He does so in the former case, however, because his project fails (he cannot escape his ethnic liminality), but in the latter because, although he is humiliated, his project succeeds (his physical inaptitude for cannery work is, for Arturo, proof that he is not meant for such menial pursuits).

Bandini's humiliation by the cannery is compounded by the fact that it is not confined *to* the cannery; rather, he carries the cannery around with him even after his shifts end. His shame acquires a sensory dimension, detectable on his person as an odor.[54] "Asleep or awake, it did not matter, I hated the cannery, and I always smelled like a basket of mackerel. It never left me, that stench of a dead horse at the edge of the road. It followed me in the streets. It went with me into buildings. When I crawled into bed at night, there it was, like a blanket."[55] This cannery is the geographical locus of Bandini's twin shames, but its true horror is in its capacity to act as a *mobile* geography: the cannery isn't merely a space that Bandini enters but a space that enters *him* through its unshakable stink. Bandini is shunned around his neighborhood because his smell is unpleasant, yes, but also because it marks him "instantly . . . as one of those cannery kids."[56] The odor is immediately recognizable to others when he enters a cinema, a physical presence attached to him "like something dead fastened to a rubber band," and that smell is synecdochic of the cannery itself: it lets others know that a "cannery worker was in the vicinity."[57] The cannery smell is a product of the industrial economy's oppressive presence in daily life that simultaneously functions as an ineffable but inescapable sensory representation of difference. The walls in which Bandini is spatially sequestered during his working hours, and the social/racial sequestration they connote, are able to relocate themselves constantly to wherever Bandini finds himself at a given moment. If a frontier was immediately redesignated as such from its previous state as "unclaimed" wilderness the instant a frontiersman entered it, any space Bandini should enter is instantly claimed by smell as an extension of the cannery, the hazardous edge-zone of socioeconomic marginality and racial shame from which he cannot escape.

Tellingly, only one figure in the cannery embodies the elusive frontierist combination of the full American whiteness to which Bandini cannot ascend *and* the physical constitution that the hostile environment demands: Shorty Naylor, the manager. Naylor on some level represents the place itself: "he seemed a part of the strange, vast loneliness of the cannery, he belonged to it, like a girder across the roof."[58] Thus the geography of racial and social marginality that the cannery imposes upon Bandini is in fact a superstructure of Naylor's unintellectual, rough-and-ready Anglo-masculinity, itself a collation of frontierist traits. Naylor is a miserable specimen of humanity both intellectually and physically—he attains perfection *only* in his whiteness (as opposed to Bandini's compromised variety). As upon Julio Sal's frontier of leisure, this new industrial frontier may require the labor of ethnic incomers to play out frontier dynamics, but those dynamics remain—like those of the Turnerian mythos—determined by, embodied in, and placed in the service of whiteness. That Naylor's tolerance for the cannery elevates him to the managerial class, while the same capacity condemns his underling to manual toil, is purely a matter of race.

LA's Italian population had reached 36,000 by 1934 but was overwhelmingly concentrated in central areas of the city.[59] The position Bandini occupies in the industrial edgelands twenty miles south of downtown not only distances him socially from the racial and class positions he wishes to claim but also serves as another, literal, claim of distance from his own ethnic community (his family and the "Dago" shopkeeper notwithstanding). In leaving Wilmington at the end of the novel, therefore, Bandini certainly seeks a social center in the lights and bustle of downtown, but it is not a center of whiteness. Rather, he attempts to find home in an area of the city even more ethnically diverse than the harbor district with its Mexican, Filipino, and Japanese communities, and indeed also a place where his specific ethnicity would not mark him as an outlier. It may be that Bandini hopes to enter that area as a white racial frontiersman, testing himself against a hostile landscape of ethnic others. Given the failures of his attempts to claim such an identity in the cannery, however, it seems more likely that, in making for downtown at the end of the novel, Bandini moves closer to an accommodation with his own ethnicity, to abandoning the rigged game of ascent to whiteness through frontiersmanlike labor.

The Petroracial Uncanny: Hisaye Yamamoto's Oilfield Frontier

"Life Among the Oil Fields: A Memoir," which depicts the relationship between a Japanese American farming family and the emergent Los Angeles petrolandscape of 1929, is a formally ambiguous piece of writing. The tale's narrator looks back from adulthood upon a youth that reproduces several facts of Yamamoto's own, and the text is described in its own title as a memoir. Yet "Oil Fields" appears in the collection *Seventeen Syllables and Other Stories* (1988). While the quality of being autobiographically informed is typical of Yamamoto's fiction, the fact that "Oil Fields" makes an explicit claim to the status of memoir while occupying a position in what is otherwise a fiction collection renders it a work especially and explicitly resistant to categorization of form or genre.[60] "Oil Fields" is a record of a pre–World War II Japanese American childhood and of circumstances in which such childhoods were historically lived: whether it is Yamamoto's memoir or that of a woman whose life resembles Yamamoto's but is lived exclusively within the pages of *Seventeen Syllables*, though, the text refuses to disclose definitively. In that refusal the text shields a past from the intrusion of a readerly present even as it seems to expose history to view, and thus in formal ambiguity mirrors its central thematic preoccupation: this is a story about paradoxical exposures that hide and disguises that reveal.

For eight of its ten pages "Oil Fields" does not appear to be much of a story at all, in that it offers extended description rather than action—narrative progression is essentially absent. Tenderly detailed are schools attended and neighbors befriended, songs sung and books read, crops grown and vehicles driven. Tiny routines and processes are memorialized: we learn the correct way to clean a kerosene lamp and the trick to turning "white one-pound blocks of oleomargarine . . . butter-colored with a small packet of red powder."[61] This is a fine-grained portrait of the minutiae that characterize the unnamed family's existence, but very little actually *happens* until, suddenly, in the story's final two pages, a chaotic irruption of near-tragedy breaks the text's hitherto placid surface. Jemo, the narrator's brother, is struck by a speeding car. Jemo escapes with minor injuries, but the greater hurt is that the car's white occupants escape *any* consequence. They do not stop after hitting Jemo, and when subsequently tracked down refuse all culpability, safe in the knowledge that social superiority, conferred by racial difference, enables them to act with impunity.

Abrupt as it first seems, though, this suddenly dramatic turn of events can be seen retrospectively to have been foretold. Not only does the narrator conclude that the neighbor who identifies the car must have had "some kind of foreboding" to have noticed it before the accident, but the story begins with an epigraph (itself autobiographical) from F. Scott

Fitzgerald, describing a pair of glamorous jazz-age motorists who speed through life without regard for danger, collisions, or other lives.[62] The narrator invokes this epigraph in the story's final lines, as if to admonish us that we should not have been shocked by the ending: unlike Jemo, we had been given the knowledge with which to see it coming. With hindsight, the story's very uneventfulness is recast as ominously conspicuous. What appears shocking in the conclusion is revealed as having been inevitable; indeed, it had been present in the text all along, the fond childhood recollections that intervene between epigraph and denouement creating only a false sense of security. The ending thus suggests again the text's central epistemological concern: namely, that which appears unexpected and aberrant, on closer inspection is anything but. That which seems to appear out of nowhere was always latent; that which seems most dramatically obtrusive is that which hides in plain sight.

The text uses oil's dynamics of latent presence, discovery, and extraction, combined with its own historical remove from the events it describes, to suggest how the racial atmospheres of the 1920s in fact anticipated, even rendered inevitable, the apparently sudden escalation in anti-Japanese sentiment that accompanied World War II and was made most dramatically manifest in the horrors of incarceration. "Suddenly," indeed, is the very word Carey McWilliams used to describe how the war made the West Coast into "the nation's new racial frontier." McWilliams was referring, accurately, to the rapidity with which African American populations grew in California, Oregon, and Washington during the war years, but his own extensive writing on anti-Japanese discrimination ought to have told him that the West Coast had by the 1940s already been a racial frontier for decades.[63] If McWilliams harmonized with Lawrence Reddick, who wrote in 1945 that wartime Black migration had "shifted" the nation's "race-relations frontier" westward, Reddick also noted rightly that to claim the prewar West Coast "never had a Negro problem . . . is not the same as saying that the West had never had a race problem."[64] Significant as the 1940s mass migration of African Americans to the West Coast was in rapidly modulating America's sense of its racial sociogeography, California's indigenous, Latinx, and Asian inhabitants could all testify of a place not newly made a racial frontier by World War II but, if anything, merely affirmed and compounded in that identity by the war's social tumult and political exigencies. Indeed, as McWilliams himself put it, "for nearly fifty years prior to December 7, 1941, a state of undeclared war existed between California and Japan."[65] Yamamoto's "Oil Fields" is, in its mostly quiet and understated way, an account of that war, the undeclared one that augured an even greater conflagration to come.

Anti-Asian violence is, in fact, one of Los Angeles's founding stories: when still a literal frontier town infamous for mob justice, it had been a site of "alarming" aggression perpetrated against (and sometimes reciprocated by) its small Chinese community.[66] If that culture of violence was most dramatically exemplified by 1871's Chinese Massacre, in which an Anglo and Hispanic mob killed a full 10 percent of the nascent city's Chinese population, the shame of that mass lynching by no means brought about an end to anti-Asian sentiment in the region. The Chinese immigrants who had arrived in California first to mine gold and build the railroads came to be resented for the very thing that had made them attractive laborers: they were perceived as being willing to toil in hardship and squalor for lower wages than a white man would accept, undermining him socially by undercutting him economically. Indeed, when Japanese migrants began arriving in California in increasing numbers toward the end of the century, they did so to fill labor shortfalls created by the Chinese Exclusion Act of 1882 and its subsequent extensions, seizing an economic opportunity that anti-Chinese sentiment had itself created.

The racist attitudes that greeted California's Japanese community from those very earliest moments of its existence bore clear continuities with the reasons Chinese immigrants had been detested—namely, a work ethic that white capitalism was happy to exploit but white laborers resented. There was, however, a distinctly new inflection to the racial anxieties that attended the Japanese. As John Modell writes, anti-Japanese groups rapidly came to believe that these new arrivals rendered California a "racial frontier," and thus in combating the Japanese presence saw themselves as "racial frontiersmen."[67] As early as 1910 "the racial frontier idea" was already "clearly impressed upon the minds of defenders and opponents of the Japanese" alike; battle lines were drawn.[68] Bearing out Lisa Lowe's characterization of Asian Americans as "contradictory, confusing, unintelligible elements" of the American body politic "on which the manifold anxieties of the US nation state have been figured," the anti-Japanese racial animus that arose in turn-of-the-century California derived not from longstanding and widespread stereotypes of Asians as "barbaric" or "subhuman" (which the Chinese had always faced), but quite the opposite.[69] In a way they never had of the Chinese, the "California chauvinists" feared the possibility that the Japanese might be (and might consider themselves) equal or even superior to white Americans, and thus that their presence on America's West Coast might call into question the finality of Anglo-Saxon continental conquest.[70]

Japanese Americans on the West Coast, conscious that they shared with their continent-ending environs a special place in America's history of migratory pioneering, also saw themselves as frontiersmen. As Eiichiro Azuma writes, they embarked on a "transnational . . . intellectual endeavor' to effect the "racialized reinvention of a collective self—as concomitantly American frontiersmen and Japanese colonists/colonialists—acceptable to both their adopted country and their homeland."[71] The qualities by which Japanese Americans in California pursued this frontiersmanlike identity—"efficiency, reliability, eagerness, and hard work"—were the same qualities that prompted the racial agitators' "fear that the Japanese were not merely as good as white Americans, they were better."[72] The very same qualities, indeed, were also those by which even by the elements of the region's white population who initially received the Japanese presence more warmly did so in terms of reductive stereotype. Reputed Japanese skills in agriculture and horticulture were especially lauded, but fetishistically so, as an Orientalized racial trait.[73]

Two competing-but-overlapping images of the Japanese American as frontiersman thus existed simultaneously in the early twentieth century: self-perception as dogged self-starters in the pioneer mold, and racial agitators' image of a threat to white America's conquest of the continent. In either reading, to be ethnically Japanese in California did indeed continue to mean occupying a social frontier—"situated between a clearly dominant group and its clear inferiors."[74] In Claire Jean Kim's phrase, Japanese Americans were "racially triangulated vis-à-vis blacks and whites"—"valorized" relative to the former but still "ostracized" by the latter.[75] Despite broad appreciation of the Japanese work ethic and perceived skills, Japanese Californians found themselves generally in positions of socioeconomic subservience to white Americans, but there remained "a color line separating them from black and brown people."[76] The Japanese-born *Issei* generation not only largely accepted that situation but, exemplifying what Natalia Molina identifies as the "relational" construction of race, sought pragmatically to "argue they [were] on the right side of the color line rather than challenge the color line itself."[77] They made that argument, and thus consolidated the California Japanese community's "middle position" in the social-racial hierarchy, by cultivating community institutions that promoted "self-censorship" and assimilation—the goal was to become "acceptable to white opinion."[78] The American-born

Nisei generation expressed Japanese identity more confidently. Tellingly, however, they found their precedents for doing so in the celebrations of ethnicity presented by such local literary lights as the Italian American Fante and the Armenian American William Saroyan, conspicuously identifying themselves with cultural figures who may have represented minority communities but claimed at least adjacency to whiteness.[79]

We might, indeed, usefully contrast the social position of the prewar California Japanese with the contemporary Italian American experience of racial hierarchy that Fante describes in *The Road*. If Italians like Bandini were considered ambiguously white but definitively inferior to "Anglo-Saxons," the Japanese were an even more troublesome prospect: definitively non-white but with the troubling potential to be the racial equals or even superiors of established white groups.[80] It is perhaps revealing that, although Japanese Americans constituted a major element of the workforce of Los Angeles's fishing economy (with a thriving community on Terminal Island), and Bandini in *The Road* does briefly mention having Japanese co-workers, he never makes them the target of his efforts to assert his own racial standing, as he does the Mexicans and Filipinos.

Particularly in agriculture, Japanese Americans carved an increasingly significant economic niche across the Los Angeles area.[81] They could only do so, however, "by exploiting the fringes of Caucasian economic enterprise, where initiative, hard work, and the willingness to put up with . . . discomfort can make a great deal of difference"—an economic frontier often experienced as a physical one.[82] They were compelled toward such positions because, despite some appreciation of Japanese work ethic and civic pride, and broad acceptance by white society of Japanese racial "superiority" to African Americans or Mexican Americans, anti-Japanese sentiment in Los Angeles steadily grew throughout the early decades of the twentieth century, in proportion with the city's Japanese population and its socioeconomic successes. Efforts to assimilate did not quell the strange and toxic mixture of contempt and fear in which, increasingly, the Japanese were held. Raymond Chandler's Marlowe exemplifies the mistrust with which many of his contemporary white Angelenos regarded their Japanese neighbors when he expresses paranoia about the duplicitous "Jap" who betrays his "nice-mannered" subservience by "hiss[ing] at you."[83] Anti-Japanese legislation followed where anti-Chinese legislation had gone before, commencing with the Alien Land Laws of 1913 and 1920, the latter of which hit the California Japanese agricultural economy particularly hard.[84] By the mid-1920s the California Japanese community found itself "engulfed by the politics of racial exclusion led by organized labor, the press, and nativist groups." Japanese Americans became subject to increasingly "rigid white control," denied access to landownership, naturalization, and the political process; any further Japanese immigration was prevented by the 1924 Immigration Act, which would remain in place until 1952.[85]

Los Angeles Japanese American community had thus come to occupy, by the time at which Yamamoto's story is set, a social, economic, and legal frontier state that itself derived from two clashing visions of the Japanese American as pioneer. If the community's industrious ability to carve for itself a proud and prosperous niche in the area's economic, civic, and cultural landscape affirmed a growing perception of itself as a group of latter-day frontiersmen, it also seemed to confirm racist agitators' worst fears that a thriving Japanese community would restore to California powerful frontier energies of civilizational conquest, endangering white America. If fears of Japanese superiority compelled discriminatory measures and sentiments that enforced distance between Japanese racial identity and whiteness, they also elevated Japanese Americans from the social categories of "inferior" races. If Japanese commerce was welcomed by the local economy, it also compelled efforts to limit its ability to compete with and potentially damage white enterprises.

Yamamoto's "Oil Fields" produces spatially these multiple frontier-like characteristics of the prewar California Japanese experience. Although the narrator's family's farming operation seems successful (groceries are plentiful, they have a car; they take English-language newspapers), it is conducted, and the family lives, upon marginal land in the undesirable industrial environs of the oilfield, immediately "adjoining a derrick" (see figure 3.2).[86] The presence of infrastructure belonging to the oil company implies leased land: due to the effects of the Alien Land Laws the vast majority of Japanese farmers in this period were tenants, and it was extremely common for them to "work surplus lands of absentee landlords, subdividers, homeowners with large plots, oil companies, and utility companies looking for short-term profits."[87] The transient whims of such landlords are perhaps indicated in the fact that the family have relocated several times during the narrator's childhood. Like many California Japanese of the period, they thus occupy an economic liminality—at once prosperous and precarious. Their occupation of a racial liminality between two color lines is also suggested: on one neighboring tract is another Japanese family, while another is occupied first by Mexicans, then by

Figure 3.2. Oilfields and orange groves north of Huntington Beach (c. 1920). This view shows the narrow interstices between agricultural land and oil's extractive apparatus that became a feature of Southern Californian landscapes in the early twentieth century—exactly the kind of marginal spaces where Japanese American families like those in Yamamoto's text made their lives. Source: California Historical Society Collection, 1860–1960, University of Southern California Libraries and California Historical Society. Public domain.

Italians. The one immediately proximate white household is conspicuous by its exceptionality, but the children do also have white schoolfriends.

The family thereby claims literal adjacency to whiteness, but also maintains (and cannot escape) proximity to ethnic groups that the California Japanese deemed their inferiors.[88] The racial arrangement of the neighborhood spatially produces Kim's "triangulated" racial position. Moreover, while Yamamoto's narrator describes her family as living in Redondo Beach, that municipality, seeking to maintain its "resort-like quality," banned oil drilling within its boundaries in 1922, seven years before the story is set.[89] Thus, the narrator's family must in fact live in a zone beyond the city's limits—they locate themselves, like the pioneers of Turner's frontier, outside the land claimed formally by civic structures, but the choice to do so, unlike that of Turner's pioneers, is not their own. Working these legally nebulous and physically hazardous margins around the oil wells, they exemplify both Modell's description of Japanese Americans "exploiting the fringes of Caucasian economic enterprises" and Azuma's identification of a hardy pioneer spirit in Japanese American self-perception during this period.

Stephanie LeMenager notes that as "derricks blocked ocean views and made surrounding communities ugly," the arrival of the oil economy in Southern California presented "a huge problem for regional planners," necessitating "generous plantings and carefully constructed views" to hide "the sights and sounds of industry."[90] Yamamoto's Japanese American children, however, live in a place where planners have no such anxieties. No attempt has been made to insulate these individuals from extraction's impacts. Yamamoto's narrator notes that "derricks then were not disguised by environmental designers to be the relatively unobtrusive, sometimes pastel-colored pumps that one comes across nowadays."[91] LeMenager, however, makes clear that in the period described by Yamamoto's story "environmental designers" were already hard at work elsewhere. Their absence from this setting, in fact, reflects not its chronological moment but rather the social status of its inhabitants. In Chandler's *The Big Sleep*, by contrast, the wealthy, white Sternwoods also live among oilfields but the derricks are their own, their domestic proximity thereto freely chosen. Indeed, Marlowe cannot fathom why "they would want to" look out at "what had made them rich," yet they do: the Sternwoods' apparent desire to maintain contact with their oilfields (when they could easily insulate themselves from their visual impacts) is a signifier of their perversity.[92]

In more normative wealthy white neighborhoods Marlowe encounters a fierce determination to maintain a uniform and pristinely manicured environment. Here too, though, instructive counterpoints present themselves to Yamamoto's articulation of how racial marginality, environmental beautification, and labors of subterranean extraction intersect in prewar Los Angeles. Observing the lush lawn of a mansion "completely screened" from public view by hedges, Marlowe notices with characteristic contempt a "Jap gardener," whom he finds "pulling a piece of weed out of the vast velvet expanse and sneering at it the way Jap gardeners do."[93] No description of the way Japanese gardeners sneer is necessary. Chandler can coyly exchange with his reader this racist confidence about the man's expression because the role of gardener was so often performed by Japanese Americans (the combined effect of horticultural repute and exclusion from other professions) that it had become an immediately recognizable stereotype. The most prominent popular image of the prewar California Japanese community, invoked here by Chandler, was a figure responsible for beautifying and regulating the immediate environments of well-to-do white communities, maintaining a spatial practice of "civilized" domestication by suppressing any hint of disorder emerging from below ground (or beyond the hedge). In this community of wealthy whiteness, a miniature act of extraction from the soil, delegated to the labor of an ethnic other, serves to defrontierize the landscape.

In Yamamoto's story, extractive acts have precisely the opposite effect, refrontierizing a landscape in which ethnic others have been compelled to live: as an industrial contest with a hazardous, unstable geography, oil extraction suggests an especially literal manifestation of Hoover's belief that technological advancement could reconstitute the frontier. The invidious conditions in which Yamamoto's characters must live are thus both the consequence of the racial frontier they occupy and a physical analogue of its characteristics. Yamamoto, however, complexifies her text's discourse on the means and effects of racial marginalization by suggesting that oil's obtrusive presence in the landscape of her characters' lives is simultaneously an elusive absence: "We must have lived day and night to the thumping pulse of the black oil being sucked out from deep within the earth. Our ambiance must have been permeated with that pungency, which we must have inhaled at every breath. Yet the skies of our years there come back to me blue and limpid and filled with sunlight."[94] The narrator persistently suggests how curious it is that, despite growing up in this dirty, noisy, dangerous environment, where the apparatus of heavy industry was ubiquitously proximate, she does not remember that presence substantially shaping the patterns, habits, and consciousness of her young life. In offering such vivid and detailed descriptions of her youth's industrial surroundings, however, the narrator belies her own insistence that while she "must have" experienced the effects of oilfield living they have not colored her childhood memories.

The sense of supposition or inference implied by "must have" is at odds with the richness of sensory, experiential immediacy in descriptions of the oil's "pungency" and "thumping pulse" as it is "sucked" upward. Similarly, while acknowledging that she and her peers could not "ignore" the derricks and sump holes, the narrator claims that they "played around them," making "respectful allowances" for the wells' "considerable presence." Immediately, though, she revises this memory, conceding that she "might venture" onto the platforms in play but maintaining that such "investigations were conducted gingerly."⁹⁵ Then follows a further sleight of revision—that contact with the pistons and pulleys was avoided "except that we sometimes tried to ride the long steel bars." This seems a large, striking, and dangerous exception to "avoid[ing] contact," and certainly throws into doubt the notion that play upon the platforms was "conducted gingerly"—let alone the idea that the children "worked and played around" the wells or that their presence "did not interfere" with their routines.⁹⁶ Rather, Yamamoto's narrator progressively concedes that the derricks and sump holes *were* her peer group's daily routine. It is as if they are so powerfully present that they dominate or occlude the environment to the point of no longer seeming like obstacles or features within it—filling the field of vision so fully that they are no longer identifiable. When Amitav Ghosh coined the genre classifier "petrofiction" to describe oil-centric narratives, he also introduced "Oil Encounter" as a term to describe the experience of human interaction with oil, but it is an inadequate one for Yamamoto's story.⁹⁷ Here, the means of oil's industrial extraction are at once completely dominant and unavoidable in their heady, multisensory all-pervasiveness, and yet somehow elusive: oil is a constant presence, but one so integral to the texture of life that it becomes paradoxically indistinct. There is nothing as straightforward or discrete as an "encounter" here.

What Yamamoto delineates here is a vision of the uncanny in its truest Freudian sense: Freud deployed Friedrich Schelling's definition of the *unheimlich* as that which "ought to have remained secret and hidden but has come to light," but augmented it with a suggestion that uncanniness occurs when the hidden thing "coincides with its opposite."⁹⁸ As the act of extracting oil from beneath the earth makes an invisible thing visible, but is performed by machinery that is, for Yamamoto's narrator, somehow so visible as to become invisible, there is thus a compound or meta-uncanniness to Yamamoto's oil and its apparatus. That which would naturally be hidden is brought "unnaturally" to the surface, but the obtrusive, blatant visibility of the extractive machinery by which that uncanny effect is created simultaneously coincides uncannily with its own opposite state of hiddenness. Uncanniness itself is rendered uncanny.

The conditions of living with this uncannily elusive omnipresence, as described by Yamamoto, are strongly suggestive of the Japanese American experience as an oppressed non-white group in an insoluble atmosphere of racial foment, because they model how whiteness itself operates in

American culture. Valerie Babb has described whiteness as, like Yamamoto's oil, at once "everywhere and nowhere," a state that reflects the "synonymity [of whiteness] with American identity."[99] There is similarly an intimation of Coco Fusco's observation that "to ignore white ethnicity is to redouble its hegemony by naturalizing it."[100] Fusco suggests that whiteness derives its othering power precisely from being ignored or treated as a mere default state; failure to identify it as a distinct construction grants it its oppressive omnipresence, but that oppressive omnipresence (inherent in its synonymity with Americanness) is exactly what makes it so hard to grasp distinctly. Such characteristics of whiteness thus replicate Yamamoto's paradoxical description of the children's experience with the apparatus of oil. This renders the text's account of the effects of the geography and economy of oil legible as a reflection on the characters' encounter with white America—and not merely in the historical moment described, but in the one anticipated.

Over a decade would elapse between the sunlit days when the children of Yamamoto's story played among the derricks and February 19th, 1942, when Franklin Roosevelt's Executive Order 9066 gave General John DeWitt, head of the Western Defense Command, jurisdiction to declare a 100-mile-wide strip running the length of the Pacific Coast "Military Area No. 1." From that area, "all persons of Japanese ancestry, both alien and non-alien" were "evacuated" almost immediately by supplementary local orders.[101] At a stroke, the entire West Coast became once more a frontier—only now one that had, like the earlier figuration of Japanese Americans as frontiersmanlike figures, two countervailing inflections. Japanese Americans found their settled home redesignated as a hostile environment, their ability to move within and claim its space as their own challenged and ultimately extinguished. For supporters of internment, an area hitherto claimed by and emplaced firmly within the purview of American "civilization" had been contested afresh by a dangerous other and required resecuring. A space of settled sociopolitical meaning had been reengineered as a precarious civic liminality, rendering as law the turn-of-the-century anti-Japanese agitators' fantasia of a West Coast racial frontier.

By July 1942, 110,000 Japanese Americans were incarcerated. Before the war they had numbered 80,000 in Los Angeles alone—a majority of all Japanese Americans in the US.[102] There was thus a particularity to internment as a Los Angeles experience. Moreover, anti-Japanese paranoia must be understood as inextricable from the area's coterminous transformation into an industrial hub of national strategic importance, because that transformation and the belief that it would be crucial to winning the war provided the object against which Japanese Americans could be suspected as "potential saboteurs and fifth columnists."[103] A *Los Angeles Times* editorial that demanded "Action on Japs" and was published on the same day as Executive Order 9066 suggested that racial panic about Japanese Americans was indivisible from panic about the security of America's industrial spaces. The editorial names "oil refineries" and "airplane factories" in the same category of vulnerability and importance as military facilities.[104] Two days later, a follow-up editorial bearing the same headline and praising the Executive Order appeared immediately adjacent to one condemning "Southern California factories" for a war-jeopardizing and "unpatriotic" failure to increase productivity.[105] Ironically, having been compelled by racial discrimination to live in undesirable industrial locations, families like those in Yamamoto's story found that their conspicuous presence there intensified the racist suspicions to which they were subject in wartime.

As Kim writes, "racial triangulation (defining the other)" was what made "internment (rounding up the alien within)" possible, the latter not an "aberration from" but an "extension of" the former.[106] Thus, when Kevin Starr terms incarceration the "fate" of the California Japanese, he does not use the term casually: as horrifying as the rapidity with which incarceration itself happened was the sense in which its conditions had been in the making for decades.[107] The peculiar compound uncanniness of Yamamoto's petrolandscape signifies precisely this double horror. Yamamoto's narrator experiences oil's extractive machinery as an everywhere-and-nowhere omnipresent invisibility, while oil itself—its pressurized secretion beneath the ground containing a potential to gush forth chaotically if disturbed—is threateningly present in its very hiddenness. The narrator's strange sense of being somehow both aware and unaware of her proximity to latent combustibility thus suggests the conditions under which she can retrospectively be seen to have lived—conditions where the cataclysmic racial explosions of wartime had yet to occur but were already present in potentiality, in smaller fires and ominous rumbles beneath a social surface that only seemed placid to those disinclined to see it otherwise. That Yamamoto's characters live in a place characterized by its *lack* of protective separation from the ugliness and danger of oil extraction ironically undergirds the logic of separation from society that Japanese Americans would experience in wartime. The former becomes legible as a preexisting means of effecting the latter: gradually, then suddenly.

If oil stands in for something like the tangible feeling of being othered by an everywhere-and-nowhere whiteness, then because oil extraction is a process that effects the productive harnessing of oil's explosive potentialities, racial othering is also revealed to be the very fuel on which America runs. To represent whiteness's seen-unseenness as an industrial presence in the lives of an ethnic group whose social marginalization increased in proportion with their contributions to California's economy is to assert that the exploitation of such groups' labor *through* ideologies of whiteness is itself the dirty open secret of the modern American economy. In an oil experience that somehow hides its own apparent revelation of the hidden through a compound uncanniness of coinciding opposites, American modernity reveals its dependence on whiteness as political and economic fuel *only* to the extent of revealing that dependence to possess the same hiding-in-plain-sight quality as whiteness itself.

Indeed, to represent racial othering as extractive machinery with untrammeled power over the narrator's geography is to imply precisely the capability (and anticipate the wartime efforts) of the racist machinery of the white American state to "extract" an ethnic population from that geography and others like it. Delia Byrnes has suggested that cultural representations of the "geography of oil" are inevitably records of "the long relationship between the pleasures of petromodernity and the material violence of its extractive regime."[108] Yamamoto's oil geography derives its most terrible uncanniness from making the same individuals subject to both very literal pleasures of petromodernity (childhood oilfield play) *and* the violence of an extractive regime (the foreshadowed trauma of incarceration), the latter simultaneously hidden and revealed in the former.

If, however, the dangerous, extractive apparatuses of industry that become the children's default landscape are legible as representing the present effects and future horrors of the everywhere-and-nowhere whiteness under which those children live, then the racial implications of oil's literal blackness are also impossible to ignore. Of course, Japanese Americans, however disfavored in prewar California, were not "Black" in any literal legal or social sense. Both Modell's "middle position" and Kim's "triangulated position" articulate the existence of an understanding shared between the Japanese American community and white Americans of mutual superiority to other racial groups, with African Americans at the foot of the racial hierarchy.[109] If the Japanese could never be "quite like the whites," through assimilation they sought to emphasize their differences from other ethnic communities.[110] Masao Suzuki notes, however, that the California Japanese—especially those engaged, like Yamamoto's narrator's family, in agriculture—had more in common economically with African Americans than social self-perception and racial pride permitted them to admit.[111]

Further, Jeannie Shinozuka notes the frequent insidious association from the 1910s onwards between Japanese immigration and the contemporary arrival of the invasive, destructive *popillia Japonica*—the Japanese beetle.[112] While it was as a "yellow" peril that the growing Japanese American population was held in suspicion, the Japanese beetle is identifiable by its prominently iridescent body.[113] As oil shares that conspicuous iridescence, its presence in Yamamoto's story visually recalls the pestilential insect with which Japanese immigrants were dehumanizingly identified, and therein suggests an ontological connection in contemporary racist discourse between blackness and "yellowness." Moreover, as Richard Dyer notes, in a similar mode to Babb and Fusco, in cultures and discourses wherein whiteness is dominant or default, "white is virtually unthinkable except in opposition to black": blackness exists in such a paradigm as an *anti-whiteness*.[114] By that token, the blackness of the oil constantly being extracted from the earth as the children play throughout Yamamoto's story, a blackness that characterizes their personal geographies, that flows just beneath the surface of and always has the potential to erupt into their lives, is a perpetual reminder of the children's immutable separation from a dominant whiteness.

Yamamoto's mobilization of oil as a discomfortingly proximate blackness anticipates a suggestion made in Chester Himes's *If He Hollers Let Him Go* that white panic and paranoia during wartime would collapse into an absolute binary of white and non-white any racial positions previously triangulated between white and Black. Scott Kurashige describes how "the bombing of Pearl Harbor drove a wedge between" LA's Black and Japanese communities, as "their relationships to the white majority and to the nation-state now diverged acutely," especially when "some Blacks in Los Angeles saw opportunity" in the jobs, businesses, properties, and neighborhoods from which Japanese residents had been forcibly removed.[115] What had been Little Tokyo became Bronzeville, as newly arrived African Americans moved into the Japanese ghost town having found themselves barred from other areas by restrictive housing covenants. A February 1943 editorial in the Los Angeles–based Black newspaper the *California Eagle* suggested that African Americans could only surmount racist resistance to their growing presence in the city by promoting solidarity with and between other racially marginalized local groups, but the only ones mentioned were Mexicans and Jews. "Notable for their absence from this statement," writes Kurashige, "were Japanese Americans."[116] Himes, though, believed powerfully in the "linked fates" of Japanese and African Americans.[117] His protagonist Bob Jones does too. In the post–Pearl Harbor climate of anti-Japanese panic, Jones realizes starkly that he is now "the same color as the Japanese." Correlatively, Japanese Americans are no longer any closer to whiteness than he is; not only can white Americans not "tell the difference," neither can he.[118] In voicing that realization Jones suggests a model of Black-Japanese interaction in which the two groups meet each other not in a zero-sum contest for rights and space in the city, but in the solidarity of overlapping relationships with whiteness.

Jones acknowledges here the power of what Molina terms a "racial script," by which "the ways in which the lives of racialized groups affect each other across time and space, even when they do not directly cross paths."[119] Jones does not need to experience being racialized as a Japanese American in order for that experience to impact him as an African American. Jones's identification (and internalization) of white society's loss of its ability (or willingness) to distinguish between an African American and a "yeller-bellied Jap" is his testament to having seen white racial thinking exposed in its barest rudiments.[120] To borrow Turner's infamous terms, his is a society revealed by the exigencies of wartime to run, ultimately, on the old, unreconstructed, frontierist binary of "civilization" versus "savagery." White society's prior self-interested promulgation of divisions and distinctions between minority groups, Jones suggests, dissolves in crisis, revealing that the only racial differentiation white Americans ultimately care about is that between white and non-white.

If the revelatory clarity of Jones's realization was initially occluded in historical reality by tensions over Little Tokyo/Bronzeville, as the war wore on and Japanese Americans eventually began to return home from the camps, his position on Black-Japanese mutual interest would come to be mirrored by African American community leaders. If a newspaper like the *California Eagle* had once been "complicit in the face of anti-Japanese agitation," by 1945 it was calling for Japanese Americans to "reclaim their former homes," despite the problems this could cause for its own readers.[121] As the war drew to a close, another Black LA paper, the *Tribune*, expressed its commitment to "cross-racial dialogue" by hiring a Japanese columnist, whose task would be "explaining the *Nisei* perspective to readers."[122] That columnist was a young woman who had honed her writerly craft while incarcerated at the Poston internment camp in Arizona. Her name was Hisaye Yamamoto, and her work at the *Tribune* "made her especially sensitive to the suffering of other communities of color."[123] Such a historical tessellation renders even more compelling a reading of "Oil Fields" in which oil's multifold significations comment on the complex dynamics that governed (and changed) relationships between LA's nonwhite populations during the war and in the years preceding it. As a journalist, Yamamoto was employed to think about—even to promote the improvement of—precisely those relationships, and "Oil Fields" is legible as an extension of that earlier project.

In it we can thus divine a relationship between how the everywhere-and-nowhere quality of the oil experience represents whiteness and how the blackness of oil itself co-opts Japanese American characters into a generalized non-whiteness. Distinctions between non-white ethnic groups are themselves both everywhere and nowhere, because whiteness's power to enforce them simultaneously threatens their removal. Kim implies as much in suggesting that the "valorization" by which racial triangulation elevates one ethnic group above another always already contains its own potential rescindment.[124] The breaking, through triangulation, of a "civilized" versus "savage" racial binary presupposes the existence of such a binary and thus the possibility of its restoration. As an "exercise of [white] racial power," triangulation's very enforcement of social distinctions between non-white groups is simultaneously a declaration of white society's power to erase such distinctions at will. On a similar basis Lowe notes that legal frameworks that periodically and partially enfranchised certain groups of Asian Americans while maintaining the disenfranchisement of others ensured that "the status of Asians as *nonwhite* [was] restated and reestablished" as a default. This paradoxical process, Lowe writes, of legally separating and stratifying Asian immigrant groups precisely in order to aggregate them as non-white, simultaneously "support[ed] and "obscure[ed]" the powerful centrality of the white racial category."[125] Again, whiteness's power to enforce sociolegal hierarchies between non-white ethnic groups (and thereby threaten to collapse them) is both the key to and the result of its ability to remain invisible.

Bob Jones fears in World War II the violent potential of whiteness's ability to elide and enforce racial distinctions simultaneously; Yamamoto anticipates that ability in the oily blackness that seeps through her

Japanese American characters' lives on the fringes of a white world. Thus the oil geography illustrates that the racial position Yamamoto's characters occupy is frontierlike not merely in its socially intermediate quality, triangulated between white and Black, but in the insoluble precarity and instability of that position. The proximity of oil's blackness to Yamamoto's characters becomes an indicator that their relative proximity to the "civilization" of whiteness is ultimately the gift *of* whiteness, and thus constantly threatens the collapse of the triangulated position into a racial wilderness of absolute and total *non*-whiteness. Tellingly, the only time the children in Yamamoto's story come "face-to-face with oil field danger" is when the young Jemo falls into a sump hole, becoming a "tar baby."[126] He is rescued, but the greatest "danger" possible in the socially and physically precarious space of the oilfield is to be immersed and covered in the blackness that has otherwise merely been in close and constant proximity. Perhaps there is a further anticipation here of the anxieties that would beset LA's Japanese community during the war—the fear of what had been Japanese being rendered Black, its Japaneseness erased through the arrival of African Americans in neighborhoods vacated by incarceration. The phrase "face-to-face" indicates that the danger here is less the possibility of Jemo's death than that of looking at one's brother and seeing, uncannily, a Black face—a previously secret double whose revelation is the revelation that non-whiteness is inescapable and ultimately binary. Jemo in the sump hole is thus a figure both of the conflict that wartime would invite between LA's Black and Japanese populations *and* of the way the same war would clarify their mutual interest as possessors of a common racialized subjecthood in the eyes of whiteness.

Jemo is a child even more doggedly marked by oil than are his siblings: gasoline siphoned from the family car is used to clean the oil from him, and the automobile that strikes him is of course the great symbol of the consumer oil economy.[127] It is the literal impact of highly pressurized petroleum combusting into kinetic energy that causes the narrator's parents to conclude, defeated, that "we Japanese [were] in a category with animals . . . to be left beside the road to die."[128] In Jemo there is thus a notion that oil as a symbol of racial difference grants mobility to some and entraps others. J. Arnold Ross, the white tycoon at the heart of a better-known Southern California petrofiction, Upton Sinclair's *Oil!* (1926), glories in the same petrocultural pleasures of automobility by which white drivers immobilize Jemo. For Sinclair as for Yamamoto, the symbolic racial overtones of the novel's titular substance are inescapable:

Sinclair's last line characterizes its titular substance as a "black and cruel demon" that must be "chain[ed]."[129] As in Yamamoto, too, connections are apparent between the oilfield and the frontier.

Sinclair's novel suggests that the values of the frontier can be recuperated via the oil encounter, which reawakens a conflict between humankind and the land. In this he participates in a longstanding American petrocultural discourse. Frederick Buell notes how Ida Tarbell, writing on America's first nineteenth-century oil rush, saw "oil extraction as signaling a resurgence of the old epic-heroic ideology of democratic, self-reliant, community- and nation-building individualism."[130] Sinclair's image of Prospect Hill (standing in for the Long Beach/Signal Hill oilfield) is of a similar refrontierizing process.[131] The neighborhood is initially an image of sleepy domestication and small-scale agriculture until oil is struck. When the black gold begins to gush, "men had to run for their lives."[132] Nature that seemed to have been pacified suddenly regains both its terrifying potency and the "mysteriously thrilling" quality of frontier flux.[133] The old geographic liminality is replicated by a new one—the westward impulse redirected downward. The surface of the earth may yield up no more conquerable space, but the frontier's challenge to "the ingenuity by which men overc[o]me Nature's obstacles" reemerges below ground.[134] As Buell notes, what fascinates Sinclair about the business of oil extraction is "how an American experience of space as freedom cuts against the necessity for enclosure in its exploration," and this is exactly the conundrum of frontierism, which expresses a desire for "space as freedom" in acts that render space no longer free.[135]

Joshua Schuster writes that "there is something too easy in the celebration of the 'great' and the 'American' that Sinclair buys into . . . a particularly boosterish national fantasy about the impact of oil on state power and the dirty but heroic work of extraction."[136] It is the linkage of oil speculation and frontier values that at once enables and demands this "too easy" celebration of "dirty heroism": Ross's status as a corrupt agent of the machinations of modern capitalism, interrogated so doggedly elsewhere by Sinclair, becomes secondary to his simpler symbolic value as a latter-day frontiersman, an "epic individualist and adventurer."[137] The nature of the connection Sinclair draws between the oilfield and the frontier is markedly different from that witnessed in Yamamoto's story precisely because the stakes of race and power in the two texts are so divergent. Where the locus of Yamamoto's text is a group of non-white children for whom oil is an inescapable reality in which they live but over which they have no agency, Sinclair's is a white man who controls oil's means of production and therefore is not spatially tied to them. Buell characterizes *Oil!* as being about "American exceptionalism leav[ing] the frontier and invest[ing] itself in the modernity of the United States," but it is more accurate to say that oil is the vehicle by which the exceptionalism *of* the frontier invests itself in modernity, as Hoover would claim it could. The garden enters the machine.

Comparison between the oilfield frontiers of Yamamoto and Sinclair suggests the ways in which any relationship with the legacies of the frontier is always bound up in a relationship with whiteness. Ross makes a straightforward claim to inherit the frontiersman's mantle as an individualist man of action who subdues nature to the benefit of "civilization." That this claim resides in his ability to "chain" oil's "black and cruel demon" (and the fact that he uses conspicuously non-white—Mexican—crews to actually perform such work) emphasizes the pertinence of his own whiteness in claiming a pioneer identity. Yamamoto's characters, by contrast, are ineluctably associated *with* the very blackness that Ross acts upon in order to claim a frontiersmanlike role. Yamamoto's description of the precarious prewar social position of the California Japanese, and its foreshadowed wartime deterioration, identify that community as participating in multiple forms of frontier dynamic—spatial, social, racial, economic. Some of these manifestations of a pioneer identity were actively claimed by Japanese Americans, but always within a context that placed whiteness in the position of the "civilization" into which non-white immigrants struggled to ingress and against whose values they were tested.

In that context, Yamamoto's characters' frontierism can only be read as an inverted one, akin to that of Fante's Julio Sal and Arturo Bandini (though the specific historical and political stakes of race and ethnicity do of course differ in each case). All these figures reimagine, contest, and expand the margins of settled American society by moving toward them from an othered beyond (whereas Sinclair's Ross employs the privilege of a conventional frontiersmanlike move from settlement *to* wilderness). Applied to Yamamoto's text, such a reading would corroborate Lowe's thesis that "the lives of Japanese Americans . . . cannot be narrated" by a plot or form or literary tradition that "reconciles the individual to the social order."[138] In "Oil Fields," autofictional ambiguity of form certainly suggests a stubborn refusal on the part of the text to reconcile itself (and thus its Japanese American inhabitants) to categorical expectations and distinctions imposed from without. Moreover, though, the inextricability of Yamamoto's children from the apparatus of oil suggests precisely the irreconcilability of prewar Californian society to its growing Japanese population—at once a valued contributor to the rapidly developing economy and an object of increasing paranoia and racial distaste. That ambivalence in turn indicates the role such a community played in reviving the frontier on its new nation's behalf. The presence of Japanese Americans reinvested the spaces they occupied with frontier qualities, but such proof of the frontier's persistence demanded (and indeed was partially manifest in) the reopening of American soil to contest with a suspicious alien force. If Yamamoto's use of oil suggests a society fueled by frontierlike forces of racial separation and contest, Sinclair corroborates that notion with the persistent image of a frontier brought into being by and perpetuated as a pioneering white individual's exploitation of a pressurized non-whiteness.

Atlas Slugged? Chester Himes's *If He Hollers Let Him Go*

The tensions that would arise between Los Angeles's Black and Japanese communities over Little Tokyo/Bronzeville, and mutual suspicions that neither had demonstrated sufficient solidarity with the other in the face of prejudice, were a cruel irony given the striking parallels—intimated by *If He Hollers Let Him Go*'s Bob Jones—between the two groups' experiences of living with whiteness. At the start of the twentieth century, like its Japanese counterpart, LA's Black community was small but thriving. A color line existed, of course, sometimes brutally so, but Jefferson Edmonds, editor of local Black newspaper the *Liberator*, could nevertheless in 1902 be as boosterish as any white civic father, citing the opportunities afforded by Los Angeles as proof of his claim that California was "the greatest state for the Negro."[139] In 1910, Black homeownership reached a nationwide high of 36.1 percent in LA.[140] As the Black population grew, though (from 1,258 in 1890 to 15,579 in 1920), segregated public services proliferated, competition for non-color-barred work increased, and racially restrictive property covenants became more widespread.[141] African Americans in LA, just like the Japanese, were increasingly being punished for their own initial success. Despite this climate of rising anti-Black hostility, the first great migration did take more hopeful pioneers westward: LA's Black population continued to grow, but modestly. World War II, however, would have a transformational effect on both the community's size and its social position.

Wartime heralded new liberties for African Americans in California just as it stripped them from the Japanese population. As California became America's arsenal, LA's shipyards and aircraft plants mushroomed: prewar, shipbuilding in LA employed barely 1,000 people; at its peak of wartime production, the figure was 90,000—with a further 230,000 at work in aerospace.[142] This constituted a regional revolution that was not just industrial but social. Sheer demand for labor, as Gerald D. Nash writes, "act[ed] as a catalyst to break down various barriers in the way of racial equality."[143] The admission of African Americans to the wartime industrial workforce—ardently campaigned for by civil rights leaders, demanded by President Roosevelt's Executive Order 8802, enabled by the Fair Employment Practices Committee (FEPC), and maintained against resistance from segregationist trade unions—inaugurated a twenty-year period in which, per Josh Sides, Los Angeles's African Americans enjoyed the "the greatest economic advances they had ever experienced."[144] Those advances were enthusiastically embraced by hopeful new arrivals. As Kurashige observes, "the Black population of the Los Angeles area expanded by 59,000 persons between April 1940 and April 1944—an increase of 78.2 percent that more than tripled the overall rate of population growth for the region."[145] When the FEPC held hearings in Los Angeles in October 1941, it had found that of Douglas Aircraft's 33,000 workers only ten were Black, and of Lockheed-Vega only fifty-four.[146] Those figures, moreover, included low-paid menial and auxiliary roles; when it came to actual production personnel, records David Wyatt, all the aircraft builders in California combined employed precisely four Black workers in 1941.[147] By early 1943, though, both Douglas and Lockheed-Vega had Black workforces in the low thousands, and other aircraft manufacturers and shipbuilders reported similar increases, as the overall size of the war industry ballooned.[148] Certainly, Black employees remained a minority, but just months earlier they had been scarcely imaginable. Once more, as Arna Bontemps remembered, "Los Angeles in legend became 'Paradise West' to Negroes still languishing in the Egyptland of the south, and not without some justification."[149]

Complicating this positivist history, though, were the "many barriers" to African American socioeconomic progress that remained—"disheartening and capricious restrictions" in labor, in housing, and in social life. In fact, as the contestation of Little Tokyo/Bronzeville indicated, if LA's acceptance of Black labor created new opportunities, a swelling Black population also heightened racial resentments. Such tension was not unique to Los Angeles. Indeed, across the country, "the heat and pace of racial struggle, conflict, and fear" rose as Black migrants "streamed into urban centers in search of war work" and were met with hostility and even violence."[150] As in so much of its mid-century history, though, what distinguished LA's experience of this demographic shift and the febrile atmosphere it fostered was enormity of scale and rapidity of pace. We can locate here perhaps a final ironic parallel between Black and Japanese experiences of racial intolerance in Los Angeles before and during the war. World War II did change things, dramatically, for African Americans in Los Angeles, but the fact that the Black community's increasing size and economic prosperity elevated racial resentments toward it is best understood as a redoubling of processes that had been in train since the beginning of the century, rather than something novel or anomalous. In wartime, both African Americans invited to Los Angeles and Japanese residents simultaneously expelled from it (both by dint of a Rooseveltian decree) experienced forms of discrimination that *were* particular to the bewildering circumstances of that moment but that should not, for that, be mistaken for unprecedented anomalies. Instead, just as implied by Yamamoto's imageries of latent combustibility, what both groups faced from 1941 onwards had been amply anticipated by and was contiguous with prewar trajectories of steadily accruing hatred. War simply steepened the angle of attack. The same, indeed, might be said of LA's Mexican and Mexican-descended population: the open violence of white sailors in the so-called Zoot Suit Riots of 1943 may have been shocking in its flagrant abandon, but was it truly inconsistent with (or surprising given) attitudes consistently displayed by Anglos toward Latinx people since California's admission to the union? War brought no new hatreds to LA; it merely broadened the imaginative horizons of the old.

Chester Himes was himself one of the thousands of African Americans who came to Los Angeles "initially optimistic" about the social gains of wartime industry only to find that "migration had not freed [them] from hurt."[151] Throughout *If He Hollers*, Bob Jones likewise finds the physical structures of his workplace, the Atlas Shipyard, to model his wider surroundings' restrictive and punitive sociogeography of race—a set of cruelly impassable frontiers. LA's war economy opens opportunities to him, but in doing so it only increases his social precarity as a Black man. When LA's wartime mayor, Fletcher Bowron, "call[ed] for unity, either in the face of Axis resistance or against the many eastern urban competitors for military wealth," he elided democratic global and capitalistic local goals.[152] Black intellectuals, including Himes, saw precisely such elision as the means by which and the reason why "white capitalist power, in the triad of government, Army and Business" co-opted African American labor to "destroy external fascism while allowing the brute processes of domestic racism . . . to pass unchecked."[153] As Nikhil Pal Singh writes, "a discourse of antifascism, freedom, and democracy" appeared to coincide with "black aspirations for justice" at home, but ultimately the global freedom struggle only extended the "promise of American universalism" to African Americans as a demand for their labor rather than as its reward.[154] In making his protagonist an African American shipyard employee, and locating much of the novel spatially within the belly of a ship built for a wartime government contract, Himes reifies the tension between a domestic racist capitalism and a global antifascist struggle. The barriers that Jones encounters in his supposedly "open" workplace thus give the lie to the contemporary assertions of union chiefs, politicians, company bosses, and even some African Americans, that Black labor's admission to previously restricted trades was a generous emancipatory benison. Himes in this period remarked that such acts and attitudes, precisely because they attested to white America's magnanimous "tolerance" of non-white groups, in fact continued to undermine the democratic ideal that "all men are created equal": a genuine opening simultaneously enforced a barrier.[155] In such ways workplace integration's signification of racial progress was only ever partial: Jones's navigations of his industrial workplace are a spatial staging of the hard limits to the supposed wartime social advancement of African Americans, of the difference between tolerance and equality.

The particular material characteristics of the half-built ship that is at once Jones's workplace and the product of that work distinguish his acts of social boundary transgression from those of characters discussed thus far. For Julio Sal on the dancefloor, or Walter Huff subversively negotiating the office, many of the boundaries and barriers that either impede or indicate the progress of their frontierist labors are primarily metaphorical: as a purely bodily challenge, Julio could easily breach the wicker gate that separates the dancing area from it surrounds; Walter faces no physical difficulty in accessing his office after dark. The tangible boundaries they cross merely denote the social frontiers through which they pass. It is a condition of maritime architecture, however, that the boundaries stratifying and striating the ship on which Jones works have qualities of literal resistiveness—hardness, smallness, incomprehensibility. Jones shares with Philip Marlowe and Walter Huff a sense of frontiersmanlike spatial audacity conferred by a particular professional skillset, but Jones's navigational feats are rendered specially virtuosic by their contention with the particular physical and technical obstacles manifest in his workplace and the particular social obstacles manifest in his own racial status. The ship is a "maze of shapes," a lattice of treacherous ladders, narrow gangways, and impenetrable bulkheads that are transparent only in their suggestion of the hazards Jones must likewise face in navigating America's racial landscape as a Black man.[156] The Atlas yard is thus both a world unto itself and a scale model of racially riven America at large.

Bob Jones's apprehension of an intrinsic link between capacities for spatial and social power is first indicated by his description of his arrival in Los Angeles in 1941. Despite being fully aware that "race was a handicap," Jones "felt fine about everything" and "knew [he'd] get along" in LA.[157] The source of his confidence is his knowledge that he is "taller than the average man, six feet two, broad-shouldered." He is confident that sheer physical presence—the ability to occupy more space than most men and to defend it more effectively—will serve to offset sufficiently the social disadvantages at which his race places him. Suggesting a Lefebvrian worldview in which the triadic elements that constitute space are perpetually unstable because they are always contingent upon and modified by each other, Jones believes that the greater *physical* space his body claims can compensate for the reduced *social* space he can access.[158]

In this economy a surfeit of one type of space is exchangeable to fill a shortfall in another. When Jones claims that he would have "hit a paddy . . . without any thought," the act is figured in language redolent of spatial discovery and ingress: "I'd have busted him wide open" remarks Jones.[159] The claim to an equal racial footing expressed in the confidence with which Jones would punch a white man is rendered analogous to making "wide open" space—even if an epithet that originates as an anti-Irish slur perhaps attenuates the ambition of Jones's willingness to assert racial parity through violence, considering the Irish American community's own complex historical relationship with whiteness.[160] There is a continuity of purpose here with Fante's Bandini—who, in his own assertions of racial agency, characterizes one of his verbal assaults on a Filipino colleague in explicitly spatial terms: it leaves the man "open to the whole world" (i.e., it redefines his relationship to the space around him).[161] Their methods are different, but these acts of aggression confirm that both characters perceive race in geographic terms, as a restricted, liminal space from which one can (attempt to) fight one's way out.

The Atlas Shipyard immediately proves a rude awakening to Jones because, having derived so much of his self-confidence from an ability to take up space, he finds that in shipbuilding his large size is, in fact, a disadvantage, a hindrance to his ability to move through the cramped spaces of the half-built vessel. Here, he must "pick every step to find a foot-size clearance of deck space," while at the same time "looking up" lest he "tear off an ear or knock out an eye against some overhanging shape."[162] A smaller man would not have to carry himself with such constant conscious regulation of the space he occupies—and in another sense, neither would a white man. Dyer writes that a fear of "white bodily inferiority," the suspicion (and stereotype) that "non-whites have better bodies . . . bigger muscles," has long prompted white culture to seek ways of defensively suffusing images of "heightened muscularity" with "connotations of whiteness" (in film, in sculpture, in bodybuilding culture), making an ideal of the "hard, visibly bounded body [that] can resist being submerged into the horror of . . . non-whiteness."[163]

This ideal—a white maleness that could preserve its integrity in hostile space (and assert superiority over that space's non-white inhabitants) by dint of physical robustness—is of course the vision of masculinity that found its paradigmatic (and, in an American context, most culturally definitional) expression in frontier myth. Jones repurposes that paradigm by inverting it, trusting to the strength and size of his Black body to prevent him from being submerged into the horror of whiteness, but is punished for doing so by the ship's hostile internal geography. Jones's punishment is anticipated in the name of his workplace, which invokes both the mythical Atlas and his latter-day namesake Charles, both archetypes of the whiteness-as-muscularity culture Dyer identifies.[164] "It put me on my muscle," says Jones of the act of donning his work clothes. This "muscle" is figurative, but nevertheless makes him "bigger . . . stronger than the average citizen, stronger than a white-collar worker—stronger even than an executive" (whiteness in more than just the collar implied in all cases).[165] In its spatial constrictions, "Atlas" checks not only Jones's mobility but the temerity of his attempts to subvert a cultural figuration of muscularity as protection *for* rather than *from* whiteness, his frontiersmanlike effort to claim space in the world through physical ruggedness. David Wyatt is right when he punningly calls Bob Jones, his prickly physicality always tensed and ready to explode in self-preservation, a "one-man defense industry," but the wordplay demands its logical extension: "defense" means getting hit in the first place.[166]

At Atlas, Jones will realize that he cannot escape or surmount, through physical power or otherwise, the social disadvantages at which his racial status places him. The spatial characteristics of the yard and the limitations they place on Jones's bodily agency are thus metonymic of the novel's racial concerns. Restricted spatial movement in the vessel's superstructure, the *impossibility* of fighting one's way out as Jones often wishes and attempts to, maps restricted social movement in the world at large. True enough, Jones and his colleagues leave mocking notes imploring their white co-workers to run afoul of the ship's compressed spaces—"Don't duck, Okie, you're tough"—but this in itself rather suggests the disadvantage at which the ship's Black workers find themselves.[167] To leave such notes, jokingly hoping that the white employees find their freedom of (spatial) movement bluntly curtailed, is to acknowledge that the white employees enjoy a greater freedom of (social) movement. If the Okies ran into barriers (social *or* spatial) of their own accord, there would be no need to exhort them to do so.

Jones's initial confidence on arriving in Los Angeles turns to an all-encompassing fear that leaves him "shriveled, paralyzed" when war breaks out—despite the fact that it is the outbreak of war that enables him to land a job at the shipyard where he had previously been rejected on racial grounds.[168] As noted, seeing Japanese Americans being interned prompts Robert's realization that white American society would have no qualms about doing the same to any non-white group. War brings about an epiphany that his own racial foothold in the American societal mainstream is even less firm than he imagined it. Himes's other wartime writings disclose his own similar slow-motion epiphany. In 1942, he still harbored hope that war's "leveling influences of common peril and common objectives" created unique opportunities to defeat racism at home, but by the following year he was so disillusioned by what the Zoot Suit Riots said about race in America as to remark that "the South [had] won Los Angeles."[169] By 1944 Himes held that white Americans were in fact moving ever "farther away from the ideology of democracy" that he had so recently expected war to retrench.[170] In the novel, such disquieting epiphanies about race are conceived in spatial terms: Pearl Harbor caused racial hatred to be "let loose in a flood." Echoing Bandini's apprehension of racial difference as olfactorily sensible in the cannery odor, Jones detects the "tight, crazy feeling of race as thick in the street as gas fumes."[171] Framed in quick succession as alternately a liquid or a gas, overwhelming in both cases, "race" is for Jones a tangible entity unto itself, possessed of physical, spatial properties. Moreover, the fear leaves him feeling "walled in, locked up," again drawing a direct link between racial security and the ability to occupy and maneuver through space: the direct correlative of Jones's feeling of increased racial precarity is a feeling that he has been spatially constricted.[172]

It is all the more curious, then, that although this fear arises with the onset of war, it is only upon being made a leaderman, and receiving a draft deferment, that it starts "really getting" to Jones.[173] If Jones's abiding anxiety was brought about by the feeling that the war rendered his place in society increasingly precarious, one might reasonably expect the leaderman job to reduce that fear. As James Lundquist asks: "Why the fear? Why the anger? Bob has a good job. He has had two years of college. He has a draft deferment."[174] The answers to those questions further suggest the extent to which the novel figures the Atlas Yard as a map of both the social disadvantages Jones suffers because of his race and the strategies he employs in the hope of overcoming the same. As Jones drives his colleagues to work, the blurring of literal and racial topographies is evident. In the "mad, fast, and furious" traffic, the drive becomes a fraught contest with white drivers and even white pedestrians: Bob deliberately drives dangerously, hoping for a collision and a pretext for injuring a white man.

> The huge industrial plants flanking the ribbon of road—shipyards, refineries, oil wells, steel mills, construction companies—the thousands of rushing workers, the low-hanging barrage balloons, the close hard roar of Diesel trucks and the distant drone of patrolling planes, the sharp, pungent smell of exhaust that used to send me driving clear across Ohio on a sunny summer morning, and the snow-capped mountains in the background, like picture post-cards, didn't mean a thing to me. I didn't even see them; all I wanted in the world was to push my Buick Roadmaster over some peckerwood's face.[175]

This passage is riven with paradox. Jones describes the industrial landscape not merely at length, in detail and with vibrancy, but also in a manner that conveys the way in which these surrounds are so large in scale and so sensorily all-enveloping, oppressive even, that they occlude and dominate the other potential visions with which they compete. They make the "mountains in the background" so removed and otherworldly as to become "picture post-cards," while "Ohio on a sunny summer morning" is relegated to irretrievable pastness. Thus both the richness of Jones's description and the particular qualities it ascribes to the sights of this landscape seem to contradict his claims that he "didn't even see them" and that they "didn't mean a thing" to him due to his overriding fixation on running over a white man. Jones clearly does see his physical surroundings, in all their sense-overpowering immediacy, yet claims to be unable to see them because that sense-overpowering immediacy is the very quality that defines his racial hatred. There is contiguity here with Yamamoto's suggestion that the effects of racism are so omnipresent as to become paradoxically invisible.

The dimensions of hostile race relations appear to overlay the dimensions of physical space; the physical landscape *becomes* Jones's psychic landscape of violent racial contest. His claim to be unable to see his actual surroundings thus derives not from a literal inability to "see" the materiality of the world around him, but from the fact that, for Jones, that materiality has *become* "race thick in the street" and vice versa; race permeates the tangible parameters of the "shipyards, refineries, oil wells, steel mills, construction companies" to such a degree that they are no longer visible merely as themselves. The Atlas Yard will prove the same, its internal geographies inevitably racial ones. This is what Jones means when he remarks that a "white boy" might enjoy the "scramble" and "tight competition" of the traffic but "to me it was racial."[176] The racial and the spatial are inextricable from each other now.

Perhaps the clearest indicator of how the Atlas Yard demands connection between spatial and racial navigation lies in the linguistic liminality in which Bob works. In the social hybridity of his speech, which fluidly sublates multiple culturally specific registers into an original form, while continuing to modulate between its constituent elements in different contexts, Bob exhibits something of what Gloria Anzaldúa would later term a "border consciousness."[177] Two of the components of this hybridity—the standard American English spoken by most of the novel's white characters and Jones's middle-class girlfriend Alice, and the African American Vernacular English deployed in rendering the speech of Jones and his fellows—present themselves obviously. A third register is that of the shipyard's many white southern employees. Himes ironically renders the dialect of the capricious Madge, Bob's nemesis, in a manner indistinguishable on the page—"yo'self," "le's"—from that of his African American characters, conjuring a hint of Roediger's thesis about the tragedy of working-class whites' unwillingness to realize grounds for solidarity across racial lines.[178] The fourth main linguistic register in which the text operates is less immediately obvious than the others, signified as they are by distinctions of race and class, but it reveals itself as essential to the novel's treatment of those very subjects.

By this I refer to the abiding sense throughout *If He Hollers* that the Atlas Yard itself has its own language, one made up of specialist technical terms and workplace-specific slang. Lundquist set the tone for decades of critical framings of Himes's style when he emphasized Bob Jones's "unremittingly tough" language, but the most distinctive characteristic of Jones's navigation of his workplace is rather that it is unremittingly *technical*.[179] This is a place rendered in "companionways," "leadermen," the "transverse bulkhead," "the chippers, the blowers, the burners, the light lines, the wooden staging," "the ventilation trunks and ducts, reducers, dividers, transformers," "gants," and "prints," the "jack ladder" and the "copper shop."[180] The cumulative effect is in such opaque exchanges as this:

> Willie said, "While you're here, Bob, you can show me where to hang these stays and save me from having to go get the print." He was crouched on the staging beneath the upper deck, trying to hang his duct.
>
> I knew he couldn't read blueprints, but he was drawing a mechanic's pay. I flashed my light on the job and said, "Hang the first two by the split and the other two just back of the joint. What's your X?"
>
> "That's what I don't know," he said, "I ain't seen the print yet."
>
> "It's three-nine off the bulkhead," I said.[181]

Jones here seeks to call Willie's bluff with the cryptic question about his "X," the letter itself redolent of mystery, forcing his underling to admit that greater ignorance of the job than initially confessed. Bob's assertion of specialist knowledge is twofold, however, because it also confounds and excludes the reader, who is unlikely to know exactly what "X" is signifies in this context, let alone the physical position of this particular "X."

Understanding the operation of this technical register is invaluable to understanding the ship as a racialized geography because, as we see in the exchange with Willie, Bob's fluency in the technical language of his job is a proxy for his knowledge of space. Bob's acts of naming are how he shows himself to have the level of specialist knowledge that has made him Atlas's first Black leaderman. By maintaining their own exclusivity, those acts of naming also model for the reader the fluency with which Bob moves around the ship, withholding the secrets of how Bob understands his work and the vessel by refusing to translate them. To read how Bob describes the activity in the yard and his movements through it is to feel everything that he does not—disorientated and slow, alienated from and uncertain of spatial meanings. The reader fumbles clumsily through the ship by fumbling clumsily through Bob's opaque jargon, in so doing recognizing his supple facility as a navigator of space both social and spatial. Thus, when Wyatt suggests that Himes helps the reader appreciate the restricted movement Bob experiences in both his "external world" (the ship) and his "inner one" (his consciousness as a Black American) by "confin[ing] the reader inside the wariness of a mind," he doesn't go quite far enough.[182] It is truer to say that the reader, though experiencing the Atlas Yard through Jones's eyes, is often confined *outside* the wariness of his expert mind—an even more alienated position, and one that ironically stages for the reader Bob's own experience of blackness as epistemological exclusion via the one aspect of his life in which he revels as a consummate insider. A. Robert Lee writes that Himes's "supporting metaphoric use of Atlas's world of heavy machines and industry" makes the shipyard "appear predatory" as it "mechanicalizes human vitality."[183] This is undeniably true of Bob's ultimate fate and the novel's conclusion, but Lee fails to observe that the yard is described in a narrative voice that is ostensibly Bob's own. The fact that Atlas is mediated to the reader through Bob's navigations of its spaces via specialist argot suggests that, at least provisionally, he has mastered his environment rather than the reverse.

Recursively, moreover, the spatial fluency Bob demonstrates through his use of a specialist linguistic register also models how his mobility between *other* linguistic registers denotes his corresponding qualities as a navigator of the social. Bob's specialist engineering language is the means by which the reader experiences his flexibility in moving through the ship as a physical space, but it is because Bob has mastered everyone else's language that he has moved through the shipyard's industrial-corporate structure. Bob constantly code-switches between his narrator's voice (incorporating some elements of African American Vernacular English but in muted form), the voice he uses to speak to his Black co-workers (where the vernacular element is more prominent), a casual workplace *lingua franca* emphasizing commonalities between AAVE and the speech of the white southern co-workers when talking to them, and the "standard"

English he uses when talking to Alice and her family or white authority figures. (Bob even code-switches in thought: in one episode where he briefly resolves to accept quiescent middle-class Black respectability with Alice, he imagines that he "sounded like Clarence Darrow himself."[184])

The frontierist implications of Bob Jones's ability to move between linguistic codes convincingly and confidently are reciprocal with and inextricable from those of his skill (represented in his knowledge of a further linguistic code) in compassing the ship. Jones initially appears to be on a path to social success, despite the racial prejudice he faces, in part because of his level of professional skill, and in part because of his linguistically manifest level of social skill in managing his relationships with the varying communities who make claims on his loyalty and identity (working-class Black, middle-class Black, working-class white, middle-class authority-holding white). He makes himself a useful resource, as the frontier itself did, by being able to function, as his boss MacDougal suggests, as a connective zone between disparate spaces of class and race, someone who could "keep down trouble between the white and colored workers."[185] Technical and social skill cannot be teased apart here: good at his job Bob Jones may be, but he has also learned to speak to white men in a way that enables him to be recognized for his skill. Not only does Bob's linguistic hybridity attest to his occupation of a frontierlike liminality between racial and class identities, it also discloses that his success has come as a result of his frontiersmanlike ability to test and push successfully against the edges of that liminality. In being made the first Black leaderman, he has been permitted authority exceeding that available to his African American peers for advancing in aptitude beyond the level his employer formerly associated with his race—less a "talented tenth" than, considering the numbers of Black men who began to be employed in LA's wartime shipyards, a talented thousandth. His "reward" is also, however, the result of his ability to present himself in a certain way—the fact that he has been able to persuade MacDougal that he is not merely skilled but exceptional among his race: "the most intelligent colored boy I knew."[186]

The workplace in which Jones operates, which is itself metonymic of the wider racialized society in which he lives, requires him to step outside the boundaries of what is considered normative for his race if he is to be valued and respected. He cannot merely be valued and respected as a Black man, he must prove himself an exceptional one. Jones does not choose to become a kind of spatial-racial frontiersman; he is compelled into that identity by the society in which he lives and by the institutional apparatus of Atlas in particular. Just as Julio Sal found, however, Jones quickly discovers that a white-centric society that compels its minority members to perform the frontierist role of stepping beyond the social bounds of their own racial marginality is also one that will quickly assert its authority in the matter of how far those bounds can be overstepped. To "overcome 'em with yeses," as the narrator's Delphic grandfather explains in Ellison's *Invisible Man*, is no quietist path toward immunity from the power of whiteness, but quite the opposite—it is to "live with your head in the lion's mouth," "a spy in the enemy's country."[187] The decision as to when the confounding of racial expectation is praiseworthy and when it is to be condemned always rests with the force representative of white societal authority, be it the dancehall management or the shipyard bosses.

The lion's mouth begins to close on Bob with his demotion from leaderman, which is the consequence of his calling Madge a "cracker bitch."[188] Bob is sociolinguistically skilled enough to know this not how he "should" speak to a white woman, but he *chooses* to demonstrate his ability to switch social codes beyond a level that is deemed acceptable. Bob is possessed of what bell hooks describes as a "contradictory longing to possess the reality of the Other, even though that reality is one that wounds and negates"—to model the "values, speech, habits of being" of a culture that engenders "suspicion, fear, and even hatred."[189] When those contradictions overwhelm Bob, he responds with aggressive assertions of difference. Mosley's Easy Rawlins will make a similar error, losing his aircraft plant job because he refuses to show a level of deference to authority greater than that demanded of even a tenuously white colleague like Benny Giacomo.[190] Both Rawlins and Jones are fluent code-switchers who run afoul of the fact that an ability to speak the white man's language is only rewarded when it is to the white man's (or woman's) edification. If their society demands that they perform as racial frontiersmen, then frontier logic dictates that their ingress into the space of whiteness must be resisted *by* whiteness in order to maintain that space's requisite unconquerability.

Madge's presence suffuses the novel as the ultimate example of a white reality that Bob wishes to possess despite its negating effects upon him. In the novel's climactic meeting between the pair, the nexus between the ship's spatial qualities and Bob's role as a social navigator is once again made manifest. A former member of Bob's team, seeing his demoted erstwhile manager crestfallen at finding his old crew reassigned to more desirable work under a white leaderman, sympathetically asks him for his expertise on the new job. When Bob goes to inspect the area, however, "peeping into various rooms," he realizes that he has no idea "what they were all for," and can only surmise possibilities for their use. Where previously he flaunted his ability to understand the ship's complex geography unaided, now he acknowledges that he would, like Willie, "have to get a print to tell anything about it."[191] The frontiersman has moved into territory where his prior knowledge no longer serves him. It is precisely because of his inability to navigate this space that he finds himself unwittingly in a room alone with Madge, who first attempts to seduce him, then loudly accuses him of rape when he refuses to return her advances.

All of Bob's various frontiersmanlike tools fail him in a single terrible moment. First, the navigational abilities that are his professional skillset desert him in a new geography (one under the explicitly white authority of the new leaderman), leading him to walk directly into a hazard. Second, the wary social resourcefulness of his self-protective code-switching proves useless. Upon discovering Madge he seeks both to defuse the situation and to place himself above the suspicion of any witnesses, stating not just loudly but with a self-conscious formality that connotes simultaneously respectfulness and respectability, "I'd like to apologize . . . I was upset that morning."[192] Bob attempts to distance himself not only from Madge but, through his polite, "well-spoken" deference, from the suggestion of Black animality that he knows will accompany any suspicion of untoward behavior on his part. Madge, however, will not be dissuaded. Third, Bob's (and the frontiersman's) most basic resource, physical strength, the quality Bob always believed would underwrite his survival even in this world of rampant racial terror, is rendered useless: he dare not use his bodily power to subdue Madge, knowing this would make the situation far worse. "All she had was her color," he knows, but that alone is more potent than all the combined traits by which he has shown himself a racial frontiersman. Just like the frontier of the Turnerian imagination, Bob's surroundings remain a geography in service of whiteness.[193]

In this instant, Jones finds with horror that his identity has been transformed from one of motility to one of entrapment, or rather that his motility was only ever illusory. Torn between remaining in the room with Madge and running from her, he no longer has any power to control the meaning of either of those spatial gestures; either will be interpreted negatively by the Atlas Yard's white arbiters of spatial practice. The eventual result will be military conscription, a fitting punishment for one who oversteps the bounds of the frontier work his society has asked him to perform: military service retains all of the frontier's emphasis on mortal danger, hostile environments, and brutal physicality, but institutionally strips away every vestige of its supposed values of individual agency, creative freedom, and self-determination. The psychological trauma wrought by military life's simultaneous demands and denials of a frontiersmanlike mode of living will reveal themselves further in my next chapter, in the white protagonists of novels by Dorothy B. Hughes and Frank Fenton. In Jones's case, though, being forced to join the army as his punishment for an errant navigation further affirms that Atlas is another frontier space in which the frontiersman's labor falls to minorities while the rules governing their performance are determined by (and benefit) white society.

The marginalized, oppressed figure is challenged, even required, by his surrounding society to approach life (and particularly working life) from a frontierist perspective, to labor as a frontiersman, only to be struck down, as Turner says he must be, should his frontiersmanship prove too successful—that is, *too transgressive* and thus at risk of erasing the frontier entirely. Indeed, if Bob periodically uses shows or fantasies of violence toward white individuals to reject assimilative demands that he surpass white expectations of Black behavior, then even these reveal the extent of his entrapment by those demands. As Roediger notes, in observations on W. E. B. Du Bois's *Black Reconstruction*, "white labor does not just receive and resist racist ideas but embraces, adopts and, at times, murderously acts upon those ideas."[194] In adopting racialized violence as a strategy to resist white demands that he perform frontiersmanship, therefore, Jones unwittingly continues that performance by embracing another of the logics upon which his white-run workplace operates.

The revelation that the invitation to African Americans to perform war work (in previously restricted trades) is in fact an invitation, symbolically, to perform frontier work thus discloses that the promise of racial advancement, of admission to the socioeconomic heart of whiteness, is illusory. If the frontiersman's task is to seem momentarily to conquer the frontier while in fact proving its viability and endurance, then it was inevitable that Bob Jones's supposed weakening of white edifices in becoming leaderman at Atlas would only ever affirm the power and robustness of those edifices. At one point Bob describes himself as "a machine being run by white people."[195] His experiences at Atlas, however, bring him to the realization that the whiteness machine is in fact America at large and he only a cog within it; like Yamamoto's oil apparatus he has struggled to see it only because it is omnipresent—the recurring sense of oppressive whiteness as everywhere and nowhere.

Bob Jones's Los Angeles of 1945 was markedly changed from that of Yamamoto's pre-Depression oilfield in many respects, not least the scale and variety of its industries. The structures and nature of oppression faced by Yamamoto's children, Arturo Bandini in *The Road*, and Jones in *If He Hollers* are not the same. They share, however, a sense that the dominant Anglo-American society in which they live demands that they move in certain spatial and social directions, namely those that would see them transcend their ethnic identity and ascend into the higher echelons of what that dominant group deems "civilized," only to restrict or deny the possibility (or at least the permanence) of that movement. As a result, they share a sense that race is experienced in profoundly and inescapably spatial terms. They explore and test the limits of social, spatial, and ethnic liminalities, while simultaneously embodying liminality within their own personhood. In all such respects, these experiences of industrial Los Angeles certainly affirm the endurance of frontier dynamics and principles, but in doing so they constitute an incisive critique of the same. They respond to the debates within which Roosevelt and Hoover explored the possibility of perpetuating frontier spirit in an age of industry not by providing an answer but by modifying the underlying question—asking not whether a modern America *could* sustain itself upon frontier values, but whether it *should*.

4

Ephemeral Accommodations
Hughes, Fenton, and the Architecture of Postwar Masculine Crisis

> He is a queer, annoying creature. . . . I have lived in rooming houses so long that I have acquired an eye for the type.
>
> —Saul Bellow, *Dangling Man*

Kenneth T. Jackson claims that "throughout history, the treatment and arrangement of shelter have revealed more about a particular people than have any other products of the creative arts."[1] On that basis we might ask what is revealed about the condition of Los Angeles at mid-century by the fact that, in the period's fiction, "multi-family" housing occupies a position of prominence disproportionate to its role in the real city's contemporaneous urban form.[2] Here I suggest that such housing's outsize textual presences constitute another manifestation of the widespread fictional determination to claim 1930s and 1940s LA as a site of enduring frontier dynamics. I do so principally via two novels that depict LA at the moment of World War II's end through the traumatized visions and traumatizing behaviors of returning veterans—Dorothy B. Hughes's *In a Lonely Place* (1947) and *What Way My Journey Lies* (1946), the second novel by the largely forgotten Frank Fenton.

In both texts, the protagonists' personal crises articulate anxieties about the viability in a postwar world of forms of masculinity that embody and seek to maintain the values of the frontier. Those stakes are revealed spatially, through the opposition both novels draw between the politics of multi-family housing (masculinist, individualist, unstable, socially marginal, frontierist) and those of the single-family home (feminized, familial, secure, socially normative, anti-frontierist). In order to identify how these texts stage a contest between those sets of values, however, it is first necessary to apprehend how and why such values vest themselves in different forms of accommodation.

Los Angeles Lifestyles: The Changing Shape of Home

"The single freestanding house" has long been regarded as "the predominant and favored item" of Los Angeles's urban landscape.[3] Such an image is most readily associated with the sprawl of the city's post–World War II development, when an "unprecedented housing boom resulted in the proliferation of suburban tracts . . . and the built-up area of the metropolis expanded ever more insistently outward" to house an estimated three million new arrivals between 1945 and 1960. "Building sprawled across the San Fernando Valley, east into the San Gabriel Valley and south, spilling over into Orange County"—LA became less a single city than a grouping of interconnected "lesser commercial and industrial centers which would provide jobs and services for neighborhoods of mostly single-family homes."[4] This increasingly dispersed and decentralized (sub)urban form was rendered comprehensible and logistically viable by the freeway network, which grew tenfold between the end of the war and 1960.[5] By 1971, Reyner Banham could assert that the "world's image of Los Angeles" was "an endless plain endlessly gridded with endless streets, peppered endlessly with ticky-tack houses clustered in indistinguishable neighborhoods, slashed across by endless freeways that have destroyed any community."[6]

Such postwar decentralization is often situated in a narrative of contrast with a prewar LA defined by greater compactness and density, organized around a central core, closer to the more "typical" urban forms of New York or Chicago. Ed Dimendberg exemplifies this position in comparing prewar and postwar "centripetal" and "centrifugal" cities. The former manifests "urban density and the visible—the skyline, monuments, recognizable public spaces, and inner-city neighborhoods," the latter "immateriality, invisibility, and speed." The prewar city's dense center gives it "focal points for collective life" that its postwar counterpart lacks.[7] In this vision, the prewar LA experience is typified by the Bunker Hill apartment house, the postwar city by the detached suburban tract home. As Ed Soja notes, however, LA already exhibited a "highly decentralized urban morphology" by the 1920s.[8] Indeed, while the ever-increasing sprawl and the hollowing-out of the central city that Dimendberg notes are undeniable realities of LA's postwar history, LA's "ability to realize the ideal of the low-density, horizontal city," an ideal embodied in the single-family detached home, was in fact at its greatest *before* the war.[9] Postwar, even as it sprawled ever further, LA became in its density and incidence of multi-family housing much more like other urban centers.

In 1930, the only other major US city with a population density about as low as LA's was Detroit, yet whereas 79.7 percent of Detroit's housing was single-family residences, the figure was 93.9 percent in Los Angeles.[10] Anton Wagner claimed in 1935 that such low density was "not due to the predominance of single-family houses but rather to the size of the plots," yet excluding two-household "duplex" residences only 2.4 percent of LA's dwellings in 1930 were "multi-family."[11] By way of comparison, in the same year 52.8 percent of New York's housing was single-family.[12] Municipal planning documents from 1941 reveal that in that year 39.6 percent of the urban used land in the LA metropolitan area (119.6 out of 302 square miles) was occupied by single-family residences and a very small proportion of two-family units. Multi-family units occupied just 7.4 square miles, or 2.45 percent of the total urban used land.[13]

In 1940, 81.6 percent of LA's populace lived in single-family homes, but the figure had already fallen from its 1930 peak.[14] This shift continued after the war. By 1950 only 65.9 percent of dwelling units in the LA metropolitan area, and 54.8 percent in the city proper, were single-family; from the 1950s onwards, "apartments outnumbered single-family units in the city's construction statistics."[15] Proportions of single-family housing would never again reach their prewar heights. Higher-density (i.e., multi-family) forms of housing became more prominent (and increasingly so) in LA's urban makeup postwar than they had been prewar. This is not, however, the impression given by fictional depictions of LA housing in the period up to and including World War II and its immediate aftermath.

Raymond Chandler's novels are peppered with single-family homes of various sizes and forms, from Arthur Geiger's bungalow to the Sternwood mansion in *The Big Sleep*, and from Mrs. Florian's "dried-out brown house" to Jules Amthor's hilltop retreat in *Farewell, My Lovely*.[16] John Fante's *Dreams from Bunker Hill*, casting a nostalgic backward glance from 1982 to the mid-'30s, finds Arturo Bandini lodging for a spell in the Hollywood hills house of his screenwriter friend Frank Edgington—a stand-in for Frank Fenton, Fante's real-life associate and a central subject of this chapter—but the arrangement proves unsustainable. In Nathanael West's *The Day of the Locust*, Homer Simpson lives alone in a cottage, but this denotes his atypicality—a "queer" house for a queer person.[17] Tod Hackett meanwhile marvels at the garish, ersatz eclecticism of a cityscape improvised lot-by-lot by each individual "builder's fancy."[18] Aldous Huxley's *After Many a Summer* (1939) takes the single-family home to its grotesque extreme in Jo Stoyte's "doubly baronial" estate, but again this is a vision of exceptionality.[19] All of this is to acknowledge that single-family homes are, of course, present in the domestic space of fictional Los Angeles in the first half of the twentieth century—but they are not infrequently signifiers of the unusual. Undeniably, moreover, the texts of this period exhibit a preponderance of multi-family housing disproportionate to and unrepresentative of a real city that exhibited a historically and nationally unique dearth thereof. Multi-family housing takes many forms in these texts, and distinctions between those forms are at times blurred. It is nonetheless possible to taxonomize them roughly, and in so doing map their superfluity in the corpus.

RESIDENTIAL HOTELS

As Paul Groth writes, "until about 1960 . . . a majority of hotel keepers not only offered travelers rooms for the night but also provided rooms or suites for permanent residents."[20] In LA, the premises that offered such services ranged widely in quality and social status, from poor-quality establishments concentrated downtown to grand affairs in otherwise "high-class single-family residence areas."[21] They are suggested in the fiction by Bunker Hill's Alta Loma, where Bandini lives in Fante's *Ask the Dust*, the Chateau Mirabella on Hollywood's Ivar Street, briefly home to Tod Hackett in West's *Locust*, or the more respectable Rossmore Arms, where Florence Almore's parents can be found in Chandler's *The Lady in the Lake*.

ROOMING HOUSES

Rooming houses also populate Fante's Bunker Hill, not only in *Ask the Dust* but in such short stories as "Mary Osaka, I Love You" (1942), "The Dreamer" (1947), and the unpublished "The Cat" (undated). They likewise appear in Chandler's portrayals of the same neighborhood—the tumbledown converted Gothic mansions of a "lost town."²² The rooming house provides basic rooms, sometimes shared, often has a live-in manager or landlord/lady, and typically does not provide board. Whereas the hotel is likely to be (if not always) purpose-built, the rooming house is almost always a converted former single-family home.

BOARDING/LODGING HOUSES

The boarding or lodging house is distinguished from the rooming house in that it is first and foremost a private home in which lodgers are taken, as opposed to the rooming house's more "professional" enterprise. The provision of board brings residents into regular—but only passing and perfunctory—contact. The worst boarding houses were regarded as "bestial nests," not least because they were historically home to large immigrant populations.²³ When Theodore Roosevelt decried the "divided allegiance[s]" of unassimilated ethnic minority immigrants in 1919, he feared America becoming a "polyglot boarding-house."²⁴ The metaphor invoked simultaneously the association of the boarding house with immigrants and its related popular image as a depthless, rootless community, a place where individuals shared space out of expedience, rather than out of mutual values or obligations. The boarding house had become unfashionable by the 1930s, but one persists postwar in Fenton's *What Way My Journey Lies*.²⁵

APARTMENT BUILDINGS

Apartments traversed a considerable breadth of the social spectrum in mid-century LA. In *The Big Sleep*, an irate building manager objects to Philip Marlowe calling his premises a "flop" but ultimately cannot argue with the description, suggesting a form that at least pretended but could not always maintain social distinction from the stigmatized boarding and rooming house.²⁶ As well as those of many of his clients and suspects, fictional examples include Marlowe's own homes in the Hobart Arms and Bristol Apartments, or the less respectable San Bernardino Arms, where West's Hackett moves from the Mirabella.

APARTMENT AND BUNGALOW COURTS

The apartment court and its close cousin the bungalow court, which compress multiple self-contained (but attached) dwellings into single lots with shared central spaces, are quintessentially Los Angeles forms—"the dominant southern California multifamily dwelling type."[27] Chandler uses them frequently: Marlowe chases a client of Geiger's through one; Helen Morrison lives in one in the Chandler-scripted *The Blue Dahlia* (1946); something like one is central to "The King in Yellow" (1938). See also the Lilac Court Apartments where Sachetti resides in Cain's *Double Indemnity*, or the Virginibus Arms of Hughes's *Lonely Place*. Sam Hall Kaplan hypothesizes that courts became popular in LA because "with their common areas encouraging neighborly mingling, [they] made pleasant enclaves in a city that in the crush of growth was becoming increasingly anonymous and alienating," creating "a sense of place and community."[28] As I will show, however, Hughes's novel identifies an opposite set of characteristics in the apartment court of the immediate postwar period.

Multi-Family Accommodation: A Frontierist Reading

This preponderance of multi-family housing in the fiction of LA in the 1930s and 1940s thus suggests an urban composition quite at odds with the city's contemporary reality of overwhelming single-family living. Dimendberg's prewar-centripetal/postwar-centrifugal paradigm is constructed principally in response to fictional visions of the city—in his case those created by *noir* cinema—and prior to the 1950s such visions *are* largely of a centripetal city defined by a high-density urban center. The LA of fiction is, however, to some degree misleading as to the condition of what was a broader city in more ways than one.

The likes of Fante and West brought to their fictions personal experiences of multi-family accommodation in the areas of the city where it did predominate. Parts of the city *were* relatively dense, even if the whole was not—in 1941, 60 percent of the population of the central district lived in multi-family residences, when the citywide mean was only 18 percent—and the writers whose chronicles of prewar Los Angeles have stuck with us were powerfully shaped by the experience of those denser quarters.[29] Fante's letters to his mother from the early 1930s offer an intimate portrait of life in a "new, little, clean hotel" downtown, "pretty near the Mexican Quarter," and a vision of the centripetal city: from his window Fante watches "the City Hall tower shooting into the air."[30] Narrative imperatives also create an (over)emphasis on the denser inner core. Although Marlowe may track criminality to the single-family homes of the city's finest districts, trails often begin with "poor little slum-bred hard guys," in whose lower-status neighborhoods the incidence of multi-family accommodation was far higher than elsewhere in the city. Thus, although Chandler himself only briefly slummed it downtown, the exigencies of detective story plots inevitably take Marlowe down mean streets that were in fact far less typical of LA's overall residential character than Chandler's long shadow has made them seem to have been.[31] There is, however, a further significant reason as to why the fictional LA of the 1930s and 1940s contains more multi-family housing than did its real-life counterpart: a literary culture preoccupied with frontier dynamics finds those dynamics recuperated more readily in the sociospatial characteristics of multi-family housing forms than in their single-family equivalents.

That recuperation takes many forms, the first of which is the quality of repetition or reproduction intrinsic to multi-family housing. In *The Big Sleep*, Marlowe tails a suspicious character to the cypress-lined doorways of a bungalow court. The repetition of those trees (Marlowe retrieves his mark's discarded pornography from behind "the third cypress") is nested within the larger repeating pattern of the multiple bungalows themselves; that repetition subdivides the mirrored "two rows" in which the bungalows sit, and the double rows within each court are in turn a further sub-factor of lot-level or block-level repetition (there are three adjacent bungalow courts on the street).[32] The effect is fractal-like: the architectural form unfolds its own procedurally generated maze, layering compounded series of identical images. Even the court's name, "The La Baba," contains a redundancy.[33] The "staggered row of six bungalows" of the earlier Chandler story "The King in Yellow," although described as "not strictly a bungalow court," has the same Escherian quality of an intersecting, hard-to-parse visual puzzle composed of duplicate structures, "all facing the same way, but so-arranged that no two of their front entrances overlooked each other."[34]

Such *mise-en-abyme* proliferation, created by the court's intrinsic multiplicity (see figure 4.1), produces a space of frontierlike character: an arrangement of cognitive obstacles, it challenges and resists Marlowe, it is hard to read and navigate, it lends itself to confusion and deception. Marlowe encounters difficulties in navigating certain single-family dwellings too, but it is not, crucially, any specific characteristic or quirk of the La Baba as an individual *example* of the apartment court that generates its challenge to Marlowe's interrogative faculties.[35] Rather, the difficulties presented to the spatial progress of Marlowe's investigation inhere in

192 | The Recursive Frontier

Figure 4.1. La Vista Terrace, Westlake (c. 1925). This typical prewar California bungalow court stood a mile or so northwest of downtown at 327 Columbia Avenue. Like so much Los Angeles of that era, it no longer exists, but the vast Mary Andrews Clark Memorial Home, looming in the background, still does, helping to mark the spot that La Vista Terrace once occupied. *Source*: Los Angeles Area Chamber of Commerce Collection 1890–1960, University of Southern California Libraries and California Historical Society. Public domain.

the nature of the court as a building *type*. The multiplicity innate to *all* multi-family structures is what generates a frontierist obstructive landscape. Like Chandler's plots, the multi-family dwelling structure is itself a compilation of convincing aliases.

This intrinsic formal repetition more broadly suggests the frontier's (impossible) demand for inexhaustible iterability. If the form of an apartment can be generated twenty times within a single building, it implies the possibility of twenty more. While those repetitions *could* be external (as in the case of three adjacent courts of the same design), they will *always* appear internally to each example of the form, as an inevitable consequence of its containing multiple units. The multi-family unit thereby makes a claim to frontier characteristics far more fundamental than those that have historically been attributed to the single-family home. The single-family dwelling, in California even more than elsewhere in the country, was held to symbolize the homesteading values of the early settlers who tamed the frontier.[36] It did so not only in the architectural echoes of pioneer-day structures (the ranch house, the mission revival style) that were so popular from the late nineteenth- to at least the mid-twentieth century, but in the connotations of individual freedom and the agrarian ideal present in a detached home standing free on its own large plot.[37] Early twentieth-century suburban America sought to "domesticate" the "themes" of the frontier ideal, with the front lawn as a "middle-class embodiment" of the "subjugation of nature to the rule of civilization."[38]

Characteristics intrinsic to the single-family home, however, preclude the frontierist suggestion of perpetual repeatability that multi-family dwellings are able to make.[39] This is particularly apparent in the case of LA's prewar residential architecture, mocked by Tod Hackett for the relentless inauthenticity of its heterogeneous appropriation of alien architectural styles. Yet the capacity of the single-family house to suggest its own ongoing replication remains limited even in the postwar era of Banham's ticky-tacky flatland, when prefabrication, mass production, and the increasing tyranny of homeowners' associations created greater uniformity within neighborhoods' residential architectures. In the single-family dwelling, the occupant (especially when that occupant is the owner, as became increasingly likely following the 1949 Housing Act's mortgage insurance provisions) retains at least some degree of control over the external appearance of their home.[40] A bank of ranch bungalows or tract homes, therefore, however standardized, contains the potential for variation and thus cannot imply the spatially infinite and inexhaustible as can the perfect repetition of a bungalow court or a corridor of hotel rooms.

This may appear counterintuitive. The lack of formal and visual distinctions in multi-family housing might intuitively suggest (like the repeating patterns of the office block) the regimented overdetermination of post-frontier modernity. In that vein Theodor Adorno and Max Horkheimer wrote, observing Los Angeles, that "town-planning projects, which are supposed to perpetuate individuals as autonomous units in hygienic small apartments, subjugate them only more completely to their adversary, the total power of capital."[41] That observation, however, is in fact truer of single-family homes, precisely because they promise the "architectural embodiment of individual freedom" only to reveal that promise as wholly false.[42] The single-family home's individualism is disclosed in the moment of its expression as a false veneer, because it resides in and is inextricable from its condition of singular finitude, a condition absolutely antithetical to an open frontier's essential condition of always containing the potential to be found again elsewhere. If one of the properties of a structure is uniqueness, then it cannot, by nature, imply the existence of more things like itself. Difference precludes the prediction of repetition.

Indeed, the larger the tranche of single-family homes, the more likely it is, in diametric opposition to frontier values, to suggest its own participation in spatial exhaustion and depletion—"sing[ing] the praises," per Adorno and Horkheimer, "of technical progress while inviting their users to throw them away after short use like tin cans."[43] Marlowe attests to the literal flimsiness of any claims made by California's single-family homes to embody ideals of individual sovereignty when he remarks that "the only part of a California house you can't put your foot through is the front door."[44] The multi-family dwelling's suggestion of its own capacity to be reiterated endlessly, by contrast, is fundamentally frontierist precisely because it exists as implied possibility rather than actuality. In its existential reliance upon the persistence of future space-to-be-conquered the frontier was always imaginary. The repetitions of the multiple-family dwelling therefore offer an analogue to frontier spatial mechanics but, in the very fact of the theoretical infinite rooming house or apartment court's *nonexistence*, their quality of being always-but-only-ever implied, they evade the exhaustion of the continental frontier.

Referring to a 1931 polemic that decried apartment living as "a sinister trend in American life," Dana Cuff notes that in the early to mid-twentieth century "not only did the house . . . denote a dedication to democracy, but apartments were [seen as] downright un-American."[45] Again the multi-family unit at first glance appears anti-frontierist: living cheek-by-jowl with others suggested compromise not only on space but on individualism and self-determination (and, per Roosevelt's "polyglot boarding-house," proximity to immigrant groups whose absent or debatable whiteness ran counter to the frontierist ideal). In fact, however, the crowded intimacy of the multi-family dwelling proves another means by which it embodies frontierist characteristics in ways unavailable to more visually immediate analogues like the ranch house or tract home, because it confers qualities of spatial conflict and contest. With communal areas, access routes, services, and in some cases even bedrooms themselves shared with others, the multi-family unit takes on the character of a disputed landscape. Spaces are permeable and unstable in designation and ownership; they must be claimed and claimed again. In contrast to what Sean McCann calls the "false privacy of suburbia," in which single-family dwellers constantly surveil each other but cannot name and challenge their surveillance as such because it works to maintain distance and separation between them, active and direct contestation of personal spatial sovereignty and privacy is an inbuilt environmental condition of multi-family housing.[46]

In *The Day of the Locust*, Tod Hackett's first encounter with a furious Abe Kusich is entirely unsolicited and the direct result of an argument between Kusich and another Mirabella resident. In *Ask the Dust*, Camilla Lopez can occupy Arturo Bandini's Bunker Hill hotel room uninvited, entering via the window. The same author's "The Dreamer" finds Cristo Serra jealously guarding his privacy from his rooming house's intrusive proprietor and trading access to his bathroom for favors from other residents. Likewise, in the boarding house of Fenton's *What Way My Journey Lies*, John Norman is constantly imposed and intruded upon by his eccentric neighbors Ray Bowen and Elisha Hare. Exploiting the spatial porousness of the boarding house, Bowen and Hare continually draw Norman into philosophical discourses, seeking to claim him on behalf of their respective worldviews. In occupying the space of the boarding house, each individual has his conception of the world persistently challenged; intellectual self-defense is required at all times to preserve a coherence and sovereignty in one's own sense of being. The walls of the men's respective bedrooms, in which their various conversations occur, model the personal interiorities that are intruded upon and challenged by the alternate consciousnesses (and physical presences) of others.

The sociolegal conditions of single-family living (especially in its "ideal" state of owner-occupancy), on the other hand, ultimately secure and celebrate the very *lack* of spatial contest that denotes the frontier's absence. John Laslett writes that "the frontier, its history, and the theory of property rights" conspired to an "ideal of private property" that was "one of complete freedom for the owner, as if, once across the property boundaries, the 'law of the land' was one's own."[47] This notion that in buying a single-family home one buys a plot of land that is sovereign through property rights, impregnably one's own and impossible for others to seize, may recall the frontier's "aggressive legacy of taking and laying claim to land," as Cuff suggests, but is in fact entirely *counter* to the frontier's values of restless, protean instability.[48] On the frontier, there is no such thing as "home"; if the conditions of stability, familiarity, comfort, and security have arrived, the frontier has departed. Indeed, Cuff notes that within the ideal of single-family living only "detached, privately owned houses . . . deserved to be called 'home' at all."[49] Such a distinction reflects the extent to which the affective qualities that are popularly held to differentiate a "home" from a mere dwelling place, which are also qualities antithetical to the frontier, were deemed unachievable in multi-family housing. The single-family home embodies the characteristics not of those who *opened* the frontier but of those who *closed* it, who sought stable, permanent claims to home and harvest.

By contrast, the close-quartered, semi-communal qualities of living in multi-family housing suggest, especially in their predominant less salubrious forms, the frontierlike qualities of social marginality, provisionality, instability, and ephemerality.[50] Like the frontier, they represent a mode of living in which mobility is not only possible but necessary: the rooming house or apartment hotel, paid for by the night, week, or month, is a space for a resident unable or unwilling to seek long-term commitments or a stable base. Prewar LA boosters touted the socially "stabilizing" effects of the single-family, owner-occupied home, and even the idea that the security of Southern Californian home ownership offered "redemption" to internal migrants who had arrived from cities with higher rental rates.[51] Likewise, the Goodyear Tire Company's 1919 plan to build a company town of affordable houses close to its Los Angeles plant was underpinned by a "belief in homeownership as a stabilizing social influence" and confident association between possession of a single-family home and civic complaisance.[52] Multi-family housing, meanwhile, was firmly "associated with populations that were transient, indigent, or transitioning to single-family accommodation"—the yet-to-be-redeemed or the irredeemable.[53] A 1950 citywide survey found only 12.8 percent of LA's owner-occupied residences were multi-family, compared with 75.5 percent of the rented structures.[54] Thus multi-family residences permit, indeed demand, the kind of restless, unstable mobility that characterized the frontier, in a way that the single-family home cannot. This is evocatively suggested by a document compiled by Joyce Fante using her husband John's surviving correspondence, which discloses that he changed his address at least twenty-nine times in his early rooming-house days in Los Angeles, the years 1932–1935—once, on average, every fifty days.[55]

Multi-family units thereby have the potential to enmesh their occupants less than their single-family counterparts in the formal administrative structures of law, government, and capital—the inbuilt "contractual nature" of such communities.⁵⁶ The owner-occupied single-family home appears to give the resident personal sovereignty but in fact grips them inextricably in a governmental-legal complex of mortgages, covenants, and deeds—the very structures that frontiersmen sought to escape. The single-family home's notional manifestation of a frontierist "ideal of autonomy" could never be "fully achieved" because it depended paradoxically for its perpetuation on the binding anti-frontier structures of law, civic administration, and community standards.⁵⁷ The rented room, by contrast, the space of false names, short notice periods, and cash rents, grants its occupants a freedom from societal ties concomitant with its double-edged grant of enforced spatial mobility.

The sense that multi-family housing betokens a frontierlike sense of detachment from intrusive sociolegal structures takes on its most uncomfortable inflection among the seedy rooming houses and hotels of neglected downtown areas, identified by city planners as semi-lawless "blighted" slums that required reformation or demolition. A 1947 municipal report describes Bunker Hill and surrounding areas as "visibly blighted and occupied by old rooming houses, transient hotels, and single-family slum-like structures," implying both that the presence of poor-quality single-family housing is symptomatic of its proximity to multi-family housing, and that "blight" is the inevitable consequence of a neighborhood so composed.⁵⁸ The multi-family slums of "blighted" downtown are figured not only in such planners' reports but also in fiction as semi-lawless spaces of danger, uncertainty, marginality, ephemerality, and resistance to the intervening hand of paternalistic government. Consider Philip Marlowe's comment about Bunker Hill hotels in which "only Smith and Jones sign the register."⁵⁹ Similarly, Marlowe can ascertain information on Agnes Lozelle's whereabouts from the manager of her "flop" by threatening that he "know[s] all about Bunker Hill apartment houses" as places where (criminal) living seeks privacy and leaves a light footprint.⁶⁰ Likewise, Arturo Bandini is subject only to a perfunctory interview before being admitted to the Alta Loma—Mrs. Hargreaves cares not for Bandini's proof of income (i.e., his writing work); he must simply promise that he is neither Mexican nor Jewish.⁶¹

Like Roosevelt's invocation of the "polyglot boarding-house," however, Hargreaves's paranoia about Mexican or Jewish presences in her rooms provides a reminder that multi-family accommodation, especially the insalubrious manifestations thereof that characterized the city's "blighted" central areas, was disproportionately populated by ethnic minorities. A 1944 report recorded that LA's central core was in 1940 not only the city's only majority-minority area but also the area with the lowest proportion of single-family dwellings, the highest proportion of multi-family units, and the lowest proportion of home ownership.[62] The same area contained by far the city's highest proportion of unsanitary dwellings and dwellings without running water, as well as the city's oldest housing stock.[63] Indeed, there was a direct association between multi-family housing, age of housing, and unsanitary conditions, because much of LA's cheap downtown multi-family units had been converted shoddily from older, single-family houses. A 1938 report assesses Bunker Hill and surrounding areas thus:

> Old families moved away, leaving their homes behind for transformation into boarding and rooming houses. . . . Living and sanitary conditions . . . are poor. . . . The rooming houses are practically all from forty-five to fifty years old. . . . Plumbing and sanitary equipment are of the oldest type and generally in bad repair. . . . No reasonable provision was made for light or air in the construction of these barracks.[64]

As the 1947 report on "blighted" conditions admits, ethnic minorities were concentrated in such areas both because of economic circumstances and because they were "precluded from settling [elsewhere] by restrictive covenants."[65] The latter factor was felt particularly acutely by the city's African American population, who "had long chafed at the racial restrictions they faced in their search for housing," restrictions among the nation's most extensive.[66] Those restrictions were not substantially challenged until after World War II. The vast wartime increases in LA's African American population discussed in the previous chapter had "overtaxed the city's already crowded black neighborhoods" and created tensions in newly multiethnic neighborhoods like Little Tokyo/Bronzeville, rendering a challenge to LA's "legal ghetto" newly urgent.[67] (Even then, however, vehement white resistance persisted.) Thus, to be a member of an ethnic minority in prewar or wartime LA was to occupy in likelihood the lowest quality multi-family housing, in the city's most deprived areas. It was therefore also to experience a mode of living that may have predominated in those particular areas (as it does in LA fiction of the period) but that, in the broader context of a city where single-family living was the norm, matched and enforced one's own social marginality.[68]

The characters who receive extended readings later in this chapter are white and have at least some agency in actively choosing multi-family housing, with its qualities of transience, contest, and social detachment, as the mode of life best suited to their frontierist traits. The association between racial marginality and multi-family accommodation, however, has implications for my earlier discussions of ethnic/racial minority characters who find themselves "forced" to perform frontiersmanship without ever benefiting from it—Bob Jones, Arturo Bandini, Julio Sal, Chu Chu Ramirez. Indeed, of those four characters only Bob Jones lives in a single-family house, and even his "small, four-room cottage" exhibits characteristics more commonly associated with multi-family housing. It sits "back in a court" rather than on its own sovereign plot and is so perfunctory in its form as to become a contested space where one cannot avoid "casual intimacy."[69] If multi-family housing evinces frontierlike characteristics, then ethnic minorities' economic and legal compulsions to occupy it suggest once more a setting and a culture in which frontier conditions may be sought by white figures but are imposed upon nonwhite figures—ironically, by the same racist logic that denies them the possibility of fully occupying the frontiersman's (white) image.

The sense that multi-family living, whether by individual choice or structural disadvantage, enfolds its occupants less fully than single-family living in the social bonds of a contractual community is paralleled by a sense that, because multi-family housing is often intended for lone individuals, it lacks the "linkage [with] the nuclear family" that defines the single-family home.[70] In chapter 2, we saw how the supposedly feminizing effects of the office placed "American manhood [in] crisis as the frontier gave way to urban sprawl"; another of the "feminine institutions of civilization" by which the "masculine frontier was . . . crowded out" was the "'woman's world' of the home."[71] The frontier is figured in Turnerian and post-Turnerian discourse as a rejection of the social expectations, structures, and routines of domestic life, and their supposedly "feminizing" influence. Thus, the end of the frontier presented "a crisis for American males" because it forced them "to accept living in a *place*, in a community, in a social environment, interacting with other men doing the same," becoming "fathers with children to support."[72] Modern domestic life, in other words, represents the kinds of sociospatial ties and commitments that were antithetical to frontiersmanship. Multi-family accommodation seems to offer a sociospatial escape from a domestic world of antifrontierist demasculinization. As on the frontier, this is not necessarily because women were not present in multi-family accommodation. Orrin Quest in Chandler's *The Little Sister* (1949), *In a Lonely Place*'s Laurel Gray, and *What Way My Journey Lies*'s Mary Carter all live in multi-family settings (the latter two challenging, as I will later show, male characters' attempts to assert gendered control over their living environments). Contemporary reportage likewise records women of varying social classes living in both single- and mixed-sex multi-family accommodation.[73]

Multi-family housing can nevertheless stand, for its male occupants, in opposition to the domestic ideal simply by virtue of *not* being a single-family home and because the social and physical characteristics of multi-family housing in themselves suggest the rejection of domesticity. Some families *were* forced through privation to live in multi-family accommodation, but the emphasis on single-room units in many multi-family housing forms (the hotel, the rooming house, the boarding house) conveys their ill-suitedness to family life. We still speak in tellingly gendered terms of a "bachelor apartment." To live in a single room or small apartment is to identify oneself as the man alone, free of family ties and the feminizing influence of long-term attachments to women and children. A man's decision to live in multi-family housing may be conceived as a frontierist gesture because it represents an evasion of the restrictions placed upon independent movement and action by the spaces, structures, and conventions of anti-frontierist domesticity. When Frank Seiberling, Goodyear's founder-president, declared in 1919 that his LA company town was for "family men," he opined that a lack of single-family homes in which to express familial domesticity engendered social "unrest."[74] Seiberling unwittingly commented on the inimicality of the single-family home to any frontierlike existence: conditions of "unrest" are what frontiersmanship demands and perpetuates.

Paradoxically, to live in the contested spaces of multi-family housing enables the profoundly individualist and frontierist gesture of fitting one's space to oneself, of choosing a unit of space that indulges no excess of social commitment, accommodating the needs of the individual only and thus refusing to admit the possibility of any non-individualist mode of living. It may seem contradictory to claim, as I have, that multi-family housing exhibits frontierist spatial practice both because its occupants' personal space is constantly vulnerable to contest from others' ingress *and* because it represents a redoubt of individualism uncompromised by invasive bonds of legal commitment, communitarian responsibility, or feminizing domesticity. In fact, these two qualities reinforce each other, as an episode in *The Big Sleep* illustrates. Marlowe's Hobart Arms apartment is a space so pared back to the basic needs of the lone ascetic that it has only a Murphy bed, implying no need of readiness for intimate company; such small indulgences as the apartment does accommodate are the solitary, "masculine" pleasures of smoking, drinking, and chess problems. The space is both Marlowe's literal refuge from female interest and a metaphor for his aloofness from women. When Carmen Sternwood enters unauthorized, she demonstrates the apartment building's quality of spatial contestation and permeability: assuring the manager that she is expected merely by flashing Marlowe's card, she exploits the spatial practice of a place where "mysterious" women are par for the course and nobody much cares who comes or goes.[75] The contest she instigates with Marlowe is premised not merely on her spatial presence in the apartment but on her femininity's threat to the apartment's values of lone masculinity.

It isn't Carmen's proximity to his person that Marlowe cannot stand, but explicitly her presence in "that room," because this is "the room" he "had to live in."[76] This is accommodation choice as existential necessity: he has to live there because this is the only kind of living space that can sustain a man of Marlowe's (frontiersmanlike) character. As its values have hitherto been of exclusive masculinity, "that room" ceases to exist with the introduction of a feminine presence. A new space is produced, one Marlowe cannot "live in": the spatial threat is a mortal one. In rejecting Carmen's advances and ejecting her from the apartment, however, Marlowe proves the possibility of making "that room" new through strength of male character and thereby reasserts that the space and he within it *are* defined by values of masculine individualism. The apartment thus replicates the paradox whereby the frontier is a space suited to the heroic individual precisely because it is hostile to him. The frontiersman cannot prove his ruggedness without conditions that threaten to overmaster his ruggedness; vulnerability occasions strength. Likewise, Marlowe is enabled to assert his apartment's values of lone masculinity precisely by the space's vulnerability to the threat of an incursive feminine presence. He thereby illustrates that the multi-family unit's identity as a space that facilitates evasion (or, for the less privileged, denies the possibility) of social entanglements does not undermine but rather compounds the frontierist identity that such accommodations simultaneously derive from their quality of continual spatial contest.

War Machines: The Veteran Problem as Frontier (Dis)closure

Dorothy B. Hughes's *In a Lonely Place* and Frank Fenton's *What Way My Journey Lies* both stage oppositions between the cultural values of single- and multi-family accommodation as a contest over the contemporary viability of their protagonists' frontier-aligned masculinities. Although their chronological settings are slightly different, both novels sit in a corridor of uncertainty around the end of World War II, wherein the shape of the world to come, and within it the role of men like Hughes's Dix Steele and Fenton's John Norman, were yet to be determined.[77] The experiences of World War II and uncertainties about how to build a post-discharge life and masculine identity plunge these men into divergent forms of crisis.

These texts occupy, along with Chandler's *The Long Goodbye*, a wider contemporary genre of narratives about traumatized veterans.[78] Such works were particularly prominent in cinema: examples include *The Best Years of Our Lives* (1946), the Hughes adaptation *Ride the Pink Horse* (1947), *Crossfire* (1947), *Home of the Brave* (1949), and *The Men* (1950). These narratives bespoke widespread concerns, voiced elsewhere in public discourse by "experts in social work, the military, and the social sciences," about "combat fatigue" or "the veterans problem."[79] The return of vast numbers of demobilized soldiers, it was feared, could provoke a "social crisis," if the veterans could not "revers[e] some of the 'hard-boiled' habits which the army demands," reconcile themselves to "the normal pace of civilian life," and productively sublimate antisocial instincts arising from the "anger and isolation" of combat trauma.[80]

In 1944, sociologist Willard Waller summarized the unique challenges presented by the veteran to society:

> The veteran who comes home is . . . the major social problem of the next few years . . . because we have used him up, sacrificed him, wasted him. No man could have a better moral claim to the consideration of his fellows. And no man could have a better right to bitterness.
>
> But the veteran, so justly entitled to move us to pity and to shame, can also put us in fear. Destitute he may be . . . but weak he is not. That makes him a different kind of problem. That hand that does know how to earn its owner's bread knows how to take your bread, knows very well how to kill you, if

need be, in the process. . . . Unless and until he can be renaturalized into his native land, the veteran is a threat to society.[81]

For Waller, the veteran presents a conundrum because he has undertaken actions that place "his fellows" in moral and material debt to him but that have simultaneously rendered him incompatible with those "fellows" and the values governing their world. Waller thereby suggests why a veteran masculinity reproduces a frontier masculinity. The soldier inherits the frontiersman's paradoxical condition of stepping beyond the bounds of society, not just spatially but in his actions and values, in order to act on behalf of that society.[82] Reed Bonadonna's description of the solider—"both the least and most civilized of persons . . . walk[ing] the weird wall at the edge of civilization . . . prepared to serve their civilization and society without stint or limit" but "constantly in danger of forsaking that which they serve"—could be applied to the Turnerian frontiersman without emendation.[83] Indeed, "the weird wall at the edge of civilization" is near-synonymous with Turner's mutable "hither edge."

Wallerite anxieties about reintegrating the returning soldier into civilian life anticipate the concept of the "war machine" advanced by Gilles Deleuze and Félix Guattari, who write that the "military institution" is not intrinsic to the state; the latter can only "appropriate" the former.[84] This, however, will "continually cause [the state] problems" because the military institution is appropriated by and to serve a set of values to which its own are antithetical. The state's self-professed civil identity is compromised by its complicity with and dependence upon "another kind of justice, one of incomprehensible cruelty at times."[85] The state requires and must internalize a war machine in order to assert itself, but cannot reconcile itself to the fact that "the war machine is . . . of another species, of another nature, of another origin."[86] Just as the frontiersman abnegates himself in discharging his social purpose of frontier conquest, the soldier (especially the wartime volunteer or conscript, as opposed to the career professional) becomes existentially redundant ("used up") at the moment he succeeds in his task of defeating the enemy. In the very moment of achieving the purpose assigned to him by society, the soldier/frontiersman is, per Deleuze and Guattari, "returned to [his] milieu of exteriority" in relation to that society, revealed as an actor with values counter to those on behalf of which he has been acting.[87] It is thus at this moment—the end of the war, the end of the frontier—that the soldier/frontiersman, still possessed of all the traits by which he had come to define himself on the battlefield or in the wilderness but suddenly shorn of the capacity to exercise them, is at his most dangerous as a socially destabilizing force.

In the process of suggesting possible manifestations of this destabilization, Hughes's and Fenton's novels further reveal the salience of a frontiersman-veteran ideological lineage. On being invalided out of combat and returning to America, John Norman is plunged into existential crisis by the war's revelation of "the limitless stupidity of the earth"—yet in some sense he wishes a return to the conditions of war, because the peacetime world by contrast seems "unreal."[88] The phrase "we're dead, aren't we?" recurs frequently in his inner monologue, suggesting that to have survived war (and thus to be forced to live on into peacetime) is as much a death as those of his fallen comrades.[89] Dix Steele exhibits a striking contiguity of sentiment in his belief that war "was so real that there wasn't any other life" afterward.[90] Neither man can self-define absent the wartime conditions that have shaped his consciousness.

Dix Steele's conception of this predicament collocates his loss of the spatial liberation he had felt as a pilot, an ironic sense that only in wartime did he feel in control of his destiny, and a belief that peacetime's expectations of "feminizing" domesticity undermine his masculinity. Replicating the thrill of war in the violent subjugation of women lends Dix not only the feeling of "power and exhilaration and freedom" he once felt in flight, but also its "loneness," because the murders he commits are acts that simultaneously possess women and reject women.[91] In spatial terms, each of Dix's crimes manifests itself as at once a drawing-close and a casting-out: he picks up women then, after raping and murdering them, discards them on beaches or in canyons. He thereby violently asserts that "loneness" is a state he can choose rather than one imposed upon him by women's perceived caprices. Frontierist concerns are implicit in a psychopathy that so closely associates spatial freedom with the violent assertion of masculine selfhood in supposed defense of itself. Where the frontiersman was threatened both by the "civilization" he escaped and by the wilderness he conquered, women for Dix appear to perform both threats: his claims to rugged, individualist masculinity reside simultaneously in proving himself able to possess them as territory *and* in cutting himself free of their feminizing influence. He echoes Marlowe, who struggles to resolve heteromasculine attraction to Carmen Sternwood's body with a revolted sense that her body's presence in his apartment attenuates its, and his, masculinity: Dix makes explicit the violence latent in Marlowe's crisis.

John Norman's complexes are more prosaic and less overtly destructive but underpinned by comparable concerns. Fenton's novel is peopled with characters trying to make sense of the change the war has wrought upon the world, but where John's many interlocutors seem confident in their competing visions of the future and their places within it, he is gripped by uncertainty. John, we are told, "knew nothing . . . because of the war."[92] Like Terry Lennox, Chandler's literally scarred veteran, John is struck repeatedly by "the uselessness of himself" in the face of the postwar world's unknowability.[93] For John, this results in a paradox of stasis and restlessness—something he holds in common with the mythic frontiersman, whose perpetual need for further free land is a moving-to-stay-still. Like the frontiersman, who exists in the moment of being *about* to move into always-open "free land" rather than in its actual conquest and consequent (self-)erasure, John "live[s] on the verge of doing something."[94] Throughout the novel he makes impulsive, seemingly decisive spatial departures, only to follow these with counteractive retreats, a repeating process that maps his characteristic combination of psychological restiveness and paralysis.

That this spatially expressed crisis of selfhood is ultimately, like Dix's, a crisis of masculinity is disclosed in the fact that these cycles of motion and retreat track the dynamics of John's romantic relationships. He shares, albeit without violence, Dix's confusion as to whether he craves or wishes to reject female companionship. John's acts of evading the overwhelming uncertainty of the postwar condition are always acts of distancing himself from, then returning to, the influence of women and their supposed domesticating effects on the male psyche. As a friend tells him, John is an "escapist," and like those of the frontiersman John's escapes are from restrictions imposed upon his mobility and agency by social entanglements.[95] He is also like the frontiersman, though, in that he fears making his escapes final because to do so would in fact represent a termination of his motile agency (in which he vests a selfhood of masculine individualism) far more conclusive than an act of choosing *not* to escape. Where Hughes's murderous protagonist vindicates the very worst "veterans problem" anxieties, Fenton offers something closer to what Christopher Breu terms a "sentimentalized" image of 'the soldier out of step with postwar life."[96] Both men's crises of frontierist masculinity, however, reveal themselves in their navigations of and between multi-family accommodation and the single-family home.

"A Hell of a House": Frank Fenton's *What Way My Journey Lies*

Throughout Frank Fenton's *What Way My Journey Lies* the domesticity of single-family living denotes safety and comfort—but also stasis, a blunting of the senses, an atrophying of masculinity and individualism. It stands in contrast to the boarding house, populated largely by single men possessed of both their own individual spaces and the ability to make periodic incursions into each other's. The novel is structured around feints away from (and, ultimately, returns to) domesticity by John Norman. First, he abandons a cottage bequeathed to him by his fallen comrade Clark when the initially comforting presence of Clark's former girlfriend Carol ultimately proves an entrapment, and seeks out a boarding house. When its qualities of masculine self-determination become compromised by the feminine presence of schoolteacher Mary Carter, however, John withdraws again to Clark's cottage. He returns to Mary, weds and buys a home with her, but makes one final attempt at evading the life she represents before finally submitting to it.

"I used to remember how he described this place and how good it was," John tells Carol when they meet in Clark's cottage on the California coast. "I thought I needed something like this."[97] Like McCoy's pier-end dancehall, the San Pedro bunkhouses of Fante's Filipino laborers, or Himes's Atlas Yard, "this place" draws attention to the California shoreline's identity as a symbolic as well as geographic point of continental termination. John recalls Clark describing the house's end-of-the-world isolation in positive terms: "Behind it, across the road, are the hills. The front yard is the beach, and the sea goes all the way to the South Pole. You get in there between the sea and the hills and you'll be in good shape, Johnny."[98] John's initial reactions to the house's proximity to continent's end are likewise of wonder: a window on the sea is a "magic casement."[99] Terror, however, is latent within Clark's description of the house's geographic location. This is a place from which there is nowhere left to go, with nothing ahead but sea and only hills behind; to seek Chandler's "country beyond the hill" here is to retreat. John discovers this entrapment when walking the beach on foggy days, "as the hills shut off the continent, the fog shut out the horizon . . . reducing his world to this long curving strip of sand."[100]

Initially, Carol's presence betokens a comforting return to a prewar order. "For the first time in a long time . . . he had a telephone number to remember. . . . It was like old times . . . like being home again."[101] Thoughts of Carol initially give John "inrushes" of the "reality" he finds so elusive elsewhere in postwar life.[102] Almost as soon as he has these fond thoughts, however, John experiences a sudden change of heart and escapes to Los Angeles. A relationship with a woman makes life at the cottage "feel like home again," but that is precisely the problem. "Home" is immediately refigured as a space produced by female presence, whereas previously the cottage, although a single-family home, had been for John a male preserve (representing the homosocial bond of his friendship with Clark). As soon as a house becomes a home, John must leave.

The urge to move on is subconscious; John cannot "account for" this "impulse," a "reflex action working separate from his consciousness," yet he obeys it.[103] This "reflex" to absent himself "without even waiting for another night to pass" from the comforts of secure and stable lodging, a warm fire, Clark's copious library, and Carol's affections, discloses a frontier psychology. John is seized by "irresistible restlessness," but moreover a sense that in leaving the cottage he is fleeing "an unrealized peril."[104] Because the frontierist mindset is defined by persistent movement and deliberate exposure to hazard, stability and comfort paradoxically become "peril," and vice versa: so it is for John. To a frontiersman, Clark's one-time glowing description of "a hell of a house," one that could offer "the damnedest vacation," revises itself as horribly literal.[105]

John knows LA well: his arrival there is a joyous return. "Even the confusion of the city streets, though sometimes momentarily disconcerting, was good again."[106] Fenton apprehends the same feeling as Fante's Bandini, returning to early 1930s LA after his own self-imposed exile in *Dreams from Bunker Hill*. Arturo describes the cobblestones as "soft and comforting as old shoes," but his definition of comfort is counterintuitive: it inheres in the streets' "tempting" and "beckoning" invitation to discover the yet-unknown.[107] Through a ritual of retreat and return, Arturo revivifies the place, making it new, and it is likewise for John Norman. He is greeted by the "iron rumble of the street cars," by pedestrians who "scurry" between "enormous beehives of office buildings," by "grave façades" of civic structures and the "self-absorbed and antlike" traffic.[108]

The hymenopteric imagery has the potential to suggest the dehumanized institutionalism of the modern corporate city that Marlowe and Huff protest in their office negotiations. For Norman, though, this potentially disorienting, alienating scene is preferable to Clark's house because "it was not dreaming on its tail in the sand of some lonely and wasted beach": John has sought out the city not despite its "devious ways" but because of them.[109] This swarming metropolis makes a constant multisensory assault upon the individual body, offering conditions of contest and hazard unattainable in the sovereign isolation of Clark's comfortable cottage. Although Fenton describes the city John sees as "the familiar pattern of civilization at work," his enjoyment of the "confusion" of the "devious," "disconcerting" city suggests that its appeal lies in the potential for a surfeit of "civilization" to be (as it was for Marlowe and Huff) a wilderness as challenging to individual will as the literal one it supplants.[110]

That John's new environment is defined by spatial contest and conquest is affirmed as he strikes up a barroom conversation with Chester, a marine on furlough. "I can't find a room," says John. "It's a crowded city."[111] Chester is a man of straightforward solutions:

> "What you ought to do is easy," Chester said. "You oughta take one of them punks and throw them out in the street. Then you got a room."
> Norman laughed.
> "Nah," Chester said seriously. "I'll go along with you on your side. We'll find some punk and toss him out. You done nineteen months belting out Krauts and then come home with your pratt full of steel, so the least you got coming is a soft seat in a nice room. Did a guy come up to you in a foxhole and ask for the rent?"
> Norman shook his head.
> "Nah, you could stay there free."
> "Chester, you come back and there's a big change."[112]

John and Chester's remarks on a spatially contested city where rooms are hard to find reflect a genuine housing crisis that afflicted LA at the end of the war, attested to by a 1945 municipal report. Demand for public war housing had already been inflated by vast wartime in-migrations of industrial workers; when the influx of demobilized veterans exacerbated that situation it caused "a housing shortage unexcelled in the city's history."¹¹³ Seventy-three percent of LA's war housing comprised temporary accommodations, including dormitory beds and trailers, furthering the sense that veterans returned to a city where their defense of "civilization" on the battlefield was rewarded only with another frontierlike landscape to navigate: a residential paradigm characterized by instability and provisionality.¹¹⁴ For Chester, men who have proved themselves patriotically and physically in combat have both the moral right to expect precedence in occupying the city's spaces and the bodily wherewithal to assert forcibly that precedence over less deserving occupants. Chester envisions precisely the kind of violent calling-in of wartime debts that Waller feared.

These undeserving occupants are termed "punks," implying inexperience and unworldliness (set against the well-traveled, battle-scarred veterans) and of apprentice-level, petty criminality ("punk" implies pretensions to criminal violence against John and Chester's history of both real and righteous killing).¹¹⁵ Also unavoidable in this context of ejecting from their beds unsuspecting men who lack a veteran masculinity is the archaic sense of "punk" as denoting an older man's passive same-sex partner or a homosexual more generally.¹¹⁶ The term's use also deepens Chester's veteran fraternity with John by invoking a mutual understanding of additional pejorative (and emasculating) implications of "punk" specific to military slang.¹¹⁷ For Chester, the hierarchical distinction between veterans and the imagined "punk" is (ironically, given the geopolitical aims of the wartime service from which he draws his authority) a near fascistic one. It not only pits a combative, war-burnished, performatively patriotic, strong-willed masculinity against a cowardly, callow, scapegoated effeminacy, it also depends on its own continual violent self-assertion. In proposing such masculinist social vigilantism, Chester simultaneously recalls LA's reputation for bloody vigilante justice in the frontier era and attests to the flimsiness of any sense of community, contractual or otherwise, in the rented room.¹¹⁸ Even prior legal agreement between tenant and landlord, vested in the systems of the paper-based modern world, can be dismissed with brute strength.

There is thus a close communion between Chester's worldview and discourses that framed the clerking types of the new, office-bound, corporate America as lacking the rugged, nation-building manhood of the frontiersman. The kind of spatial acquisition that Chester proposes envisions a restoration of a supposed "natural" masculine order not merely for the veteran but also for the defenestrated punk. The veterans penetrate the room from the outdoor world effeminately avoided by the punk, to seize a figure who, like the clerk of antimodernist invective, luxuriates in a closeted interiority unearned by masculine toil. Moreover, though, in "throw[ing] him out on the street" Chester would demand he reenter a competitive, contested environment against which he would be compelled to assert and impose himself. Thus, while the conquest of the punk's space enforces metaphorically the image of the passive homosexual—the violation of the intimate space of his room, the non-consensual seizure of his body—it would, Chester implies, simultaneously restore to him the potential for masculine agency. For Chester, to enact quasi-sexually his and John's heteromasculine superiority over the punk is ironically a way to "make a man" of their effeminate inferior.

Chester assures John that this is a time when the "real" men will return and reclaim a feminized "punk" world for and through hypermasculinity. John, meanwhile, suspects that the "big change" to which they are subject is a postwar domestic culture's embarrassed rejection of the conquistadorial ethics of wartime. Not only does Norman consider his first glorious hours back in Los Angeles "a day of gold out of an age of iron," that thought occurs amid a conversation about killing "Japs" and "Krauts," and Chester's idea of a returning soldier's rights. It thereby obtains the context of the war as well as the literal day itself, affirming that for men of John's kind this is a diminished world in which the best they can hope for is a momentary last hurrah.[119] Chester and John embody a dialectic about how war has changed the destiny of American manhood. One reading suggests a land primed by war for the revival of the dynamic individualist masculinity that had powered its advance across the continent a century before. Otherwise, the very fact that war alone could provide a contemporary theatre for the revival of those values might prove their peacetime obsolescence.

Having figured the contest to secure short-term accommodation in the "crowded city" as one battle in a violent national contest *between* masculinities, however, Chester reveals that Norman's ingress upon an intimate fraction of LA is in fact in the gift of women: Chester's girlfriend's mother runs a boarding house. Phoning Mrs. Cramer, "the old lady," Chester clears a social path for Norman, "pour[ing] it on" to secure the entrée.[120] Immediately after boasting about war-proven power of his and John's masculine physicality, Chester is reduced to petitioning women to offer John a room by the rather less martial arts of sweet talk and persuasion. Women (not punks) prove the gatekeepers of the boarding house, and do not yield up its space without consent: it cannot be claimed by a frontiersman's or soldier's direct assault.[121]

While this is no "free land" for frontierist men to claim as they please, however, Cramer determinedly assumes menial subservience to her (almost exclusively) male tenants—despite her status as the space's owner and gatekeeper. Cramer seldom rents John's third-floor room because "it's a long climb up there to clean it" and she deems unconscionable the idea of a male tenant cleaning it himself.[122] Upon Chester's pleading, however, "she'll clean the sonafabitch herself or get some broad to do it."[123] This is, in Cramer's view, woman's labor; she cannot countenance permitting a man to perform it, however willingly he may do so.[124] This defines the spatial practice of the boarding-house room: it is for men to live in but not to work in.

This suggests that, even if Chester's dreams of frontierist forcible seizure of rooms are merely futile boasts, one characteristic of the boarding house that does align it with the sociospatial ethics of the frontier is that of uncompromising, uncompromised masculinity. It is not merely a space in which men dominate (such a qualification would surely exclude few spaces in 1940s America). It is a space conceived as existing for the performance of normative masculinity, and one that thus rejects alternatives thereto, much as Turner and his contemporaries conceived of the frontier as an enormous testing ground for American manhood, a space that "demanded manly exertion."[125] No man who is willing to perform the decidedly *unmanly* exertions of housework will be granted ingress to the space Cramer guards. Paradoxically, the frontierist codes of masculine practice that govern the boarding house and its residents are themselves policed by a woman. These peculiar roles are confirmed as Cramer interrogates her prospective new tenant:

> "There's a bathroom down the hall, with a shower. Are you a man after girls?"
> "I'm a man," he said.
> "There'll be none up here," she said.
> "I doubt it myself."[126]

Mrs. Cramer asks the question about girls with a dual purpose: she impresses upon her boarder that he will not be permitted women in his room, but a satisfactory answer is one that indicates forbearance of his "natural" masculine urges rather than any disclamation of those urges themselves. John's response indicates that Cramer's question is as much about confirming that her guest is indeed "a man" as it is about reminding him of the limits to which he will be permitted to express that masculinity under her roof. John's "I doubt it myself," however, jokingly implies that even though he assuredly has the urges expected of "a man," any lack of girls in his room will be the result of his own aversion to romantic attachments rather than submission to Cramer's rules. A self-deprecating gesture immediately recodes itself as an attempt to subvert female authority, as John (like Marlowe and like Dix) expresses the conundrum of a masculinity that secures itself simultaneously in performing heterosexual desire and in insulating itself from feminine influences.

These exchanges extend the boarding house's implicit promise of a solitary, unfeminized way of life among men (though Mrs. Cramer is a woman, the text persistently figures her as desexualized by her age, widowhood, and physical appearance), but John unexpectedly finds schoolteacher Mary Carter in residence. Although the two fall in love, their relationship is defined by John's persistent attempts to maintain distance from what he perceives as Mary's embodiment of a kind of suffocating domesticity. Just as when he left Carol, John betrays his frontiersmanlike instincts in suddenly abandoning Mary and the boarding house: in the very moment of acquiring the comfort and stability of conjugal domesticity he elects to return to the cottage, gripped by fear of stasis. Where once he saw vivifying excitement in the city's tumult, now he can only see "a dreary march of self-conscious dunces." He is disgusted by these "wonderless children" who embody, he now sees, a "hypnotized" participation in capitalism: "how little their lives had to show for all the storm of energies they poured out . . . all rallying round the dollar bill that was their flag . . . in the murder and catastrophe of their times."[127] John has in most regards refused such a way of living. He does not at this point have a job, and lives in the marginal space of the boarding house. The only respect in which John has capitulated to the codes of postwar American normativity, the twin pursuits of the nuclear family and the dollar bill, is in accepting proto-domestication through his relationship with Mary Carter. John's newfound anxieties about the forms and structures of urban life, expressed in the act of spatially dislocating himself from Mary, result from his participation in them through his relationship with her.

John eventually returns from the cottage to Mary but the cycle of escape and return continues. They marry and buy a house, acceding to the stability of single-family living. Soon, though, John's restlessness surfaces again. Sensing this, Mary suggests that "[a] man" must "have a den with his own things in it." John responds: "What? Tackle and golf clubs? Whiskies on a shelf behind a bar? Hunting prints and a card table for rummy and poker? A closet for outdoor clothes and boots? A blowup snapshot of a string of trout? God, I never want to touch a gun again for the rest of my life. Even if I go fishing I never want to catch a fish. Let the bastards swim."[128] John identifies, and rejects, precisely the ways in which the ideal of suburban single-family domesticity claims a frontier lineage but in fact only offers a superficial burlesque of pioneer life. Where once individualist masculinity had the entire western United States as its psychodramatic proving ground, it is now bathetically reduced to an adult playroom, the outdoors present only in prints, photographs, dead fish. Having experienced in wartime a truly frontiersmanlike life, surviving by one's wits in a hostile environment under the constant threat of death, John is disgusted by the den's transformation of frontier violence into a set of props for the obligatory social performance of mid-century American suburban manhood—something, as Mary says, he "should" have.[129]

The vision of familial domesticity Mary encourages in the den suggestion—a man's life of stable leisure in a single-family home facilitated by a subservient wife—is one she repeatedly advances. Almost a parody of feminine subservience to patriarchal authority, she belittles her own achievements and value, declares her inadequacy to be John's partner, and performs all domestic duties smiling and unprompted. The height of her ambition is, she suggests, to "marry and start a home," thereby "becoming a kitchen-busy housewife."[130] She protests that she is "not beautiful," doesn't drink, abhors swearing, and refers to herself as "dumb" despite an academic background.[131] She tells John that "a man must get tired of looking at the same woman every night, even his wife."[132] That line reflects her equanimous tolerance of John's unexplained absence when he returns to Clark's cottage. When he returns, Mary is an image of domestic servitude, "wearing a white apron and standing by the stove."[133] She accepts his protestations of love within moments and without a word of protest or a demand for any explanation, betraying no frustration at John's soul-searching emotional unavailability while asserting no need for her own spaces of self-discovery or loneliness. Mary appears to present herself in a way that is precisely designed not to threaten John's masculinity: she shrinks herself to inflate his patriarchal authority, attempting to secure and steer in the direction of self-rediscovery a man who no longer knows himself. In thus seeking to please John and restore his masculine selfhood, however, she only plunges him deeper into crisis. That is because she does not apprehend John's frontierist consciousness—his ineluctable tendency to conceive of stability, domesticity, and familial and social commitment as paralyzing threats to individualist agency. By seeking to quell his restlessness, she only increases it.

John's final expression of that restlessness comes after he takes a job in a bookshop owned by the gregarious Deirdre Dodd. Deirdre, though female, is defeminized by the text to a greater extent even than Cramer—distinctly implied in her manner, appearance, and lifestyle to be a lesbian. Evenings carousing with Deirdre and her friends become, for John, another way to avoid marital domesticity. Indeed, Deirdre's combination of masculine presentation and intellectual interests simulate the homosocial camaraderie of wartime drinking sessions with Clark.[134] At the end of an evening spent carousing with Deirdre, John does not want to go home, and rejects Deirdre's advice to phone Mary. He awakes later, downtown, in the bedroom of a pianist named Marie, who has extricated him from a bar fight that he cannot recall. She assures him that nothing untoward has occurred between them, but the similarity between her name and Mary's affirms that John's mere presence here is a kind of spatial infidelity.

John's early-hours walk home across Los Angeles is an arduous westward trek, ending on the verdant greens of a golf course near his house. The tension between California's frontierist and Edenic identities is bathetically modeled: a grueling, hard-to-navigate landscape gives way to an artificial arcadia, signaling that John's hopes of perpetuating a frontiersmanlike existence, evading through perpetual motion the enervating effects of a life of leisure, are forlorn. Mary confirms what the golf course foreshadows. She again accepts John's return instantly and without rancor or query, but makes one stipulation: "don't leave me any more, even for a while."[135] This is not a request but an absolute command. She may, just like Helen in the reverie of Fante's Julio Sal, scramble John's eggs, but it is he who is described as behaving "obediently" in sitting down to eat them.[136] Mary submits to the patriarchal authority of her era, but also demands (as Cramer had) that John submit to his role within that structure. She elevates, privileges, and indulges his masculinity, but on the condition that it is expressed in a particular form. Mary demands a domesticated vision of manhood defined by its place within conjugal, familial life in the single-family home.

A frontier masculinity of course "centers" the singular (white) male in both narrative and power dynamics, but the frontiersman must continually fight for power and space, through individual will and struggle—as in the war, as in the boarding house. The postwar patriarchal domesticity of the single-family home, the offer that Mary makes, by contrast presents patriarchal masculinity as supreme and unchallenged by its immediate environment, but thereby blunts the sociospatial agency of the masculine individualist, subjecting him to no vivifying frontierist insecurity or danger but holding him static in the bonds of family, community, and mortgage payments. John tries to envisage his new life in frontierist terms, imagining "man and wife and child, cat and dog and canary, fighting the battle for survival within the picket moat of their stucco castle." By acknowledging the bathetic form this modern "battle" takes, however, he confesses the tragicomic impossibility of it ever representing a frontierist life. He is now entirely subservient to and subsumed within by property lines, civic obligations, tax demands, and municipal legalese: "Lot 47, tract 6939, in the City of Los Angeles, State of California, as per Map recorded in Book 93, page 50 of Maps in the office of the County Recorder of said county."[137] In finally coming home to the single-family house, John Norman accepts that a frontier masculinity is no longer tenable.

"She Was at Home Here": Dorothy B. Hughes's *In a Lonely Place*

Mary's quiet assault-through-subservience upon John's frontier-veteran masculinity stands in contrast to the sexually and socially confident women who threaten Dix Steele's sense of selfhood throughout *In a Lonely Place* by being individualists themselves. The morning after murdering one such woman, Dix awakes to a ringing telephone in the courtyard apartment he occupies (having murdered its tenant, his friend Mel Terriss). When Steele opens his front door, Hughes signals an intimate textual engagement with frontier logic. "There [is] nothing unusual on the front page" of the newspaper that Steele retrieves from the doormat, only "the ways of civilization." As "civilization" is one of the absolute poles of the Turnerian universe, its perpetual opposite being "savagery," we might wonder about the implications for the setting of this novel in a suggestion that the "ways of civilization" arrive here as news, that "civilization" is something that happens elsewhere, to be consumed vicariously rather than part of the experience of this location.

The paper carries national and international news on its "civilization"-focused front page, but "savage" local stories within—Dix checks page two for any report of the prior night's murder. If the newspaper's arrival denotes a place characterized by "savagery" rather than "civilization," however, the place denoted is not merely Los Angeles in general but the specific doorstep where it lands. Dix's borrowed apartment performs the refinements of "civilization," right down to the quality of the coffee ("Terriss had good stuff"), but this of course only obscures its harboring of the novel's singular "savage" force, the murderous Steele.[138] Dix's apartment, like the frontier, is a place to which "the ways of civilization" must be delivered from without, because they are not the space's "native" conditions. As the inhabitant of that space, Dix immediately occupies a position akin to that of *Double Indemnity*'s Walter Huff—embodying the frontiersman's paradoxical disdain for the very "civilization" he notionally served and rendering explicit the original frontiersman's latent complicity with "savagery" by making himself the agent of its introduction to, rather than its eradication from, his environment. Throughout Hughes's novel, the peculiar spatiality of the apartment court continues to model these complex ambiguities of Dix's toxic frontiersmanship.

Breu notes that *In a Lonely Place* is intimately concerned with conflicts between men and women over "definition[s] of public and private space," but we can be more specific: the novel articulates such "gendered antagonism" over space's meaning most persistently in the peculiarly mutable dynamics of public and private that define its recurring apartment court setting.[139] Hughes's Virginibus Arms enables its residents to present a semblance of sociable community while in fact jealously guarding their privacy. As in Marlowe's apartment the frontierist sense prevails that this space is both individualist (in that these apartments are intended for single people) and contested (in that the presence of others nearby necessitates the jealous guarding and defense of one's own sovereign space). The Virginibus suggests that the apartment court's typological and social characteristics fall somewhere between those of the private dwelling and the more transient, provisional world of the rooming house or residential hotel. Residents occupy self-contained dwellings with direct access to the world outside, yet this access is not to the public realm of the street but to either the balcony or the patio—shared, semi-communal spaces. Those communal areas are prevented from becoming fully public by the court's spatial enclosure and the institutional surveillance of a building manager and janitorial staff. Despite such protection, residents keep to themselves—the patio and its pool are never used. Residents have garages but these are not attached to their homes, and Dix regularly plans his routes to avoid arousing suspicion when walking between the apartments and the garages. There is a productive tension here. The sociospatial form of the building is one that both requires residents to devise strategies to remain hidden *and* permits and enables such strategies.

As Stefanos Polyzoides et al. identify, because the "space enveloped by the court . . . becomes the primary organizing element," the apartment court represents a striking "alternative to the illusory American dream of the freestanding house."[140] External space is made *internal* to the form of the building, unsettling the familiar dichotomy of a sovereign home surrounded by an "outside" world. Thus, the meaning of this internal-external space—shared but not public, a space occupied when outside one's home and yet *part of* one's home—becomes resistant to stable definition. Lewis Mumford once lamented that twentieth-century architecture had "turned from enclosure to exposure . . . all sense of intimacy and privacy . . . forfeited . . . to create a kind of exposed public space for every moment."[141] The apartment court, more radically and unsettlingly, blends enclosure and enclosure imperceptibly, in the same space, to constitute an unstable liminality between the two: its spatial conditions are dangerously ambiguous. For Turner, the frontier denoted the land between the safely, stably settled world and complete wilderness: the apartment court's inscrutable equivocation between the public and private, the communal and the discrete (and, indeed, discreet) seems to model something very similar in an urban context. All these qualities, and what they suggest about the subtle ambiguities of Dix's frontiersmanship, are made apparent when Dix first encounters Laurel:

> He was walking fast. That was why he didn't see the girl until he almost collided with her at the arched street entrance of the patio. It shocked him that he hadn't noticed her, that he hadn't been aware. He stepped back quickly. "I beg your pardon," he said. It wasn't a formality as he said it; shock made each word apology for a grave error. . . .
>
> He didn't move. He stood and watched her. . . . She took her time, skirting the small sky-blue oblong of the pool which lay in the center of the patio. She started up the stairway to the balcony of the second-floor apartments. He swung out of the archway fast. He wouldn't let her reach the balcony, look over the balustrade and see him standing there. He'd find out about her some other way, if she lived here, or whom she visited.[142]

Here, Dix is leaving the court, Laurel entering it. They collide at the very point that marks the division between the liminal public-private space of the patio and the wholly public space of the world outside—the city-as-wilderness. Dix at this point finds himself at the very furthest edge of the apartment court's spatial frontier zone, about to move into the space of greater danger and uncertainty beyond.

Laurel is figured as making an incursion from that space, representative of the unknown and unstable—that which Dix cannot control. The "grave error" that "shocks" him is a failure to have mastered the immediate territory surrounding him—he allows himself to be surprised, ambushed (again the physical characteristics of the court, Dix's vision blocked by a physical barrier to the street beyond, facilitate this). Dix then realizes he remains subject to spatial vulnerability (being captured in the watchful eye of another's surveillance), caught in the public-private netherspace of the patio as Laurel proceeds to the relative sovereignty of her apartment. In either the courtyard or her own apartment, he cannot control her. The power dynamics here are further swayed in her direction by the elevation of her apartment: the insecure Dix is worried about quite literally being looked down upon by a woman, caught in a tactically disadvantageous position.

Dix emerges from the relative safety of his own apartment, and making a journey out into the world is assailed on its "hither edge" by a figure from outside, like the frontiersman journeying from settled land into wilderness. Yet in that very instant the dynamics shift. As Laurel makes for her apartment, the external force threateningly penetrates the boundaries of the court, first destabilizing the idea of the court as a settled space but immediately revealing itself in doing so to in fact be a rightful occupant of that space (which Dix, of course, is not). In this moment, as Laurel heads for her balcony, Dix finds himself a vulnerable entity in the contested, outer-inner space of the patio, yet the force to whose power he is subject has been revealed not to be a "wild" incursion from outside but a resident part of the court's internal condition. Dix seems at once to travel toward and be assailed by forces emanating from the wildness of the external world *and* to represent the wildness of the external world assailed by forces that emanate from within the purview of settled, ordered space. As in his own description of himself as a "lone wolf" (recalling the ambiguous animal imagery of Fante's "To Be a Monstrous Clever Fellow"), it is uncertain if Dix is hunter or hunted, frontiersman or frontier.[143] Dix's first encounter with Laurel thus suggests the complexity and mutability of frontier identity in *In a Lonely Place* and its apartment court.

The court's spatial practice continues to be defined by ambiguous, shifting dynamics of public and private that imply a frontierist tension between the preservation of the individual and an embrace of spatial conflict. The spatial vulnerability Dix feels in his first encounter with Laurel is perpetuated in persistent intrusions upon his privacy by the building manager and maid. His powers to limit these incursions are limited partly because he is not legitimately resident (through violently physical self-assertion he has claimed living space from a man he perceived as undeserving of it, fulfilling the fantasy of Fenton's Chester) and fears drawing attention to the circumstances by which he has "replaced" Terriss. There is, however, no suggestion that either manager or maid ever suspect Dix of killing Mel, while Laurel too invokes their prying eyes as a means of extricating herself from Dix's attentions. The ever-intrusive presence of staff surveillance thus seems suggestive less of Dix's particular anxieties as murderer than the general conditions of apartment court living. Not only space itself but what it signifies is contested: Dix must work continually to keep private space private.

Precisely because Dix is aware of his own vulnerability to surveillance in the court, however, he also knows that Laurel's spatial sovereignty can be undermined. He jokes that he could inveigle himself into her life and space "get[ting] a job reading the light meter or delivering laundry."[144] Like Carmen Sternwood entering Marlowe's apartment, Dix intends to exploit the expectations of multi-family residences as permeable spaces where casual intrusions upon private space are the norm, literally part of the service. Dix proposes such possibilities, however, for the very reason that they are somehow less aberrant within the spatial practice of the court than simply engaging Laurel in open conversation, the approach he will ultimately choose. Dix retrospectively justifies the boldness of that approach as the institution of a new and overdue "good-neighbor policy" at the Virginibus, acknowledging that he understands it as a breach of accepted spatial practice.[145] The sense of unstable bivalence in the court's simultaneous spatial identities of enclosure and exposure is thus present once more. Dix's direct approach to Laurel is aberrant because it breaks the codes of a space designed for privacy and maintained as such by its residents, where "you don't even see" your neighbor, but the alternative methods of approach he imagines exploit the conditions of a space where residents actively *expect* to find their privacy intruded upon.[146]

The space's combination of privacy and permeability simultaneously threatens and benefits Dix, further revealing his character as a frontierist—both a lone individualist and a spatial ingressor. The qualities that make the court challenging and obstructive to him (watchful eyes, the inability to claim a space as entirely sovereign) also provide the conditions under which he can maintain the relative anonymity and lack of a social "footprint" that enable his criminality (a transient space of short tenancies, multiple mobile occupants, regular visitors, and informal sublettings). Again, multi-family housing evinces frontierist characteristics in ways that appear to contradict but in fact articulate each other. It invites the presence of those who want to prevent their individualism from being sociospatially compromised but who also demand the opportunity to assert that individualism by defending their sociospatial integrity against incursions from others and making such incursions themselves.

The Virginibus Arms' spatial mutability, the difficulty of determining whether spaces in an apartment court are public or private, enclosed or exposed, is compounded by a text that keeps its own counsel about exactly what those spaces look like. Apartment courts in this period took many forms; Polyzoides et al. record single blocks, parallel blocks, "L"-shapes, "U"-shapes, and completed courtyards.[147] The Virginibus appears to belong to the last category, but Hughes's description of its form is remarkably opaque. Around its square interior patio are "Spanish bungalows boxing the court on three sides," while on an upper level are apartments "off the Spanish-Colonial balcony."[148] It is unclear, however, how many sides of the court are covered by this balcony. Hughes at times calls Dix's ground-floor home a "bungalow," which by most definitions would imply that it has no further floor of housing above it, but at other times it receives the designation "apartment," opening the possibility that Hughes may simply use "bungalow" to mean "single-story, ground-floor dwelling," suggesting that a dwelling may have further stories above it and still be called a "bungalow." There is precedent for this in architectural literature.[149] This ambiguity in the architectural terminology Hughes applies to the ground floor of the Virginibus leaves us unclear as to whether, when the text describes a balcony above the bungalows, this runs *over* the bungalows on anything up to three sides of the court, and/or on the fourth side of the court where there are no bungalows—i.e., with a void beneath forming an entranceway to the court. The presence of an "arched street entrance" and its implied location on a fourth, enclosing side of the court do little to clarify whether the upper "balcony" apartments run only on one side of the court with the walled entrance (thus making the ground-floor apartments "true" bungalows), atop the ground-floor apartments, or both.

As in the bungalow court that challenged Philip Marlowe's interrogative faculties with its series of repeated forms, repetition that might seem to suggest a predictable space in fact engenders ambiguity. Where Marlowe sought to divine an interrogative passage into the court, however, here our protagonist is resident within its ambiguous structures, which therefore serve to compound his own unknowability. Many of Dix's most significant actions in the novel take place in between-chapter blackouts, always withheld from the reader, and these blackouts find their spatial analogue in the court—Dix's space resists, like his most critical actions, readerly attempts at epistemic penetration. The concrete yet protean court, confounding in that contradiction, presents itself as fundamentally frontier-like because, like Dix's own psyche, it proves to the reader treacherously changeable and hard to navigate. The court's true dimensions and form, like the "lonely place" of the killer's psychological isolation and like the frontier, remain elusive to all those outside the space itself. Even the frontiersman only finds the frontier "knowable" in the sense that he embraces it as that which cannot be known: once fully compassed, it is no longer a frontier. Dix, likewise, privileged with experiential knowledge of the court's spaces that the text denies the reader, finds that the meanings of those spaces shift from moment to moment as violently and unpredictably as does his own temperament. A frontier-oriented architectural composition models a frontier-oriented psyche.

Such mapping of spatial conditions to frontierlike psychological makeup is complicated, however, by the fact that Laurel too lives in the apartments, a complication exemplified by the spatial role-reversal of her first meeting with Dix. He is threatened by a woman whose association with and ability to navigate this contested, mutable, blurry space suggests that she may be as unknowable, changeable, and elusive as he intends to be. Her spatial identity implies the threat that Walter Huff could not apprehend in Phyllis Nirdlinger—that of a woman also possessed by frontierist characteristics—and thus presents a direct challenge to Dix's urge to control and subdue women. That Laurel lives alone suggests a woman who has rejected social convention and male control (in this case that of an ex-husband). Her gender marks her living alone in an apartment as a resistive act of *not* living with a husband in a single-family home, inverting the multi-family unit's familiar role as a space where a man can evade the domesticating, feminizing norms of a post-frontier world. This renders Laurel to Dix simultaneously alluring (in her frontier-individualist rejection of social conventions and bonds) and infuriating (because such frontier-individualism is vested "improperly" in a woman).

Those domesticating, feminizing norms of the single-family home, which in *What Way My Journey Lies* were represented by Mary Carter, here find their champion in Sylvia Nicolai—wife of Brub Nicolai, Dix's former comrade-in-arms and now, as a cop, ostensible investigator of his crimes. As the primary residential space in the novel, the Virginibus Arms is contrasted persistently with the Nicolais' Santa Monica home, which stands on the frontier-landscape-evoking "Mesa Road" but ultimately confirms for Dix that the single-family home's claim to the imaginary of frontier living is at best superficial and at worst dangerously deceptive.[150] When Dix first contacts Brub, he does not know his friend is married, so to meet Sylvia when he visits their home is a shock. On meeting her, rather than engage her in conversation, he turns immediately to Brub. "Why didn't you tell me you were married?" Dix asks. There is no jocularity here, only angry urgency: the answer is "demanded," and the demand then repeated.[151] Dix had envisaged a homosocial encounter with Brub, reproducing their wartime dynamic. Sylvia, though, as emblem of Brub's new peacetime existence, has precluded that, corrupting a purely masculine Brub-Dix relationship by enmeshing her husband in the feminized structures of domesticity.

Even before being introduced to Sylvia, on first sight Dix knows that "she was at home here; she was mistress of the house and she was beautiful in her content."[152] Dix thus recognizes Brub and Sylvia's home instantly as a place of female security and power: Sylvia represents the house, the house Sylvia. Even though the traditional, patriarchal family unit privileges and elevates Brub above his wife, in Dix's view it has placed Brub under undue female influence, spatially fixing him within a sphere where Sylvia is the force truly in control. She is as tall as Brub, physically manifesting the demasculinizing diminution Dix believes her to have wrought. Deeming her far more malign than Mary ever seems to John Norman, Dix perceives Sylvia as having entrapped Brub in a sociospatial construct that precludes him from functioning as an exclusively and independently masculine individual. That Sylvia is rendered "beautiful" precisely by this state of affairs discloses Dix's conflicted attitudes toward her: as with Laurel, or Marlowe with Carmen, Dix's perception of Sylvia's independent agency (and its threat to that of men) generates simultaneous revulsion and desire. Dix finds Sylvia's threat, as John finds Mary's, especially insidious because in a frontierist mindset where comfort is entrapment and stability is stasis, Sylvia's "submission" to a domestic ideal of apparent male agency and female subservience is in fact the very source of her independent agency and the loss of Brub's. She becomes a dangerously individuated threat to masculinity by appearing not to be one, thereby testifying once more that the single-family house's superficial redolence of the pioneer homestead in fact disguises its deeper treachery to frontier values.

If the unknowability of the Virginibus Arms represents the elusive inner self Dix attempts to hide and protect, Sylvia's feminized realm of domesticated certainty enables her to "see under the covering of a man."[153] Thus she instantly sees under Dix's covering to identify his most obviously frontiersmanlike trait, calling him a "stubborn individualist," the clarity with which his frontiersmanship appears to her marking it as conspicuously aberrant to the space of her home and signaling her ability to challenge it.[154] Sylvia indeed vindicates Dix's worst fears about female agency and its capacity to diminish men through domesticity when she (aided by Laurel), not Brub, proves to be his captor. Unlike John Norman, Dix never willingly submits to the anti-frontierist, emasculating tyranny of the single-family home, its stability, its easily identifiable boundaries, and its stultifying domestic comforts. It is, however, the novel's principal symbol of that domestic paradigm who first suspects and ultimately conquers him.

In *Double Indemnity*, Barton Keyes's pursuit of Walter Huff demonstrates the extent to which Huff's final antagonist is no individual, not even his lover-turned-tormentor Phyllis Nirdlinger, but the office itself. In *In a Lonely Place*, Sylvia is similarly suggestive of the extent to which Dix's ultimate enemy (and vanquisher) is not simply or only a feminine presence but the conjugal domesticity of the family home itself. Dix's murderous attempts to resist that familial ideal, to seek a way of life more individualistic, more socially marginal, and less diluted by feminine agency, are far more brutal and extreme than John Norman's cold feet—but, for that, no more successful.

Homes of the Future; Men of the Past

Something happens at the end of World War II to the latter-day frontiersmen of fictional Los Angeles. A crisis of manhood and its place in the postwar world plays out between two opposed spaces—provisional, ephemeral, multi-occupancy accommodation denoting masculine individualism at society's hither edge, and the normative, bloodless, familial domesticity of the single-family home. These dynamics and their reflection of a crisis of post-frontier masculinity are by no means limited to Dix

Steele and John Norman. As Sarah Trott writes on Chandler's *The Little Sister*, "the war became a pivotal event for [Philip] Marlowe because it heralded the advent of a new Los Angeles."[155] Between *The Little Sister* in 1949 and *The Long Goodbye* in 1953, Marlowe, a longstanding apartment denizen who once vested his selfhood of lone maleness with existential urgency in his Hobart Arms rooms, trades that "urban transience for a furnished house" on Yucca Avenue in Laurel Canyon.[156]

That move seems to suggest that Marlowe, like John Norman and unlike Dix Steele, is coming with age to accept being drawn toward domesticity and conjugality. Marlowe is not living with a woman when he takes the Yucca Avenue house, but *The Long Goodbye* is also the novel in which he first meets Linda Loring, who recurs in *Playback* (1958) and has married Marlowe by the time of the unfinished, posthumously published "The Poodle Springs Story" (1962). Throughout *The Long Goodbye* and *Playback*, Marlowe starts to doubt the viability of the identity he embodied in the earlier novels. The phone rings at Yucca Avenue in the dead of night and the occupant is asked if he is, indeed, Marlowe: "I guess so," comes the uncertain response.[157] Moving to a single-family home seems to anticipate spatially a retreat to the safety and comfort of the domestic, away from the earlier novels' resolutely masculinist individualism, a retreat later corroborated by Linda's arrival. Similarly, when thirteen years after *Ask the Dust* John Fante finally came to publish another novel, his mode remained heavily autobiographical, but *Full of Life* (1952) and its protagonist (now simply called "John Fante") had left the grubby if invigoratingly ephemeral hotel lifestyle far behind. A domestic comedy of early middle age, tender but flecked with darkness, *Full of Life* follows its protagonist and his heavily pregnant wife as they purchase and renovate the home where they intend to make a family—the deliberate cliché of a four-bed, picket-fenced affair, a few miles out of downtown, not far from John Norman's place.[158] The mood is far less desperate than that of *What Way My Journey Lies*, but Fante's novel shares with his friend Fenton's a conflicted sense of a generation of wild men belatedly brought to ground by the very patriarchal expectations that simultaneously uphold their social status.

These shifts suggest aging authors, of course, but also the changing sociospatial makeup of the city in the postwar era. The outward moves from the urban core made by Marlowe, Norman, and Fante's protagonist anticipate the white flight to the suburbs that would define LA's changing demography in the 1950s and 1960s. Marlowe's move may reflect perhaps that in an expanding, centrifugalized city, it is less important to have immediate access to the neon fleshpots of Hollywood and the "decaying mansions and sinister rooming houses" of Bunker Hill.[159] Indeed, much of the latter would, having been condemned as irredeemably "blighted" by 1947, begin to be torn down in 1960, an act of social cleansing that disproportionately displaced low-income Black, Latinx, and indigenous communities—the experiences of the latter notably documented in Kent Mackenzie's 1961 film *The Exiles*.[160] In distancing himself further from the central city, Marlowe anticipates the imminent replacement of its "diversity, complexity, and locality" with monumental homogeneity, and therein the loss of its "occult power" to furnish the "nocturnal imagination" of the crime narrative.[161] Fante's fictional alter ego's departure from downtown likewise reflects the fact that, while multi-family housing may have become, contrary to popular imagery, more common in postwar Los Angeles, the day of the downtown tumbledown flophouse was over.

By the onset of the 1950s, then, Philip Marlowe is unsure if he can sustain himself as the lone, danger-braving trouble seeker of Chandler's earlier books. Fante's fictional alter ego is avowedly no longer the sociosexual boundary pusher and convention breaker of *Ask the Dust* or "Clever Fellow." Dix Steele and John Norman cannot reconcile themselves to peacetime life after the brutal viscerality of wartime experience renders any other existence unreal and meaningless. All four find that after the war they can no longer sustain aspects of their characters that denoted individualist masculinity, willful self-endangerment, and various expressions of a roving spatial agency. The traits that marked them out as latter-day inheritors or manipulators of the frontierist ideal are somehow no longer tenable. All respond by attempting to share experiences and spaces with women, accepting or inviting a feminine domestic presence.

These responses are variably successful, Dix's indeed "failing" entirely purposefully and in the most violent and shocking terms. In the other cases, the act of coming to accept domesticity, conjugality, and the familial is figured in acts of swapping multi-family accommodation for the single-family home. These are in turn acts that swap a form of housing that in multiple dimensions reflects the dynamics and values of the frontier for one that perhaps superficially suggests the open plain but is revealed as only a flimsy assemblage of superficial frontier images and indeed fundamentally anti-frontierist in its deeper bases. There is, further, an abiding strangeness that these men make their moves at the moment when multi-family housing was in fact becoming more rather than less popular in Los Angeles. Just as the form of housing that most effectively models or supports the values of the frontier seems about to become a more normative way to live in LA, these former frontiersmen abandon it—because as a frontier experience ceases to be marginal it ceases to be a frontier.

As David Gebhard and Harriette von Breton write, "by the end of the 1930s, LA was the only city where all of the essential ingredients of the horizontal, private-auto oriented city were firmly established. Only the outbreak of . . . World War II prevented their full realization in 1942 and 1943."[162] By the same token, although LA was a city of single-family homes long before the war, it is only at war's end that these men abandon to a greater or lesser extent frontierist spatial practices of multi-family living (bar Dix, whose murderous resistance to the entrapments of domesticity is his downfall). It is perhaps as John and Dix fear: the horrors of war have rendered men like them placeless; a postwar world is wary of the frontierist values of physical force, violence, spatial incursion, individualism, and unpredictability. Now it prizes regimentation and systematization (embodied in LA's urban form by freeways and tract homes) to curtail the dangerous will of men. Indeed, on the horizon was Eisenhower's America of picket fences and patriotic procreation, and with it the fear that "American traditions of individualism were vanishing and being buried beneath . . . prefabricated towns."[163] The conformist familial fantasia of the 1950s was at odds with frontierism's valorization of singular figures on the unpredictable social margin, a conflict *Invasion of the Body Snatchers* (1956) would stage in the takeover of a suburban Southern California setting, with all its regional "last frontier" resonances, by blank, unthinking pod people.

If incipient white flight is a further (unarticulated) undercurrent to the suburbanizing moves made by Marlowe, John Norman, and Fante's fictionalized self in *Full of Life*, it too is consistent with a diminution of frontiersmanlike identity as a tool for marshaling the city's geography: white flight is a reluctant acknowledgment of whiteness's loss of interpretative and designatory hegemony over space. The frontiersman's ancestral powers—to make and remake space in the image of whiteness—are now contested. John Norman self-abjectingly accepts, and Dix Steele violently protests, that a certain visceral form of frontier-inherited masculinity—defined by its rejection of spatial stability, of socially normative routine, of feminizing influence, of familial domesticity—is exhausted. In leaving the apartment and the boarding house, these men and their fictional peers participate in the sprawling, decentralizing postwar city and thus acknowledge that Los Angeles will now be less navigable by and legible to the individual who defines himself by his powers of spatial divination. In so doing they acknowledge that white masculine identity too, as the solipsistic certainties of its frontier-derived hermeneutics grow less relevant in a changing world, will itself become harder to navigate.

Epilogue

"Steaming Remnants of the Fire"

> I don't know how this story ends. I'm sort of hoping that because it's set in Los Angeles, the usual process will reverse itself in an LA double flip. An LA change.
>
> —Eve Babitz, "Heroine"

Making his first appearance in 1949's *The Moving Target*, Ross Macdonald's Southern California private eye Lew Archer emerges into the world of John Norman, Dix Steele, and Philip Marlowe, but outlives it, making his final appearance in 1976's *The Blue Hammer*. Archer is not Marlowe, but in inheriting the generational mantle of fictional LA's premier detective he serves as a thought experiment into what happens when a figure who embodies a 1940s urban frontiersmanship finds himself gradually extruded into the years of Nixonian malaise. Per Terry Curtis Fox, Archer is a "sensibility through which we view [how] California society . . . had changed" over the course of the 1950s and 1960s.[1] He is therefore strategically placed to test whether my claims about the frontier's modern endurance as the structuring logic of Southern California fiction sustain themselves beyond this book's purview—the few years preceding and succeeding World War II—or speak only of the particular weirdness and heat of that liminal juncture in American, Californian, and Angeleno life. If we light out for the future, with Lew Archer as our guide, does the fictive neofrontiersmanship of the 1930s and 1940s persist, or peter out?

Certainly, plenty of weirdness and heat persists in *The Underground Man* (1971), the antepenultimate novel in the Archer series, throughout which an enormous wildfire rages in the mountains around Los Angeles. Most of the novel's action is concentrated further up the California coast and a little closer to the blaze's heart, in Santa Teresa (Macdonald's analogue for Santa Barbara). Archer, however, can already smell burning as he awakes in his West LA apartment; the usual "cool air, smelling of fresh ocean" becomes a "hot wind" blowing in his face within the space of the first chapter.[2] Even miles from the blaze, the conditions are identifiable as "fire weather"—and the fire is always identifiable closer to LA than Archer expects.[3] Driving from his apartment to Santa Teresa, Archer has barely begun the descent into the San Fernando Valley when he sees a firefighting plane.[4] On a later trip by the same route, the fire comes into view above the freeway "sooner than . . . expected."[5] Macdonald's ominously hot wind is in part a declaration of debt to (or emancipation from) Chandler, who wrote in "Red Wind" (1938) about how everyone in Southern California goes a little crazy when the Santa Anas start to blow. To sense imminent fire in the atmosphere of a fictional Los Angeles, though, is also to recall the city's best-known imagined conflagration—"The Burning of Los Angeles," the apocalyptic masterwork of Tod Hackett, Nathanael West's painter-protagonist in *The Day of the Locust*.

West's novel is one of the defining texts of the critical school against which I initially framed my case that fictional representations of Los Angeles in the 1930s and 1940s suggest the disturbing consequences of the frontier's endurance rather than the disturbing consequences of its closure. As early as 1967 George Pisk contended that West's "fire in dreamland" should be taken for a broader "state of decay" in the "American spiritual life" of the 1930s.[6] Later, Steven Weisenburger characterized *Locust* as a text intimately engaged with its own spatial entrapment, one that "begins and ends at the western boundary of American culture" and therefore becomes characterized by "circular" acts of "destructive regress" that grimly satirize the limits of the "westward course of empire."[7] David Fine calls West's novel "the single most powerful metaphor" for an American Dream that collapsed on contact with Southern California's coastline.[8] He sets it alongside Cain and Chandler in defining a literary LA that poses as "the land of the new beginning" only to reveal its true self as "the land of the disastrous finale, the place where the American road ends and turns back on itself at the edge of the continent."[9]

Hackett's painting, for such critics, is a singular statement of eschatological prophecy, not merely symbolizing the novel's descent into scenes of violent chaos but signifying an America that, in the absence of a frontier, will inevitably implode beneath the pressures of entropic modernity. Such readings rely on an obvious omission, one that Fine admits seemingly without realizing the consequences of doing so: it's only a painting. There is much violence, horror, and catastrophe in *Locust*, but Los Angeles does not and will not burn down. "The Burning of Los Angeles" might in fact be viewed, through the prism of the framework I have established over the preceding chapters, as the fever dream of an East Coast boy traumatized by a Far West that still has *too much* of the frontier about it, rather than too little. The city doesn't burn down in *The Underground Man* either, but unlike in West's novel the threat that it might is a real one.

Crucially, Macdonald's possibility of a disaster that combines Southern Californian regional specificity with quasi-apocalyptic impact does *not*, as appearances might superficially suggest, betoken the persistence of a frontier. It may reveal the natural environment's recalcitrant danger within urban modernity, but this is no mere negotiation between a self-defined "civilized" world and the unsettled wilderness beyond, the reopening of a liminal space between the two; rather, it is the demand by the latter to reclaim the former wholesale. Frontier myth demands that the wilderness must be always present but also always conquerable by human forces; Macdonald's fire reverses that threat. The fire does recede eventually, but by nature's caprice. First "a mass of air" moves in from the sea and appears to hold the fire "back from the coastal plain and the city."[10] As a radio announcer makes clear, whatever firefighting procedures might be undertaken, the region remains entirely at the whim of the Santa Ana winds; only if they stop blowing will the fire's progress be arrested.[11]

Macdonald's fire echoes a scene in Alison Lurie's LA social satire *The Nowhere City*, published in 1965 but set a few years earlier, at the turn of the decade. Academic Paul Cattleman attempts to explain to film starlet Glory Green that natural destruction is inevitable in Southern California because "a fault in the rock structure" means the Santa Monica mountains are "gradually disintegrating." Glory, however, takes him to mean something far more immediate, a "landslide and explosion above Sunset Boulevard, scattering trees and cars and houses and fragments of earth."[12] Likewise, Macdonald's fire prefigures the magical-realist natural catastrophes of Karen Tei Yamashita's postmodernist LA epic, *Tropic of Orange* (1997), which defy logic and understanding. Human means are inadequate to fight Macdonald's and Lurie's catastrophes; they are inadequate even to comprehend Yamashita's.

Natural disaster has always been both a threat and a facet of identity in Southern California. As Mike Davis notes, Los Angeles had in the geographic conditions of its location from the outset seemed to "put itself in harm's way," subjecting the dream of an American Eden to inevitable challenges—the very tension in which resides the frontier condition. The catastrophes of Macdonald, Lurie, and Yamashita, however, speak to Davis's description of how, as the twentieth century drew toward a close and natural disasters began to occur in "virtually biblical conjugation," the relationship between LA's inhabitants and their environment took on a more urgently millenarian inflection.[13] A "popular apprehension that the former Land of Sunshine [was] 'reinventing' itself . . . as a Book of the Apocalypse theme park" took hold: the "Last Days," for so long confined to such "Los Angeles disaster fiction" as West's *Locust*, suddenly seemed inevitable and thus in a sense already here.[14]

Sometime in the early 1960s, Gore Vidal encountered an LA cab driver who thought as much. Asking news of a fire's progress, Vidal was corrected in his nomenclature: the blaze's proper name was "the holocaust."[15] Similarly, Joan Didion's 1989 statement that "there is nothing unusual about fires in Los Angeles" was not a blasé dismissal of environmental danger but an acceptance of it as a condition of life, the apocalyptic all-the-time.[16] As Didion wrote of earthquakes the previous year, Angelenos' "apparent equanimity" about the constant threat of natural catastrophe was in fact a "protective detachment," a "fatalism."[17] If the earthquake is "the Big One" or the fire a "true big hitter," no amount of individualist human hardiness will be capable of resisting it.[18] Macdonald's fire never seizes Santa Teresa or Los Angeles, and Lurie's regional disintegration theoretically remains in the geological future, but in both cases it is posited that the moment of catastrophe *could* be now and could not be thwarted if it were. The implication of Yamashita's reality-bending text, meanwhile, is that the disasters of which she writes are happening to *a* Los Angeles right now: we are merely fortunate enough not to be living in that permutation of the present. In each case, only sheer dumb luck of timing or circumstance, not any feat of frontierist heroism, allows the human edifice to escape destruction by its natural adversary.

Eric Avila notes that in 1965 a record-breaking LA heatwave "echoed the chants of 'burn, baby, burn!' emanating from South Central Los Angeles," where the Watts Rebellion raged. Such an echo suggests how the increasingly volatile natural environment of later twentieth-century LA and increasingly turbulent human dynamics in the same period's changing city became metaphors for each other.[19] Throughout Macdonald's novel, likewise, the natural danger looming just beyond the city appears of a piece with a social fire threatening an older LA, and in so doing further suggests the exhaustion of the frontier revival moment proposed in prior chapters. In his late 1960s novels, Macdonald had already begun engaging with Southern California's contemporary climate of generational and social conflict—be it "the explosive racial situation" or "a youth culture abandoned to pleasure"—but in *The Underground Man* the pressure comes to a head.[20] The burning hillsides are redolent of an era in which, writes Avila, "Los Angeles itself seemed on the verge of a nervous breakdown."[21] That breakdown is experienced in *The Underground Man* by white, middle-class, "middle-ageing men" adrift in a changing world that they no longer know how to navigate, uncertain as to either the attainability or the viability of frontierist selfhood.[22]

Archer is probably in his early fifties at the time of the events of *The Underground Man*.[23] Leo Broadhurst, who disappeared in 1955 but becomes the novel's absent center as Archer investigates Broadhurst's son Stanley's ill-fated attempts to trace his father's whereabouts, is of a similar generation, having been "a captain of infantry in the Pacific."[24] These are men of John Norman and Dix Steele's generation. Generational kinship is also implied between Archer and two other major male characters. Brian Kilpatrick, with whom Archer enjoys an "angry brotherhood," is forty-five; Lester Crandall, euphemistically described by his wife as "no longer young," is fifty-nine.[25] Other men in the novel are still relatively young but already find themselves enduring rather than enjoying the trappings of respectably well-heeled marital domesticity, entrenched despite their relative youth (like John Norman at the end of *What Way My Journey Lies*) in its social and material significations—the job, the house, the car, the boat. They are coded as staring at the rapid onset of "middle-ageing" despite ostensibly still being some years from its arrival. Roger Armistead is "youngish" but his thinning hair and status as the considerably older Kilpatrick's social peer code him as older. Stanley Broadhurst is only twenty-seven but, with a marriage in crisis and a bitter suspicion that the much older Archer may be his wife's "playmate" and about to become "a substitute father" to his six-year-old son, already carries the cares of midlife.[26]

These men are united by fraught relationships with both an escaping past and an onrushing present. Such relationships find their psychological "intersection" within the very landscape of Southern California, as Lee Clark Mitchell notes is common in Macdonald's work.[27] The past-present "intersection" is located in the soil itself, via the plot of long-buried and lately discovered bodies that gives the novel its title. There is thus a structural evocation throughout *The Underground Man* of the Turnerian sense that the frontier was a temporal liminality as well as a geographic one—it only exists in and as the present, a constantly moving point along a linear progression through both time and space, because what lies behind is now ossified by prior settlement, and what lies ahead remains unknowable wilderness. On similar lines runs Van Wyck Brooks's 1918 claim that the American cultural present had become void-like because it contained a past that was always already dead.[28] Although Brooks saw "pioneer instinct" in the great figures of the American literary past (Emerson, Thoreau, Whitman), the "past without living value" he saw as deadening the nation's cultural present was unmistakably that of the frontier's already powerful mythos, a stultifying over-regard for "the age of pioneering" from which arose resistance to "finer ideals."[29]

The Underground Man attests to such claims in literal fashion: the present is a hole where bodies are buried, a gaping void in the landscape containing a dead past. Confrontation with this dead, buried past is for the novel's characters a confrontation with the long-delayed exhaustion of the frontier's utility as a mythic structuring device for their world, rendering void-like the culture they inhabit. Stanley Broadhurst has long been "hipped on the subject of his father's desertion" and preoccupied with an obsessive quest to discover his whereabouts, believing that Leo left with a mistress for Hawaii in 1955.[30] Such an act would be an immediately frontierist gesture, a response to sociospatial entrapment (in California, in marriage) that takes advantage of the United States' post-Turner extension of its western frontier beyond continental bounds.[31] Moreover, Leo Broadhurst's status as a World War II veteran aligns him with a moment that, John Norman's and Dix Steele's experiences suggest, gave the frontierlike masculine individualist a new, modern stage upon which to assert himself—but perhaps a final one, a rallying call for the martial pioneer but also his death rattle. That the search for the lost father is also a grasping for that lost moment is further implied in the one image of Leo that Stanley possesses: "a picture of him in uniform."[32] Such an implication echoes elsewhere in the text: the firefighting plane that Archer sees is in fact a converted World War II bomber. A symbol of a moment when American men were asked once more to define themselves by frontierist values is now an indicator of an unfrontiersmanlike inability to master nature's forces.

Leo Broadhurst's embodiment of a proud, martial masculinity stands in stark contrast with his son, who rages impotently at his wife and at Archer, and who works for an insurance firm. The nothing-making, deskbound entity that exemplified the overcivilized world against which Walter Huff strained here resurfaces as the antithesis of the rugged wartime manhood that Stanley seeks to reclaim by seeking out his father. Yet the man who solves the mystery of the Broadhursts, Archer, is emphatically *not* one who embodies an association between the war years and a revival of frontierist masculinity. Archer may be of Broadhurst Sr.'s generation, and served in World War II, but elsewhere in Macdonald's oeuvre it is emphasized that, unlike Dix Steele and John Norman, he remembers his army days not as a frontierlike liberation of masculine individualism but as something much more like the corporate bureaucracy against which Huff rails: "channels, red tape, protocol, buck-passing, hurry up and wait."[33] That such a man should, in solving the Broadhurst mysteries, foreclose what was never merely a son's search for a father but also a vicarious attempt to recover a romanticized memory of an older, war-forged generation's rugged masculinity powerfully demystifies any notion that the legacies of World War II portended a viable revival of frontier values. That demystification is compounded in the ultimate revelation that Leo Broadhurst never in fact made his neofrontierist gesture of escape to Hawaii. He had been lying dead and buried in the California soil of his home all along, a blunt continental circumscription suggesting hard limits to any frontiersmanlike quality he may have embodied.

When Leo Broadhurst's body is discovered, the autopsy reveals the murder weapon. To Archer, it initially appears to be "an Indian arrowhead"—a relic of the frontier, and one that has transposed frontier violence into the present. It is, however, a trick of the eye: the "discolored triangle" proves to be only the "tip of a butcher knife."[34] Shortly after this discovery, Archer is ushered out of the mortuary because he is "not authorized personnel."[35] The contrast with Philip Marlowe two or three decades earlier is striking. As noted in chapter 2, Marlowe's investigative efforts actively benefited from his frontiersmanlike identity as a semi-outsider to official crimefighting apparatus, his ability to embody justice while remaining only quasi-judicial in his official role and thereby existing as a conductive liminality between law and lawlessness, truth and lies, visible present and hidden past. Archer, however, finds that such an ambiguity in his identity is now a hindrance to his investigation. The world is changing: the structures of officialdom have closed more firmly upon the detective's realm; playing the pioneer is now distinctly frowned upon.

If Macdonald's men grapple continually with their dislocation from older, frontier-oriented ways of constructing masculine selfhood and navigating the world, they feel equally alienated from the "just to get by" attitude of the next generation—a youth that professes to believe in neither the force that motivated frontier conquest (capital) nor the one by which it occurred (violence).[36] This Californian youth refuses, as Didion wrote in 1967, to "learn the games that had held the society together."[37] Everyone from the young Broadhursts to Lester Crandall, a full three decades apart in age, is suspicious of the world of the "teenage drop-out," a world of "acid in a Coke" where any authority figure is a "grungy pig."[38] Traditional values are collapsing and even an only slightly older cohort struggles to read its successors: nobody is entirely certain as to which of the adult men may or may not be involved with Lester Crandall's teenage daughter—who discomforts Jean Broadhurst less because of her assumed affair with Stanley than because it is impossible to tell if she is "absolutely innocent" or "absolutely cold and amoral."[39] Nobody is even entirely sure if one of the married men may be involved with Brian Kilpatrick's hippie boathand son Jerry. As Archer notes, when Kilpatrick Sr. complains that "we're losing a whole generation," it makes him "sound like an old man."[40] Yet Archer himself, confronted by a beach "littered with bodies" of guitar-playing youths lying atop each other, betrays an uncomfortable conservatism of his own. He sees "a warning vision of the future, when every square foot of the world would be populated." Suggesting now in human rather than ecological terms Davis's millenarian mode of late twentieth-century Californian fiction, Archer feels "as if everybody but me was paired off like the animals in the ark."[41] This is the ultimate vision of post-frontier finitude: an apocalyptically Malthusian exhaustion of space upon the California coastline.

It befits this changing world that the only character in the novel who succeeds to any degree in continuing to suggest the legacies of the pioneer generations is not a frontiersman but a frontierswoman—Elizabeth Broadhurst, Stanley's widow. She is figured as both a fearless conqueror of nature in herself and a link with the era of its initial white conquest. Inverting the familiar gendered metaphor for frontiersmanship, in which the pioneer is male and subdued nature figured as female (not to mention young and virginal), Elizabeth drives a truck into the heart of the fire "as if it was a male animal resisting control." Archer worries that, with "the smell of burning growing stronger," he and Mrs. Broadhurst were "going against nature," but elects not to reveal his fears because "she wasn't the sort of woman you confessed human weakness to."[42] The name of the neighborhood in which she lives—Canyon Estates—contains a tension redolent of human imposition upon nature, and she in turn dominates the place so completely that it is known informally as "Mrs. Broadhurst's canyon."⁴³ As the fire approaches, Elizabeth is urged to flee a home in which everything "is some kind of relic" of the frontier era but refuses, stating that "if the house goes, I might as well go with it."⁴⁴ Remarkably, though, miraculously even, the house survives, "scorched but intact," while others around it perish, suggesting Elizabeth's embodiment of a frontierswomanlike ability to withstand the assaults of nature.⁴⁵

Hers is a family that has been emplaced in the region since the pioneer days. She was born in the "white stucco ranch-house," which is "full of Victorian furniture" and "dark Victorian portraits on the walls"—"ancestral tintypes" of men with "mutton-chop whiskers." Alongside are trinkets commemorating human conquest of nature—"cabinets full of stuffed native birds" and the inherited antique pistols that killed them.⁴⁶ Archer discovers writings by Elizabeth about her father and grandfather, who came to the region and acquired the land on which the house stands in the 1860s. Her notes are marked by the same obsessive reverence with which Stanley pursues his own absent father, but Elizabeth's writings seek to undermine the frontiersman myth. Her father, she is desperate to affirm, was more a "scholar than a rancher"; he was the third of his line to attend Harvard; he was the subject of "false rumors" that he was a "wanton killer of songbirds" when in fact, she claims, he only killed them "for scientific reasons" and was in fact a deeply sensitive man who loved to commune with nature.⁴⁷

Elizabeth Broadhurst doubly subverts expectations of how ideological legacies of the frontier might be inherited. First, a woman appears to be the text's lone holdout of frontierist values in a changing world that frightens and defeats men of both her husband's and her son's generations. Second, however, in her revisionist history of her family's arrival in the West she challenges the myth of those frontierist values themselves. Paradoxically, although her pioneer resonances place her even further out of step with the modern world than the novel's more urban and urbane characters, the ways in which she complexifies the figure of the modern-day frontierist holdout indicate the inadequacy of the conventional frontiersman type to negotiate and survive that modern world's conditions. The only character in the novel who is successfully able to use frontier identity to survive a changing world is one who simultaneously issues a radical challenge to the premises of such an identity.

There are similar stakes at play in Lurie's *The Nowhere City*. This is a novel full of characters who voice popular clichés about LA—as a city lacking either a sense of place, per the novel's title, or "the dimension of time"—that I hope this book has challenged.[48] Like Macdonald, though, Lurie attests to the frontiersman character's increasing inability to navigate the city in the later twentieth century. Paul Cattleman and his wife, Katherine, are East Coast transplants but, as a near synonym for "cowboy," Cattleman's surname immediately suggests a mythic birthright with which to live out fantasies of conquering the Far West. Indeed, he thinks explicitly of LA as "the last American frontier" and arrives "in the spirit of the explorer"; his "dream about Los Angeles" is a dream of "limitless freedom and opportunity . . . straight out of America [sic] history: 'Go West, Young Man.'"[49]

For Paul, limitless freedom is supposed to manifest itself in opportunities for financial, intellectual, social, and sexual conquest of his new surroundings, but all such opportunities prove short-lived or failures. Meanwhile, Katherine follows an exactly opposite trajectory. She begins the novel hating LA, its cars and buildings, its sunshine and customs—seldom leaving the house, complaining of chronic sinus conditions, trapped in and by her loveless marriage. At the start of the novel, in effect, the Cattlemans represent either side of Davis's "sunshine" versus "*noir*" dichotomy; Paul sees a land of abundance there for the taking, Katherine a dystopian "hell" and "a great big advertisement for *nothing*."[50] After Katherine begins an affair with swinging psychiatrist Iz Eisnam and a friendship with Eisnam's film-star wife, however, she is liberated in her relationship both with herself and with the city. Katherine, not Paul, becomes the figure who conquers LA, and is herself transformed in the process—in mannerisms, dress, voice, physical appearance—to the point that Paul can no longer recognize her. Nor can he even conceive of the possibility that she has engaged in the kind of infidelity that had been commonplace for him. Having secured another teaching appointment back on the East Coast, he begs her to return with him, but she refuses. The tables are turned. The man who sought to assail LA as a frontiersman, and saw his wife as at best a mere accessory and worse an active hindrance to that process, has been rejected, defeated by the city, while she has claimed it as her own, in so doing rejecting patriarchal repression and asserting herself as a liberated individualist.

It is not merely his assumptions about the gendered stakes of his fantasy frontiersmanship that Paul finds humiliatingly overturned, but also its racial dimensions. In conversation with Chinese American Walter Wong, Paul offers a cringing apology for a tasteless joke about Japanese internment. In response, Wong reminds him that "we minority groups have got to stick together." Paul is having an affair with Wong's wife, and Wong (wholly sanguine about this situation) reasons that "Ceci wouldn't be interested" in him were he not part of "some underprivileged order." Paul is confused, then insulted, especially when Walter admits that initially he "thought maybe you were a Jew."[51] Eventually Wong solves the mystery: "I know what group you represent. You're a square."[52] From his assumed position of hegemonic whiteness, Paul is laughingly reduced by Walter to just one of many minorities in an act that radically decenters him from his own narrative. Not only that, but the "minority" he is deemed to represent is one that humiliatingly undercuts his own image of himself as a bold frontiersman. Walter regards the "Protestant ethic," so closely adjacent to the frontier ideal, as indicative of a dull conformism—Paul's "squareness."[53] For Wong, the whiteness that has lost the privileged position to which frontier myth once attested so powerfully is precisely the whiteness that continues to believe in the frontier myth. The crux of Paul's failure to master LA is in his failure to accept that individuals who sit further from the frontierist ideal can, in the 1960s, claim its freedoms too. "Freedom and opportunity" still exist here, but Paul's inability to accept that they are no longer, per the frontier myth that drew him to LA, the sole desert of the individualist white male renders him unable to seize them. Turner enshrined a vision of the frontierist mindset's axis of temporality and space as one in which "the west looks to the future," leaving the past in the East.[54] As Didion has it, California was "the reward for having left the past."[55] Ironically, precisely that worldview has in Lurie's text become outmoded, an ossified historical dogma. It is Paul's adherence to such a frontierist history that causes Ceci to remark that he is simply "too hung up on the past," and Katherine to declare him "squeezed up between the past and the future."[56]

The valence of Lurie's central theme—an East Coast sixties sophisticate who goes west seeking libertine reinvention but finds a world no longer made for him—is echoed conspicuously in a rather more prominent and recent cultural artifact, the AMC TV series *Mad Men* (2007–2015). Advertising executive Don Draper (John Hamm) first flies to Los Angeles in the second of the show's seven seasons, after which its narrative becomes an increasingly bicoastal one. On arrival, Draper seems to undergo a rapid Californian transformation. We seem him first standing awkwardly by a Los Angeles swimming pool in a sport coat, tie, and trilby, New York cool rendered desperately unhip by California sun.[57] By the end of the next episode, he is standing waist-deep and shirtless in the Pacific (having fallen in with a group of sexually liberated bohemians), seemingly in a state of blissful freedom.[58] Don appears to have escaped Paul Cattleman's fate. Yet it is also during the course of these episodes that Don, who has been living under another man's name since the Korean War, for the first time reassumes the moniker with which he was born— that of Dick Whitman.

If this is an appropriate place in which to acknowledge oneself as a namesake of the poet who faced "west from California's shores" to "find the circle almost circled," such acknowledgment is also a signal that California for Don will not and cannot mean a straightforward unshackling of the self from the past.[59] Whereas the Far West had once been sought by the frontiersman as a place where the governance of an older and more restrictive world no longer applied, this white male individualist immediately figures California as the very opposite—somewhere that demands a reckoning with a former life he once thought he had outrun. In texts of the 1930s and 1940s the past coming back often means the frontier coming back, but not in *Mad Men*'s millennial (and in some respects millenarian) vision of the 1960s. This past returns not to enable reinvention but to compromise a reinvention Draper had imagined entirely secure. He goes to California, and becomes less frontiersmanlike. By the show's sixth season, we a confront a stark mirroring of his first—poolside and Pacific—brushes with clear Californian water. After smoking hashish he can't handle, Don hallucinates badly before ending up face-down in another Los Angeles pool, almost drowning.[60] It's a rare moment of literal-mindedness in a frequently cryptic drama: in the LA of 1968, Draper is out of his depth.

Like Paul Cattleman and Lew Archer, Draper discovers that as the world changes, he cannot navigate it as sure-footedly as he had imagined his birthright would always allow him to. In this respect it's again significant that Don Draper is really Dick Whitman: if he had once believed no world impregnable to someone imbued with the rugged, white, sexually and economically self-confident mid-century masculinity of which he appears a paragon, his own past reminds us (and him) just how arbitrarily and unequally such sociospatial agency has always been doled out among the population. In taking his wartime comrade's identity, Don once profited from the American truth that frontier myth manifests—that we're all tasked with being bold and fearless adventurers, but not all of us are permitted to be. He only learns that truth, however, when it is to his disadvantage. That terrible knowledge used to accrue only to minoritized would-be frontiersmen, the likes of Julio Sal and Bob Jones; in this later Los Angeles it is finally visited upon a white man. Even he now finds the frontier closing.

Mad Men's seventh and final season ends in California, not in Los Angeles but further up the coast, at a clifftop spiritual retreat. In its final scene, Don still appears a little out of place in this new world. He sticks to a white collared shirt (albeit with a few buttons undone) and is still short-haired and clean-shaven, while all around him are hippyish types. Yet he has happily joined them here, and meditates alongside them with his eyes closed and a peaceful smile.[61] *Mad Men*'s ending is ambiguous, but it does at the very least suggest that Don Draper has had to become a different kind of man in order to be at peace in these surroundings. If California is to be his reward for leaving the past, that past must include the self. Draper survives by changing what he is. Elizabeth Broadhurst survives by changing what it means to inherit the frontier. Paul Cattleman can do neither, but is changed regardless: leaving California without his wife, his loneness now is involuntary and undesired rather than a badge of rugged honor. In these different ways *Mad Men*, Macdonald, and Lurie all reflect upon the fact that as the postwar era progresses, it becomes impossible to continue to use the frontier as a device for structuring the spaces of LA. It is impossible because, as Wong's humiliation of Cattleman suggests, the values that defined and were represented in Turnerian ideology—values that exclusively valorized white masculinity—no longer reflect the changing city.

White men in the fictions that this book has explored, men like Dix Steele, John Norman, Walter Huff, and Philip Marlowe, work to restore frontier dynamics to the city because their identities and claims to social primacy are vested in the legacy of those dynamics and must be asserted against forces antithetical to frontier myth—the urban, the modern, the female or feminizing, the non-white Meanwhile non-white characters, like the African American Bob Jones, Fante's Filipino and racially ambiguous Italian American characters, and the Japanese family of Yamamoto's oilfield, seek to perform frontiersmanship in exchange for greater proximity to social advantages that only white men can typically claim. White women with prominent roles in LA fictions of the 1930s and 1940s largely exist either to grant physical form to the elusive whiteness that non-white male characters wish to pursue through their social frontiersmanship (Fante's Helen, Himes's Madge), or as figures against which white male characters define and assert their frontier masculinity. This may be most obvious in the case of the feminizing domesticity represented by Hughes's and Fenton's women, but even the *femmes fatales* of Chandler and Cain, while possessed of agency, individualism, and a sense of danger that aligns them with the values of the frontier, always serve to provide the presence that is hazardous to a central male protagonist who is able to claim a frontiersmanlike identity more fully on the basis of his maleness. Even if women in these texts problematize the psychodrama of frontier masculinity, they remain ineluctably co-opted into it, their very challenges to it providing the conditions for its expression. By contrast, while white men are still central for both Lurie and Macdonald, they are so as absences or redundancies, the dying past hanging on into a void-like present. Don Draper only narrowly escapes the same fate.

Just as Patricia Nelson Limerick and Richard White would come to challenge the narrative primacy of whiteness, maleness, and Turnerism in new tellings of western American history, so did a changing world, and a changing LA, render itself untenable as the vehicle for a mythic structure that can only accommodate non-male, non-white voices in functions that serve further to center whiteness and maleness. As early as the war years, human counterparts to the natural conflagrations that stalk the pages of LA fiction had begun to reverberate around the city as an increasingly diverse population began to assert its right to the city. If 1943's Zoot Suit Riots were started by white servicemen, they were in part a response to the supposed provocations of Mexican American youths who, in the aftermath of the Sleepy Lagoon murder trial, refused to "accept the racialized norms of segregated America" and "the privilege of whiteness."[62] Both Watts in 1965 and the Los Angeles Uprising of 1992 were refusals to accept acts of police brutality against African Americans.[63] Mexican Americans fought for a decade to forestall their eviction from Chavez Ravine.[64] It was to Los Angeles that Cesar Chavez moved in 1959 in order to take up his national directorship of the Community Service Organization, anticipating and contributing to LA's future centrality to the Latinx civil rights and labor movement.[65] In 1973 the Feminist Studio Workshop (later the Woman's Building) opened, making Los Angeles a radical hub for feminist art and politics.[66] In 1967, two years before Stonewall, police raids on Silver Lake's Black Cat tavern were answered with America's first gay street protest; in 1970 Hollywood Boulevard played host to the nation's first officially recognized pride parade.[67]

Such manifold and variegated acts of political self-assertion and resistance to marginalization occurred in the context of and were in part occasioned by equally radical demographic shifts. Although, as the fictions I have explored affirm, Los Angeles has always been a multiethnic city, it became far more comprehensively so during the period this book addresses. Robert Fogelson writes that LA was home to an exceptionally "diverse . . . mixture of racial groups" by the 1920s, but the city's ethnic diversity was in the number rather than the size of those groups.[68] There is something instructive in the fact that in 1940 LA's population of English and Welsh émigrés (20,454) was almost the equal of its ethnically Japanese population (23,321), and almost twice the size of the total population of all other groups contemporarily categorized as "Oriental" (10,752, including Filipinos, Chinese, Koreans, and "Hindus").[69] Roger Waldinger argues that only since the 1960s "has the immigrant presence transformed and ultimately redefined Los Angeles."[70] In 1960, as Mike Davis notes, LA was still "the most [demographically] WASPish of big [American] cities," but by 1970 had a countywide non-Anglo majority and by 1989 was more ethnically diverse than New York.[71]

None of this is to suggest that whiteness, or maleness, or straightness, entirely lost their positions of social privilege in later twentieth-century Los Angeles. It would be no less absurd to make such a claim about LA than to make it about the United States as a whole, however radically Southern California's cultural politics shifted in the postwar era. Many of the aforementioned political conflagrations (Watts, Chavez Ravine, the Zoot Suit Riots, the Black Cat protest) are in themselves stories how of marginalized groups' attempts at spatial self-assertion were suppressed by white interests, and in the first two postwar decades demographic change and its spatial impacts met especially fierce resistance. Eric Avila reads the suburbanization in which John Norman, later Marlowe, the fictionalized Fante of *Full of Life*, and the "middle-ageing" men of *The Underground Man* participate as a last-gasp attempt by threatened white citizens to recover an earlier era's "racialized fantasies" of the LA as a "southwestern outpost of white supremacy."[72] White Angelenos sought to maintain their centrality in the city's social makeup by relocating to (and policing the racial exclusivity of) its spatial edges. Ultimately, though, attempts to forestall the demographic and cultural transformation of LA only "flickered momentarily," unable to withstand a pace of change that only increased from the 1960s onwards.[73] LA today remains a city where privileges of race and gender, spatial mobility, and socioeconomic opportunity are invidiously connected, but it has undeniably become "a cultural kaleidoscope of global proportions."[74]

This cultural transformation has especially profound implications for the frontierist ethic's equation of spatial agency with racial identity because, in Julian Murphet's words, the polydiversity of late twentieth-century LA "emerges as patterns of interference on the spatial itself."[75] The various political acts and demographic shifts just described were all ultimately claims upon the space of Los Angeles, and thus claims of a type that the literature of an earlier era suggested demanded a frontiersman's guise. A space where "what is dominant is precisely the becoming minor of all populations" is incompatible with a frontierist logic that so closely associates the capacity to dominate space with the inviolable social dominance of a single racial identity—whiteness.[76] That incompatibility is borne out in Davis's observation that the increasing numbers of wealthy white Angelenos who "escape[d] to the idyllic canyons above Malibu and Hollywood" in the 1970s, 1980s, and 1990s purported to be motivated by "love of the great outdoors or frontier rusticity" but in fact sought insulation against and privacy from "the dense fabric of common citizenship and urban life."[77] That is, a frontierist ethic became, ironically, something invoked as a means to cede rather than to make white claims upon the spaces of a threateningly diverse LA, suggesting its own redundancy as a way of figuring the city.

LA became more determinedly pluralistic through the concerted resistance of marginalized groups to their own marginality, through a persistent refusal to submit to logics that socially center whiteness and/or maleness. If, to borrow Marshall Berman's phrasing for acts of urban rebellion, those "gigantic engines" of power were not stopped by "passionate shouts from the street," they at least had their premises epistemically undermined.[78] The non-white, non-male characters of the texts I have analyzed often find themselves co-opted, even to their own disadvantage, into perpetuating the dynamics of frontierism, dynamics that facilitate and are facilitated by the vision of a particular form of white masculinity as a social ideal, because they are not politically empowered to consider a future outside those dynamics, a world that does not run on frontierist myth. They can hope only for some marginal participation in the myths of the world they find. As the sociopolitical picture changes after the war, however, with the increasing "importance of ethnicity as a mobilizing force" in politics, and comparable appeals to sex or gender as bases for "mobilizing group interest,' so must change the mythic structures underpinning the literature, if it is adequately to represent its place.[79]

Los Angeles's literature of the later twentieth century, and the twenty-first, reflects this in a tremendous diversification of the authorial backgrounds and narrative perspectives it centers. The voices of female authors came to be heard more loudly and frequently from the 1960s onwards, in the works of Eve Babitz, Kate Braverman, and Carolyn See, among many others, as well as in Lurie's *Nowhere City* or, especially pertinently, in Joan Didion's deconstructions of California's frontier-mythic identity. More recently have come Edan Lepucki and Claire Vaye Watkins. In 1963 John Rechy made the first major statement of queer LA fiction in *City of Night*, and simultaneously participated in the early flowering of the Chicanx literary movement. That movement, vast and multifarious in its own right, sits at the center but does not represent the entirety of an even larger profusion of Latinx LA writing since the 1960s, exemplified by such figures as Helena María Viramontes, Oscar Zeta Acosta, Luis Valdez, Luis J. Rodriguez, Manazar Gamboa, Gil Cuadros, and Héctor Tobar.[80] In the aftermath of the 1965 rebellion, the Watts Writers' Workshop provided a platform for and an institutional culture in which to foster new African American voices; kaleidoscopic literary visions of Los Angeles that centered Black consciousness would unfold from Workshop alumna Wanda Coleman, from Al Young, from Octavia Butler, and later from Walter Mosley, Dana Johnson, and Paul Beatty, to name just a few.[81]

The categories I have employed to organize this incomplete list are, of course, by no means mutually exclusive, and a determined intersectionality is conspicuous in the representational politics of the new Los Angeles literature. This is true not only in the fact that the post-'60s regional corpus is exemplified by authors who in many cases personally occupy convergences of multiple insurgent and historically marginalized social perspectives, but also in choices made about which stories to tell, and how to tell them. If Karen Tei Yamashita, Nina Revoyr, and Joe Ide, for example, all exemplify a proliferation in Asian American LA fiction that has been particularly notable since the 1990s, their works are equally notable for a commitment to articulating the city's multiethnicity. All three are as likely to tell Black, white, and Latinx stories as they are to give voice to Asian perspectives. The cast of characters in Yamashita's *Tropic of Orange* is positively Dickensian in both its size and its attempt to range across the full span of the city's sociocultural sprawl; Revoyr's *Southland* (2003) is invested in the tension between mutual solidarity and mutual suspicion that marks the complex sociospatial histories of LA's Black and Japanese communities; Ide created a Black detective protagonist, Isaiah Quintabe, in reflection of his own South LA youth in a mostly Black peer group, his Japanese family having chosen not to leave for suburbs as the area's demography changed.[82]

This flowering of a more diverse literary LA, of which I have given only the most cursory and partial account precisely to indicate how much richness and depth I cannot encompass here, is to a degree simply reflective of wider trends in American publishing. The book industry is, mercifully, less white and male than it used to be, even if vital recent work by Richard Jean So reminds us that reports of publishing's belatedly discovered commitment to social justice and equitable representation have been greatly exaggerated.[83] LA's literary diversification, though, seems particular and significant in the scale and suddenness of the change it betokens, even if we ought to guard against celebrating great writing "just" because it represents diversity, when that term has been weakened by so much cynical corporate co-opting. To do so would be, ironically, to homogenize these authors, circumscribing them within the very confines of minoritization that their work challenges—often in the politics of its content, and always by simply existing. As Ignacio López-Calvo notes, drawing on Henri Lefebvre, "symbolic image making carries with it an impetus of taking possession of social space in both its territorial and political manifestations."[84] In its diversity, then, for want of a better word, LA's literature in the later twentieth and early twenty-first centuries represents a shift away from the enshrinement of white maleness that was intrinsic to an older literary culture, one in part beholden to frontier myth. *Within* that mythic context, though, any reclamation of space from dominant culture of whiteness and maleness likewise represents a rebellious inversion of frontier logic's "savage"/"civilized" certainties. This later literature simultaneously rejects the premises of frontierism and uses them as the instrument of their own demise.[85]

Perhaps no single text embodies this twofold rejection more thoroughly than *Mambo Hips and Make Believe* (1999), Wanda Coleman's only novel in a career best known for poetry. *Mambo Hips* charts the course of a friendship between Erlene, a Black woman, and a white-passing Latina, Tamala. They build their friendship in LA in the 1970s, but as Tamala begins to roam more widely across the state the two keep in touch mostly by mail. The postmarks of Tamala's letters tell a story in their own right, tracing a restless personal geography. Tamala is always on the move—chasing work, chasing dreams of being a writer, chasing and being chased by men, running or on the run from herself, always with the specter of her insecure and ambiguous proximity to whiteness hovering just ahead or just behind. This is a firmly frontierless world: there is never anywhere new to go, only circuits to run around California. So frequent are her moves that "Erlene found it difficult to keep track. Information on Tamala crowded an entire page in her phone diary."[36] The further Tamala travels from LA, moreover, the likelier it is that Coleman uses an invented name rather than a real one for the locale in which she finds herself. Eventually, the only spaces into which Tamala can move are imaginary, and such unreal space never satisfies or proves stable for long. Tamala does not survive the novel.

Erlene, meanwhile, stays more or less still, in Los Angeles. There is, for her, no urge to roam, no need to chase the new and uncharted space before its promises are (inevitably) revealed as illusory. Erlene knows where she is and who she is, and the answer to both questions is Los Angeles. This is not because Coleman's city has fulfilled the paradisical promises of its early twentieth-century boosters: those promises were always racially exclusive, and *Mambo Hips* is unflinching and unsentimental in accounting the ways in which Erlene's identity as a Black woman in the 1970s and '80s still makes LA a tougher place to navigate than it otherwise would be. That frankness, though, is never accompanied in Erlene by a desire to imagine or an attempt to flee elsewhere. Los Angeles is home: it represents in *Mambo Hips* not instability and flux but groundedness and solidity—the rejection of which brings Tamala no happiness. It is hard to imagine a novel with a less frontierist sense of how one might build a relationship between space, place, race, and self.

It seems similarly notable how frequently writers from marginalized and minoritized communities have chosen to write back to the LA of the mid-twentieth century, and to the whiteness of the frontierist literary corpus through which it has been enduringly memorialized. Naomi Hirahara, for example, has stated that her LA detective, elderly Japanese gardener Mas Arai, is a direct rejoinder to the cruel stereotypes that Raymond Chandler deployed in such figures—Arai thus acts to subvert and complicate the image of the archetypal hardboiled investigator as the frontiersman's inheritor.[37] Mosley's Easy Rawlins does something similar, offering a kind of revisionist fictional history that asks how different a mid-century LA we might have come to know had its greatest detective been, instead of Marlowe, a Black man first drawn to the city from Texas by the promise of war work. (Or, what if Bob Jones's fate had been different?) Ide's Quintabe, who owes a substantial debt to Rawlins, transposes such perspective-altering questions to the contemporary city. Meanwhile in *The Goodbye Coast* (2022), a contemporary Philip Marlowe reboot, Ide's present-day version of the king of the LA sleuths is, simply, no longer a racist—though we might wonder accordingly wonder if he is no longer Philip Marlowe either. If the Sleepy Lagoon murder trial and the Zoot Suit Riots were racist attempts to silence the voices of a burgeoning Mexican American youth, Luis Valdez's play *Zoot Suit* (1979) acted to reamplify those same voices retroactively. In so doing, Valdez wrote reparatively not only against a social injustice but also into a cognate literary-historical gap—the dearth of LA literature published by Latinx authors in the mid-century decades that I have acknowledged as creating a historical aporia at the heart of this book. Revoyr's *Southland* and Viramontes's *Their Dogs Came with Them* (2007) perform similar acts of historical reparation—reaching backward to 1960s Watts and 1930s Crenshaw (in Revoyr's novel) and 1960s East LA (in Viramontes's) to resist what Norman Klein terms LA's willful "history of forgetting" its past acts of violence toward the marginalized and even to itself.[88]

When more recent white male authors have written back to the white male mid-century LA canon, meanwhile, there is typically at least an acknowledgment that one cannot do so straightforwardly. When James Ellroy takes up the discarded champion's belt of mid-century California noir, he invokes his inspirations in a manner so steroidally hypertrophied—in the style and politics of both his novels and his theatrical public persona—as to cloud the water between irony, provocation, and a sincerely reactionary conservatism that borders on the fascistic. If Ellroy attests to the continuing popular viability of LA fiction that champions the kind of unreconstructed and uncompromising white masculinity that Macdonald knew was out of style by the late '60s, he does so from an explicitly revanchist position, one that acknowledges a changed world in proclaiming embattlement by and resistance to it. Thomas Pynchon, meanwhile, being Thomas Pynchon, updates the mid-century LA detective simply by realizing what a deeply strange figure he is, and testing his pathologically peculiar mind to its psychogeographic limits. One way or another, everyone agrees: things aren't what they were.

None of this is to declare the frontier's pernicious cultural influence "gone at last"—to make such a claim now would demand no less credulity than when Frank Norris made it 120 years ago. Greg Grandin, for example, has framed Donald Trump's determination to wall off the United States' southern border as "the final closing of the frontier," a political strategy prompted by a crisis of realization that "the world's horizon is not infinite."[89] As I argued in my introduction, however, and as Grandin himself acknowledges, this "argument isn't new": plenty of America's brightest minds believed the nation had reached "the end of its myth" a century ago, but they underestimated that myth's stubborn adhesiveness and mutability, its ability to pour itself into even the tightest cultural and social spaces.[90] We would be naive, therefore, to state that any more contemporary assertion of frontier closure is final or total (whether we find it in the Trumpian wall of the 2010s or the increasingly diverse literary culture of post-1960s LA). As Grandin writes, the frontier's legacy retains the potential to make Americans "prisoners of the past."[91]

In the final scene of *The Underground Man*, Lew Archer is in a car with Jean Broadhurst and her son Ronny, whose father and grandfather have both been murdered in the process of frontiersmanlike attempts to assert individualist masculinity. "I hoped it was over," Archer recalls. "I hoped that Ronny's life wouldn't turn back toward his father's death as his father's life had turned, in a narrowing circle. I wished the boy a benign failure of memory."[92] Perhaps there is no such thing as a "benign failure of memory" when, as Klein emphasizes, the history of forgetting—who gets to forget, what gets forgotten—is itself a history of the very same privileges as those embodied by the figure of the frontiersman. Certainly, we should not would not wish to erase frontier myth from memory, as we must not forget whose dreams its irruptive legacies centered and whose it derogated. Indeed, this book has sought precisely to chart how the myth's legacies continued to suffuse the culture of LA long after the geographic frontier had gone.

In the fiction, those legacies place "narrowing circles" of human possibility most obviously and punitively around non-white characters like Julio Sal and Bob Jones—demanding a perpetual cycle of futile attempts to possess the frontier ideal. The very same myths, though, also narrow the possibilities afforded to white characters like Walter Huff, John Norman, even Philip Marlowe—who suffer greatly in their inability to escape a frontierist vision of what whiteness and masculinity are permitted to be. Fictive as all these lives are, they are real inasmuch as they respond to a real world, and what they share and memorialize of that world is a quality of being circumscribed not by the closure of the frontier but by its closing upon them. So, as a cleansing rain falls upon the "steaming remnants of the fire," Archer's hope for a "benign failure of memory" is to be welcomed as a hope that Southern California might move beyond such restrictive and destructive myths.[93] Archer, Ronny, and Jean drive south. Ahead of them lies Los Angeles—just, as it always seems to be, slightly in the future, where it would indeed demand and discharge new possibilities for structuring the world.

Notes

Introduction

1. "Raymond Chandler to Hamish Hamilton, 4 December 1949," in *Raymond Chandler Speaking*, ed. Dorothy Gardiner and Kathrine Sorley Walker (Berkeley: University of California Press, 1997), 84.

2. Frederick Jackson Turner, "The Significance of the Frontier in American History," in *The Frontier in American History* (New York: Henry Holt, 1921), 1. *The Frontier in American History* collects Turner's writings on the frontier and thus constitutes the most complete accounting of Turnerism in its various historical, political, theoretical, and philosophical dimensions.

3. J. Hector St. John de Crèvecœur, "Letter III: What is an American?" in *Letters from an American Farmer and Other Essays*, ed. Dennis D. Moore (Cambridge, MA: Harvard University Press, 2013), 29–32 and throughout.

4. Francis Joseph Grund, *The Americans, in Their Moral, Social, and Political Relations* (Boston, MA: Marsh, Capen and Lyon, 1837), 206.

5. Richard Slotkin, "Nostalgia and Progress: Theodore Roosevelt's Myth of the Frontier," *American Quarterly* 33, no. 5 (Winter 1981): 608, https://doi.org/10.2307/2712805. Roosevelt would ultimately be influenced by and champion Turner as a figure who lent academic authority to his own worldview, but in fact "wrote much of" *The Winning of the West* before the 1893 speech in which Turner first outlined his frontier thesis. Michael Allen, review of *The Winning of the West*, by Theodore Roosevelt, *Tennessee Historical Quarterly* 55, no. 1 (1996): 88. Turner himself reviewed the first volumes of *The Winning of the West* favorably, as noted in George B. Utley, "Theodore Roosevelt's *The Winning of the West*: Some Unpublished Letters," *Mississippi Valley Historical Review* 30, no. 4 (March 1944): 496, https://doi.org/10.2307/1916697.

6. Michael C. Steiner, "From Frontier to Region: Frederick Jackson Turner and the New Western History," *Pacific Historical Review* 64, no. 4 (November 1995): 479–80.

7. William Cronon, "Turner's First Stand: The Significance of Significance in American History," in *Writing Western History: Essays on Major Western Historians*, ed. Richard W. Etulain (Reno: University of Nevada Press, 2002), 87.

8. Richard W. Etulain, "The Rise of Western Historiography," in *Writing Western History: Essays on Major Western Historians*, ed. Richard W. Etulain (Reno: University of Nevada Press, 2002), 12.

9. Walter Prescott Webb, *The Great Frontier: An Interpretation of World History Since Columbus* (London: Secker and Warburg, 1953), 5. Webb's mature academic career is conterminous with and emblematic of my period of investigation as one in which Turnerian frontier history flourished: *The Great Frontier*'s 1951 American publication came exactly twenty years after Webb's first major work, *The Great Plains* (Boston: Ginn, 1931).

10. Paxson's major contributions are *The Last American Frontier* (New York: Macmillan, 1910); *The New Nation* (Boston: Houghton Mifflin, 1915); *History of the American Frontier, 1763–1893* (Dunwoody, GA: Norman S. Berg, 1924).

11. John Pettegrew, *Brutes in Suits: Male Sensibility in America, 1890–1920* (Baltimore: Johns Hopkins University Press, 2007), 22. Its prevalence notwithstanding, Turnerism did have its academic dissenters in this period. Turner's former student Herbert Bolton challenged the frontier's theoretical primacy with a proto-transnationalist call for a "history of the Americas." Nevertheless, he maintained Turner's framing of the American West as a "nationalizing force," per Russell M. Magnaghi, *Herbert E. Bolton and the Historiography of the Americas* (Westport, CT: Greenwood Press, 1998), 121. Bolton's contributions include *Colonization of North America, 1492–1783* (with Thomas Maitland Marshall; New York: Macmillan, 1920), *The Spanish Borderlands: A Chronicle of Old Florida and the Southwest* (New Haven, CT: Yale University Press, 1921), and *Wider Horizons of American History* (New York: D. Appleton-Century, 1939). George Pierson would more directly interrogate Turnerism: see *The Frontier and Frontiersmen of Turner's Essays: A Scrutiny of the Foundations of the Middle Western Tradition* (Indianapolis: Bobbs-Merrill, 1940) and "The Frontier and American Institutions: A Criticism of the Turner Theory," *New England Quarterly: A Historical Review of New England Life and Letters* 15, no. 2 (June 1942): 224–55, https://doi.org/10.2307/360525.

12. Kerwin Lee Klein, *Frontiers of Historical Imagination: Narrating the European Conquest of Native America, 1890–1990* (Berkeley: University of California Press, 1999), 8.

13. Robert P. Porter, *Extra Census Bulletin: Distribution of Population According to Density: 1890* (Washington, DC: Census Office, Department of the Interior, 1891), 4. Cited by Turner in "Significance," 1.

14. Turner, "Significance," 36.

15. Cronon, "Turner's First Stand," 86.

16. Frederick Jackson Turner, "The Problem of the West," in *The Frontier in American History* (New York: Henry Holt, 1921), 219; Turner, "Significance," 37.

17. Turner, "Problem of the West," 219–20.
18. Turner, "Significance," 4.
19. Turner, "Problem of the West," 205.
20. Pettegrew, *Brutes in Suits*, 42.
21. Pettegrew, *Brutes in Suits*, 44; Turner, "Significance," 37.
22. Philip Fisher, *Still the New World: American Literature in a Culture of Creative Destruction* (Cambridge, MA: Harvard University Press, 1999), 3.
23. E. Douglas Branch, *Westward: The Romance of the American Frontier* (New York: Appleton, 1930), vii.
24. Webb, *Great Frontier*, 284.
25. Webb, *Great Frontier*, 281.
26. Frank Norris, "The Frontier Gone at Last," *The World's Work*, February 1902, 1731.
27. The fullest discussion of the turn-of-the-century antimodernist movement and fears of "overcivilization" remains T. J. Jackson Lears's *No Place of Grace: Antimodernism and the Transformation of American Culture, 1880–1920*, 2nd ed. (Chicago: University of Chicago Press, 1994). Although dated, Roderick Nash's *Wilderness and the American Mind* (New Haven, CT: Yale University Press, 1967) is still an essential account of changing American attitudes to wilderness, including post-frontier trends towards conservation and the "wilderness cult." Both Nash and Lears are further discussed in chapter 2.
28. Turner, "Problem of the West," 209; Waldo Frank, *Our America* (New York: Ams Press, 1972), 19.
29. Frank, *Our America*, 29.
30. Turner, "Problem of the West," 210.
31. Such themes recur in Frank's later work. The title of *The Re-Discovery of America: An Introduction to a Philosophy of American Life* (New York: Charles Scribner's Sons, 1929) is powerfully suggestive of the extent to which Frank urgently believed that America had devoted too many resources to spatial exploration of itself and now demanded an equivalent intellectual self-exploration in redress.
32. I return to Hoover and Roosevelt's frontier debates in chapter 3
33. Pettegrew, *Brutes in Suits*, 47.
34. John Dewey, *Individualism: Old and New* (London: G. Allen and Unwin, 1931), 87.
35. Dewey, *Individualism*, 88.
36. Dewey, *Individualism*, 88.
37. Turner likewise claimed (pre-Depression), in one of his statements of advocacy for the frontier's endurance, that "masters of industry and capital" like Carnegie and Rockefeller emerged from a frontier society and thus could continue to "profess its principles" even as they represented its depredation. Frederick Jackson Turner, "Contributions of the West to American Democracy," in *The Frontier in American History* (New York: Henry Holt, 1921), 264.

38. William Hollingsworth Whyte, *The Organization Man* (New York: Simon and Schuster, 1956), 15.

39. Webb, *Great Frontier*, 48.

40. Whyte, *Organization Man*, 16.

41. Weber suggests the conceptual proximity between his ethic and Turnerian claims about the frontier's environmental influence on character and society when he writes that "the simple fact of working in quite different surroundings from those to which one is accustomed breaks through the tradition and is the educative force. It is hardly necessary to remark how much of American economic development is the result of such factors." *The Protestant Ethic and the Spirit of Capitalism*, trans. Talcott Parsons (London: Routledge, 2005), 137.

42. Peter Stanfield, *Hollywood, Westerns, and the 1930s: The Lost Trail* (Exeter: University of Exeter Press, 2001), 10.

43. Robert L. Sklar, *City Boys: Cagney, Bogart, Garfield* (Princeton: Princeton University Press, 1992), 8.

44. Stanfield, *Hollywood, Westerns, and the 1930s*, 10.

45. Jimmie Rodgers, "Waiting for a Train" (Victor, 1928).

46. Webb, *Great Frontier*, 281, 283.

47. Carey McWilliams, "Myths of the West," *North American Review*, November 1931, 425.

48. McWilliams, "Myths of the West," 429.

49. McWilliams, "Myths of the West," 432.

50. McWilliams, "Myths of the West," 432.

51. Fisher, *Still the New World*, 7.

52. See Henry Nash Smith, *Virgin Land: The American West as Symbol and Myth* (Cambridge, MA: Harvard University Press, 1950). Slotkin's towering contribution consists principally of *Regeneration through Violence: The Mythology of the American Frontier, 1600–1860* (Middletown, CT: Wesleyan University Press, 1973), *The Fatal Environment: The Myth of the Frontier in the Age of Industrialization, 1800–1890* (New York: Atheneum, 1985), and *Gunfighter Nation: The Myth of the Frontier in Twentieth-Century America* (Norman: University of Oklahoma Press, 1998). The most enthusiastic and thoroughgoing Turnerian of the post-'50s period was Ray Allen Billington. Yet even his oeuvre is less Turnerian history per se than an apologetic historiography of Turnerism, suggesting a period in which a Turner-accommodating view remained defensible but required defending. See *The American Frontier Thesis: Attack and Defense* (Washington, DC: American Historical Association, 1971) and *The Genesis of the Frontier Thesis: A Study in Historical Creativity* (San Marino, CA: Huntington Library, 1971).

53. Stanfield, *Hollywood, Westerns, and the 1930s*, 10. Among the essential fundaments of the New Western History are Patricia Nelson Limerick's *The Legacy of Conquest: The Unbroken Past of the American West* (New York: W. W. Norton, 1987) and Richard White's *"It's Your Misfortune and None of My Own": A New History of the American West* (Norman: University of Oklahoma Press, 1991).

54. Cronon, "Turner's First Stand," 91.
55. Turner, "Significance," 3.
56. Turner, "Significance," 3, 8, 21, 1.
57. Turner, "Significance," 3.
58. Turner, "Significance," 2 (emphasis mine).
59. Kerwin Lee Klein, *Apocalypse Noir: Carey McWilliams and Posthistorical California* (Berkeley: Doe Library, University of California, 1997), 6.
60. Michael C. Steiner, "Frederick Jackson Turner and Western Regionalism," in *Writing Western History: Essays on Major Western Historians*, ed. Richard W. Etulain (Reno: University of Nevada Press, 2002), 103.
61. Turner, "Significance," 2.
62. Indeed, because the frontiers I identify depart from Turner's in *not* being constructed on the inevitably finite possibilities of westward advance into free land, my fictional frontiers, for good or ill, in fact prove to possess a greater facility for cyclical repetition than their geographic forebears.
63. Frederick Jackson Turner, "The West and American Ideals," in *The Frontier in American History* (New York: Henry Holt, 1921), 294.
64. Frederick Jackson Turner, "Pioneer Ideals and the State University," in *The Frontier in American History* (New York: Henry Holt, 1921), 270.
65. Cronon, "Turner's First Stand," 90.
66. Slotkin, *Gunfighter Nation*, 59.
67. Slotkin, *Gunfighter Nation*, 59; Slotkin, "Nostalgia and Progress," 612.
68. Klein, *Frontiers of Historical Imagination*, 9.
69. Klein, *Frontiers of Historical Imagination*, 19.
70. Pettegrew, *Brutes in Suits*, 39.
71. Turner, "Contributions," 1921, 253.
72. Turner, "Problem of the West," 213.
73. Turner, "Significance," 9.
74. Slotkin, "Nostalgia and Progress," 611.
75. Cronon, "Turner's First Stand," 82–83.
76. Slotkin, *Gunfighter Nation*, 59.
77. Ray Allen Billington and Martin Ridge, *Westward Expansion: A History of the American Frontier*, 6th ed. (Albuquerque: University of New Mexico Press, 2001), 5. The more recent editions of Billington's *Westward Expansion* (one of the most comprehensive elaborations on the Turner thesis, originally published in 1949) constitute a particularly intriguing example of the revisionism to which Turnerism has been subject in recent decades. Ridge has updated and amended Billington's text, preserving its structure and argument but endeavoring to compensate for some gaps of perspective that are symptomatic of its time of writing. It thus becomes, in effect, a synthesis of old and new modes of thinking about and producing history—a New Western Turnerism.
78. Webb, *Great Frontier*, 49.
79. Billington and Ridge, *Westward Expansion*, 2.

80. Turner, "Problem of the West," 212.

81. Turner, "Contributions," 1921, 250; Turner, "Problem of the West," 213; Turner, "Pioneer Ideals," 272.

82. Pettegrew, *Brutes in Suits*, 21; Richard Dyer, *White* (London: Routledge, 1997), 35.

83. Turner, "Contributions," 1921, 252.

84. Valerie Babb, *Whiteness Visible: The Meaning of Whiteness in American Literature and Culture* (New York: New York University Press, 1998), 91.

85. Babb, 169.

86. Dyer, *White*, 33.

87. These figures are derived from my own corpus analysis of *The Frontier in American History*.

88. Billington and Ridge, *Westward Expansion*, 11.

89. Carla J. McDonough, *Staging Masculinity: Male Identity in Contemporary American Drama* (Jefferson, NC: McFarland, 2006), 36.

90. Klein, *Frontiers of Historical Imagination*, 8–9.

91. Klein, *Frontiers of Historical Imagination*, 12.

92. Pettegrew, *Brutes in Suits*, 21.

93. Billington and Ridge, *Westward Expansion*, x.

94. Billington and Ridge, *Westward Expansion*, 12.

95. Turner, "Significance," 15; Turner, "Problem of the West," 214.

96. Frederick Jackson Turner, "The First Official Frontier of the Massachusetts Bay," in *The Frontier in American History* (New York: Henry Holt, 1921), 46; Turner, "Problem of the West," 212.

97. Turner, "Significance," 12.

98. Klein, *Frontiers of Historical Imagination*, 12. For Klein, this is the irony of the New Western History's critique of Turner's supposed narrowness of perspective—that perspective is in fact, suggests Klein, the progenitor of later historiographical emphases on marginal and subaltern voices.

99. Slotkin, "Nostalgia and Progress," 612.

100. Turner, "Contributions," 256, 254.

101. Harold P. Simonson, *Beyond the Frontier: Writers, Western Regionalism, and a Sense of Place* (Fort Worth: Texas Christian University Press, 1989), 18.

102. Turner, "Problem of the West," 205.

103. Fisher, *Still the New World*, 3–4.

104. *Fifteenth Census of the United States, 1930: Population*, vol. 1: Number and Distribution of Inhabitants (Washington, DC: United States Government Printing Office, 1931).

105. Something like the LA of today perhaps began to become recognizable in the 1960s, when an increasingly sprawling, increasingly multiethnic, increasingly freeway-striated and car-dependent conurbation headed towards a population of three million. This later city is one to which I return in my epilogue.

106. Edward W. Soja and Allen J. Scott, "Introduction to Los Angeles: City and Region," in *The City: Los Angeles and Urban Theory at the End of the Twentieth Century*, ed. Edward W. Soja and Allen J. Scott (Berkeley: University of California Press, 1996), 3.

107. J. Scott Bryson, "Los Angeles Literature: Exiles, Natives, and (Mis) Representation," *American Literary History* 16, no. 4 (December 2004): 711, https://doi.org/10.1093/ALH/AJH039.

108. Mike Davis, *City of Quartz: Excavating the Future in Los Angeles* (London: Verso, 2006), 24, 30. Davis deploys this dichotomy throughout *City of Quartz*, most prominently in its first section; these references denote the points at which he introduces each term.

109. Edward Dimendberg, introduction to *Los Angeles: The Development, Life, and Structure of the City of Two Million in Southern California*, by Anton Wagner, ed. Edward Dimendberg, trans. Timothy Grundy (Los Angeles: Getty Research Institute, 2022), 16.

110. John D. Keyes, Preface to *Los Angeles: A Guide to the City and Its Environs* (New York: Hastings House, 1941), v.

111. Morrow Mayo, *Los Angeles* (New York: Alfred A. Knopf, 1933), 30.

112. Anton Wagner, *Los Angeles: The Development, Life, and Structure of the City of Two Million in Southern California*, ed. Edward Dimendberg, trans. Timothy Grundy (Los Angeles: Getty Research Institute, 2022), 287.

113. Wagner, *Los Angeles*, 288.

114. Mark Wild, *Street Meeting: Multiethnic Neighborhoods in Early Twentieth-Century Los Angeles* (Berkeley: University of California Press, 2005), 38; Eric Avila, *Popular Culture in the Age of White Flight: Fear and Fantasy in Suburban Los Angeles* (Berkeley: University of California Press, 2006), 22.

115. Avila, *Popular Culture in the Age of White Flight*, 22.

116. Harry Carr, *Los Angeles: City of Dreams* (New York: D. Appleton-Century, 1935), 5.

117. Avila, *Popular Culture in the Age of White Flight*, 22, 25.

118. Mayo, *Los Angeles*, 35.

119. Wagner, *Los Angeles*, 212.

120. Margaret Sarah Climie, "Southern California in American Fiction" (Los Angeles: University of Southern California, 1925), 3.

121. Edmund Wilson, *Boys in the Back Room: Notes on California Novelists* (San Francisco: The Colt Press, 1941), 59.

122. Kevin Starr identifies the key members of the literary circle that formed around Rose's store and the adjacent Musso and Frank Grill at the turn of the 1930s as James M. Cain, Erskine Caldwell, John Fante, A. I. Bezzerides, Frank Fenton, Jo Pagano, Raymond Chandler, Louis Adamic, Budd Schulberg, William Saroyan, William Faulkner, and Nathanael West. Kevin Starr, *Material Dreams: Southern California through the 1920s* (Oxford: Oxford University Press, 1990), 348.

123. Carey McWilliams, *Southern California: An Island on the Land* (Layton, UT: Gibbs-Smith, 2010), 364. McWilliams's other candidates are Fante, West, and Luther.

124. Blake Allmendinger, conclusion to *A History of California Literature*, ed. Blake Allmendinger (New York: Cambridge University Press, 2015), 385.

125. *Double Indemnity* first appeared in serial form in in *Liberty* magazine in 1936, before being collected as part of the Cain anthology *Three of a Kind* in 1943.

126. Peter Lunenfeld, *City at the Edge of Forever: Los Angeles Reimagined* (New York: Viking, 2020), 5. Readers seeking a clear account of the Hollywood novel as a discrete phenomenon in the history of LA literature would do well to start with Chip Rhodes, "Hollywood Fictions," in *The Cambridge Companion to the Literature of Los Angeles*, ed. Kevin R. McNamara (Cambridge: Cambridge University Press, 2010).

127. Ignacio López-Calvo, *Latino Los Angeles in Film and Fiction: The Cultural Production of Social Anxiety* (Tucson: University of Arizona Press, 2011), 13–14, 20.

128. López-Calvo, *Latino Los Angeles*, 177.

129. George J. Sanchez, *Becoming Mexican American: Ethnicity, Culture, and Identity in Chicano Los Angeles, 1900–1945* (Oxford: Oxford University Press, 1993).

130. Slotkin, *Gunfighter Nation*, 2.

131. John F. Kennedy, "Acceptance Speech at the 1960 Democratic National Convention," www.jfklibrary.org/Asset-Viewer/AS08q5oYz0SFUZg9uOi4iw.aspx.

132. Harold P. Simonson, *The Closed Frontier: Studies in American Literary Tragedy* (New York: Holt, Rinehart, and Winston, 1970).

133. James D. Houston, " 'The Circle Almost Circled': Some Notes on California's Fiction," in *Reading the West: New Essays on the Literature of the American West*, ed. Michael Kowalewski (Cambridge: Cambridge University Press, 1996), 238.

134. David M. Fine, *Imagining Los Angeles: A City in Fiction* (Reno: University of Nevada Press, 2004), 82.

135. Simonson, *Beyond the Frontier*, 54.

136. Davis, *City of Quartz*, 18.

137. William Alexander McClung, *Landscapes of Desire: Anglo Mythologies of Los Angeles* (Berkeley: University of California Press, 2000), 41.

138. Joseph C. Porter, "The End of the Trail: The American West of Dashiell Hammett and Raymond Chandler," *Western Historical Quarterly* 6, no. 4 (October 1975): 411–12, https://doi.org/10.2307/967777.

139. Porter, "The End of the Trail," 424.

140. David Wyatt, *The Fall into Eden: Landscape and Imagination in California* (Cambridge: Cambridge University Press, 1986), 158.

141. Wyatt, *The Fall into Eden*, 158.

142. As Mike Davis shows, both boosters and debunkers of Southern California have investments in the popular but untrue notion that Los Angeles sits in what would, if not for titanic and perpetual acts of human geoengineering, be a desert, completely barren and inhospitable. For the former, this discloses the

triumph of the region as man-made Eden or conquered frontier where nature has been subdued; for the latter, it only reveals the superficiality and precarity of the edifice constructed there. See Davis's *Ecology of Fear: Los Angeles and the Imagination of Disaster* (London: Picador, 2000), 10–11.

143. Fine, *Imagining Los Angeles*, 22–23.

144. Fine, *Imagining Los Angeles*, 23.

145. Houston, "The Circle Almost Circled," 236.

146. John Scaggs, *Crime Fiction* (London: Routledge, 2005), 68.

147. Hugh T. Hodges, "Charles Maclay: California Missionary, San Fernando Valley Pioneer: Part III," *Southern California Quarterly* 68 no. 4 (December 1986): 357, https://doi.org/10.2307/41171239.

148. Mayo, *Los Angeles*, 329.

149. Woody Guthrie, "Do Re Mi" (RCA Victor, 1940).

150. Dora Beale Polk, *The Island of California: A History of the Myth* (Lincoln: University of Nebraska Press, 1995), 125. As Houston notes, because it draws its name from a work of fantastical fiction, there is a sense that California is a place where 'the dream came first. The place came later." Houston, "The Circle Almost Circled," 231–32.

151. Porter, "End of the Trail," 412.

152. Laurence Culver embodies this paradox in the title of his study *The Frontier of Leisure: Southern California and the Shaping of Modern America* (Oxford: Oxford University Press, 2010). A land of leisure may represent the triumph (or imagined triumph) of an Edenic myth but it is, in Turnerian terms, no frontier at all.

153. Wyatt, *The Fall into Eden*, 132.

154. Wyatt, *The Fall into Eden*, 132, 148, 149.

155. Scaggs, *Crime Fiction*, 68–69.

156. Davis, *City of Quartz*, 23.

157. Davis, *City of Quartz*, 20, 38.

158. Aldous Huxley, *Jesting Pilate: The Diary of a Journey* (London: Triad/Paladin Books, 1985), 192.

159. Davis refers to LA's predilection for producing *noir* fiction as a response to Depression-era conditions that were felt disproportionately acutely among the middle classes in early-'30s LA, as its blue-collar economy was less well developed than those of Eastern cities. He suggests, like the "closed frontier" critical school, that *noir* invokes ideas of LA as the "terminus of American history," and indeed briefly quotes David Fine, that critical tendency's leading exponent, to the same effect. Davis, *City of Quartz*, 20, 38. The implications of the fact that these ideas are rooted in the frontier myth, frontier history, and the anxious Depression-era discourse around frontier closure, however, go unpursued by Davis.

160. Michael Sorkin, "Explaining Los Angeles," in *California Counterpoint: New West Coast Architecture 1982* (New York: Rizzoli International Publications, 1982), 8. Also cited in in Davis, *City of Quartz*, 20.

161. Julian Murphet, *Race and Literature in Los Angeles* (Cambridge: Cambridge University Press, 2001), 9.

162. Casey Shoop, "Corpse and Accomplice: Fredric Jameson, Raymond Chandler, and the Representation of History in California," *Cultural Critique* 77 (Winter 2011): 236, https://doi.org/10.5749/culturalcritique.77.2011.0205.

163. Murphet, *Race and Literature in Los Angeles*, 8.

164. Murphet, *Race and Literature in Los Angeles*, 13.

165. Karen Tei Yamashita, *Tropic of Orange* (Minneapolis: Coffee House Press, 2017), 53.

166. Joan Didion, *Play It as It Lays* (London: Fourth Estate, 2011), 15.

167. Joan Didion, "Bureaucrats," in *We Tell Ourselves Stories in Order to Live: Collected Nonfiction* (New York: Alfred A. Knopf, 2006), 238.

168. Edward Dimendberg, "The Kinetic Icon: Reyner Banham on Los Angeles as Mobile Metropolis," *Urban History* 33, no. 1 (May 2006): 113, https://doi.org/10.1017/S0963926806003543.

169. Dimendberg, 120.

170. Dean Franco, *The Border and the Line: Race and Literature in Los Angeles* (Stanford, CA: Stanford University Press, 2019), 6.

171. Robert M. Fogelson, *The Fragmented Metropolis: Los Angeles 1850–1930* (Berkeley: University of California Press, 1993), 185.

172. Carr, *City of Dreams*, 6, 257.

173. John Fante, *Ask the Dust*, in *The Bandini Quartet* (Edinburgh: Canongate Books, 2004), 588.

174. Fante, *Ask the Dust*, 556.

175. Carey McWilliams, *Southern California*, 314.

176. Franco, *The Border and the Line*, 1.

177. Franco, *The Border and the Line*, 4.

178. John Fante, "Mary Osaka, I Love You," in *The Big Hunger: Stories 1932–1959*, ed. Cooper, Stephen (New York: Ecco, 2000), 193.

179. As quoted by Rosencrans Baldwin from a conversation with Tobar, in Baldwin's *Everything Now: Lessons from the City-State of Los Angeles* (New York: Farrar, Straus and Giroux, 2021), 250.

180. Blake Allmendinger, *Ten Most Wanted: The New Western Literature* (New York: Routledge, 1998), 1–2.

Chapter 1

1. Russel B. Nye, "Saturday Night at the Paradise Ballroom: Or, Dance Halls in the Twenties," *Journal of Popular Culture* 7, no. 1 (Summer 1973): 15, https://doi.org/10.1111/j.0022-3840.1973.00014.x.

2. Paul Goalby Cressey, *The Taxi-Dance Hall: A Sociological Study in Commercialized Recreation and City Life* (Chicago: University of Chicago Press, 1932), xvii.

3. Nye, "Saturday Night at the Paradise Ballroom," 16.

4. Nye, "Saturday Night at the Paradise Ballroom," 16–17.

5. Henri Lefebvre, *The Production of Space*, trans. Donald Nicholson-Smith (Oxford: Blackwell, 1991), 38–40. Lefebvre respectively glosses "representations of space," "spatial practice," and "representational space" as the "conceived," the "perceived," and the "lived." Lefebvre, 39.

6. Fine, *Imagining Los Angeles*, 92.

7. Fine, *Imagining Los Angeles*, 104–5.

8. David M. Fine, "The Emergence of Los Angeles as a Literary Territory," *California History* 79, no. 1 (April 2000): 7, https://doi.org/10.2307/25591571.

9. Philip E. Melling, "The West in Fiction," in *Nothing Else to Fear: New Perspectives on America in the Thirties*, ed. Stephen W. Baskerville and Ralph Willett (Manchester: Manchester University Press, 1985), 121–22.

10. Jan Goggans, "Dreams, Denial, and Depression-Era Fiction," in *A History of California Literature*, ed. Blake Allmendinger (New York: Cambridge University Press, 2015), 175.

11. William Hare, *Pulp Fiction to Film Noir: The Great Depression and the Development of a Genre* (Jefferson, NC: McFarland, 2012), 73–74.

12. Carol J. Martin, *Dance Marathons: Performing American Culture of the 1920s and 1930s* (Jackson: University Press of Mississippi, 1994), 5.

13. Martin, *Dance Marathons*, 15–21.

14. Martin, *Dance Marathons*, 7.

15. Ralph G. Giordano, *Social Dancing in America*, vol. 2 (Westport, CT: Greenwood Press, 2007), 79–80.

16. Martin, *Dance Marathons*, 33–34. Giordano suggests that the typical format comprised 45- to 50-minute periods of motion followed by 10-minute rest breaks, but in McCoy's novel the 10-minute break is only granted every two hours. Giordano, *Social Dancing in America*, 2:61; Horace McCoy, *They Shoot Horses, Don't They?* (London: Serpent's Tail, 1995), 16.

17. Giordano, *Social Dancing in America*, 2:61.

18. Martin, *Dance Marathons*, 43.

19. Giordano, *Social Dancing in America*, 2:76.

20. McCoy, *Horses*, 14.

21. Santa Monica-Ocean Park Chamber of Commerce, *Santa Monica: Southern California's Home City of Culture and Recreation* (Santa Monica, CA: Santa Monica-Ocean Park Chamber of Commerce, 1930), 14.

22. Philip L. Fradkin and Alex L. Fradkin, *The Left Coast: California on the Edge* (Berkeley: University of California Press, 2011), 49; Jeffrey Stanton,

Venice of America: "Coney Island of the Pacific" (Los Angeles: Donahue, 1987), 55, 76.

23. Sydney Pollack's 1969 film adaptation of *Horses* identified the dancehall as the Aragon Ballroom on Lick Pier. Hare, *Pulp Fiction to Film Noir*, 67. The Lick Pier straddled the Santa Monica-Venice municipal boundary and opened in 1924, following the destruction of a previous pier in a fire. During the time in which McCoy's novel is set, however, the ballroom on Lick Pier was not in fact the Aragon but the Bon Ton, per Stanton, *Venice of America*, 94. Months after the release of Pollack's film, the Aragon itself would itself burn down. "Pier Fire Destroys Aragon Ballroom," *Los Angeles Times*, May 27, 1970.

24. McCoy, *Horses*, 14.

25. Giordano, *Social Dancing in America*, 2:103; Paula A. Scott, *Santa Monica: A History on the Edge* (Charleston, SC: Arcadia, 2004), 66.

26. Giordano, *Social Dancing in America*, 2:69.

27. McCoy, *Horses*, 116.

28. Dimendberg, introduction to *Los Angeles*, 59.

29. Lefebvre, *The Production of Space*, 21.

30. Martin, *Dance Marathons*, 41.

31. McCoy, *Horses*, 116.

32. Goggans, "Dreams, Denial, and Depression-Era Fiction," 175.

33. Giordano, *Social Dancing in America*, 2:80.

34. Stephen Cooper, editor's notes to *The Big Hunger: Stories 1932–1959*, by John Fante, ed. Stephen Cooper (New York: Ecco, 2000), 310; Stephen Cooper, *Full of Life: A Biography of John Fante* (New York: North Point Press, 2000), 133.

35. References in the text to the presence at San Pedro of two aircraft carriers, the *Lexington* and *Saratoga*, exclude any date prior to April 1928, when both ships came to be moored at the port. The protagonist is young, but old enough both to manage the work of a longshoreman and to momentarily convince a woman that he is a professor, while there is contemporary evidence that most dancehalls were relatively diligent in ensuring minors were not admitted: see Ella Gardner, *Public Dance Halls: Their Regulation and Place in the Recreation of Adolescents* (Washington, DC: United States Government Printing Office, 1929), http://hdl.loc.gov/loc.music/musdi.205. We may thus infer that this protagonist is in his early twenties. If, like most of Fante's protagonists, he shares Fante's age (Fante was born in 1909 but often claimed 1911), we can therefore assume that "Clever Fellow" is set between 1930 and 1932. The frequency with which Fante's fiction contains autobiographical elements supports such a conclusion: 1930–32 was the period in which he himself lived and worked odd jobs in LA's southernmost maritime fringe. Cooper, *Full of Life*, 73.

36. "Clever Fellow" takes its title from Cabell's *Jurgen: A Comedy of Justice* (New York: Robert M. McBride, 1919), 20.

37. The theme within Fante's fiction of crises of Italian American identity, typically manifest as a tension between ethnic pride and assimilative aspirations, has defined the still-underplanted field of Fante criticism. Key treatments include Catherine J. Kordich, "John Fante's *Ask the Dust*: A Border Reading," *MELUS* 20, no. 4 (December 1995): 17–27, https://doi.org/10.2307/467887; Stefano Luconi, "The Protean Ethnic Identities of John Fante's Italian-American Characters," in *John Fante: A Critical Gathering*, ed. David M. Fine and Stephen Cooper (Madison, NJ: Fairleigh Dickinson University Press, 1999), 54–64; and Rocco Marinaccio, "'Tea and Cookies, Diavolo!': Italian American Masculinity in John Fante's *Wait until Spring, Bandini*," *MELUS* 34, no. 3 (Fall 2009): 43–69, https://doi.org/10.1353/mel.0.0040. In chapter 3, I offer my own analysis of Fante texts that address this theme, applying a frontierist dialectic to the uncertain ethnic liminality occupied by Fante's Italian Americans.

38. John Fante, "To Be a Monstrous Clever Fellow," in *The Big Hunger: Stories 1932–1959*, ed. Stephen Cooper (New York: Ecco, 2000), 108–9.

39. For example: "'*Mamma mia!*' he blubbered. 'Tummy Murray, he calla me Wopa.'" John Fante, "The Odyssey of a Wop," in *The Wine of Youth* (New York: Ecco, 2002), 133.

40. The fullest treatment of this theme perhaps occurs in *Ask the Dust*, wherein Bandini's abusive romantic relationship with the Mexican American Camilla Lopez mobilizes his fears that to be a "wop" is no better than to be a "greaser." See Meagan Meylor, "'Sad Flower in the Sand': Camilla Lopez and the Erasure of Memory in *Ask the Dust*," in *John Fante's Ask the Dust: A Joining of Voices and Views* (New York: Fordham University Press, 2020), 58–82.

41. Steve Garner, *Whiteness: An Introduction* (Abingdon: Routledge, 2007), 34.

42. Fante, "Clever Fellow," 87–88.
43. Fante, "Clever Fellow," 89.
44. Fante, "Clever Fellow," 94.
45. Fante, "Clever Fellow," 95.
46. Fante, "Clever Fellow," 96.
47. Fante, "Clever Fellow," 97.
48. Fante, "Clever Fellow," 97.
49. Fante, "Clever Fellow," 88.
50. Fante, "Clever Fellow," 94.
51. Fante, "Clever Fellow," 94.

52. John Fante, "Helen, Thy Beauty Is to Me—," *Saturday Evening Post*, March 1, 1941.

53. "Helen" must be set near-contemporaneously with its 1941 publication; Julio's consideration of his countrymen's preference for Betty Grable among young American actresses makes it impossible that "Helen" could be set any earlier than October 1940, when Grable had her first leading film role in *Down Argentine*

Way. John Fante, "Helen, Thy Beauty Is to Me—," in *The Wine of Youth* (New York: Ecco, 2002), 259.

54. Linda España-Maram, *Creating Masculinity in Los Angeles's Little Manila: Working-Class Filipinos and Popular Culture, 1920s–1950s* (New York: Columbia University Press, 2006), 4–5.

55. Giordano, *Social Dancing in America*, 2:69; Lawrence K. Hong and Robert W. Duff, "Becoming a Taxi-Dancer: The Significance of Neutralization in a Semi-Deviant Occupation," *Sociology of Work and Occupations* 4, no. 3 (August 1, 1977): 327, https://doi.org/10.1177/003803857700400305.

56. Giordano, *Social Dancing in America*, 2:69.

57. Ernest Burgess, introduction to *The Taxi-Dance Hall: A Sociological Study in Commercialized Recreation and City Life*, by Paul Goalby Cressey (Chicago: University of Chicago Press, 1932), xi.

58. Gregory Mason, "Satan in the Dance-Hall," *The American Mercury*, June 1924, 178.

59. Giordano, *Social Dancing in America*, 2:70.

60. Jesse Frederick Steiner, *Americans at Play: Recent Trends in Recreation and Leisure Time Activities* (New York: McGraw-Hill, 1933), 113.

61. Illustrative of moral criticism directed at dance more generally is a pamphlet produced by the Los Angeles–based dance teacher turned anti-dance preacher T. A. Faulkner in 1916. Through the course of such unambiguously titled chapters as "The Whispering of Demon Temptation to the Poor Girl," Faulkner details dance's inextricable links with Satan and the inevitably of its slippery slope towards prostitution for women and dissolution for men. Thomas A. Faulkner, *The Lure of the Dance* (Los Angeles: T. A. Faulkner, 1916), 26.

62. Steiner, *Americans at Play*, 113.

63. Mason, "Satan in the Dance-Hall," 177–78.

64. Steiner, *Americans at Play*, 113; Gardner, *Public Dance Halls*, 34.

65. Cressey, *The Taxi-Dance Hall*, 49.

66. Clyde Bennett Vedder, "An Analysis of the Taxi-Dance Hall as a Social Institution with Special Reference to Los Angeles and Detroit" (PhD diss., Los Angeles, CA, University of Southern California, 1947), 252.

67. Vedder, "An Analysis of the Taxi-Dance Hall," 308–9; España-Maram, *Creating Masculinity*, 116. LA's only dedicated dancehall-regulation ordinance as of 1929 was a ban on under-18s. Gardner, *Public Dance Halls*, 14.

68. España-Maram, *Creating Masculinity*, 106.

69. España-Maram, *Creating Masculinity*, 109.

70. España-Maram, 4, 8; Giordano, *Social Dancing in America*, 2:70.

71. España-Maram, *Creating Masculinity*, 111.

72. España-Maram, *Creating Masculinity*, 110.

73. Manuel Buaken, *I Have Lived with the American People* (Caldwell, ID: Caxton Printers, 1948), 181, 179.

74. Marcelino A. Foronda, "America Is in the Heart: Ilokano Immigration to the United States, 1906–1930," De La Salle University Occasional Paper no. 3, August 1976, 39.

75. Augusto Espiritu, review of *Creating Masculinity in Los Angeles's Little Manila: Working-Class Filipinos and Popular Culture, 1920s–1950s*, by Linda España-Maram, *Philippine Studies* 56, no. 1 (March 2008): 105.

76. Use of the term "little brown brothers" to refer to Filipinos originated in the vision of supposedly benevolent colonialism advocated by William Howard Taft as the first US civil governor-general of the Philippines, and also provided the title of a short story by Fante's friend William Saroyan. Gideon Lasco, " 'Little Brown Brothers': Height and the Philippine–American Colonial Encounter (1898–1946)," *Philippine Studies: Historical and Ethnographic Viewpoints* 66, no. 3 (September 2018): 376, 381, https://doi.org/10.1353/phs.2018.0029; William Saroyan, "Our Little Brown Brothers the Filipinos," *Fiction Parade and Golden Book*, April 1936.

77. Richard Collins, "Fante, Family, and the Fiction of Confession," in *John Fante: A Critical Gathering*, ed. David M. Fine and Stephen Cooper (Madison, NJ: Fairleigh Dickinson University Press, 1999), 109.

78. Pasquale Verdicchio, *Devils in Paradise: Writings on Post-Emigrant Culture* (Toronto: Guernica Editions, 1997), 57–58.

79. Fante, "Helen, Thy Beauty Is to Me—," 2002, 252. I have elected to use page references from the printing of "Helen" in *The Wine of Youth* as this is more helpfully paginated for ease of reference than the *Saturday Evening Post* printing. I have confirmed that the two texts are identical.

80. Cressey, *The Taxi-Dance Hall*, 51.

81. Fante, "Helen," 2002, 264.

82. Fante, "Helen," 2002, 251; Rick Baldoz, *The Third Asiatic Invasion: Empire and Migration in Filipino America, 1898–1946* (New York: New York University Press, 2011), 89–100.

83. Peggy Pascoe, "Miscegenation Law, Court Cases, and Ideologies of 'Race' in Twentieth-Century America," *Journal of American History* 83, no. 1 (June 1996): 49, https://doi.org/10.2307/2945474.

84. Herbert W. Krieger, "Races and Peoples in the Philippines," *Far Eastern Quarterly* 4, no. 2 (February 1945): 96–97, https://doi.org/10.2307/2048958.

85. Notions of Filipino indigeneity are themselves hard to define. Krieger's piece represents an early ethnological attempt to appreciate the full complexity of ethnic groupings within the Philippines, but his frustration at erroneous popular ideas of the "Malay race" suggests how poorly even Americans who "observed Filipinos going about their daily business" understood such complexity in the 1940s. Fante appears no exception. Krieger, "Races and Peoples in the Philippines," 94.

86. Fante, "Helen," 2002, 260.

87. Grayson Kirk, "The Filipinos," *Annals of the American Academy of Political and Social Science* 223 (September 1942): 45. Kirk's comment is applicable to

Filipinos who had entered the United States before 1934, who had "had not been granted United States citizenship" but "were not to be classed as aliens" either. Kirk, 45. The Tydings-McDuffie Act of 1934, prompted by nativist sentiment especially within the agriculture industry, changed this status; "future Filipino immigrants were declared to be deportable as ordinary aliens." Kirk, 46; Rick Bonus, *Locating Filipino Americans: Ethnicity and the Cultural Politics of Space* (Philadelphia: Temple University Press, 2000), 41. This change of status was not, however, applied retroactively to Filipinos already in the country, such as Julio: Fante tells us he arrived in America in the late 1920s. Fante, "Helen," 2002, 254.

88. Kirk, "The Filipinos," 46.

89. Kirk, "The Filipinos," 45.

90. España-Maram, *Creating Masculinity*, 37; John H. Burma, "The Background of the Current Situation of Filipino-Americans," *Social Forces* 30, no. 1 (October 1951): 42–43, https://doi.org/10.2307/2571739.

91. Fante, "Helen," 2002, 251.

92. Fante, "Helen," 2002, 251.

93. Fante, "Helen," 2002, 252.

94. The average height of early twentieth-century Filipino men has been estimated at around 160 cm; it has not appreciably changed over the ensuing century. John E. Murray, "Height and Weight of Early 20th Century Filipino Men," *Annals of Human Biology* 29, no. 3 (June 2002): 326, https://doi.org/10.1080/03014460110086826.

95. Fante, "Helen," 2002, 252.

96. Fante, "Helen," 2002, 253.

97. Fante, "Helen," 2002, 253; Constantine Panunzio, "Intermarriage in Los Angeles, 1924–33," *American Journal of Sociology* 47, no. 5 (March 1942): 691, https://doi.org/10.1086/219000.

98. With "The Dreamer," first published in *Woman's Home Companion* in 1947, Fante would reuse the theme of an LA-dwelling Filipino who, infatuated with a glamorous American woman, must implore a more literate friend to write love letters on his behalf. In "The Dreamer," however, the unattainable object of desire is a cabaret artiste rather than a taxi-dancer, and the letter-writer an Anglo-American rather than a fellow Filipino. An inevitable rejection by the dream girl of course makes Cristo Serra realize that true beauty comes from within; he runs to the open arms of his unprepossessing but devoted Mexican American landlady. John Fante, "The Dreamer," in *The Wine of Youth* (New York: Ecco, 2002), 237–50.

99. In her analysis of race and gender relations in the taxi-dancehalls of the 1920s and 1930s, Rhacel Salazar Parreñas affirms this sense of a genuinely transformative sense of social liberation. Even if the opportunities the taxi-dancehall afforded "Filipino men to interact socially with [white] women" were strictly limited

and always fundamentally transactional, that they extended such opportunities at all was rare and precious to their patrons in an era of strict "racial segregation and stringent anti-miscegenation." Rhacel Salazar Parreñas, "'White Trash' Meets the 'Little Brown Monkeys': The Taxi Dance Hall as a Site of Interracial and Gender Alliances between White Working Class Women and Filipino Immigrant Men in the 1920s and 30s," *Amerasia Journal* 24, no. 2 (January 1998): 115, https://doi.org/10.17953/amer.24.2.760h5w08630ql643.

100. España-Maram, *Creating Masculinity*, 110.

101. Although Buaken criticizes Fante for depicting Filipino men as "suckers," obsessed with appearance, libidinous, and endlessly tempted by another roll of dance tickets, España-Maram confirms that this kind of performative, conspicuous consumerism, centered around the dance hall and its opportunities to be seen as a "sporting man" with women, was indeed widespread in the Los Angeles Filipino community at this time. Buaken, *I Have Lived with the American People*, 179–81; España-Maram, *Creating Masculinity*, 112–15.

102. Fante, "Helen," 2002, 262.

103. Fante, "Helen," 2002, 264.

104. Fante, "Helen," 2002, 265.

105. Describing the then-recent history of Filipino Americans in 1951, John Burma remarked that "the crux of the most active and bitter [anti-Filipino] discrimination and dislike seems to be the Filipino's refusal to accept his 'place' as an inferior," ignoring that being made to accept such a place was surely a *symptom* of "discrimination and dislike." Burma, "The Background of the Current Situation of Filipino-Americans," 47. Julio Sal's experience with the waiter illustrates the flaws in Burma's logic: Julio's momentary act of resistance to his "inferiority" may cause discrimination to redound upon him, but in doing so proves that the discrimination already existed.

106. Fante, "Helen," 2002, 264.

107. Fante, "Helen," 2002, 266.

108. Cressey, *The Taxi-Dance Hall*, 52–53. Published in 1932 and containing research that commenced in 1925, Cressey's study largely predates the legal contestation of Filipinos' racial status in respect of anti-miscegenation legislation and certainly California's outright ban on Filipino-Caucasian intermarriage. Cressey, xvii.

109. Panunzio, "Intermarriage in Los Angeles, 1924–33," 695–96.

110. Cressey, *The Taxi-Dance Hall*, 52–53.

111. Parreñas, "'White Trash' Meets the 'Little Brown Monkeys,'" 130–31.

112. David M. Fine, "California: Part of—or West of—the West?," *Western American Literature* 34, no. 2 (1999): 211. Theodore Roosevelt famously remarked that in California he felt that he was not in the West but somewhere "west of the West." Fine, 210. The phrase has proven irresistible for scholars grappling with notions of Californian exceptionalism; see Leonard Michaels, David Reid, and

Raquel Scherr, eds., *West of the West: Imagining California* (Berkeley: University of California Press, 1995), or Mark Arax, *West of the West: Dreamers, Believers, Builders, and Killers in the Golden State* (New York: PublicAffairs, 2009).

113. Harry Carr wrote of Los Angeles as a "gateway into a new era of the Pacific" as early as 1935. *City of Dreams*, 5. Even earlier than that, as chapter 3 of this book explores, white Californians had begun to worry that migration to their state from China and Japan represented a malign recontestation of the frontier, unsettling constructions of the place as a fulfilment of westwardly mobile Aryan destiny. Nevertheless it was from "the late seventies and eighties" that California began in earnest to "be constructed ideologically as a multicultural, new world semi-nation" on a Pacific axis, fueled by "Japanese, Taiwanese, and South Korean capital." In such visions LA takes the "central role . . . as capital of the twenty-first century, serving as a financial conduit to the Pacific . . . and enlivened by the 'new immigrants,' largely from Asia (read: 'good' immigrants who have money and work hard)." Christopher L. Connery, "Pacific Rim Discourse: The U.S. Global Imaginary in the Late Cold War Years," *Boundary 2* 21, no. 1 (Spring 1994): 43, https://doi.org/10.2307/303396. Julio endeavors precisely to be such a "good" Pacific immigrant, but is not welcomed as such.

114. Fante, "Helen," 2002, 253.

115. España-Maram, *Creating Masculinity in Los Angeles's Little Manila*, 111.

116. Fante, "Helen," 2002, 253.

117. *President* was ultimately filmed, in substantially altered form and with Ricardo Montalbán as Chu Chu, as *My Man and I* (Metro-Goldwyn-Mayer, 1952). The film was a flop.

118. By the time of Vedder's 1947 investigation, "the majority of taxi-dance halls no longer cater[ed] to Filipinos or the Oriental trade." Vedder, "An Analysis of the Taxi-Dance Hall," 49. The Tydings-McDuffie act had imposed an annual limit of just fifty Filipino immigrants per year in 1934; meanwhile, the 1935 Filipino Repatriation Act incentivized a return home, and the California Filipino population suffered. Bonus, *Locating Filipino Americans*, 41. As the dancehalls were robbed of clientele, the remaining Filipinos became still less desirable as customers, caught up as they were in increasing fears of an "Oriental Menace" throughout the 1930s. Burma, "The Background of the Current Situation of Filipino-Americans," 48. That Fante's shift from a Filipino to a Mexican American protagonist thus seems at least in part a practical matter of contemporary verisimilitude further supports a reading of *President* as an outgrowth of the *Brown Brothers* material.

119. John Fante and Jack Leonard, *A Letter from the President*, 1950, 5, Box 14, Folder 1. John Fante Papers (Collection 1832), UCLA Library Special Collections, Charles E. Young Research Library, University of California, Los Angeles, 3.

120. Fante and Leonard, *A Letter from the President*, 25.

121. Fante and Leonard, *A Letter from the President*, 27.

122. Fante and Leonard, *A Letter from the President*, 36.

123. Fante and Leonard, *A Letter from the President*, 37.

124. Fante and Leonard, *A Letter from the President*, 33.
125. Fante and Leonard, *A Letter from the President*, 42.
126. Fante and Leonard, *A Letter from the President*, 44–45.
127. Fante and Leonard, *A Letter from the President*, 56–57.
128. Janet Sturman, *The Course of Mexican Music* (New York: Routledge, 2015), 154.
129. Kirk, "The Filipinos," 46.
130. Fante, "Clever Fellow," 108.
131. Kirk, "The Filipinos," 45.

Chapter 2

1. Clark Davis, "'You Are the Company': The Demands of Employment in the Emerging Corporate Culture, Los Angeles, 1900–1930," *Business History Review* 70, no. 3 (Autumn 1996): 332, https://doi.org/10.2307/3117241.
2. Davis, "'You Are the Company,'" 333.
3. André Siegfried, "L'Age Administratif," *Revue des Deux Mondes*, May 1951, 3; Nikil Saval, *Cubed: A Secret History of the Workplace* (New York: Doubleday, 2014), 13–14.
4. Evelyn Nakano Glenn and Roslyn L. Feldberg, "Degraded and Deskilled: The Proletarianization of Clerical Work," *Social Problems* 25, no. 1 (October 1977): 54, https://doi.org/10.2307/800467.
5. Saval, *Cubed*, 14.
6. Saval, *Cubed*, 27.
7. Given that the rise of the office is often (correctly) associated with an "extraordinary growth in women's employment," it is worth emphasizing in the context of a discourse about the impact of clerking upon masculinity that the clerking class of the mid-to-late nineteenth century *was* overwhelmingly male. Saval, *Cubed*, 74. Women entered the office later: in 1870 only 2.4 percent of clerical workers were women; by 1900 the figure was 26.5 percent, but women did not constitute a majority of American clerical workers until 1930. Glenn and Feldberg, "Degraded and Deskilled," 54.
8. Saval, *Cubed*, 16.
9. Edgar Allan Poe similarly felt that clerks' labor had a visible impact on their physical comportment, rendering them identifiable by "a certain dapperness of carriage, which may be termed *deskism*." "The Man of the Crowd," in *Tales of Mystery and Imagination* (Ware: Wordsworth Editions, 2008), 256.
10. Walt Whitman, "New York Dissected: IV.—Broadway," *Life Illustrated*, August 9, 1856, 116.
11. Michael Zakim, "The Business Clerk as Social Revolutionary; or, a Labor History of the Nonproducing Classes," *Journal of the Early Republic* 26, no. 4 (Winter 2006): 571, https://doi.org/10.1353/jer.2006.0079.

12. Herman Melville, "Bartleby, the Scrivener," in *The Piazza Tales* (New York: Dix and Edwards, 1856), 49; Zakim, "The Business Clerk as Social Revolutionary," 571, 564.

13. Michael Zakim, "Producing Capitalism: The Clerk at Work," in *Capitalism Takes Command: The Social Transformation of Nineteenth-Century America*, ed. Michael Zakim and Gary J. Kornblith (Chicago: University of Chicago Press, 2012), 225; "'Mother Goose' for Counter Jumpers," *Vanity Fair*, March 17, 1860, 188.

14. Zakim, "Producing Capitalism," 225–26; Zakim, "The Business Clerk as Social Revolutionary," 569; "Know Thyself," *Vanity Fair*, February 18, 1860, 115; "'Mother Goose' for Counter Jumpers," 188.

15. Zakim, "The Business Clerk as Social Revolutionary," 569.

16. Nash, *Wilderness and the American Mind*, 152.

17. Nash, *Wilderness and the American Mind*, 152.

18. Lears, *No Place of Grace*, xv.

19. Nash, *Wilderness and the American Mind*, 145.

20. Henry Childs Merwin, "On Being Civilized Too Much," *Atlantic Monthly*, June 1897, 838.

21. Merwin, "On Being Civilized Too Much," 839.

22. Merwin, "On Being Civilized Too Much," 846.

23. Graham Thompson, *Male Sexuality Under Surveillance: The Office in American Literature* (Iowa City, IA: University of Iowa Press, 2003), 47.

24. Thompson, *Male Sexuality Under Surveillance*, 72.

25. Michel Crozier, *The World of the Office Worker*, trans. David Landau (Chicago: University of Chicago Press, 1971), 1.

26. Whyte, *The Organization Man*, 51.

27. Arthur M. Schlesinger Jr., "Freedom: A Fighting Faith," in *The Vital Center: The Politics of Freedom* (New York: Da Capo Press, 1988), 247; Adlai Stevenson, "A Purpose for Modern Woman," *Woman's Home Companion*, September 1955, 30.

28. Whyte, *The Organization Man*, 14, 15, 18. Whyte's historical basis for these claims draws directly on Weber's Protestant ethic rather than on Turner's frontier theory but in doing so only emphasizes the proximity between the two men's conceptual frameworks, as discussed in this book's introduction.

29. Saval, *Cubed*, 170.

30. Saval, *Cubed*, 38–39, 43.

31. Michael Saphier, *Office Planning and Design* (New York: McGraw-Hill, 1968), 1–2.

32. Saval, *Cubed*, 54–60.

33. Glenn and Feldberg, "Degraded and Deskilled," 55.

34. David Graeber, *Bullshit Jobs* (London: Allen Lane, 2018), 2–3.

35. Thompson, *Male Sexuality Under Surveillance*, 71; Glenn and Feldberg, "Degraded and Deskilled," 54.

36. Contemporary reports disclose the optimism with which the office building was hailed in the 1910s, 1920s, and 1930s. See, for example, the *Los*

Angeles Times on the luxuriant modernity of a proposed new office block in 1915, or Waldemar Kaempffert on the new national Patent Office building in the *New York Times Magazine* in 1932. "Classic Grace to Adorn City," *Los Angeles Times*, March 30, 1915; Waldemar Kaempffert, "A New Patent Office for a New Age," *New York Times Magazine*, April 10, 1932. The unfortunately named architect William Boring hoped in 1924 that "the vast experimental laboratory the building industry affords"—embodied nowhere more so than in "the skyscraping office building"—would create a "beautiful, logical, modern American style of architecture." William A. Boring, "America Groping in Architecture," *New York Times*, August 3, 1924. In the same year, even Turner himself saw the skyscraper, ultimate architectural embodiment of frontier closure in both its urban modernity and its acceptance of verticality as the new axis of spatial conquest, as in fact the "best expression" of "American artistic genius" in the modern age, a fresh space to vest the frontierist exploratory spirit. Frederick Jackson Turner, "Since the Foundation of Clark University 1889–1924," in *The Significance of Sections in American History* (Gloucester, MA: Peter Smith, 1959), 225.

37. Frederick Winslow Taylor, *The Principles of Scientific Management* (New York: Harper and Brothers, 1911), 8.

38. Taylor, *The Principles of Scientific Management*, 7.

39. John Maynard Keynes, "Economic Possibilities for Our Grandchildren," in *Essays in Persuasion* (New York: W. W. Norton, 1963), 373.

40. Herbert Marcuse, *One-Dimensional Man: Studies in the Ideology of Advanced Industrial Society* (Boston: Beacon Press, 1991), 2.

41. Turner, "Since the Foundation," 212.

42. Huff and Marlowe also enter the office at a particularly significant point in the history of workplace gender dynamics: the 1930s were the decade when women first outnumbered men in the United States' clerical workforce, having represented only 2.4 percent of clerical workers 60 years earlier. Glenn and Feldberg, "Degraded and Deskilled," 54. The implications of that demographic shift for any masculinist, frontierist, anti-office discourse are, however, ambiguous. The office becoming a space populated mostly by women might appear to confirm (and even increase) earlier fears that the office was a space with feminine and feminizing qualities. Equally, however, it might seem that men had been fortuitously spared the feminizing effects of the office by the delegation to women of almost all its "detail work" and the tacit demarcation therein of white-collar *management* as a distinctly male realm, conceptually secured against the demasculinizing effects of mere clerking. Glenn and Feldberg, 54–55. Accordingly, it is difficult to make any claim that any anti-office discourse manifested by Huff and Marlowe represents a direct or specific response to women's contemporaneous achievement of (numerical) superiority in the office workforce, and I do not do so here.

43. Taylor, *The Principles of Scientific Management*, 7.

44. Sean McCann, *Gumshoe America: Hard-Boiled Crime Fiction and the Rise and Fall of New Deal Liberalism* (Durham, NC: Duke University Press, 2000), 175.

45. Franz Alexander, *Our Age of Unreason: A Study of the Irrational Forces in Social Life* (New York: J. B. Lippincott, 1942), 302–3. Also cited in Webb, *The Great Frontier*, 124.
46. Webb, *The Great Frontier*, 123.
47. Webb, *The Great Frontier*, 124, 123.
48. Alexander, *Our Age of Unreason*, 302.
49. David Madden and Kristopher Mecholsky, *James M. Cain: Hard-Boiled Mythmaker* (Lanham, MD: Scarecrow Press, 2011), 38; Frank MacShane, *The Life of Raymond Chandler* (New York: E. P. Dutton, 1976), 101.
50. John T. Irwin, "Beating the Boss: Cain's *Double Indemnity*," *American Literary History* 14, no. 2 (April 1, 2002): 264.
51. Billy Wilder, dir., *Double Indemnity* (Paramount Pictures, 1944).
52. Lefebvre, *The Production of Space*, 39–40.
53. Lefebvre, *The Production of Space*, 77.
54. Census sample statistics estimated that, in 1940, 6.3 million urban-dwelling Americans were employed in clerical and "kindred" occupations, of a total of 27.7 million urban workers. *1940 Census of Population: The Labor Force (Sample Statistics)* (Washington, DC: United States Government Printing Office, 1943), 134. Glenn and Feldberg give a lower figure of 4.8 million clerical workers in the total population, a figure that appears to strip out the "kindred" jobs from the census tables. "Degraded and Deskilled," 54. I cite the census's broader definition here because it in itself suggests the conceptual creep of "clericalization" into other forms of work and because it gives a sense of how many Americans were not strictly clerical workers but worked in proximity to those who were. By 1940, you may not have been an office worker but there was a good chance that you knew somebody who was and/or recognized elements of clerical life in your own employment (at least, if you were white—the same census statistics suggest that less than 4 percent of non-white urban workers occupied clerical and kindred positions).
55. James M. Cain, *Double Indemnity* (London: Orion, 2005), 3.
56. Raymond Chandler, *The Big Sleep*, in *The Big Sleep and Other Novels* (London: Penguin, 2000), 118.
57. Robert Whaples and David Buffum, "Fraternalism, Paternalism, the Family, and the Market: Insurance a Century Ago," *Social Science History* 15, no. 1 (Spring 1991): 98, https://doi.org/10.2307/1171484.
58. Frederick Whiting, "Playing Against Type: Statistical Personhood, Depth Narrative, and the Business of Genre in James M. Cain's *Double Indemnity*," *Journal of Narrative Theory* 36, no. 2 (Summer 2006): 198, https://doi.org/10.1353/jnt.2007.0006.
59. Cain, *Double Indemnity*, 26.
60. Roy Hoopes, *Cain: The Biography of James M. Cain*, 2nd ed. (Carbondale: Southern Illinois University Press, 1987), 258.
61. Cain, *Double Indemnity*, 21–22.

62. Cain, *Double Indemnity*, 24.

63. On rail's significance specifically in Southern California's development from frontier to major center of population and commerce, see Paul R. Spitzzeri, "The Road to Independence: The Los Angeles and Independence Railroad and the Conception of a City," *Southern California Quarterly* 83, no. 1 (Spring 2001): 23–58, https://doi.org/10.2307/41172051, or Edna Monch Parker, "The Southern Pacific Railroad and Settlement in Southern California," *Pacific Historical Review* 6, no. 2 (1937): 103–19, https://doi.org/10.2307/3633158. A succinct account of the railroad's broader role in the West's (and America's) nineteenth-century socioeconomic transformation can be found in H. W Brands, *American Colossus: The Triumph of Capitalism, 1865–1900* (New York: Doubleday, 2010), 43–69.

64. Christian Wolmar *The Great Railway Revolution* (London: Atlantic Books, 2012), 203–4, 206.

65. Joan Didion, "The Insidious Ethic of Conscience," *American Scholar* 34, no. 3 (Autumn 1965): 626.

66. James M. Cain, *The Postman Always Rings Twice* (London: Orion, 2005), 7.

67. Irwin, "Beating the Boss," 260.

68. Cain, *Postman*, 87–88.

69. James M. Cain, "Paradise," *The American Mercury*, March 1933, 273.

70. Cain, *Double Indemnity*, 26–27.

71. Cain, *Double Indemnity*, 26.

72. Turner, "Significance," 4.

73. Cain, *Double Indemnity*, 23–24.

74. Cain, *Double Indemnity*, 22.

75. Cain, *Double Indemnity*, 42.

76. Cain, *Double Indemnity*, 24, 42.

77. Thompson, *Male Sexuality Under Surveillance*, xiv, 5, 7, 12.

78. Cain, *Double Indemnity*, 66.

79. Cain, *Double Indemnity*, 67.

80. Cain, *Double Indemnity*, 78.

81. Cain, *Double Indemnity*, 91–92.

82. Cain, *Double Indemnity*, 66, 68.

83. Raymond Chandler, "Raymond Chandler to D. J. Ibberson, 19 April 1951," in *Raymond Chandler: Later Novels and Other Writings*, ed. Frank MacShane (New York: Library of America, 1995), 1043–44. As the novels make clear, Marlowe has also had a spell working for the district attorney. When Marlowe visits former colleague Bernie Ohls in *The Big Sleep* there are conspicuous references to the confinements of Ohls's office, suggesting that the Hall of Justice was also too spatially and systemically restricted a life for Marlowe. Ohls ruefully refers to his own working environment as his "hutch," while Marlowe notes that the offices are "small," and that Ohls's is "no larger" than those of his juniors "but he had it to himself." Chandler, *The Big Sleep*, 31–32.

84. Raymond Chandler, *Farewell, My Lovely*, in *The Big Sleep and Other Novels* (London: Penguin, 2000), 330.

85. Scaggs, *Crime Fiction*, 64.

86. Philip Durham, *Down These Mean Streets: Raymond Chandler's Knight* (Chapel Hill: University of North Carolina Press, 1963), 147.

87. McCann, *Gumshoe America*, 149; Scaggs, *Crime Fiction*, 64.

88. Megan E. Abbott, *The Street Was Mine: White Masculinity in Hardboiled Fiction and Film Noir* (New York: Palgrave Macmillan, 2002), 2.

89. Richard Lehan, *The City in Literature: An Intellectual and Cultural History* (Berkeley: University of California Press, 1998), 252.

90. Lee Horsley, *Twentieth-Century Crime Fiction* (Oxford: Oxford University Press, 2005), 74.

91. Ross Macdonald, "The Writer as Detective Hero," in *On Crime Writing* (Santa Barbara, CA: Capra Press, 1973), 15 (emphasis mine).

92. Like the critics quoted here, I am principally interested in how the detective inherits aspects of the frontiersman's identity as a mythic archetype. That inheritance was, however, compounded by and reflected in material relationships between the two figures. As protagonists of fiction, both "detectives . . . and western outlaws . . . proliferated" alongside each other in late nineteenth- and early twentieth-century dime novels and pulp magazines. Michael Denning, *The Cultural Front: The Laboring of American Culture in the Twentieth Century* (London: Verso, 1998), 242. See also Marcus Klein, *Easterns, Westerns, and Private Eyes: American Matters, 1870–1900* (Madison: University of Wisconsin Press, 1994). Indeed, the detective to some extent developed from and supplanted figures of the pre-urban West in such literature—the popular late nineteenth-century character Deadwood Dick started life as a stage driver, but as time passed and the West changed was "transformed into a detective." Smith, *Virgin Land*, 119. As Blake Allmendinger notes, such fictional elision between the detective and cowboy in turn reflected the historical reality of "livestock detectives," cowboys who took to working for ranches or even detective agencies to catch cattle rustlers. Blake Allmendinger, *The Cowboy: Representations of Labor in an American Work Culture* (New York: Oxford University Press, 1992), 115–18.

93. Turner, "Contributions," 253–54.

94. Macdonald, "The Writer as Detective Hero," 20.

95. Fredric Jameson, *Raymond Chandler: The Detections of Totality* (London: Verso, 2016), 7.

96. Raymond Chandler, "The Simple Art of Murder," in *The Simple Art of Murder* (New York: Vintage, 1988), 18.

97. Liahna K. Babener, "Raymond Chandler's City of Lies," in *Los Angeles in Fiction: A Collection of Original Essays*, ed. David M. Fine (Albuquerque: University of New Mexico Press, 1984), 110.

98. Chandler, *Farewell, My Lovely*, 171.

99. Stanley Orr, *Darkly Perfect World: Colonial Adventure, Postmodernism, and American Noir* (Columbus: The Ohio State University Press, 2010), 52.

100. Tzvetan Todorov, "Typology of Detective Fiction," in *Modern Criticism and Theory: A Reader*, ed. David Lodge and Nigel Wood, 3rd ed. (London: Routledge, 2014), 231.

101. Chandler, *The Big Sleep*, 20.

102. Raymond Chandler, *The Lady in the Lake* (London: Penguin, 2011), 122, 52, 94.

103. Raymond Chandler, *The Long Goodbye*, in *The Big Sleep and Other Novels* (London: Penguin, 2000), 654–55.

104. Jameson, *Raymond Chandler*, 46, 7 (emphasis mine).

105. Orr, *Darkly Perfect World*, 42.

106. Eve Kosofsky Sedgwick, *The Coherence of Gothic Conventions* (New York: Arno Press, 1980), 13.

107. Although they emerge in markedly different traditions and to divergent ends, there is contiguity between Sedgwick's sense of the simultaneous, inextricable inside/outside and the fundamental notion underpinning Lefebvre's thought—that space is always-already an inseparable, codependent, total contingency of its constituent elements. That contingency, Lefebvre's "production of space," may find something conceptually analogical in what Sedgwick more lyrically terms the "weight of space." Sedgwick, *The Coherence of Gothic Conventions*, 29–30.

108. Sedgwick, *The Coherence of Gothic Conventions*, 13.

109. Chandler, *The Big Sleep*, 6.

110. Orr, *Darkly Perfect World*, 54.

111. Orr, *Darkly Perfect World*, 56.

112. Orr, *Darkly Perfect World*, 56.

113. Raymond Chandler, *The High Window* (London: Penguin, 2011), 196.

114. Chandler, *The Long Goodbye*, 578.

115. Jameson, *Raymond Chandler*, 47.

116. Jameson, *Raymond Chandler*, 46.

117. Davis, *City of Quartz*, 38.

118. Chandler, "Chandler to Ibberson, 19 April 1951," 1047.

119. Chandler, *The Big Sleep*, 40.

120. In offering this reading of filing cases containing "California climate," it is incumbent upon me to acknowledge that in a description of Marlowe's office in *The High Window*, highly consistent with that found in *The Big Sleep*, three of the five filing cases *are* simply "full of nothing." Chandler, *High Window*, 23. This variability between two otherwise near-identical descriptions, however, attests in itself to the notion that one may never be entirely certain as to what one will find when one enters Marlowe's world.

121. John H. M. Laslett, *Sunshine Was Never Enough: Los Angeles Workers, 1880–2010* (Berkeley: University of California Press, 2012), 116.

122. Mayo, *Los Angeles*, 67.
123. Raymond Chandler, "Red Wind," in *Trouble Is My Business and Other Stories* (London: Penguin, 1988), 69.
124. Cain, *Double Indemnity*, 39.
125. Chandler, *The Big Sleep*, 40.
126. Murphet, *Race and Literature in Los Angeles*, 37.
127. Turner, "Significance," 4.
128. Tanja M. Laden, "Best Art Deco (1928)," *LA Weekly*, October 6, 2010, www.laweekly.com/best-art-deco-1928/; Tyler Dilts, "Chandler's Shadow," Los Angeles Review of Books, January 1, 2015, https://lareviewofbooks.org/article/chandlers-shadow/.
129. Ray Hebert, "No Tall Buildings: Aesthetics, Not Quakes, Kept Lid On," *Los Angeles Times*, July 8, 1985.
130. Hadley Meares, "The James Oviatt Building: The Bespoke Brilliance and Pretension Behind an Art Deco Masterpiece," KCET.org, September 6, 2013, www.kcet.org/history-society/the-james-oviatt-building-the-bespoke-brilliance-and-pretension-behind-an-art-deco.
131. Laden, "Best Art Deco (1928)"; Meares, "The James Oviatt Building."
132. Olive Gray, "Doors Open at New Men's Shop," *Los Angeles Times*, May 16, 1928.
133. Meares, "The James Oviatt Building."
134. Gray, "Doors Open at New Men's Shop," 7; Ray Hebert, "There's Lots of Room at the Top of This Building," *Los Angeles Times*, June 5, 1988.
135. Edward Dimendberg, *Film Noir and the Spaces of Modernity* (Cambridge, MA: Harvard University Press, 2004), 18.
136. I return in greater detail in chapter 4 to competing visions of verticality and horizontality in prewar and postwar Los Angeles, finding that widespread conceptions of a prewar city that maintained concentrated verticality versus a postwar city defined by horizontal forms are at least partially complicated by historical reality.
137. Jameson, *Raymond Chandler*, 7.
138. McCann, *Gumshoe America*, 142.
139. Chandler, *Lady in the Lake*, 1.
140. Dennis Porter, "The Private Eye," in *The Cambridge Companion to Crime Fiction* (Cambridge: Cambridge University Press, 2003), 95.
141. Chandler, *Lady in the Lake*, 1.
142. Thompson, *Male Sexuality Under Surveillance*, 87.
143. Chandler, *Lady in the Lake*, 1.
144. Chandler, *Lady in the Lake*, 1–2 (emphasis in original).
145. Chandler, *Lady in the Lake*, 2.
146. Chandler, *Lady in the Lake*, 135.
147. Chandler, *Lady in the Lake*, 2.

148. Chandler, *Lady in the Lake*, 2.
149. Chandler, *Lady in the Lake*, 2, 4.
150. Chandler, *Lady in the Lake*, 3.
151. Chandler, *Lady in the Lake*, 7.
152. Chandler, *Lady in the Lake*, 5.
153. Marcus Klein, *Easterns, Westerns, and Private Eyes*, 155.
154. Abbott, *The Street Was Mine*, 6.
155. Ralph Ellison, *Invisible Man* (London: Penguin, 2014), 170.

Chapter 3

1. Ruth Wallach et al., *Los Angeles in World War II* (Charleston, SC: Arcadia, 2011), 7.
2. Michael Kazin, "The Great Exception Revisited: Organized Labor and Politics in San Francisco and Los Angeles, 1870–1940," *Pacific Historical Review* 55, no. 3 (August 1986): 374–373, https://doi.org/10.2307/3639704.
3. Soja and Scott, "Introduction to Los Angeles," 3; Gerald D. Nash, *The American West Transformed: The Impact of the Second World War* (Bloomington: Indiana University Press, 1985), 7.
4. Becky M. Nicolaides, *My Blue Heaven: Life and Politics in the Working-Class Suburbs of Los Angeles, 1920–1965* (Chicago: University of Chicago Press, 2002), 187.
5. Nicolaides, *My Blue Heaven*, 187.
6. Josh Sides, *LA City Limits: African American Los Angeles from the Great Depression to the Present* (Berkeley: University of California Press, 2003), 55.
7. Prior to the 1920s, when several major fields were discovered in quick succession in the Los Angeles basin, the San Joaquin valley was California's biggest oil producing region. Los Angeles had, however, experienced its first, smaller, oil boom in the 1890s. Nancy Quam-Wickham, "'Cities Sacrificed on the Altar of Oil': Popular Opposition to Oil Development in 1920s Los Angeles," *Environmental History* 3, no. 2 (April 1998): 191, https://doi.org/10.2307/3985379.
8. Kazin, "The Great Exception Revisited," 373.
9. Arthur M. Schlesinger Jr., *The Crisis of the Old Order, 1919–1933* (Boston: Houghton Mifflin Harcourt, 2003), 425.
10. Franklin D. Roosevelt, "New Conditions Impose New Requirements Upon Government and Those Who Conduct Government," in *The Public Papers and Addresses of Franklin D. Roosevelt: The Genesis of the New Deal, 1928–1932*, vol. 1 (New York: Random House, 1938), 750–52.
11. Roosevelt, "New Conditions," 751, 746.
12. Roosevelt, "New Conditions," 753.
13. Roosevelt, "New Conditions," 747, 755, 751.

14. Schlesinger, *The Crisis of the Old Order*, 425–26.
15. Roosevelt, "New Conditions," 743.
16. Herbert Hoover, "Speech at Madison Square Garden," in *Public Papers of the Presidents of the United States: Herbert Hoover* (Washington, DC: United States Government Printing Office, 1977), 674.
17. Hoover, "Speech at Madison Square Garden," 674; Leo Marx, *The Machine in the Garden: Technology and the Pastoral Ideal in America* (Oxford: Oxford University Press, 2000), 193, 153.
18. Fante's longstanding fascination with and use of the cannery as a setting reflects his own traumatic employment in one prior to his literary career. Cooper, *Full of Life*, 59.
19. Fante and Leonard, *A Letter from the President*, 17.
20. John Fante, "Synopsis of *The Left-Handed Virgin/1933 Was a Bad Year*, Version C" (c. 1960), Box 4, Folder 3, John Fante Papers (Collection 1832), UCLA Library Special Collections, Charles E. Young Research Library, University of California, Los Angeles, 4; John Fante, "Synopsis of *The Left-Handed Virgin/1933 Was a Bad Year*, Version B" (c. 1960), Box 4, Folder 3, John Fante Papers (Collection 1832). UCLA Library Special Collections, Charles E. Young Research Library, University of California, Los Angeles, 3.
21. Another unpublished text, a film or TV treatment from 1955, hinges on the fate of a fishing and canning business in a small city in the greater Los Angeles area, but is slight, offering little suggestion of the politics with which I am concerned here. It is, though, further evidence of Fante's recurrent preoccupation with the business of fish and fishing as a spur to and site for drama. John Fante, "Untitled Manuscript" (1955), Box 24, Folder 4, John Fante Papers (Collection 1832), UCLA Library Special Collections, Charles E. Young Research Library, University of California, Los Angeles.
22. Cooper, *Full of Life*, 133.
23. John Fante, "Fish Cannery" (n.d.), 1, Box 1, Folder 4, John Fante Papers (Collection 1832), UCLA Library Special Collections, Charles E. Young Research Library, University of California, Los Angeles, 1.
24. If we entertain the possibility of an intertextual geography of Fantean Los Angeles, Arturo may even live next door to Julio: unlike Dom Molise, Arturo may not have to bunk with Filipinos, but his family's apartment house lodgings are adjacent to "a place where a lot of Filipinos lived." *The Road to Los Angeles*, in *The Bandini Quartet* (Edinburgh: Canongate Books, 2004), 226.
25. "Soyo" is clearly a thinly veiled analogue for Wilmington's actual Toyo Fisheries—referred to by their true name in the *1933 Was a Bad Year/The Left-Handed Virgin* synopses. Richard Symonds Croker, *The California Mackerel Fishery* (Sacramento, CA: California State Printing Office, 1933), 26, Special Collections and Archives, University of California, San Diego; Fante, *The Road to Los Angeles*, 273.

26. Fante, *The Road*, 275.
27. Fante, *The Road*, 276.
28. Thomas Guglielmo *White on Arrival: Italians, Race, Color, and Power in Chicago, 1890–1945* (Oxford: Oxford University Press, 2003), 8.
29. Guglielmo, *White on Arrival*, 5–6.
30. Guglielmo, *White on Arrival*, 6, 7 (emphasis in original).
31. Gloria Ricci Lothrop, "Italians of Los Angeles: An Historical Overview," *Southern California Quarterly* 85, no. 3 (Fall 2003): 262, https://doi.org/10.2307/41172173.
32. Guglielmo, *White on Arrival*, 9 (emphasis in original).
33. David R. Roediger, *Towards the Abolition of Whiteness: Essays on Race, Politics, and Working Class History* (London: Verso, 1994), 184.
34. Fante, *The Road*, 221, 254.
35. Fante, *The Road*, 275.
36. Fante, *The Road*, 329.
37. Fante, *The Road*, 331.
38. Roediger, *Towards the Abolition of Whiteness*, 189.
39. Fante, *The Road*, 287.
40. Fante, "Fish Cannery," 7.
41. Cain, *Postman*, 4–5.
42. Fante, *The Road*, 284–85.
43. Fante, *The Road*, 285.
44. Fante, *The Road*, 286–87.
45. Fante, *The Road*, 287.
46. Fante, *The Road*, 288.
47. Fante, *The Road*, 289.
48. Fante, *The Road*, 290.
49. Fante, *The Road*, 291.
50. Fante, *The Road*, 286, 291.
51. Fante, "Fish Cannery," 1.
52. Walter Mosley, *Devil in a Blue Dress* (London: Serpent's Tail, 2017), 71.
53. Roediger, *Towards the Abolition of Whiteness*, 66 and throughout. Likewise throughout *The Wages of Whiteness: Race and the Making of the American Working Class* (London: Verso 2007).
54. Chester Himes, *If He Hollers Let Him Go* (London: Serpent's Tail, 2010), 4.
55. Fante, *The Road*, 305.
56. Fante, *The Road*, 310.
57. Fante, *The Road*, 310.
58. Fante, *The Road*, 333.
59. Wild, *Street Meeting*, 28–29.
60. The act of including the designation "memoir" within the work's title could itself even be taken as an ironically fictionalizing gesture, in the Defoean or

Richardsonian tradition of fictive narratives that deploy pseudo-autobiographical framing conceits.

61. Hisaye Yamamoto, "Life Among the Oil Fields, A Memoir," in *Seventeen Syllables* (New Brunswick, NJ: Rutgers University Press, 2001), 91.

62. Yamamoto, "Life Among the Oil Fields," 94.

63. Carey McWilliams, "Storm Signals," in *Fool's Paradise: A Carey McWilliams Reader* (Berkeley, CA: Heyday Books, 2001), 140. Reproduced from *Brothers Under the Skin*, revised ed. (Boston: Little, Brown, 1951). For McWilliams on the development of anti-Japanese racism in America, and in California especially, see *Prejudice: Japanese-Americans, Symbol of Racial Intolerance* (Boston: Little, Brown, 1944).

64. Lawrence D. Reddick, "The New Race-Relations Frontier," *Journal of Educational Sociology* 19, no. 3 (1945): 137, 140, https://doi.org/10.2307/2263418.

65. Carey McWilliams, *Prejudice*, 15.

66. Scott Zesch, "Chinese Los Angeles in 1870–1871: The Makings of a Massacre," *Southern California Quarterly* 90, no. 2 (2008): 127, https://doi.org/10.2307/41172418.

67. John Modell, *The Economics and Politics of Racial Accommodation: The Japanese of Los Angeles, 1900–1942* (Urbana: University of Illinois Press, 1977), 7.

68. Modell, *The Economics and Politics of Racial Accommodation*, 37.

69. Lisa Lowe, *Immigrant Acts: On Asian American Cultural Politics* (Durham, NC: Duke University Press, 1996), 4, 84.

70. Modell, *The Economics and Politics of Racial Accommodation*, 7.

71. Eiichiro Azuma, "The Politics of Transnational History Making: Japanese Immigrants on the Western 'Frontier,' 1927–1941," *Journal of American History* 89, no. 4 (March 2003): 1403, https://doi.org/10.2307/3092548.

72. Modell, *The Economics and Politics of Racial Accommodation*, 5, 8.

73. Modell, *The Economics and Politics of Racial Accommodation*, 8.

74. Modell, *The Economics and Politics of Racial Accommodation*, 9.

75. Claire Jean Kim, "The Racial Triangulation of Asian Americans," *Politics and Society* 27, no. 1 (March 1999): 107, https://doi.org/10.1177/0032329299027001005.

76. Modell, *The Economics and Politics of Racial Accommodation*, 14–15.

77. Natalia Molina, "Understanding Race as a Relational Concept," *Modern American History* 1, no. 1 (March 2018): 101–3, https://doi.org/10.1017/mah.2017.14.

78. Modell, *The Economics and Politics of Racial Accommodation*, 10, 12.

79. Valerie Matsumoto, "Desperately Seeking 'Deirdre': Gender Roles, Multicultural Relations, and Nisei Women Writers of the 1930s," *Frontiers: A Journal of Women Studies* 12, no. 1 (1991): 29, https://doi.org/10.2307/3346573.

80. Some sense of what this distinction meant practically can be gleaned from the low numbers of Italians interned in World War II. Of 3,567 Italian

nationals arrested in World War II, only 367 were interned, against 1,532 internments made from 5,428 arrests of Japanese nationals; Italians were perceived as the "least threatening" of enemy groups. Mary Elizabeth Basile Chopas, *Searching for Subversives: The Story of Italian Internment in Wartime America* (Chapel Hill: University of North Carolina Press, 2017), 2. Moreover, while US citizens of Japanese ancestry were interned *en masse*, the same approach was never taken with the far larger population of US citizens who had Italian ancestry. (A small number of "suspicious" naturalized Italian Americans were interned under "individual exclusion" measures Chopas, 138.) Of course, the West Coast's proximity to and potential as a military target for Japan was a major factor in this difference, and indeed 10,000 Italians on the West Coast who resided in prohibited zones were forced to relocate, but an equivalent fear of Italians as potential racial superiors, and a consequent panic about their presence, simply did not exist. Chopas, 57.

81. Modell, *The Economics and Politics of Racial Accommodation*, 8–9.

82. Modell, *The Economics and Politics of Racial Accommodation*, 27.

83. Chandler, *Farewell, My Lovely*, 234.

84. Dudley O. McGovney, "The Anti-Japanese Land Laws of California and Ten Other States," *California Law Review* 35, no. 1 (March 1947): 7, 14–18, https://doi.org/10.2307/3477374; Masao Suzuki, "Important or Impotent? Taking Another Look at the 1920 California Alien Land Law," *Journal of Economic History* 64, no. 1 (March 2004): 139–40, https://doi.org/10.1017/S0022050704002621.

85. Azuma, "The Politics of Transnational History Making," 1402.

86. Yamamoto "Life Among the Oil Fields," 91, 90, 88.

87. Scott Kurashige, *The Shifting Grounds of Race: Black and Japanese Americans in the Making of Multiethnic Los Angeles* (Princeton: Princeton University Press, 2010), 66.

88. Modell, *The Economics and Politics of Racial Accommodation*, 10.

89. Nancy Quam-Wickham, "Cities Sacrificed on the Altar of Oil," 198.

90. Stephanie LeMenager, *Living Oil: Petroleum Culture in the American Century* (Oxford: Oxford University Press, 2014), 79.

91. Yamamoto, "Life Among the Oil Fields," 88.

92. Chandler, *The Big Sleep*, 16.

93. Chandler, *Farewell, My Lovely*, 248.

94. Yamamoto, "Life Among the Oil Fields," 89.

95. Yamamoto, "Life Among the Oil Fields," 93.

96. Yamamoto, "Life Among the Oil Fields," 93.

97. Amitav Ghosh, "Petrofiction: The Oil Encounter and the Novel," *New Republic*, March 2, 1992, 29.

98. Sigmund Freud, "The 'Uncanny,'" in *The Standard Edition of the Complete Psychological Works*, ed. and trans. James Strachey, vol. 17 (London: Hogarth Press, 1955), 225–26.

99. Babb, *Whiteness Visible*, 168, 119.

100. Coco Fusco, "Fantasies of Oppositionality: Reflections on Recent Conferences in Boston and New York," *Screen* 29, no. 4 (Autumn 1988): 91.

101. John L. DeWitt, "Public Proclamation No. 1" (San Francisco: Western Defense Command and Fourth Army, March 2, 1942), 3–4, Special Collections, University of Washington Libraries, https://cdm16786.contentdm.oclc.org/digital/collection/pioneerlife/id/15329/rec/5.

102. Kevin Starr, *Embattled Dreams: California in War and Peace, 1940–1950* (Oxford: Oxford University Press, 2002), 94; Nash, *The American West Transformed*, 12.

103. "Action on Japs [a]," *Los Angeles Times*, February 19, 1942.

104. "Action on Japs [a]."

105. "Action on Japs [b]," *Los Angeles Times*, February 21, 1942; "Production Our Main Job—and Right Now!," *Los Angeles Times*, February 21, 1942.

106. Kim, "The Racial Triangulation of Asian Americans," 115.

107. Starr, *Embattled Dreams*, 94.

108. Delia Byrnes, "'I Get a Bad Taste in My Mouth Out Here': Oil's Intimate Ecologies in HBO's *True Detective*," *Global South* 9, no. 1 (Spring 2015): 87, https://doi.org/10.2979/globalsouth.9.1.07.

109. Modell, *The Economics and Politics of Racial Accommodation*, 5, 10, 14.

110. Modell, *The Economics and Politics of Racial Accommodation*, 13–14.

111. Suzuki, "Important or Impotent?," 141.

112. Jeannie N. Shinozuka, "Deadly Perils: Japanese Beetles and the Pestilential Immigrant, 1920s–1930s," *American Quarterly* 65, no. 4 (December 2013): 838–39, https://doi.org/10.1353/aq.2013.0056.

113. "Japanese Beetle Trap Intrigues Local Golfer," *Los Angeles Times*, July 16, 1945.

114. Dyer, *White*, 51.

115. Kurashige, *The Shifting Grounds of Race*, 102, 104.

116. Kurashige, *The Shifting Grounds of Race*, 153.

117. Lawrence P. Jackson, *Chester P. Himes* (New York: W. W. Norton, 2017), 157.

118. Himes, *If He Hollers*, 4.

119. Molina, "Understanding Race as a Relational Concept," 102.

120. Himes, *If He Hollers*, 4.

121. Kurashige, *The Shifting Grounds of Race*, 165.

122. Kurashige, *The Shifting Grounds of Race*.

123. Kurashige, *The Shifting Grounds of Race*, 194.

124. Kim, "The Racial Triangulation of Asian Americans," 115.

125. Lowe, *Immigrant Acts*, 20, italics in original.

126. Yamamoto, "Life Among the Oil Fields," 93–94.

127. Yamamoto, "Life Among the Oil Fields," 94.

128. Yamamoto, "Life Among the Oil Fields," 95.

129. Upton Sinclair, *Oil!* (London: Penguin, 2008), 548.

130. Frederick Buell, "A Short History of Oil Cultures; or, The Marriage of Catastrophe and Exuberance," in *Oil Culture*, ed. Ross Barrett and Daniel Worden (Minneapolis: University of Minnesota Press, 2014), 75.

131. Stephanie LeMenager, "The Aesthetics of Petroleum, after *Oil!*," *American Literary History* 24, no. 1 (January 2012): 69, https://doi.org/10.1093/alh/ajr057.

132. Sinclair, *Oil!*, 25.

133. Sinclair, *Oil!*, 78.

134. Sinclair, *Oil!*, 76–77.

135. Buell, "A Short History of Oil Cultures," 79.

136. Joshua Schuster, "Where Is the Oil in Modernism?," in *Petrocultures: Oil, Politics, Culture*, ed. Sheena Wilson, Adam Carlson, and Imre Szeman (Montreal: McGill-Queen's University Press, 2017), 204.

137. Buell, "A Short History of Oil Cultures," 78.

138. Lowe, *Immigrant Acts*, 175.

139. Quoted in Baldwin, *Everything Now*, 212.

140. Kurashige, *The Shifting Grounds of Race*, 19.

141. Lonnie G. Bunch III, "'The Greatest State for the Negro': Jefferson L. Edmonds, Black Propagandist of the California Dream," in *Seeking El Dorado: African Americans in California*, ed. Lawrence B. de Graaf, Kevin Mulroy, and Quintard Taylor (Seattle: University of Washington Press, 2001), 132, 142–43.

142. Kevin Allen Leonard, "'In the Interest of All Races': African Americans and Interracial Cooperation in Los Angeles during and after World War II," in *Seeking El Dorado: African Americans in California*, ed. Lawrence B. de Graaf, Kevin Mulroy, and Quintard Taylor (Seattle: University of Washington Press, 2001), 311.

143. Nash, *The American West Transformed*, 152.

144. Sides, *LA City Limits*, 57.

145. Kurashige, *The Shifting Grounds of Race*, 140.

146. Leonard, "In the Interest of All Races," 311.

147. David Wyatt, *Five Fires: Race, Catastrophe, and the Shaping of California* (Oxford: Oxford University Press, 1999), 163.

148. Leonard, "In the Interest of All Races," 312.

149. Arna Bontemps, *Anyplace But Here* (New York: Hill and Wang, 1966), 267.

150. Nikhil Pal Singh, *Black Is a Country: Race and the Unfinished Struggle for Democracy* (Cambridge, MA: Harvard University Press, 2004), 105.

151. Sides, *LA City Limits*, 54–55.

152. Roger W. Lotchin, *Fortress California 1910–1961: From Warfare to Welfare* (Champaign: University of Illinois Press, 2002), 131.

153. A. Robert Lee, "Violence Real and Imagined: The Novels of Chester Himes," in *The Critical Response to Chester Himes*, ed. Charles L. P. Silet (Westport, CT: Greenwood Press, 1999), 68.

154. Singh, *Black Is a Country*, 103–5.
155. Chester Himes, "If You're Scared, Go Home!," in *Black on Black: Baby Sister and Selected Writings* (London: Michael Joseph, 1975), 229.
156. Himes, *If He Hollers*, 20.
157. Himes, *If He Hollers*, 3.
158. Lefebvre, *The Production of Space*, 41–52, 116.
159. Himes, *If He Hollers*, 3.
160. The Irish had historically been regarded in Roediger's category of the "not-yet-white"—what whiteness they had was regarded as an inferior strain not unlike that of the Italians. Indeed, Roediger notes not only the familiar nineteenth-century association of racialized simian traits and "savagery" with the Irish, but direct associations between Irish and African Americans—"smoked Irish"—in racist slang "well into the twentieth century." Although "paddy" had the potential to denote any white person in mid-century African American slang, Jones's braggadocious challenge to whiteness is simultaneously an anti-Irish slur coined by non-Irish whites, and thus contains a reminder that Irish Americans had "only gradually fought . . . their ways into the white race." Roediger, *Towards the Abolition of Whiteness*, 184.
161. Fante, *The Road*, 286.
162. Himes, *If He Hollers*, 19.
163. Dyer, *White*, 147, 148, 153.
164. As he was an Italian American (and a Southern Italian at that), the whiteness of Charles Atlas—real name Angelo Siciliano—is not, as discussions earlier in this chapter indicate, entirely clear-cut. In making the de-Italianization of his name part of the project of making and marketing his physique, however, he affirmed the whiteness-as-muscularity paradigm. Atlas became white by becoming muscular and vice versa, but the possibility of such an act demanded at least a degree of prior proximity to "full" whiteness, which Bob Jones lacks.
165. Himes, *If He Hollers*, 10.
166. Wyatt, *Five Fires*, 165.
167. Himes, *If He Hollers*, 22.
168. Himes, *If He Hollers*, 4, 3.
169. Chester Himes, "Now Is the Time! Here Is the Place!," in *Black on Black: Baby Sister and Selected Writings* (London: Michael Joseph, 1975), 219; Chester Himes, "Zoot Riots Are Race Riots," in *Black on Black: Baby Sister and Selected Writings* (London: Michael Joseph, 1975), 225.
170. Himes, "If You're Scared, Go Home!," 228.
171. Himes, *If He Hollers*, 4.
172. Himes, *If He Hollers*, 5.
173. Himes, *If He Hollers*, 3.
174. James Lundquist, *Chester Himes* (New York: Frederick Ungar, 1976), 29.
175. Himes, *If He Hollers*, 17.

176. Himes, *If He Hollers*, 17.
177. Gloria Anzaldúa, *Borderlands: The New Mestiza*, 4th ed. (San Francisco: Aunt Lute Books, 2012), 20.
178. Himes, *If He Hollers*, 221.
179. Lundquist, *Chester Himes*, 46.
180. Himes, *If He Hollers*, 219, 34, 22, 19, 24, 25, 152, 42.
181. Himes, *If He Hollers*, 25.
182. Wyatt, *Five Fires*, 164.
183. Lee, "Violence Real and Imagined," 68.
184. Himes, *If He Hollers*, 213.
185. Himes, *If He Hollers*, 35.
186. Himes, *If He Hollers*, 35.
187. Ellison, *Invisible Man*, 16.
188. Himes, *If He Hollers*, 33.
189. bell hooks, "Representing Whiteness in the Black Imagination," in *Displacing Whiteness: Essays in Social and Cultural Criticism*, ed. Ruth Frankenberg (Durham, NC: Duke University Press, 1997), 338–39.
190. Mosley, *Devil in a Blue Dress*, 69, 73.
191. Himes, *If He Hollers*, 219.
192. Himes, *If He Hollers*, 220.
193. Himes, *If He Hollers*, 221.
194. Roediger, *The Wages of Whiteness*, 12.
195. Himes, *If He Hollers*, 206.

Chapter 4

1. Kenneth T. Jackson, *Crabgrass Frontier: The Suburbanization of the United States* (Oxford: Oxford University Press, 1985), 3.
2. For the avoidance of doubt, in line with contemporary municipal planning documents as well as more recent studies of Los Angeles's architectural history, the terms "multi-family housing" and "multi-family residence" are used throughout this chapter to refer to any type of single building or lot that contains multiple dwellings—even when those dwellings themselves are discrete and self-contained. A fuller taxonomy of the different forms multi-family housing took in mid-century Los Angeles, and takes in the fiction of the period, follows later in this chapter.
3. David Gebhard and Harriette von Breton, *LA in the Thirties* (Layton, UT: Peregrine Smith, 1975), 26.
4. Soja and Scott, "Introduction to Los Angeles," 8; Sam Hall Kaplan, *LA Lost and Found: An Architectural History of Los Angeles* (New York: Crown, 1987), 127, 129.
5. Kaplan, *LA Lost and Found*, 151.

6. Reyner Banham, *Los Angeles: The Architecture of Four Ecologies* (Berkeley: University of California Press, 2009), 143.

7. Dimendberg, *Film Noir and the Spaces of Modernity*, 177, 89.

8. Edward W. Soja, *Postmodern Geographies: The Reassertion of Space in Critical Social Theory* (London: Verso, 1989), 195.

9. Gebhard and von Breton, *LA in the Thirties*, 25.

10. Gebhard and von Breton, *LA in the Thirties*, 26.

11. Wagner, *Los Angeles*, 239; Fogelson, *The Fragmented Metropolis*, 146.

12. Fogelson, *The Fragmented Metropolis*, 146.

13. *Master Plan of Land Use, Inventory and Classification* (Los Angeles: Regional Planning Commission, County of Los Angeles, 1941), 20, Box 333, John Randolph Haynes and Dora Haynes Foundation Library (Collection 1604), UCLA Library Special Collections, Charles E. Young Research Library, University of California, Los Angeles.

14. *1940 Census of Housing*, vol. 2: General Characteristics (Washington, DC: United States Government Printing Office, 1943), 215.

15. Howard J. Nelson and William A. V. Clark, *The Los Angeles Metropolitan Experience: Uniqueness, Generality, and the Goal of the Good Life* (Cambridge, MA: Ballinger, 1976), 24.

16. Chandler, *Farewell, My Lovely*, 182.

17. Nathanael West, *The Day of the Locust and Miss Lonelyhearts* (London: Vintage, 2012).

18. West, *The Day of the Locust and Miss Lonelyhearts*, 61.

19. Aldous Huxley, *After Many a Summer* (London: Vintage, 2015), 16.

20. Paul Groth, *Living Downtown: The History of Residential Hotels in the United States* (Berkeley: University of California Press, 1999), 1.

21. *Master Plan of Land Use, Inventory and Classification*, 30.

22. Chandler, *The High Window*, 70.

23. Robert F. Harney, "Boarding and Belonging: Thoughts on Sojourner Institutions," *Urban History Review* 7, no. 2 (October 1978): 18.

24. "Theodore Roosevelt to Richard Melancthon Hurd, 3 January 1919," in *Letters of Theodore Roosevelt*, ed. Elting E. Morrison, vol. 8 (Cambridge: Cambridge University Press, 1954), 1422.

25. John Modell and Tamara K. Hareven, "Urbanization and the Malleable Household: An Examination of Boarding and Lodging in American Families," *Journal of Marriage and Family* 35, no. 3 (August 1973): 476, https://doi.org/10.2307/350582; James C. Young, "The Boarding House Era Goes with 'Miss Mary's,'" *New York Times*, October 18, 1925.

26. Chandler, *The Big Sleep*, 126.

27. Stefanos Polyzoides et al., *Courtyard Housing in Los Angeles: A Typological Analysis* (Berkeley: University of California Press, 1982), 9.

28. Kaplan, *LA Lost and Found*, 103, 105.

29. In 1941 60 percent of the population of the central district lived in multi-family residences, when the citywide mean was only 18 percent. *Master Plan of Land Use, Inventory and Classification*, 32.

30. John Fante, "John Fante to Mary Fante," January 13, 1933, Box 26, Folder 3, John Fante Papers (Collection 1832), UCLA Library Special Collections, Charles E. Young Research Library, University of California, Los Angeles. The "old address on Bunker Hill . . . at the bottom floor at the rear and corner of the hotel," from which Fante writes to his mother in late 1934, appears to have been the inspiration for *Ask the Dust*'s Alta Loma hotel. "John Fante to Mary Fante," December 9, 1934, Box 26, Folder 3, John Fante Papers (Collection 1832), UCLA Library Special Collections, Charles E. Young Research Library, University of California, Los Angeles. Correspondence between Frank Fenton and Carey McWilliams (undated, but presumably from July 1935 as it refers to recent news of the death of George Russell) suggests that the boarding house in Fenton's *What Way My Journey Lies* was at least partly inspired by its author's living circumstances in the mid-'30s. "Frank Fenton to Carey McWilliams," n.d., Carey McWilliams Correspondence (Collection 1356), UCLA Library Special Collections, Charles E. Young Research Library, University of California, Los Angeles. Meanwhile Robert Emmet Long confirms the concordance between West's period as an apartment hotel denizen on North Ivar Street and the living circumstances of Tod Hackett. Robert Emmet Long, *Nathanael West* (New York: Frederick Ungar, 1985).

31. Klein, *The History of Forgetting*, 51.

32. Chandler, *The Big Sleep*, 19.

33. The name translates as "The Spittle," "The Slime," "The Slobber," or, to be precise, "The The Slobber." Chandler seemingly mocks the tendencies of LA's ever-creative real estate boosters to dress up their bland blocks in "romantic" or "exotic" Spanish names—sometimes to nonsensical effect.

34. Raymond Chandler, "The King in Yellow," in *The Simple Art of Murder* (New York: Vintage, 1988), 113.

35. Single-family homes that impede Marlowe tend to do so, by contrast, through highly particular spatial characteristics: see, for example, the suffocating greenhouse of Sternwood's mansion in *The Big Sleep* or Lagardie's house of horrors in *The Little Sister*.

36. Nicolaides, *My Blue Heaven*, 26.

37. Harold Kirker, *California's Architectural Frontier: Style and Tradition in the Nineteenth Century* (San Marino, CA: Huntington Library, 1960), 122–28; Kaplan, *LA Lost and Found*, 133.

38. Richard Weinstein, "The First American City," in *The City: Los Angeles and Urban Theory at the End of the Twentieth Century*, ed. Allen J. Scott and Edward W. Soja (Berkeley: University of California Press, 1996), 26.

39. Laslett, *Sunshine Was Never Enough*, 16.

40. Robert E. Lang and Rebecca R. Sohmer, "Legacy of the Housing Act of 1949: The Past, Present, and Future of Federal Housing and Urban Policy," *Housing Policy Debate* 11, no. 2 (January 2000): 295, https://doi.org/10.1080/10511482.2000.9521369.

41. Theodor Adorno and Max Horkheimer, *Dialectic of Enlightenment*, ed. Gunzelin Schmid Noerr, trans. Edmund Jephcott (Stanford, CA: Stanford University Press, 2002), 94.

42. David Gebhard and Robert Winter, *Los Angeles: An Architectural Guide*, 4th ed. (Salt Lake City: Gibbs-Smith, 1994), xv.

43. Adorno and Horkheimer, *Dialectic of Enlightenment*, 94.

44. Chandler, *The Big Sleep*, 24–25.

45. S. James Herman, *Why Do You Live in an Apartment? A Study of a Sinister Trend in American Life* (Detroit: Michigan Housing Association, 1931). Cited in Dana Cuff, *The Provisional City: Los Angeles Stories of Architecture and Urbanism* (Cambridge, MA: MIT Press, 2002), 144–45.

46. McCann, *Gumshoe America*, 176.

47. Laslett, *Sunshine Was Never Enough*, 75. See also Jackson, *Crabgrass Frontier*.

48. Cuff, *The Provisional City*, 75.

49. Cuff, *The Provisional City*, 146.

50. Those less salubrious forms dominated available accommodation stocks. By the late 1920s, such was the growth in LA's more well-to-do population that "the city was facing a shortage of high-class hotels and apartment buildings, although it had plenty of the 'ordinary'—i.e., low- to mid-priced apartment lodgings." This furthers the sense that although, as previously noted, the categories of hotel and apartment did span the full range of the city's social spectrum, the spaces of multi-family housing in its various permutations tended to be spaces of relative socioeconomic precarity. Ruth Wallach, *Los Angeles Residential Architecture: Modernism Meets Eclecticism* (Charleston, SC: History Press, 2015), 86.

51. Starr, *Material Dreams*, 70. Starr's description of this ideal as an "Ozcot gospel of homes and happiness" suggests the extent to which, like so many LA dreams, it had the whiff of fantasy. Nevertheless, it is certainly true that LA's owner-occupancy rates were higher than in other major US cities—a third of LA's homes were owner-occupied in the period between 1920 and 1940. A 1944 report (using 1940 statistics) notes that such figures were to be expected precisely because LA's proportion of single-family dwellings was so high, further affirming that the dream of single-family living and the dream of home ownership were largely one and the same. Earl Henson and Paul Beckett, *Los Angeles: Its People and Its Homes* (Los Angeles: Haynes Foundation, 1944), 13, Box 153, John Randolph Haynes and Dora Haynes Foundation Library (Collection 1604), UCLA

Library Special Collections, Charles E. Young Research Library, University of California, Los Angeles.

52. Wallach, *Los Angeles Residential Architecture*, 129.

53. Wallach, *Los Angeles Residential Architecture*, 84.

54. *Housing Occupancy in the City of Los Angeles and Supplement* (Los Angeles: Peacock Research Associates, 1950), 6, Box 333, John Randolph Haynes and Dora Haynes Foundation Library (Collection 1604), UCLA Library Special Collections, Charles E. Young Research Library, University of California, Los Angeles.

55. Joyce Fante, "List of John Fante's Addresses," n.d., Box 48, Folder 3, John Fante Papers (Collection 1832), UCLA Library Special Collections, Charles E. Young Research Library, University of California, Los Angeles. The list bears no attribution but I infer Joyce Fante's authorship with confidence on the basis of consistency between the handwriting of this list and that of other documents in the Fante papers known to be written by Joyce.

56. Joseph George, *Postmodern Suburban Spaces: Philosophy, Ethics, and Community in Post-War American Fiction* (Basingstoke: Palgrave Macmillan, 2016), 11.

57. Cuff, *The Provisional City*, 75.

58. *Housing Study City of Los Angeles, Community Redevelopment, Conditions of Blight, Central Area* (Los Angeles: City Planning Commission, 1947), 13, Box 333, John Randolph Haynes and Dora Haynes Foundation Library (Collection 1604), UCLA Library Special Collections, Charles E. Young Research Library, University of California, Los Angeles.

59. Chandler, *The High Window*, 70.

60. Chandler, *The Big Sleep*, 126.

61. This is not to suggest that these are the only minority groups Hargreaves would exclude, only that they are the ones of which Bandini might pass for a member.

62. Henson and Beckett, *Los Angeles*, 35, 51, 44. In figures: 33.6 percent of dwelling units were single-family detached homes; 33.5 percent accommodated ten households or more; only 14 percent were owner-occupied.

63. Henson and Beckett, *Los Angeles*, 58, 59, 45.

64. William Burk, *Poor Housing in the Los Angeles Metropolitan Area* (Los Angeles: Works Progress Administration Delinquency Prevention Project, 1938), 2, Box 333, John Randolph Haynes and Dora Haynes Foundation Library (Collection 1604), UCLA Library Special Collections, Charles E. Young Research Library, University of California, Los Angeles. This document's pages are not numbered; in the interest of precision of reference, I have applied numbering myself by counting pages.

65. *Housing Study City of Los Angeles*, 15.

66. Sides, *LA City Limits*, 98.

67. Sides, *LA City Limits*, 98.

68. The data of the period is insufficiently granular to permit a statement of absolute certainty that the association between LA's distribution of ethnic minority populations and its distribution of multi-family housing means that multi-family housing was disproportionately populated by ethnic minorities. (Indeed, Bandini's landlady is herself indicative of the extent to which even some decidedly shabby residential hotels and apartment houses maintained "whites only" policies.) Nevertheless, the correlations outlined hitherto are strong and consistent enough to seem highly persuasive.

69. Himes, *If He Hollers*, 10.

70. Weinstein, "The First American City," 26.

71. McDonough, *Staging Masculinity*, 36.

72. Joe L. Dubbert, *A Man's Place: Masculinity in Transition* (Englewood Cliffs, NJ: Prentice-Hall, 1979), 10.

73. Young, "The Boarding House Era Goes with 'Miss Mary's,'" 23; Mary Farley, "Boarding-House Clubs: Are Serious Inroads Upon the Once Popular Boarding-House," *Los Angeles Times*, November 21, 1897.

74. "Goodyear Home Plan Approved," *Los Angeles Times*, December 21, 1919.

75. Chandler, *The Big Sleep*, 111.

76. Chandler, *The Big Sleep*, 112.

77. The main action of Hughes's novel takes place after the war has already "crashed to a finish and dribbled to an end." *In a Lonely Place* (London: Penguin, 2010), 1. Inference from the text suggests that *What Way My Journey Lies* takes place over a period of approximately one and a half years, commencing in perhaps January or February 1944 and concluding around September 1945.

78. Sarah Trott has argued that Marlowe himself occupies a form of veteran identity, and that this colors his vision of America around the years of World War II, his attitude to violence, his ethics, and his interactions with other soldiering types—most prominently *The Long Goodbye*'s Terry Lennox. Marlowe's own military identity as advanced by Trott, however, is not in itself a direct expression of post–World War II veteran panic, its specifics rooted rather in Chandler's own experiences of World War I. Sarah Trott, *War Noir: Raymond Chandler and the Hard-Boiled Detective as Veteran in American Fiction* (Jackson: University Press of Mississippi, 2016), 114–15. In *The Big Sleep*, Marlowe, Rusty Regan, General Sternwood, and the Sternwoods' Butler, Norris, all share "the soldier's eye"; Eddie Mars likewise persistently refers to Marlowe as "soldier." Chandler, *The Big Sleep*, 153.

79. Colleen Glenn, "The Traumatized Veteran: A New Look at Jimmy Stewart's Post-WWII Vertigo," *Quarterly Review of Film and Video* 31, no. 1 (January 2014): 27, https://doi.org/10.1080/10509208.2011.593957; David A. Gerber, "Heroes and Misfits: The Troubled Social Reintegration of Disabled Veterans in *The Best Years of Our Lives*," *American Quarterly* 46, no. 4 (December 1994): 545, https://doi.org/10.2307/2713383.

80. Gerber, "Heroes and Misfits," 545; Anne L. Shewring, "We Didn't Do That Did We? Representation of the Veteran Experience," *Journal of American and Comparative Cultures* 23, no. 4 (Winter 2000): 53, 51, https://doi.org/10.1111/j.1537-4726.2000.2304_51.x.

81. Willard Walter Waller, *The Veteran Comes Back* (New York: Dryden Press, 1944), 14.

82. Crèvecœur wrote in 1782 that "the few magistrates [on the frontier] are . . . often in a perfect state of war. . . . There men appear to be no better than carnivorous animals of a superior rank. . . . He who would wish to see America in its proper light, and have a true idea of its feeble beginnings and barbarous rudiments, must visit our extended line of frontiers where the last settlers dwell . . . the most hideous parts of our society. They are a kind of forlorn hope, preceding by ten or twelve years the most respectable army of veterans which come after them." Crèvecœur, "Letter III: What is an American?," 33–34.

83. Reed Robert Bonadonna, *Soldiers and Civilization: How the Profession of Arms Thought and Fought the Modern World into Existence* (Annapolis, MD: Naval Institute Press, 2017), 1.

84. Gilles Deleuze and Félix Guattari, *Nomadology: The War Machine*, trans. Brian Massumi (Seattle: Wormwood Distribution, 2010), 7.

85. Deleuze and Guattari, *Nomadology*, 7, 4.

86. Deleuze and Guattari, *Nomadology*, 7.

87. Deleuze and Guattari, *Nomadology*, 7.

88. Frank Fenton, *What Way My Journey Lies* (New York: Duell, Sloan and Pearce, 1946), 101.

89. Fenton, *Journey*, 73, 80, 86.

90. Hughes, *Lonely Place*, 96.

91. Hughes, *Lonely Place*, 1.

92. Fenton, *Journey*, 77.

93. Fenton, *Journey*, 80.

94. Fenton, *Journey*, 122.

95. Fenton, *Journey*, 148.

96. Christopher Breu, "Radical Noir: Negativity, Misogyny, and the Critique of Privatization in Dorothy Hughes's *In a Lonely Place*," *Modern Fiction Studies* 55, no. 2 (Summer 2009): 204, https://doi.org/10.1353/mfs.0.1607.

97. Fenton, *Journey*, 18–19.

98. Fenton, *Journey*, 3.

99. Fenton, *Journey*, 4.

100. Fenton, *Journey*, 25.

101. Fenton, *Journey*, 24.

102. Fenton, *Journey*, 27.

103. Fenton, *Journey*, 34.

104. Fenton, *Journey*, 34.

105. Fenton, *Journey*, 3.
106. Fenton, *Journey*, 33.
107. John Fante, *Dreams from Bunker Hill*, in *The Bandini Quartet* (Edinburgh: Canongate Books, 2004), 746.
108. Fenton, *Journey*, 34–45.
109. Fenton, *Journey*, 35.
110. Fenton, *Journey*, 35.
111. Fenton, *Journey*, 35.
112. Fenton, *Journey*, 35–36.
113. *Preliminary Report on the Disposition of Public War Housing in Los Angeles* (Los Angeles: Housing Authority of the City of Los Angeles, 1945), 3, Box 333, John Randolph Haynes and Dora Haynes Foundation Library (Collection 1604), UCLA Library Special Collections, Charles E. Young Research Library, University of California, Los Angeles.
114. *Preliminary Report on the Disposition of Public War Housing in Los Angeles*, 1, 5.
115. Harold Wentworth and Stuart Berg Flexner, *Dictionary of American Slang* (New York: Thomas Y. Crowell, 1960), 411.
116. Eric Partridge, *A Dictionary of the Underworld: British and American*, 3rd ed. (London: Routledge and Kegan Paul, 1968), 538.
117. "Punk" was at this time "the army name for bread," and the "punk sergeant" the mocking name for the attendant who dispensed it in the mess. Likewise, in both the US Army and Marine Corps the company clerk (the notion of clerks as effeminate present once more) was sometimes known as the "punk." Elbridge Colby, *Army Talk: A Familiar Dictionary of Soldier Speech* (Princeton: Princeton University Press, 1942), 161.
118. The definitive modern account of frontier-era LA's culture of violence is John Mack Faragher's *Eternity Street: Violence and Justice in Frontier Los Angeles* (New York: W. W. Norton, 2016).
119. Fenton, *Journey*, 36.
120. Fenton, *Journey*, 36–37.
121. Fante's protagonists must similarly deploy charm to navigate past the female hotel proprietors of Bunker Hill, in the forms of *Ask the Dust*'s Mrs. Hargreaves, *Dreams from Bunker Hill*'s Mrs. Brownell, and Mrs. Flores in "The Dreamer."
122. Fenton, *Journey*, 37.
123. Fenton, *Journey*, 37.
124. It should of course be noted that this account of Cramer's beliefs on the gendering of labor comes to us via Chester, whose own vision of the politics of masculinity and femininity is less than nuanced. John's later experiences in the boarding house do, however, bear out Chester's information.
125. Turner, "Contributions," 1921, 261.
126. Fenton, *Journey*, 40.

127. Fenton, *Journey*, 147.
128. Fenton, *Journey*, 213–14.
129. Fenton, *Journey*, 213.
130. Fenton, *Journey*, 103.
131. Fenton, *Journey*, 105, 131, 138, 198.
132. Fenton, *Journey*, 213.
133. Fenton, *Journey*, 161.
134. John's friendship with Deirdre is one of a string of episodes in the book (following the intensity of John's grief for Clark and domestic occupation of his home, his recurring reluctance to commit to heterosexual relationships, and the homoerotic implications of Chester's earlier discourse on "punks") that suggest the potential for a queer interpretation of *What Way My Journey Lies*—itself another potential avenue of comparison with *In a Lonely Place*. Such a reading would not preclude my frontierist analysis of John's actions and motivations (indeed, it would derive largely from similar claims), however, and the evidence for it is not so overwhelming as to suggest it is the only plausible one. One is mindful of Raymond Chandler's exhortation, however paranoid it may have been, when faced with Gershon Legman's claim that his prose encodes a gay Philip Marlowe, not to join "that rather numerous class . . . which cannot conceive of a close relationship between a couple of men as other than homosexual." Jerry Speir, *Raymond Chandler* (New York: Frederick Ungar, 1981), 111. Cited in Trott, *War Noir*, 95.
135. Fenton, *Journey*, 241.
136. Fenton, *Journey*, 243.
137. Fenton, *Journey*, 215–16.
138. Hughes, *Lonely Place*, 15.
139. Breu, "Radical Noir," 201.
140. Polyzoides et al., *Courtyard Housing in Los Angeles*, 9.
141. Lewis Mumford, *The City in History: Its Origins, Its Transformations, and Its Prospects* (Harmondsworth: Penguin, 1966), 310. Mumford's dismissal of Los Angeles as "an undifferentiated mass of houses," risible on its face, seems all the more foolish in light of the potential pertinence of the unique spatial characteristics possessed by the apartment court, that most quintessentially LA residential form, to his hermeneutics of public and private urban space. Mumford, 581.
142. Hughes, *Lonely Place*, 20–21.
143. Hughes, *Lonely Place*, 20.
144. Hughes, *Lonely Place*, 41.
145. Hughes, *Lonely Place*, 82.
146. Hughes, *Lonely Place*, 82.
147. Polyzoides et al., *Courtyard Housing in Los Angeles*, 32, 35, 38.
148. Hughes, *Lonely Place*, 46.
149. Polyzoides refers to seemingly self-contradicting "duplex or quadruplex" bungalows, "stacked shotgun house[s] on two stories"—buildings that resemble two-story single-family dwellings but in fact contain separate dwellings on each

floor, each with its own external access. "California Bungalows, Streets, and Courts," *Old-House Journal* 30, no. 3 (June 2002): 73.

150. Hughes, *Lonely Place*, 6.
151. Hughes, *Lonely Place*, 7.
152. Hughes, *Lonely Place*, 7.
153. Hughes, *Lonely Place*, 46.
154. Hughes, *Lonely Place*, 7.
155. Trott, *War Noir*, 107.
156. McCann, *Gumshoe America*, 176.
157. Raymond Chandler, *Playback* (London: Hamish Hamilton, 1958), 7.
158. Fante married Joyce Smart in 1937 and their first child was born in 1942. Although the 1940s were years of artistic disappointment for Fante (*Ask the Dust*'s failure to catapult him into the literary establishment, his failure to win a Guggenheim fellowship, the failure of *The Little Brown Brothers*), screenwriting work became increasingly lucrative. Never again would John Fante slum it in a Bunker Hill hotel.
159. Mike Davis, "Bunker Hill: Hollywood's Dark Shadow," in *Cinema and the City: Film and Urban Societies in a Global Context*, ed. Mark Shiel and Tony Fitzmaurice (Oxford: Blackwell, 2001), 33.
160. Avila, *Popular Culture in the Age of White Flight*, 60.
161. Avila, *Popular Culture in the Age of White Flight*, 60; Davis, "Bunker Hill," 33.
162. Gebhard and von Breton, *LA in the Thirties*, 9.
163. Thomas C. Frank, *The Conquest of Cool: Business Culture, Counterculture, and the Rise of Hip Consumerism* (Chicago: University of Chicago Press, 1997), 10.

Epilogue

1. Terry Curtis Fox, "City Knights," *Film Comment* 20, no. 5 (October 1984): 34.
2. Ross Macdonald, *The Underground Man* (London: Penguin, 2012), 1, 8.
3. Macdonald, *The Underground Man*, 10.
4. Macdonald, *The Underground Man*, 18.
5. Macdonald, *The Underground Man*, 133.
6. George M. Pisk, "The Graveyard of Dreams: A Study of Nathanael West's Last Novel, *The Day of the Locust*," *South Central Bulletin* 27, no. 4 (Winter 1967): 71, https://doi.org/10.2307/3188923.
7. Steven Weisenburger, "Williams, West, and the Art of Regression," *South Atlantic Review* 47, no. 4 (November 1982): 10, 7, 1, https://doi.org/10.2307/3199403.
8. David M. Fine, "James M. Cain and the Los Angeles Novel," *American Studies* 20, no. 1 (Spring 1979): 26.

9. David M. Fine, "Nathanael West, Raymond Chandler, and the Los Angeles Novel," *California History* 68, no. 4 (December 1989): 201, https://doi.org/10.2307/25158537.
10. Macdonald, *The Underground Man*, 133–34.
11. Macdonald, *The Underground Man*, 68.
12. Alison Lurie, *The Nowhere City* (London: Abacus, 1986), 238.
13. Davis, *Ecology of Fear*, 9.
14. Davis, *Ecology of Fear*, 6–8.
15. Gore Vidal, "The Ashes of Hollywood I: The Bottom 4 of the Top 10," *New York Review of Books*, May 17, 1973. Vidal does not provide a date for this encounter but does state that it occurred en route to his final meeting with Dorothy Parker, and Parker's last period of residence in LA was in the early '60s, while her previous sojourns there predate the context of Vidal's piece.
16. Joan Didion, "Fire Season," in *We Tell Ourselves Stories in Order to Live: Collected Nonfiction* (New York: Alfred A. Knopf, 2006), 656.
17. Joan Didion, "Los Angeles Days," in *We Tell Ourselves Stories in Order to Live: Collected Nonfiction* (New York: Alfred A. Knopf, 2006), 614.
18. Didion, "Los Angeles Days," 615; Didion, "Fire Season," 659.
19. Avila, *Popular Culture in the Age of White Flight*, 226.
20. Michael Kreyling, *The Novels of Ross Macdonald* (Columbia: University of South Carolina Press, 2005), 111.
21. Avila, *Popular Culture in the Age of White Flight*, 226.
22. Macdonald, *The Underground Man*, 149.
23. In *Black Money*, set approximately five years before *The Underground Man* (Macdonald maintains a fairly consistent chronology from book to book), Archer describes another character as being "fifty at most" and notes that this "wasn't much older than I was." *Black Money* (London: Collins, 1966), 30.
24. Macdonald, *The Underground Man*, 22.
25. Macdonald, *The Underground Man*, 149, 112, 292.
26. Macdonald, *The Underground Man*, 75, 23, 4.
27. Lee Clark. "Diversions of Furniture and Signature Styles: Hammett, Chandler, Macdonald," *Arizona Quarterly* 71, no. 3 (Autumn 2015): 19, https://doi.org/10.1353/arq.2015.0016.
28. Van Wyck Brooks, "On Creating a Usable Past," *The Dial*, April 11, 1918, 339.
29. Brooks, "On Creating a Usable Past," 337–39.
30. Macdonald, *The Underground Man*, 36, 225.
31. In September 1898, making the case for American seizure of the Philippines in a speech reproduced by the *Indianapolis Journal*, the imperialist Senator-historian Albert Beveridge explicitly compared the previous month's annexation of Hawaii to the earlier frontier conquest of California. "Both," he noted, demanded that American guile and hardiness test itself against "a savage

and an alien population" and had similar qualities of distance from the seat of government. When he spoke of God endowing the American people with "gifts beyond our deserts" he may not have intended a geographic pun, but one was certainly present. The claiming of Pacific territory, a mere five years after Turner's declaration of the frontier's end, was explicitly figured as an assertion that frontierism remained possible: it was merely the latest stage in "a history of statesmen who flung the boundaries of the Republic out into unexplored lands and savage wilderness." Albert J. Beveridge, "Stirred by His Words: Mr Beveridge's Magnificent Presentation of War Issues," *Indianapolis Journal*, September 17, 1898. For more on the intersecting (and often frontierist) meanings imputed to California and Hawaii in American political and cultural consciousness throughout the nineteenth and twentieth centuries, see Henry Knight Lozano's *California and Hawai'i Bound: U.S. Settler Colonialism and the Pacific West, 1848–1959* (Lincoln: University of Nebraska Press, 2021).

32. Macdonald, *The Underground Man*, 22.
33. Ross Macdonald, *The Doomsters* (London: Cassell, 1958), 20.
34. Macdonald, *The Underground Man*, 283.
35. Macdonald, *The Underground Man*, 284.
36. Macdonald, *The Underground Man*, 92, 82.
37. Joan Didion, "Slouching Towards Bethlehem," in *We Tell Ourselves Stories in Order to Live: Collected Nonfiction* (New York: Alfred A. Knopf, 2006), 67.
38. Macdonald, *The Underground Man*, 115, 112, 125, 87.
39. Macdonald, *The Underground Man*, 24.
40. Macdonald, *The Underground Man*, 91.
41. Macdonald, *The Underground Man*, 78–79.
42. Macdonald, *The Underground Man*, 35.
43. Macdonald, *The Underground Man*, 30–31.
44. Macdonald, *The Underground Man*, 166, 53.
45. Macdonald, *The Underground Man*, 160.
46. Macdonald, *The Underground Man*, 32, 53, 160, 53, 165.
47. Macdonald, *The Doomsters*, 163.
48. Lurie, *The Nowhere City*, 270.
49. Lurie, *The Nowhere City*, 5, 272, 232.
50. Lurie, *The Nowhere City*, 39, italics in original.
51. Lurie, *The Nowhere City*, 102.
52. Lurie, *The Nowhere City*, 103.
53. Lurie, *The Nowhere City*, 101.
54. "Frederick Jackson Turner to Mae Sherwood," September 5, 1887. Cited in Michael C. Steiner, "The Significance of Turner's Sectional Thesis," *Western Historical Quarterly* 10, no. 4 (October 1979): 442, https://doi.org/10.2307/968085.
55. Joan Didion, *Where I Was From*, in *We Tell Ourselves Stories in Order to Live: Collected Nonfiction* (New York: Alfred A. Knopf, 2006), 1075.

56. Lurie, *The Nowhere City*, 107, 278.

57. Phil Abraham, dir., "The Jet Set," *Mad Men*, season 2, episode 11 (AMC, October 12, 2008).

58. Alan Taylor, dir., "The Mountain King," *Mad Men*, season 2, episode 12 (AMC, October 19, 2008).

59. Walt Whitman, "Facing West from California's Shores," *The Selected Poems of Walt Whitman* (New York: Walter J. Black, 1942), 117.

60. John Slattery, dir., "A Tale of Two Cities," *Mad Men*, season 6, episode 10 (AMC, June 2, 2013).

61. Matthew Weiner, dir., "Person to Person," *Mad Men*, season 7, episode 14 (AMC, May 17, 2015).

62. Eduardo Obregón Pagán, *Murder at the Sleepy Lagoon: Zoot Suits, Race, and Riot in Wartime LA* (Chapel Hill: University of North Carolina Press, 2003), 7. Pagán's book is the definitive social history of the trial, the riot, and the circumstances of racial resistance that surrounded both.

63. For a comprehensively contextualized account, see Ronald N. Jacobs, *Race, Media and the Crisis of Civil Society: From the Watts Riots to Rodney King* (Cambridge: Cambridge University Press, 2000).

64. John Laslett has thoroughly reinvestigated the circumstances and consequences of the infamous mass eviction of Mexican Americans from their homes to clear space for the Los Angeles Dodgers' new stadium in *Shameful Victory: The Los Angeles Dodgers, the Red Scare, and the Hidden History of Chavez Ravine* (Tucson: University of Arizona Press, 2015).

65. Miriam Pawel, *The Crusades of Cesar Chavez: A Biography* (New York: Bloomsbury, 2014), 63.

66. See Laura Meyer, "The Los Angeles Woman's Building and the Feminist Art Community, 1973–1991," in *Sons and Daughters of Los: Culture and Community in LA*, ed. David E. James (Philadelphia: Temple University Press, 2003), 39–62.

67. Mike Davis and Jon Wiener, *Set the Night on Fire: LA in the Sixties* (London: Verso, 2020), 6. A fitting capstone to the late Davis's career of vital activism and scholarship, *Set the Night on Fire* is the definitive account of the many intersecting movements for radical political change that coalesced (and, at times, collided) in Los Angeles in the 1960s.

68. Fogelson, *The Fragmented Metropolis*, 83.

69. Henson and Beckett, *Los Angeles*, 41, 39.

70. Roger Waldinger, "Not the Promised City: Los Angeles and Its Immigrants," *Pacific Historical Review* 68, no. 2 (May 1999): 253, https://doi.org/10.2307/3641987.

71. Davis, *City of Quartz*, 104; Davis, *Ecology of Fear*, 282.

72. Avila, *Popular Culture in the Age of White Flight*, 20.

73. Avila, *Popular Culture in the Age of White Flight*, 21.

74. Avila, *Popular Culture in the Age of White Flight*, 20.

75. Murphet, *Race and Literature in Los Angeles*, 1.
76. Murphet, *Race and Literature in Los Angeles*, 1.
77. Davis, *Ecology of Fear*, 140–41.
78. Marshall Berman, *All That Is Solid Melts Into Air: The Experience of Modernity* (New York: Penguin, 1988), 328–29.
79. John F. Stack, "The Ethnic Citizen Confronts the Future: Los Angeles and Miami at Century's Turn," *Pacific Historical Review* 68, no. 2 (May 1999): 314, 309, https://doi.org/10.2307/3641990.
80. The sheer depth and breadth of Latinx literature produced in and about Los Angeles since the 1960s is admirably documented in López-Calvo's *Latino Los Angeles in Film and Fiction*. Dean Franco offers a persuasive reading of the role of space in Viramontes's fiction in *The Border and the Line*, 33–70.
81. Franco also offers a compelling and meticulously researched account of the history of the Writers' Workshop's checkered history, again in *The Border and the Line*, 75–99.
82. Karen Grigsby Bates, "Joe Ide: Creating A Complicated Hero From the Hood," NPR: Code Switch, November 10, 2017, https://www.npr.org/sections/code switch/2017/11/10/562935061/joe-ide-creating-a-complicated-hero-from-the-hood.
83. Richard Jean So and Gus Wezerek, "Just How White Is the Book Industry?," *New York Times*, December 11, 2020; Richard Jean So, *Redlining Culture: A Data History of Racial Inequality and Postwar Fiction* (New York: Columbia University Press, 2020).
84. López-Calvo, *Latino Los Angeles in Film and Fiction*, 2.
85. The process by which the fiction of Los Angeles became, in reflection of the city itself, less accommodating of frontier myth as a way of navigating the world and structuring experience should be located in the context of a simultaneous reckoning (albeit a reluctant and still incomplete one) in broader American popular culture with frontier myth and its representations. See the rise of the "revisionist Western," which interrogated, subverted, and deconstructed the heroic legends of the Old West—in films from John Ford's *The Man Who Shot Liberty Valance* (1962) to Clint Eastwood's *High Plains Drifter* (1973), or the literary works of Cormac McCarthy. Key critical treatments include Sara L. Spurgeon, *Exploding the Western: Myths of Empire on the Postmodern Frontier* (College Station: Texas A and M University Press, 2005) and James J. Donahue, *Failed Frontiersmen: White Men and Myth in the Post-Sixties American Historical Romance* (Charlottesville: University of Virginia Press, 2015).
86. Wanda Coleman, *Mambo Hips and Make Believe* (Santa Rosa, CA: Black Sparrow, 1999), 313.
87. Naomi Hirahara, "What Raymond Chandler Didn't Understand About LA," Zócalo Public Square, August 6, 2014, https://www.zocalopublicsquare.org/2014/08/06/what-raymond-chandler-didnt-understand-about-l-a/ideas/nexus/.
88. Klein, *The History of Forgetting*, 2–4, 12–14.

89. Greg Grandin, *The End of the Myth: From the Frontier to the Border Wall in the Mind of America* (New York: Henry Holt, 2019), 9, 8.
90. Grandin, *The End of the Myth*, 8.
91. Grandin, *The End of the Myth*, 9.
92. Macdonald, *The Underground Man*, 305.
93. Macdonald, *The Underground Man*, 305.

Bibliography

1940 Census of Housing. Vol. 2: General Characteristics. Washington, DC: United States Government Printing Office, 1943.

1940 Census of Population: The Labor Force (Sample Statistics). Washington, DC: United States Government Printing Office, 1943.

Abbott, Megan E. *The Street Was Mine: White Masculinity in Hardboiled Fiction and Film Noir.* New York: Palgrave Macmillan, 2002.

Abraham, Phil, dir. "The Jet Set." *Mad Men,* season 2, episode 11. AMC, October 12, 2008.

Adamic, Louis. *The Truth About Los Angeles.* Girard, KS: Haldeman-Julius Publications, 1927.

Adorno, Theodor, and Max Horkheimer. *Dialectic of Enlightenment.* 1947. Edited by Gunzelin Schmid Noerr. Translated by Edmund Jephcott. Stanford, CA: Stanford University Press, 2002.

Alexander, Franz. *Our Age of Unreason: A Study of the Irrational Forces in Social Life.* New York: J. B. Lippincott, 1942.

Allen, Michael. Review of *The Winning of the West,* by Theodore Roosevelt. *Tennessee Historical Quarterly* 55, no. 1 (1996): 88.

Allmendinger, Blake. Conclusion to *A History of California Literature,* edited by Blake Allmendinger, 335–90. New York: Cambridge University Press, 2015.

———. *The Cowboy: Representations of Labor in an American Work Culture.* New York: Oxford University Press, 1992.

———. *Ten Most Wanted: The New Western Literature.* New York: Routledge, 1998.

"Action on Japs [a]." *Los Angeles Times.* February 19, 1942.

"Action on Japs [b]." *Los Angeles Times.* February 21, 1942.

Anzaldúa, Gloria. *Borderlands: The New Mestiza.* 1987. 4th ed. San Francisco: Aunt Lute Books, 2012.

Arax, Mark. *West of the West: Dreamers, Believers, Builders, and Killers in the Golden State.* New York: PublicAffairs, 2009.

Avila, Eric. *Popular Culture in the Age of White Flight: Fear and Fantasy in Suburban Los Angeles.* Berkeley: University of California Press, 2006.

Azuma, Eiichiro. "The Politics of Transnational History Making: Japanese Immigrants on the Western 'Frontier,' 1927–1941." *Journal of American History* 89, no. 4 (March 2003): 1401–30. https://doi.org/10.2307/3092548.
Babb, Valerie. *Whiteness Visible: The Meaning of Whiteness in American Literature and Culture*. New York: New York University Press, 1998.
Babener, Liahna K. "Raymond Chandler's City of Lies." In *Los Angeles in Fiction: A Collection of Original Essays*, edited by David M. Fine, 109–31. Albuquerque: University of New Mexico Press, 1984.
Babitz, Eve. "Heroine." 1977. In *Slow Days, Fast Company: The World, The Flesh, and LA*, 51–63. New York: New York Review Books, 2016.
———. "Slow Days." 1977. In *Slow Days, Fast Company: The World, The Flesh, and LA*, 5–9. New York: New York Review Books, 2016.
Baldoz, Rick. *The Third Asiatic Invasion: Empire and Migration in Filipino America, 1898–1946*. New York: New York University Press, 2011.
Baldwin, Rosecrans. *Everything Now: Lessons from the City-State of Los Angeles*. New York: Farrar, Straus and Giroux, 2021.
Banham, Reyner. *Los Angeles: The Architecture of Four Ecologies*. 1971. Berkeley: University of California Press, 2009.
Barrymore, Lionel, dir. *Ten Cents a Dance*. Columbia Pictures, 1931.
Bates, Karen Grigsby. "Joe Ide: Creating A Complicated Hero From the Hood." NPR: Code Switch, November 10, 2017. https://www.npr.org/sections/codeswitch/2017/11/10/562935061/joe-ide-creating-a-complicated-hero-from-the-hood.
Bellow, Saul. *Dangling Man*. 1944. New York: Penguin, 1996.
Berman, Marshall. *All That Is Solid Melts Into Air: The Experience of Modernity*. 1982. New York: Penguin, 1988.
Beveridge, Albert J. "Stirred by His Words: Mr Beveridge's Magnificent Presentation of War Issues." *Indianapolis Journal*. September 17, 1898.
Billington, Ray Allen. *The American Frontier Thesis: Attack and Defense*. Washington, DC: American Historical Association, 1971.
———. *The Genesis of the Frontier Thesis: A Study in Historical Creativity*. San Marino, CA: Huntington Library, 1971.
Billington, Ray Allen, and Martin Ridge. *Westward Expansion: A History of the American Frontier*. 1949. 6th ed. Albuquerque: University of New Mexico Press, 2001.
Bolton, Herbert Eugene. *The Spanish Borderlands: A Chronicle of Old Florida and the Southwest*. New Haven, CT: Yale University Press, 1921.
———. *Wider Horizons of American History*. New York: D. Appleton-Century, 1939.
Bolton, Herbert Eugene, and Thomas Maitland Marshall. *Colonization of North America, 1492–1783*. New York: Macmillan, 1920.
Bonadonna, Reed Robert. *Soldiers and Civilization: How the Profession of Arms Thought and Fought the Modern World into Existence*. Annapolis, MD: Naval Institute Press, 2017.

Bontemps, Arna. *Anyplace But Here*. New York: Hill and Wang, 1966.
Bonus, Rick. *Locating Filipino Americans: Ethnicity and the Cultural Politics of Space*. Philadelphia: Temple University Press, 2000.
Boring, William A. "America Groping in Architecture." *New York Times*, August 3, 1924.
Boulding, Kenneth Ewart. *The Organizational Revolution: A Study in the Ethics of Economic Organization*. 1953. Chicago, IL: Quadrangle Books, 1968.
Branch, E. Douglas. *Westward: The Romance of the American Frontier*. New York: Appleton, 1930.
Brands, H. W. *American Colossus: The Triumph of Capitalism, 1865–1900*. New York: Doubleday, 2010.
Breu, Christopher. "Radical Noir: Negativity, Misogyny, and the Critique of Privatization in Dorothy Hughes's *In a Lonely Place*." *Modern Fiction Studies* 55, no. 2 (Summer 2009): 199–215. https //doi.org/10.1353/mfs.0.1607.
Brooks, Van Wyck. "On Creating a Usable Past." *The Dial*, April 11, 1918.
Bryson, J. Scott. "Los Angeles Literature: Exiles, Natives, and (Mis)Representation." *American Literary History* 16, no. 4 (December 2004): 707–18. https://doi.org/10.1093/ALH/AJH039.
Buaken, Manuel. *I Have Lived with the American People*. Caldwell, ID: Caxton Printers, 1948.
Buell, Frederick. "A Short History of Oil Cultures; or, The Marriage of Catastrophe and Exuberance." In *Oil Culture*, edited by Ross Barrett and Daniel Worden, 69–88. Minneapolis: University of Minnesota Press, 2014.
Bulosan, Carlos. *America Is in the Heart: A Personal History*. 1946. Seattle: University of Washington Press, 2014.
Bunch, Lonnie G., III. "'The Greatest State for the Negro': Jefferson L. Edmonds, Black Propagandist of the California Dream." In *Seeking El Dorado: African Americans in California*, edited by Lawrence B. de Graaf, Kevin Mulroy, and Quintard Taylor, 129–48. Seattle: University of Washington Press, 2001.
Burgess, Ernest. Introduction to *The Taxi-Dance Hall: A Sociological Study in Commercialized Recreation and City Life*, by Paul Goalby Cressey, xi–xvi. Chicago: University of Chicago Press, 1932.
Burk, William. *Poor Housing in the Los Angeles Metropolitan Area*. Los Angeles: Works Progress Administration Delinquency Prevention Project, 1938. Box 333, John Randolph Haynes and Dora Haynes Foundation Library (Collection 1604), UCLA Library Special Collections, Charles E. Young Research Library, University of California, Los Angeles.
Burma, John H. "The Background of the Current Situation of Filipino-Americans." *Social Forces* 30, no. 1 (October 1951): 42–48. https://doi.org/10.2307/2571739.
Byrnes, Delia. "'I Get a Bad Taste in My Mouth Out Here': Oil's Intimate Ecologies in HBO's *True Detective*." *Global South* 9, no. 1 (Spring 2015): 86–106. https://doi.org/10.2979/globalsouth.9.1.07.

Cabell, James Branch. *Jurgen: A Comedy of Justice*. New York: Robert M. McBride, 1919.

Cain, James M. *Double Indemnity*. 1936. London: Orion, 2005.

———. *Mildred Pierce*. New York: Alfred A. Knopf, 1941.

———. "Paradise." *The American Mercury*, March 1933.

———. *The Postman Always Rings Twice*. 1934. London: Orion, 2005.

Cain, Paul. *Fast One*. Garden City, NY: Doubleday, Doran, 1933.

Carpio, Genevieve. *Collisions at the Crossroads: How Place and Mobility Make Race*. Oakland: University of California Press, 2019.

Carr, Harry. *Los Angeles: City of Dreams*. New York: D. Appleton-Century, 1935.

Casey Shoop. "Corpse and Accomplice: Fredric Jameson, Raymond Chandler, and the Representation of History in California." *Cultural Critique* 77 (Winter 2011): 205–38. https://doi.org/10.5749/culturalcritique.77.2011.0205.

Chandler, Raymond. *The Big Sleep*. 1939. In *The Big Sleep and Other Novels*, 1–164. London: Penguin, 2000.

———. *Farewell, My Lovely*. 1940. In *The Big Sleep and Other Novels*, 165–366. London: Penguin, 2000.

———. *The High Window*. 1942. London: Penguin, 2011.

———. "The King in Yellow." 1938. In *The Simple Art of Murder*, 84–138. New York: Vintage, 1988.

———. *The Lady in the Lake*. 1943. London: Penguin, 2011.

———. *The Little Sister*. 1949. New York, NY: Vintage, 1988.

———. *The Long Goodbye*. 1953. In *The Big Sleep and Other Novels*, 367–659. London: Penguin, 2000.

———. *Playback*. London: Hamish Hamilton, 1958.

———. "The Poodle Springs Story." 1962. In *Raymond Chandler Speaking*, edited by Dorothy Gardiner and Kathrine Sorley Walker, 251–64. Berkeley: University of California Press, 1997.

———. "Raymond Chandler to D. J. Ibberson, 19 April 1951." In *Raymond Chandler: Later Novels and Other Writings*, edited by Frank MacShane, 1043–48. New York: Library of America, 1995.

———. "Raymond Chandler to Hamish Hamilton, 4 December 1949." In *Raymond Chandler Speaking*, edited by Dorothy Gardiner and Kathrine Sorley Walker, 84–85. Berkeley: University of California Press, 1997.

———. "Red Wind." 1938. In *Trouble Is My Business and Other Stories*, 69–124. London: Penguin, 1988.

———. "The Simple Art of Murder." 1944. In *The Simple Art of Murder*, 1–18. New York: Vintage, 1988.

Chopas, Mary Elizabeth Basile. *Searching for Subversives: The Story of Italian Internment in Wartime America*. Chapel Hill: University of North Carolina Press, 2017.

"Classic Grace to Adorn City." *Los Angeles Times*, March 30, 1915.

Climie, Margaret Sarah. "Southern California in American Fiction." Los Angeles: University of Southern California, 1925.
Colby, Elbridge. *Army Talk: A Familiar Dictionary of Soldier Speech.* Princeton: Princeton University Press, 1942.
Coleman, Wanda. *Mambo Hips and Make Believe.* Santa Rosa, CA: Black Sparrow, 1999.
Collins, Richard. "Fante, Family, and the Fiction of Confession." In *John Fante: A Critical Gathering*, edited by David M. Fine and Stephen Cooper, 95–111. Madison, NJ: Fairleigh Dickinson University Press, 1999.
Connery, Christopher L. "Pacific Rim Discourse: The U.S. Global Imaginary in the Late Cold War Years." *Boundary 2* 21, no. 1 (Spring 1994): 30–56. https://doi.org/10.2307/303396.
Cooper, Stephen. Editor's notes to *The Big Hunger: Stories 1932–1959*, by John Fante, edited by Stephen Cooper, 309–15. New York: Ecco, 2000.
———. *Full of Life: A Biography of John Fante.* New York: North Point Press, 2000.
Cressey, Paul Goalby. *The Taxi-Dance Hall: A Sociological Study in Commercialized Recreation and City Life.* Chicago: University of Chicago Press, 1932.
Crèvecœur, J. Hector St. John de. "Letter III: What is an American?" 1782. In *Letters from an American Farmer and Other Essays*, edited by Dennis D. Moore. Cambridge, MA: Harvard University Press, 2013.
Croker, Richard Symonds. *The California Mackerel Fishery.* Sacramento: California State Printing Office, 1933. Special Collections and Archives, University of California, San Diego.
Cronon, William. "Turner's First Stand: The Significance of Significance in American History." In *Writing Western History: Essays on Major Western Historians*, edited by Richard W. Etulain, 73–101. Reno: University of Nevada Press, 2002.
Crozier, Michel. *The World of the Office Worker.* 1965. Translated by David Landau. Chicago: University of Chicago Press, 1971.
Cuff, Dana. *The Provisional City: Los Angeles Stories of Architecture and Urbanism.* Cambridge, MA: MIT Press, 2002.
Culver, Lawrence. *The Frontier of Leisure: Southern California and the Shaping of Modern America.* Oxford: Oxford University Press, 2010.
Davis, Clark. "'You Are the Company': The Demands of Employment in the Emerging Corporate Culture, Los Angeles, 1900–1930." *Business History Review* 70, no. 3 (Autumn 1996): 328–62. https://doi.org/10.2307/3117241.
Davis, Floyd. Illustrations for "Helen, Thy Beauty Is to Me—." *Saturday Evening Post*, March 1, 1941.
Davis, Mike. "Bunker Hill: Hollywood's Dark Shadow." In *Cinema and the City: Film and Urban Societies in a Global Context*, edited by Mark Shiel and Tony Fitzmaurice, 33–45. Oxford: Blackwell, 2001.
———. *City of Quartz: Excavating the Future in Los Angeles.* 1990. 2nd ed. London: Verso, 2006.

———. *Ecology of Fear: Los Angeles and the Imagination of Disaster*. 1998. London: Picador, 2000.

Davis, Mike, and Jon Wiener. *Set the Night on Fire: LA in the Sixties*. London: Verso, 2020.

Deleuze, Gilles, and Félix Guattari. *Nomadology: The War Machine*. 1986. Translated by Brian Massumi. Seattle: Wormwood Distribution, 2010.

Denning, Michael. *The Cultural Front: The Laboring of American Culture in the Twentieth Century*. London: Verso, 1998.

Dewey, John. *Individualism: Old and New*. London: G. Allen and Unwin, 1931.

DeWitt, John L. "Public Proclamation No. 1." San Francisco: Western Defense Command and Fourth Army, March 2, 1942. Special Collections, University of Washington Libraries. https://cdm16786.contentdm.oclc.org/digital/collection/pioneerlife/id/15329/rec/5.

Didion, Joan. "Bureaucrats." 1976. In *We Tell Ourselves Stories in Order to Live: Collected Nonfiction*, 236–40. New York: Alfred A. Knopf, 2006.

———. "Fire Season." 1989. In *We Tell Ourselves Stories in Order to Live: Collected Nonfiction*, 656–61. New York: Alfred A. Knopf, 2006.

———. "The Insidious Ethic of Conscience." *American Scholar* 34, no. 3 (Autumn 1965): 625–27.

———. "Los Angeles Days." 1988. In *We Tell Ourselves Stories in Order to Live: Collected Nonfiction*, 614–31. New York: Alfred A. Knopf, 2006.

———. *Play It as It Lays*. 1970. London: Fourth Estate, 2011.

———. "Slouching Towards Bethlehem." 1967. In *We Tell Ourselves Stories in Order to Live: Collected Nonfiction*, 67–97. New York: Alfred A. Knopf, 2006.

———. *Where I Was From*. 2003. In *We Tell Ourselves Stories in Order to Live: Collected Nonfiction*, 949–1104. New York: Alfred A. Knopf, 2006.

Dilts, Tyler. "Chandler's Shadow." *Los Angeles Review of Books*, January 1, 2015. https://lareviewofbooks.org/article/chandlers-shadow/.

Dimendberg, Edward. *Film Noir and the Spaces of Modernity*. Cambridge, MA: Harvard University Press, 2004.

———. Introduction to *Los Angeles: The Development, Life, and Structure of the City of Two Million in Southern California*, by Anton Wagner, 1–72. edited by Edward Dimendberg, translated by Timothy Grundy. Los Angeles: Getty Research Institute, 2022.

———. "The Kinetic Icon: Reyner Banham on Los Angeles as Mobile Metropolis." *Urban History* 33, no. 1 (May 2006): 106–25. https://doi.org/10.1017/S0963926806003543.

Dmytryk, Edward, dir. *Crossfire*. RKO Radio Pictures, 1947.

Donahue, James J. *Failed Frontiersmen: White Men and Myth in the Post-Sixties American Historical Romance*. Charlottesville: University of Virginia Press, 2015.

Dubbert, Joe L. *A Man's Place: Masculinity in Transition*. Englewood Cliffs, NJ: Prentice-Hall, 1979.
Durham, Philip. *Down These Mean Streets: Raymond Chandler's Knight*. Chapel Hill: University of North Carolina Press, 1963.
Dyer, Richard. *White*. London: Routledge, 1997.
Eastwood, Clint, dir. *High Plains Drifter*. Universal Pictures, 1973.
Ellison, Ralph. *Invisible Man*. 1952. London: Penguin, 2014.
España-Maram, Linda. *Creating Masculinity in Los Angeles's Little Manila: Working-Class Filipinos and Popular Culture, 1920s–1950s*. New York: Columbia University Press, 2006.
Espiritu, Augusto. Review of *Creating Masculinity in Los Angeles's Little Manila: Working-Class Filipinos and Popular Culture, 1920s–1950s*, by Linda España-Maram. *Philippine Studies* 56, no. 1 (March 2008): 105–9.
Etting, Ruth. *Ten Cents a Dance*. Columbia, 1930.
Etulain, Richard W. "The Rise of Western Historiography." In *Writing Western History: Essays on Major Western Historians*, edited by Richard W. Etulain, 1–16. Reno: University of Nevada Press, 2002.
Evergood, Philip. *Dance Marathon*. 1934. Oil on canvas, 152.6 cm × 101.7 cm. Blanton Museum of Art, Austin, TX.
Fante, John. *Ask the Dust*. 1939. In *The Bandini Quartet*, 409–602. Edinburgh: Canongate Books, 2004.
———. "The Dreamer." 1947. In *The Wine of Youth*, 237–50. New York: Ecco, 2002.
———. *Dreams from Bunker Hill*. 1982. In *The Bandini Quartet*, 603–749. Edinburgh: Canongate Books, 2004.
———. "Fish Cannery," n.d. Box 1, Folder 4. John Fante Papers (Collection 1832). UCLA Library Special Collections, Charles E. Young Research Library, University of California, Los Angeles.
———. *Full of Life*. 1952. Boston: Little, Brown, 1952.
———. "Helen, Thy Beauty Is to Me—." *Saturday Evening Post*, March 1, 1941.
———. "Helen, Thy Beauty Is to Me—." 1941. In *The Wine of Youth*, 251–66. New York: Ecco, 2002.
———. "John Fante to Mary Fante," January 13, 1933. Box 26, Folder 3, John Fante Papers (Collection 1832), UCLA Library Special Collections, Charles E. Young Research Library, University of California, Los Angeles.
———. "John Fante to Mary Fante," December 9, 1934. Box 26, Folder 3, John Fante Papers (Collection 1832), UCLA Library Special Collections, Charles E. Young Research Library, University of California, Los Angeles.
———. "Mary Osaka, I Love You." 1942. In *The Big Hunger: Stories 1932–1959*, edited by Cooper, Stephen, 175–204. New York: Ecco, 2000.
———. "The Odyssey of a Wop." 1933. In *The Wine of Youth*, 133–46. New York: Ecco, 2002.

———. *The Road to Los Angeles*. 1936/1985. In *The Bandini Quartet*, 215–407. Edinburgh: Canongate Books, 2004.

———. "Synopsis of *The Left-Handed Virgin/1933 Was a Bad Year*, Version B," c. 1960. Box 4, Folder 3. John Fante Papers (Collection 1832). UCLA Library Special Collections, Charles E. Young Research Library, University of California, Los Angeles.

———. "Synopsis of *The Left-Handed Virgin/1933 Was a Bad Year*, Version C," c. 1960. Box 4, Folder 3. John Fante Papers (Collection 1832). UCLA Library Special Collections, Charles E. Young Research Library, University of California, Los Angeles.

———. "The Cat," n.d. Box 1, Folder 5. John Fante Papers (Collection 1832). UCLA Library Special Collections, Charles E. Young Research Library, University of California, Los Angeles.

———. "To Be a Monstrous Clever Fellow." C. 1936. In *The Big Hunger: Stories 1932–1959*, edited by Stephen Cooper, 85–110. New York: Ecco, 2000.

———. "Untitled Manuscript," 1955. Box 24, Folder 4. John Fante Papers (Collection 1832). UCLA Library Special Collections, Charles E. Young Research Library, University of California, Los Angeles.

Fante, John, and Jack Leonard. *A Letter from the President*, 1950. Box 14, Folder 1. John Fante Papers (Collection 1832). UCLA Library Special Collections, Charles E. Young Research Library, University of California, Los Angeles.

Fante, Joyce. "List of John Fante's Addresses," n.d. Box 48, Folder 3, John Fante Papers (Collection 1832), UCLA Library Special Collections, Charles E. Young Research Library, University of California, Los Angeles.

Faragher, John Mack. *Eternity Street: Violence and Justice in Frontier Los Angeles*. New York: W. W. Norton, 2016.

Farley, Mary. "Boarding-House Clubs: Are Serious Inroads Upon the Once Popular Boarding-House." *Los Angeles Times*, November 21, 1897.

Faulkner, Thomas A. *The Lure of the Dance*. Los Angeles: T. A. Faulkner, 1916.

Fenton, Frank. "Frank Fenton to Carey McWilliams," n.d. Carey McWilliams Correspondence (Collection 1356), UCLA Library Special Collections, Charles E. Young Research Library, University of California, Los Angeles.

———. *What Way My Journey Lies*. New York: Duell, Sloan and Pearce, 1946.

Fifteenth Census of the United States, 1930: Population. Vol. 1: Number and Distribution of Inhabitants. Washington, DC: United States Government Printing Office, 1931.

Fine, David M. "California: Part of—or West of—the West?" *Western American Literature* 34, no. 2 (1999): 206–11.

———. "The Emergence of Los Angeles as a Literary Territory." *California History* 79, no. 1 (April 2000): 4–9. https://doi.org/10.2307/25591571.

———. *Imagining Los Angeles: A City in Fiction*. 2000. Reno: University of Nevada Press, 2004.

———. "James M. Cain and the Los Angeles Novel." *American Studies* 20, no. 1 (Spring 1979): 25–34.

———. "Nathanael West, Raymond Chandler, and the Los Angeles Novel." *California History* 68, no. 4 (December 1989): 196–201. https://doi.org/10.2307/25158537.

Fisher, Philip. *Still the New World: American Literature in a Culture of Creative Destruction*. Cambridge, MA: Harvard University Press, 1999.

Fogelson, Robert M. *The Fragmented Metropolis: Los Angeles 1850–1930*. Berkeley: University of California Press, 1993.

Ford, John, dir. *The Man Who Shot Liberty Valance*. Paramount Pictures, 1962.

Foronda, Marcelino A. "America Is in the Heart: Ilokano Immigration to the United States, 1906–1930." De La Salle University Occasional Paper no. 3, August 1976.

Fox, Terry Curtis. "City Knights." *Film Comment* 20, no. 5 (October 1984): 30–36.

Fradkin, Philip L., and Alex L. Fradkin. *The Left Coast: California on the Edge*. Berkeley: University of California Press, 2011.

Franco, Dean. *The Border and the Line: Race and Literature in Los Angeles*. Stanford, CA: Stanford University Press, 2019.

Frank, Thomas C. *The Conquest of Cool: Business Culture, Counterculture, and the Rise of Hip Consumerism*. Chicago: University of Chicago Press, 1997.

Frank, Waldo. 1919. *Our America*. New York: Ams Press, 1972.

———. *The Re-Discovery of America: An Introduction to a Philosophy of American Life*. New York: Charles Scribner's Sons, 1929.

Freud, Sigmund. "The 'Uncanny.'" 1919. In *The Standard Edition of the Complete Psychological Works*, edited and translated by James Strachey, vol. 17. London: Hogarth Press, 1955.

Fusco, Coco. "Fantasies of Oppositionality: Reflections on Recent Conferences in Boston and New York." *Screen* 29, no. 4 (Autumn 1988): 80–95.

Gardner, Ella. *Public Dance Halls: Their Regulation and Place in the Recreation of Adolescents*. Washington, DC: United States Government Printing Office, 1929. http://hdl.loc.gov/loc.music/musdi.205.

Garner, Steve. *Whiteness: An Introduction*. Abingdon: Routledge, 2007.

Gebhard, David, and Harriette von Breton. *LA in the Thirties*. Layton, UT: Peregrine Smith, 1975.

Gebhard, David, and Robert Winter. *Los Angeles: An Architectural Guide*. 4th ed. Salt Lake City: Gibbs-Smith, 1994.

George, Joseph. *Postmodern Suburban Spaces: Philosophy, Ethics, and Community in Post-War American Fiction*. Basingstoke: Palgrave Macmillan, 2016.

Gerber, David A. "Heroes and Misfits: The Troubled Social Reintegration of Disabled Veterans in *The Best Years of Our Lives*." *American Quarterly* 46, no. 4 (December 1994): 545–74. https://doi.org/10.2307/2713383.

Ghosh, Amitav. "Petrofiction: The Oil Encounter and the Novel." *New Republic*, March 2, 1992.

Giordano, Ralph G. *Social Dancing in America*. Vol. 2. Westport, CT: Greenwood Press, 2007.

Glenn, Colleen. "The Traumatized Veteran: A New Look at Jimmy Stewart's Post-WWII Vertigo." *Quarterly Review of Film and Video* 31, no. 1 (January 2014): 27–41. https://doi.org/10.1080/10509208.2011.593957.

Glenn, Evelyn Nakano, and Roslyn L. Feldberg. "Degraded and Deskilled: The Proletarianization of Clerical Work." *Social Problems* 25, no. 1 (October 1977): 52–64. https://doi.org/10.2307/800467.

Goggans, Jan. "Dreams, Denial, and Depression-Era Fiction." In *A History of California Literature*, edited by Blake Allmendinger, 171–81. New York: Cambridge University Press, 2015.

"Goodyear Home Plan Approved." *Los Angeles Times*. December 21, 1919.

Graeber, David. *Bullshit Jobs*. London: Allen Lane, 2018.

Grandin, Greg. *The End of the Myth: From the Frontier to the Border Wall in the Mind of America*. New York: Henry Holt, 2019.

Gray, Olive. "Doors Open at New Men's Shop." *Los Angeles Times*, May 16, 1928.

Groth, Paul. *Living Downtown: The History of Residential Hotels in the United States*. Berkeley: University of California Press, 1999.

Grund, Francis Joseph. *The Americans, in Their Moral, Social, and Political Relations*. Boston: Marsh, Capen and Lyon, 1837.

Guglielmo, Thomas. *White on Arrival: Italians, Race, Color, and Power in Chicago, 1890–1945*. Oxford: Oxford University Press, 2003.

Guthrie, Woody. "Do Re Mi." RCA Victor, 1940.

Hare, William. *Pulp Fiction to Film Noir: The Great Depression and the Development of a Genre*. Jefferson, NC: McFarland, 2012.

Harney, Robert F. "Boarding and Belonging: Thoughts on Sojourner Institutions." *Urban History Review* 7, no. 2 (October 1978): 8–37.

Harrington, Alan. *Life in the Crystal Palace*. 1959. New York: Avon, 1973.

Hebert, Ray. "No Tall Buildings: Aesthetics, Not Quakes, Kept Lid On." *Los Angeles Times*, July 8, 1985.

———. "There's Lots of Room at the Top of This Building." *Los Angeles Times*, June 5, 1988.

Henson, Earl, and Paul Beckett. *Los Angeles: Its People and Its Homes*. Los Angeles: Haynes Foundation, 1944. Box 153, John Randolph Haynes and Dora Haynes Foundation Library (Collection 1604), UCLA Library Special Collections, Charles E. Young Research Library, University of California, Los Angeles.

Herman, S. James. *Why Do You Live in an Apartment? A Study of a Sinister Trend in American Life*. Detroit: Michigan Housing Association, 1931.

Himes, Chester. *If He Hollers Let Him Go*. 1945. London: Serpent's Tail, 2010.

———. "If You're Scared, Go Home!" 1944. In *Black on Black: Baby Sister and Selected Writings*, 226–29. London: Michael Joseph, 1975.

———. "Now Is the Time! Here Is the Place!" 1942. In *Black on Black: Baby Sister and Selected Writings*, 213–19. London: Michael Joseph, 1975.

———. "Zoot Riots Are Race Riots." 1943. In *Black on Black: Baby Sister and Selected Writings*, 220–25. London: Michael Joseph, 1975.

Hirahara, Naomi. "What Raymond Chandler Didn't Understand About LA." Zócalo Public Square, August 6, 2014. https://www.zocalopublicsquare.org/2014/08/06/what-raymond-chandler-didnt-understand-about-l-a/ideas/nexus/.

Hobsbawm, Eric. *Industry and Empire: From 1750 to the Present Day*. 1968. New York: The New Press, 1999.

Hodges, Hugh T. "Charles Maclay: California Missionary, San Fernando Valley Pioneer: Part III." *Southern California Quarterly* 68, no. 4 (December 1986): 329–63. https://doi.org/10.2307/41171239.

Hong, Lawrence K., and Robert W. Duff. "Becoming a Taxi-Dancer: The Significance of Neutralization in a Semi-Deviant Occupation." *Sociology of Work and Occupations* 4, no. 3 (August 1, 1977): 327–42. https://doi.org/10.1177/003803857700400305.

hooks, bell. "Representing Whiteness in the Black Imagination." In *Displacing Whiteness: Essays in Social and Cultural Criticism*, edited by Ruth Frankenberg. Durham, NC: Duke University Press, 1997.

Hoopes, Roy. *Cain: The Biography of James M. Cain*. 2nd ed. Carbondale: Southern Illinois University Press, 1987.

Hoover, Herbert. "Speech at Madison Square Garden." In *Public Papers of the Presidents of the United States: Herbert Hoover*, 656–80. Washington, DC: United States Government Printing Office, 1977.

Horsley, Lee. *Twentieth-Century Crime Fiction*. Oxford: Oxford University Press, 2005.

Housing Occupancy in the City of Los Angeles and Supplement. Los Angeles: Peacock Research Associates, 1950. Box 333, John Randolph Haynes and Dora Haynes Foundation Library (Collection 1604), UCLA Library Special Collections, Charles E. Young Research Library, University of California, Los Angeles.

Housing Study City of Los Angeles, Community Redevelopment, Conditions of Blight, Central Area. Los Angeles: City Planning Commission, 1947. Box 333, John Randolph Haynes and Dora Haynes Foundation Library (Collection 1604), UCLA Library Special Collections, Charles E. Young Research Library, University of California, Los Angeles.

Houston, James D "'The Circle Almost Circled': Some Notes on California's Fiction." In *Reading the West: New Essays on the Literature of the American West*, edited by Michael Kowalewski, 231–50. Cambridge: Cambridge University Press, 1996.

Hughes, Dorothy B. *In a Lonely Place*. 1947. London: Penguin, 2010.

Huxley, Aldous. *After Many a Summer*. 1939. London: Vintage, 2015.

———. *Jesting Pilate: The Diary of a Journey*. 1926. London: Triad/Paladin Books, 1985.

Ide, Joe. *The Goodbye Coast*. London: Weidenfeld and Nicholson, 2022.
Irwin, John T. "Beating the Boss: Cain's Double Indemnity." *American Literary History* 14, no. 2 (April 1, 2002): 255–83.
Jackson, Kenneth T. *Crabgrass Frontier: The Suburbanization of the United States*. Oxford: Oxford University Press, 1985.
Jackson, Lawrence P. *Chester P. Himes*. New York: W. W. Norton, 2017.
Jacobs, Ronald N. *Race, Media and the Crisis of Civil Society: From the Watts Riots to Rodney King*. Cambridge: Cambridge University Press, 2000.
Jameson, Fredric. *Raymond Chandler: The Detections of Totality*. London: Verso, 2016.
"Japanese Beetle Trap Intrigues Local Golfer." *Los Angeles Times*, July 16, 1945.
Kaempffert, Waldemar. "A New Patent Office for a New Age." *New York Times Magazine*, April 10, 1932.
Kaplan, Sam Hall. *LA Lost and Found: An Architectural History of Los Angeles*. New York: Crown, 1987.
Kazin, Michael. "The Great Exception Revisited: Organized Labor and Politics in San Francisco and Los Angeles, 1870–1940." *Pacific Historical Review* 55, no. 3 (August 1986): 371–402. https://doi.org/10.2307/3639704.
Kennedy, John F. "Acceptance Speech at the 1960 Democratic National Convention." July 15, 1960. www.jfklibrary.org/Asset-Viewer/AS08q5oYz0SFUZg9uOi4iw.aspx.
Keyes, John D. Preface to *Los Angeles: A Guide to the City and Its Environs*, v–vi. New York: Hastings House, 1941.
Keynes, John Maynard. "Economic Possibilities for Our Grandchildren." In *Essays in Persuasion*, 358–373. New York: W. W. Norton, 1963.
Kim, Claire Jean. "The Racial Triangulation of Asian Americans." *Politics and Society* 27, no. 1 (March 1999): 105–38. https://doi.org/10.1177/0032329299027001005.
Kirk, Grayson. "The Filipinos." *Annals of the American Academy of Political and Social Science* 223 (September 1942): 45–48.
Kirker, Harold. *California's Architectural Frontier: Style and Tradition in the Nineteenth Century*. San Marino, CA: Huntington Library, 1960.
Klein, Kerwin Lee. *Apocalypse Noir: Carey McWilliams and Posthistorical California*. Berkeley: Doe Library, University of California, 1997.
———. *Frontiers of Historical Imagination: Narrating the European Conquest of Native America, 1890–1990*. Berkeley: University of California Press, 1999.
Klein, Marcus. *Easterns, Westerns, and Private Eyes: American Matters, 1870–1900*. Madison: University of Wisconsin Press, 1994.
Klein, Norman M. *The History of Forgetting: Los Angeles and the Erasure of Memory*. London: Verso, 1997.
Knight, Eric. *You Play the Black and the Red Comes Up*. New York: Robert M. McBride, 1938.

"Know Thyself." *Vanity Fair*, February 18, 1860.
Kordich, Catherine J. "John Fante's *Ask the Dust*: A Border Reading." *MELUS* 20, no. 4 (December 1995): 17–27. https://doi.org/10.2307/467887.
Kreyling, Michael. *The Novels of Ross Macdonald*. Columbia: University of South Carolina Press, 2005.
Krieger, Herbert W. "Races and Peoples in the Philippines." *Far Eastern Quarterly* 4, no. 2 (February 1945): 94–101. https://doi.org/10.2307/2048958.
Kurashige, Scott. *The Shifting Grounds of Race: Black and Japanese Americans in the Making of Multiethnic Los Angeles*. Princeton: Princeton University Press, 2010.
Laden, Tanja M. "Best Art Deco (1928)." *LA Weekly*, October 6, 2010. www.laweekly.com/best-art-deco-1928/.
Lang, Robert E., and Rebecca R. Sohmer. "Legacy of the Housing Act of 1949: The Past, Present, and Future of Federal Housing and Urban Policy." *Housing Policy Debate* 11, no. 2 (January 2000): 291–98. https://doi.org/10.1080/10511482.2000.9521369.
Lasco, Gideon. "'Little Brown Brothers': Height and the Philippine–American Colonial Encounter (1898–1946)." *Philippine Studies: Historical and Ethnographic Viewpoints* 66, no. 3 (September 2018): 375–406. https://doi.org/10.1353/phs.2018.0029.
Laslett, John H. M. *Shameful Victory: The Los Angeles Dodgers, the Red Scare, and the Hidden History of Chavez Ravine*. Tucson: University of Arizona Press, 2015.
———. *Sunshine Was Never Enough: Los Angeles Workers, 1880–2010*. Berkeley: University of California Press, 2012.
Lears, T. J. Jackson. *No Place of Grace: Antimodernism and the Transformation of American Culture, 1880–1920*. 2nd ed. Chicago: University of Chicago Press, 1994.
Lee, A. Robert. "Violence Real and Imagined: The Novels of Chester Himes." In *The Critical Response to Chester Himes*, edited by Charles L. P. Silet, 65–81. Westport, CT: Greenwood Press, 1999.
Lefebvre, Henri. 1974. *The Production of Space*. Translated by Donald Nicholson-Smith. Oxford: Blackwell, 1991.
Lehan, Richard. *The City in Literature: An Intellectual and Cultural History*. Berkeley: University of California Press, 1998.
LeMenager, Stephanie. "The Aesthetics of Petroleum, after *Oil!*" *American Literary History* 24, no. 1 (January 2012): 59–86. https://doi.org/10.1093/alh/ajr057.
———. *Living Oil: Petroleum Culture in the American Century*. Oxford: Oxford University Press, 2014.
Leonard, Kevin Allen. "'In the Interest of All Races': African Americans and Interracial Cooperation in Los Angeles during and after World War II." In *Seeking El Dorado: African Americans in California*, edited by Lawrence B.

de Graaf, Kevin Mulroy, and Quintard Taylor, 309–40. Seattle: University of Washington Press, 2001.
Lewis, Sinclair. *Babbitt*. New York: Harcourt, Brace, 1922.
Limerick, Patricia Nelson. *The Legacy of Conquest: The Unbroken Past of the American West*. New York: W. W. Norton, 1987.
Long, Robert Emmet. *Nathanael West*. New York: Frederick Ungar, 1985.
López-Calvo, Ignacio. *Latino Los Angeles in Film and Fiction: The Cultural Production of Social Anxiety*. Tucson: University of Arizona Press, 2011.
Lotchin, Roger W. *Fortress California 1910–1961: From Warfare to Welfare*. Champaign: University of Illinois Press, 2002.
Lothrop, Gloria Ricci. "Italians of Los Angeles: An Historical Overview." *Southern California Quarterly* 85, no. 3 (Fall 2003): 249–300. https://doi.org/10.2307/41172173.
Lowe, Lisa. *Immigrant Acts: On Asian American Cultural Politics*. Durham, NC: Duke University Press, 1996.
Lozano, Henry Knight. *California and Hawai'i Bound: U.S. Settler Colonialism and the Pacific West, 1848–1959*. Lincoln: University of Nebraska Press, 2021.
Luconi, Stefano. "The Protean Ethnic Identities of John Fante's Italian-American Characters." In *John Fante: A Critical Gathering*, edited by David M. Fine and Stephen Cooper, 54–64. Madison, NJ: Fairleigh Dickinson University Press, 1999.
Lundquist, James. *Chester Himes*. New York: Frederick Ungar, 1976.
Lunenfeld, Peter. *City at the Edge of Forever: Los Angeles Reimagined*. New York: Viking, 2020.
Lurie, Alison. *The Nowhere City*. 1965. London: Abacus, 1986.
Luther, Mark Lee. *The Boosters*. Indianapolis: Bobbs-Merrill, 1924.
Macdonald, Ross. *Black Money*. London: Collins, 1966.
———. *The Blue Hammer*. New York: Alfred A. Knopf, 1976.
———. *The Doomsters*. London: Cassell, 1958.
———. *The Moving Target*. New York: Alfred A. Knopf, 1949.
———. *The Underground Man*. 1971. London: Penguin, 2012.
———. "The Writer as Detective Hero." In *On Crime Writing*, 9–24. Santa Barbara, CA: Capra Press, 1973.
Mack, Roy, dir. *Roseland*. Warner Brothers-Vitaphone, 1930.
Mackenzie, Kent, dir. *The Exiles*. Contemporary Films, 1961.
MacShane, Frank. *The Life of Raymond Chandler*. New York: E. P. Dutton, 1976.
Madden, David, and Kristopher Mecholsky. *James M. Cain: Hard-Boiled Mythmaker*. Lanham, MD: Scarecrow Press, 2011.
Magnaghi, Russell M. *Herbert E. Bolton and the Historiography of the Americas*. Westport, CT: Greenwood Press, 1998.
Marcuse, Herbert. *One-Dimensional Man: Studies in the Ideology of Advanced Industrial Society*. 1964. Boston: Beacon Press, 1991.

Marinaccio, Rocco. "'Tea and Cookies, Diavolo!': Italian American Masculinity in John Fante's *Wait until Spring, Bandini.*" *MELUS* 34, no. 3 (Fall 2009): 43–69. https://doi.org/10.1353/mel.0.0040.

Marsh, Reginald. *Ten Cents a Dance*. 1933. Tempera on composition board, 91.3 cm × 121.8 cm. Whitney Museum of American Art, New York.

Marshall, George, dir. *The Blue Dahlia*. Paramount Pictures, 1946.

Martin, Carol J. *Dance Marathons: Performing American Culture of the 1920s and 1930s*. Jackson: University Press of Mississippi, 1994.

Marx, Leo. *The Machine in the Garden: Technology and the Pastoral Ideal in America*. 1964. Oxford: Oxford University Press, 2000.

Mason, Gregory. "Satan in the Dance-Hall." *The American Mercury*, June 1924.

Master Plan of Land Use, Inventory and Classification. Los Angeles: Regional Planning Commission, County of Los Angeles, 1941. Box 333, John Randolph Haynes and Dora Haynes Foundation Library (Collection 1604), UCLA Library Special Collections, Charles E. Young Research Library, University of California, Los Angeles.

Matsumoto, Valerie. "Desperately Seeking 'Deirdre': Gender Roles, Multicultural Relations, and Nisei Women Writers of the 1930s." *Frontiers: A Journal of Women Studies* 12, no. 1 (1991): 19–32. https://doi.org/10.2307/3346573.

Mayo, Morrow. *Los Angeles*. New York: Alfred A. Knopf, 1933.

McCann, Sean. *Gumshoe America: Hard-Boiled Crime Fiction and the Rise and Fall of New Deal Liberalism*. Durham, NC: Duke University Press, 2000.

McClung, William Alexander. *Landscapes of Desire: Anglo Mythologies of Los Angeles*. Berkeley: University of California Press, 2000.

McCoy, Horace. *They Shoot Horses, Don't They?* 1935. London: Serpent's Tail, 1995.

McDonough, Carla J. *Staging Masculinity: Male Identity in Contemporary American Drama*. Jefferson, NC: McFarland, 2006.

McGovney, Dudley O. "The Anti-Japanese Land Laws of California and Ten Other States." *California Law Review* 35, no. 1 (March 1947): 7–60. https://doi.org/10.2307/3477374.

McWilliams, Carey. *Brothers Under the Skin*. 1943. Revised ed. Boston: Little, Brown, 1951.

———. "Myths of the West." *North American Review*, November 1931.

———. *Prejudice: Japanese-Americans, Symbol of Racial Intolerance*. Boston: Little, Brown, 1944.

———. *Southern California: An Island on the Land*. 1946. Layton, UT: Gibbs-Smith, 2010.

———. "Storm Signals." In *Fool's Paradise: A Carey McWilliams Reader*, 139–44. Berkeley, CA: Heyday Books, 2001.

Meares, Hadley. "The James Oviatt Building: The Bespoke Brilliance and Pretension Behind an Art Deco Masterpiece." KCET.org, September 6, 2013. www.kcet.

org/history-society/the-james-oviatt-building-the-bespoke-brilliance-and-pretension-behind-an-art-deco.

Melling, Philip E. "The West in Fiction." In *Nothing Else to Fear: New Perspectives on America in the Thirties*, edited by Stephen W. Baskerville and Ralph Willett. Manchester: Manchester University Press, 1985.

Melville, Herman. "Bartleby, the Scrivener." 1853. In *The Piazza Tales*, 32–110. New York: Dix and Edwards, 1856.

Merwin, Henry Childs. "On Being Civilized Too Much." *Atlantic Monthly*, June 1897.

Meyer, Laura. "The Los Angeles Woman's Building and the Feminist Art Community, 1973–1991." In *Sons and Daughters of Los: Culture and Community in LA*, edited by David E. James, 39–62. Philadelphia: Temple University Press, 2003.

Meylor, Meagan. "'Sad Flower in the Sand': Camilla Lopez and the Erasure of Memory in *Ask the Dust*." In *John Fante's Ask the Dust: A Joining of Voices and Views*, 58–82. New York: Fordham University Press, 2020.

Michaels, Leonard, David Reid, and Raquel Scherr, eds. *West of the West: Imagining California*. Berkeley: University of California Press, 1995.

Mills, C. Wright. *White Collar: The American Middle Classes*. 1951. Oxford: Oxford University Press, 1969.

Mitchell, Lee Clark. "Diversions of Furniture and Signature Styles: Hammett, Chandler, Macdonald." *Arizona Quarterly* 71, no. 3 (Autumn 2015): 1–26. https://doi.org/10.1353/arq.2015.0016.

Modell, John. *The Economics and Politics of Racial Accommodation: The Japanese of Los Angeles, 1900–1942*. Urbana: University of Illinois Press, 1977.

Modell, John, and Tamara K. Hareven. "Urbanization and the Malleable Household: An Examination of Boarding and Lodging in American Families." *Journal of Marriage and Family* 35, no. 3 (August 1973): 467–79. https://doi.org/10.2307/350582.

Molina, Natalia. "Understanding Race as a Relational Concept." *Modern American History* 1, no. 1 (March 2018): 101–5. https://doi.org/10.1017/mah.2017.14.

Montgomery, Robert, dir. *Ride the Pink Horse*. Universal Pictures, 1947.

Mosley, Walter. *Devil in a Blue Dress*. 1990. London: Serpent's Tail, 2017.

"'Mother Goose' for Counter Jumpers." *Vanity Fair*, March 17, 1860.

Mumford, Lewis. *The City in History: Its Origins, Its Transformations, and Its Prospects*. 1961. Harmondsworth: Penguin, 1966.

Murphet, Julian. *Race and Literature in Los Angeles*. Cambridge: Cambridge University Press, 2001.

Murray, John E. "Height and Weight of Early 20th Century Filipino Men." *Annals of Human Biology* 29, no. 3 (June 2002): 326–33. https://doi.org/10.1080/03014460110086826.

Nash, Gerald D. *The American West Transformed: The Impact of the Second World War*. Bloomington: Indiana University Press, 1985.

Nash, Roderick. *Wilderness and the American Mind.* New Haven, CT: Yale University Press, 1967.
Nelson, Howard J., and William A. V. Clark. *The Los Angeles Metropolitan Experience: Uniqueness, Generality, and the Goal of the Good Life.* Cambridge, MA: Ballinger, 1976.
Nicolaides, Becky M. *My Blue Heaven: Life and Politics in the Working-Class Suburbs of Los Angeles, 1920-1965.* Chicago: University of Chicago Press, 2002.
Norris, Frank. "The Frontier Gone at Last." *The World's Work*, February 1902.
Nye, Russel B. "Saturday Night at the Paradise Ballroom: Or, Dance Halls in the Twenties." *Journal of Popular Culture* 7, no. 1 (Summer 1973): 14-22. https://doi.org/10.1111/j.0022-3840.1973.00014.x.
Orr, Stanley. *Darkly Perfect World: Colonial Adventure, Postmodernism, and American Noir.* Columbus: The Ohio State University Press, 2010.
Pagán, Eduardo Obregón. *Murder at the Sleepy Lagoon: Zoot Suits, Race, and Riot in Wartime LA.* Chapel Hill: University of North Carolina Press, 2003.
Panunzio, Constantine. "Intermarriage in Los Angeles, 1924-33." *American Journal of Sociology* 47, no. 5 (March 1942): 690-701. https://doi.org/10.1086/219000.
Parker, Edna Monch. "The Southern Pacific Railroad and Settlement in Southern California." *Pacific Historical Review* 6, no. 2 (1937): 103-19. https://doi.org/10.2307/3633153.
Parreñas, Rhacel Salazar. "'White Trash' Meets the 'Little Brown Monkeys': The Taxi Dance Hall as a Site of Interracial and Gender Alliances between White Working Class Women and Filipino Immigrant Men in the 1920s and 30s." *Amerasia Journal* 24, no. 2 (January 1998): 115-34. https://doi.org/10.17953/amer.24.2.760h5w08630ql643.
Partridge, Eric. *A Dictionary of the Underworld: British and American.* 3rd ed. London: Routledge and Kegan Paul, 1968.
Pascoe, Peggy. "Miscegenation Law, Court Cases, and Ideologies of 'Race' in Twentieth-Century America." *Journal of American History* 83, no. 1 (June 1996): 44-69. https://doi.org/10.2307/2945474.
Pavey, Alex. "Crime, Space and Disorientation in the Literature and Cinema of Los Angeles." PhD dissertation, University College London, 2018.
Pawel, Miriam. *The Crusades of Cesar Chavez: A Biography.* New York: Bloomsbury, 2014.
Paxson, Frederic Logan. *History of the American Frontier, 1763-1893.* Dunwoody, GA: Norman S. Berg, 1924.
———. *The Last American Frontier.* New York: Macmillan, 1910.
———. *The New Nation.* Boston: Houghton Mifflin, 1915.
Pettegrew, John. *Brutes in Suits: Male Sensibility in America, 1890-1920.* Baltimore: Johns Hopkins University Press, 2007.
"Pier Fire Destroys Aragon Ballroom." *Los Angeles Times*, May 27, 1970.

Pierson, George Wilson. "The Frontier and American Institutions: A Criticism of the Turner Theory." *New England Quarterly: A Historical Review of New England Life and Letters* 15, no. 2 (June 1942): 224–55. https://doi.org/10.2307/360525.

———. *The Frontier and Frontiersmen of Turner's Essays: A Scrutiny of the Foundations of the Middle Western Tradition*. Indianapolis: Bobbs-Merrill, 1940.

Pisk, George M. "The Graveyard of Dreams: A Study of Nathanael West's Last Novel, *The Day of the Locust*." *South Central Bulletin* 27, no. 4 (Winter 1967): 64–72. https://doi.org/10.2307/3188923.

Poe, Edgar Allan. "The Man of the Crowd." 1840. In *Tales of Mystery and Imagination*, 255–62. Ware: Wordsworth Editions, 2008.

Polk, Dora Beale. *The Island of California: A History of the Myth*. Lincoln: University of Nebraska Press, 1995.

Polyzoides, Stefanos. "California Bungalows, Streets, and Courts." *Old-House Journal* 30, no. 3 (June 2002): 72–73.

Polyzoides, Stefanos, Roger Sherwood, James Tice, and Julius Shulman. *Courtyard Housing in Los Angeles: A Typological Analysis*. Berkeley: University of California Press, 1982.

Porter, Dennis. "The Private Eye." In *The Cambridge Companion to Crime Fiction*, 95–113. Cambridge: Cambridge University Press, 2003.

Porter, Joseph C. "The End of the Trail: The American West of Dashiell Hammett and Raymond Chandler." *Western Historical Quarterly* 6, no. 4 (October 1975): 411–24. https://doi.org/10.2307/967777.

Porter, Robert P. *Extra Census Bulletin: Distribution of Population According to Density: 1890*. Washington, DC: Census Office, Department of the Interior, 1891.

Preliminary Report on the Disposition of Public War Housing in Los Angeles. Los Angeles: Housing Authority of the City of Los Angeles, 1945. Box 333, John Randolph Haynes and Dora Haynes Foundation Library (Collection 1604), UCLA Library Special Collections, Charles E. Young Research Library, University of California, Los Angeles.

"Production Our Main Job—and Right Now!" *Los Angeles Times*. February 21, 1942.

Quam-Wickham, Nancy. " 'Cities Sacrificed on the Altar of Oil': Popular Opposition to Oil Development in 1920s Los Angeles." *Environmental History* 3, no. 2 (April 1998): 189–209. https://doi.org/10.2307/3985379.

Rechy, John. *City of Night*. New York: Grove Press, 1963.

Reddick, Lawrence D. "The New Race-Relations Frontier." *Journal of Educational Sociology* 19, no. 3 (1945): 129–45. https://doi.org/10.2307/2263418.

Revoyr, Nina. *Southland*. New York: Akashic Books, 2003.

Rhodes, Chip. "Hollywood Fictions." In *The Cambridge Companion to the Literature of Los Angeles*, edited by Kevin R. McNamara. Cambridge: Cambridge University Press, 2010.

Riesman, David, Reuel Denney, and Nathan Glazer. *The Lonely Crowd: A Study of the Changing American Character*. 1950. New Haven, CT: Yale University Press, 1961.

Robson, Mark, dir. *Home of the Brave*. United Artists, 1949.

Rodgers, Jimmie. "Waiting for a Train." Victor, 1928.

Roediger, David R. *Towards the Abolition of Whiteness: Essays on Race, Politics, and Working Class History*. London: Verso, 1994.

———. *The Wages of Whiteness: Race and the Making of the American Working Class*. 1991. Revised ed. London: Verso, 2007.

Roosevelt, Franklin D. "Executive Order 9066, in Which President Franklin D. Roosevelt Authorizes the Secretary of War to Prescribe Military Areas." Washington, DC: The White House, February 19, 1942. General Records of the United States Government, Record Group 11, National Archives. https://catalog.archives.gov/id/5730250.

———. "New Conditions Impose New Requirements Upon Government and Those Who Conduct Government." In *The Public Papers and Addresses of Franklin D. Roosevelt: The Genesis of the New Deal, 1928–1932*, 1:742–56. New York: Random House, 1938.

Roosevelt, Theodore. "Theodore Roosevelt to Richard Melancthon Hurd, 3 January 1919." In *Letters of Theodore Roosevelt*, edited by Elting E. Morrison, 8:1422. Cambridge: Cambridge University Press, 1954.

———. *The Winning of the West*. 1889–1896. Vols. 1–4. Lincoln: University of Nebraska Press, 1995.

Ryan, Don. *Angel's Flight*. New York: Boni and Liveright, 1927.

Sanchez, George J. *Becoming Mexican American: Ethnicity, Culture, and Identity in Chicano Los Angeles, 1900–1945*. Oxford: Oxford University Press, 1993.

Santa Monica-Ocean Park Chamber of Commerce. *Santa Monica: Southern California's Home City of Culture and Recreation*. Santa Monica, CA: Santa Monica-Ocean Park Chamber of Commerce, 1930.

Saphier, Michael. *Office Planning and Design*. New York: McGraw-Hill, 1968.

Saroyan, William. "Our Little Brown Brothers the Filipinos." *Fiction Parade and Golden Book*, April 1936.

Saval, Nikil. *Cubed: A Secret History of the Workplace*. New York: Doubleday, 2014.

Scaggs, John. *Crime Fiction*. London: Routledge, 2005.

Schlesinger, Arthur M., Jr. *The Crisis of the Old Order, 1919–1933*. 1957. Boston: Houghton Mifflin Harcourt, 2003.

———. "Freedom: A Fighting Faith." 1949. In *The Vital Center: The Politics of Freedom*, 243–56. New York: Da Capo Press, 1938.

Schuster, Joshua. "Where Is the Oil in Modernism?" In *Petrocultures: Oil, Politics, Culture*, edited by Sheena Wilson, Adam Carlson, and Imre Szeman, 197–214. Montreal: McGill-Queen's University Press, 2017.

Scott, Paula A. *Santa Monica: A History on the Edge.* Charleston, SC: Arcadia, 2004.

Sedgwick, Eve Kosofsky. *The Coherence of Gothic Conventions.* New York: Arno Press, 1980.

Shewring, Anne L. "We Didn't Do That Did We? Representation of the Veteran Experience." *Journal of American and Comparative Cultures* 23, no. 4 (Winter 2000): 51–66. https://doi.org/10.1111/j.1537-4726.2000.2304_51.x.

Shinozuka, Jeannie N. "Deadly Perils: Japanese Beetles and the Pestilential Immigrant, 1920s–1930s." *American Quarterly* 65, no. 4 (December 2013): 831–52. https://doi.org/10.1353/aq.2013.0056.

Sides, Josh. *LA City Limits: African American Los Angeles from the Great Depression to the Present.* Berkeley: University of California Press, 2003.

Siegel, Don, dir. *Invasion of the Body Snatchers.* Allied Artists Pictures, 1956.

Siegfried, André. "L'Age Administratif." *Revue des Deux Mondes*, May 1951, 3–12.

Simonson, Harold P. *Beyond the Frontier: Writers, Western Regionalism, and a Sense of Place.* Fort Worth: Texas Christian University Press, 1989.

———. *The Closed Frontier: Studies in American Literary Tragedy.* New York: Holt, Rinehart, and Winston, 1970.

Sinclair, Upton. *Oil!* 1926. London: Penguin, 2008.

Singh, Nikhil Pal. *Black Is a Country: Race and the Unfinished Struggle for Democracy.* Cambridge, MA: Harvard University Press, 2004.

Sklar, Robert L. *City Boys: Cagney, Bogart, Garfield.* Princeton: Princeton University Press, 1992.

Slattery, John, dir. "A Tale of Two Cities." *Mad Men*, season 6, episode 10. AMC, June 2, 2013.

Slotkin, Richard. *The Fatal Environment: The Myth of the Frontier in the Age of Industrialization, 1800–1890.* New York: Atheneum, 1985.

———. *Gunfighter Nation: The Myth of the Frontier in Twentieth-Century America.* 1992. Norman: University of Oklahoma Press, 1998.

———. "Nostalgia and Progress: Theodore Roosevelt's Myth of the Frontier." *American Quarterly* 33, no. 5 (Winter 1981): 608–37. https://doi.org/10.2307/2712805.

———. *Regeneration through Violence: The Mythology of the American Frontier, 1600–1860.* Middletown, CT: Wesleyan University Press, 1973.

Smith, Henry Nash. *Virgin Land: The American West as Symbol and Myth.* Cambridge, MA: Harvard University Press, 1950.

So, Richard Jean. *Redlining Culture: A Data History of Racial Inequality and Postwar Fiction.* New York: Columbia University Press, 2020.

So, Richard Jean, and Gus Wezerek. "Just How White Is the Book Industry?" *New York Times*, December 11, 2020.

Soja, Edward W. *Postmodern Geographies: The Reassertion of Space in Critical Social Theory.* London: Verso, 1989.

Soja, Edward W., and Allen J. Scott. "Introduction to Los Angeles: City and Region." In *The City: Los Angeles and Urban Theory at the End of the Twentieth Century*, edited by Edward W. Soja and Allen J. Scott, 1–21. Berkeley: University of California Press, 1996.
Sorkin, Michael. "Explaining Los Angeles." In *California Counterpoint: New West Coast Architecture 1982*, 8–14. New York: Rizzoli International Publications, 1982.
Speir, Jerry. *Raymond Chandler*. New York: Frederick Ungar, 1981.
Spitzzeri, Paul R. "The Road to Independence: The Los Angeles and Independence Railroad and the Conception of a City." *Southern California Quarterly* 83, no. 1 (Spring 2001): 23–58. https://doi.org/10.2307/41172051.
Spurgeon, Sara L. *Exploding the Western: Myths of Empire on the Postmodern Frontier*. College Station: Texas A and M University Press, 2005.
Stack, John F. "The Ethnic Citizen Confronts the Future: Los Angeles and Miami at Century's Turn." *Pacific Historical Review* 68, no. 2 (May 1999): 509–16. https://doi.org/10.2307/3641990.
Stanfield, Peter. *Hollywood, Westerns, and the 1930s: The Lost Trail*. Exeter: University of Exeter Press, 2001.
Stanton, Jeffrey. *Venice of America: "Coney Island of the Pacific."* Los Angeles: Donahue, 1987.
Starr, Kevin. *Embattled Dreams: California in War and Peace, 1940–1950*. Oxford: Oxford University Press, 2002.
———. *Material Dreams: Southern California through the 1920s*. Oxford: Oxford University Press, 1990.
Steiner, Jesse Frederick. *Americans at Play: Recent Trends in Recreation and Leisure Time Activities*. New York: McGraw-Hill, 1933.
Steiner, Michael C. "Frederick Jackson Turner and Western Regionalism." In *Writing Western History: Essays on Major Western Historians*, edited by Richard W. Etulain, 103–35. Reno: University of Nevada Press, 2002.
———. "From Frontier to Region: Frederick Jackson Turner and the New Western History." *Pacific Historical Review* 64, no. 4 (November 1995): 479–501.
———. "The Significance of Turner's Sectional Thesis." *Western Historical Quarterly* 10, no. 4 (October 1979): 437–66. https://doi.org/10.2307/968085.
Stevenson, Adlai. "A Purpose for Modern Woman." *Woman's Home Companion*, September 1955.
Sturman, Janet. *The Course of Mexican Music*. New York: Routledge, 2015.
Suzuki, Masao. "Important or Impotent? Taking Another Look at the 1920 California Alien Land Law." *Journal of Economic History* 64, no. 1 (March 2004): 125–43. https://doi.org/10.1017/S0022050704002621.
Taylor, Alan, dir. "The Mountain King." *Mad Men*, season 2, episode 12. AMC, October 19, 2008.

Taylor, Frederick Winslow. *The Principles of Scientific Management*. New York: Harper and Brothers, 1911.

Thompson, Graham. *Male Sexuality Under Surveillance: The Office in American Literature*. Iowa City: University of Iowa Press, 2003.

Todorov, Tzvetan. "Typology of Detective Fiction." 1966. In *Modern Criticism and Theory: A Reader*, edited by David Lodge and Nigel Wood, 3rd ed., 226–232. London: Routledge, 2014.

Trott, Sarah. *War Noir: Raymond Chandler and the Hard-Boiled Detective as Veteran in American Fiction*. Jackson: University Press of Mississippi, 2016.

Turner, Frederick Jackson. "Contributions of the West to American Democracy." 1903. In *The Frontier in American History*, 243–68. New York: Henry Holt, 1921.

———. "The First Official Frontier of the Massachusetts Bay." 1914. In *The Frontier in American History*, 39–66. New York: Henry Holt, 1921.

———. *The Frontier in American History*. New York: Henry Holt, 1921.

———. "Pioneer Ideals and the State University." 1910. In *The Frontier in American History*, 269–89. New York: Henry Holt, 1921.

———. "The Problem of the West." 1896. In *The Frontier in American History*, 205–42. New York: Henry Holt, 1921.

———. "The Significance of the Frontier in American History." 1893. In *The Frontier in American History*, 1–38. New York: Henry Holt, 1921.

———. "Since the Foundation of Clark University 1889–1924." 1924. In *The Significance of Sections in American History*, 207–34. Gloucester, MA: Peter Smith, 1959.

———. "The West and American Ideals." 1914. In *The Frontier in American History*, 290–310. New York: Henry Holt, 1921.

Utley, George B. "Theodore Roosevelt's *The Winning of the West*: Some Unpublished Letters." *Mississippi Valley Historical Review* 30, no. 4 (March 1944): 495–506. https://doi.org/10.2307/1916697.

Valdez, Luis. *Zoot Suit and Other Plays*. Houston: Arte Publico Press, 1992.

Valentino, Rudolph. "How Do You Dance?" *Screenland*, April 1922.

Vedder, Clyde Bennett. "An Analysis of the Taxi-Dance Hall as a Social Institution with Special Reference to Los Angeles and Detroit." PhD diss., University of Southern California, 1947.

Verdicchio, Pasquale. *Devils in Paradise: Writings on Post-Emigrant Culture*. Toronto: Guernica Editions, 1997.

Vidal, Gore. "The Ashes of Hollywood I: The Bottom 4 of the Top 10." *New York Review of Books*, May 17, 1973. https://www.nybooks.com/articles/1973/05/17/the-ashes-of-hollywood-i-the-bottom-4-of-the-top-1/.

Viramontes, Helena María. *Their Dogs Came with Them*. New York: Atria Books, 2007.

Wagner, Anton. *Los Angeles: The Development, Life, and Structure of the City of Two Million in Southern California*. 1935. Edited by Edward Dimendberg. Translated by Timothy Grundy. Los Angeles: Getty Research Institute, 2022.
Waldinger, Roger. "Not the Promised City: Los Angeles and Its Immigrants." *Pacific Historical Review* 68, no. 2 (May 1999): 253–72. https://doi.org/10.2307/3641987.
Wallach, Ruth. *Los Angeles Residential Architecture: Modernism Meets Eclecticism*. Charleston, SC: History Press, 2015.
Wallach, Ruth, Dace Taube, Claude Zachary, Linda McCann, and Curtis C. Roseman. *Los Angeles in World War II*. Charleston, SC: Arcadia, 2011.
Waller, Willard Walter. *The Veteran Comes Back*. New York: Dryden Press, 1944.
Webb, Walter Prescott. *The Great Frontier: An Interpretation of World History Since Columbus*. 1951. London: Secker and Warburg, 1953.
———. *The Great Plains*. Boston: Ginn, 1931.
Weber, Max. *The Protestant Ethic and the Spirit of Capitalism*. 1905. Translated by Talcott Parsons. London: Routledge, 2005.
Weiner, Matthew. "Person to Person." *Mad Men*, season 7, episode 14. AMC, May 17, 2015.
Weinstein, Richard. "The First American City." In *The City: Los Angeles and Urban Theory at the End of the Twentieth Century*, edited by Allen J. Scott and Edward W. Soja, 22–46. Berkeley: University of California Press, 1996.
Weisenburger, Steven. "Williams, West, and the Art of Regression." *South Atlantic Review* 47, no. 4 (November 1982): 1–16. https://doi.org/10.2307/3199403.
Wellman, William, dir. *My Man and I*. Metro-Goldwyn-Mayer, 1952.
Wentworth, Harold, and Stuart Berg Flexner. *Dictionary of American Slang*. New York: Thomas Y. Crowell, 1960.
West, Nathanael. *The Day of the Locust and Miss Lonelyhearts*. 1939/1933. London: Vintage, 2012.
Whaples, Robert, and David Buffum. "Fraternalism, Paternalism, the Family, and the Market: Insurance a Century Ago." *Social Science History* 15, no. 1 (Spring 1991): 97–122. https://doi.org/10.2307/1171484.
White, Richard. *"It's Your Misfortune and None of My Own": A New History of the American West*. Norman: University of Oklahoma Press, 1991.
Whitfield, Raoul. *Death in a Bowl*. New York: Alfred A. Knopf, 1931.
Whiting, Frederick. "Playing Against Type: Statistical Personhood, Depth Narrative, and the Business of Genre in James M. Cain's *Double Indemnity*." *Journal of Narrative Theory* 36, no. 2 (Summer 2006): 190–227. https://doi.org/10.1353/jnt.2007.0006.
Whitman, Walt. "Facing West from California's Shores." 1860. *The Selected Poems of Walt Whitman*, 117. New York: Walter J. Black, 1942.
———. "New York Dissected: IV.—Broadway." *Life Illustrated*, August 9, 1856.

Whyte, William Hollingsworth. *The Organization Man*. New York: Simon and Schuster, 1956.
Wild, Mark. *Street Meeting: Multiethnic Neighborhoods in Early Twentieth-Century Los Angeles*. Berkeley: University of California Press, 2005.
Wilder, Billy, dir. *Double Indemnity*. Paramount Pictures, 1944.
Wilson, Edmund. *Boys in the Back Room: Notes on California Novelists*. San Francisco: The Colt Press, 1941.
Wilson, Sloan. *The Man in the Gray Flannel Suit*. New York: Simon and Schuster, 1955.
Wolmar, Christian. *The Great Railway Revolution*. London: Atlantic Books, 2012.
Wyatt, David. *The Fall into Eden: Landscape and Imagination in California*. Cambridge: Cambridge University Press, 1986.
———. *Five Fires: Race, Catastrophe, and the Shaping of California*. Oxford: Oxford University Press, 1999.
Wyler, William, dir. *The Best Years of Our Lives*. RKO Radio Pictures, 1946.
Yamamoto, Hisaye. "Life Among the Oil Fields, A Memoir." 1979. In *Seventeen Syllables*, 86–95. New Brunswick, NJ: Rutgers University Press, 2001.
Yamashita, Karen Tei. *Tropic of Orange*. 1997. Minneapolis: Coffee House Press, 2017.
Yates, Richard. *Revolutionary Road*. London: Vintage, 2011.
Young, James C. "The Boarding House Era Goes with 'Miss Mary's.'" *New York Times*, October 18, 1925.
Zakim, Michael. "The Business Clerk as Social Revolutionary; or, a Labor History of the Nonproducing Classes." *Journal of the Early Republic* 26, no. 4 (Winter 2006): 563–603. https://doi.org/10.1353/jer.2006.0079.
———. "Producing Capitalism: The Clerk at Work." In *Capitalism Takes Command: The Social Transformation of Nineteenth-Century America*, edited by Michael Zakim and Gary J. Kornblith, 223–47. Chicago: University of Chicago Press, 2012.
Zesch, Scott. "Chinese Los Angeles in 1870–1871: The Makings of a Massacre." *Southern California Quarterly* 90, no. 2 (2008): 109–58. https://doi.org/10.2307/41172418.
Zinnemann, Fred, dir. *The Men*. United Artists, 1950.

Index

1933 Was a Bad Year (Fante), 137-38, 278n25

Abbott, Megan, 109, 131
Adorno, Theodor, 193-94
African Americans: admission to wartime industrial work, 170-72, 180, 183; and antifascism, 171-72; belief in opportunities afforded by California, 169; community in Los Angeles, 163-164, 166, 169, 171; contributions to literature of Los Angeles, 29, 245-47 (*see also* Himes, Chester); prejudice against, 146, 169, 170-72, 175, 180-82; and racial property restrictions, 27, 163-64, 169-70, 198; relationship with Japanese Americans, 163-65, 166, 245-46, 169-71; stereotypes of, 174, 182; westward migration of, 135, 151, 169, 170-71
After Many a Summer (Huxley), 188
Agrarianism, 14-20 passim, 193
Alexander, Franz, 96
Alien Land Laws (1913 and 1920), 154-55
Allmendinger, Blake, 31, 46, 274n92
American Mercury, 61, 102

American Phrenological Journal, 91
American Whig Review, 91
Americanness, 136, 141, 143, 146, 150. *See also* citizenship; whiteness
Angel's Flight (Ryan), 29
antimodernism, 7, 91, 111, 136, 210, 253n27
Anzaldúa, Gloria, 177
apartments, 187, 189, 194, 197, 200-201. *See also* apartment courts; housing, multi-family
apartment courts: architectural form of, 189-90, 216-21; association with Los Angeles, 189-90; in *In a Lonely Place*, 216-221; literary examples of, 189-90; public-private ambiguity of, 216-219, 293n141; spatial repetition within, 191-92, 194. See also *In a Lonely Place* (Hughes); multi-family housing
Aragon Ballroom, 262n23
Aryan race, 27, 268n113
Asian Americans: contributions to literature of Los Angeles, 245-46 (*see also* Yamamoto, Hisaye; Yamashita, Karen Tei); prejudice against, 145, 165. *See also* Chinese Americans; Filipino Americans; Japanese Americans

Ask the Dust (Fante), 2, 56; automobility in, 42; critical reputation of, 31; hotel living in, 188, 287n30, 292n121; racism in, 146, 263n40. *See also* Bandini, Arturo; Fante, John
Atlas, Charles, 174, 284n164
automobility: and freeways, 41–42, 186, 226, 256n105; and race, 42, 166, 176–77; in prewar Los Angeles, 42
Avila, Eric, 232, 233, 243
Azuma, Eiichiro, 153, 157

Babb, Valerie, 18, 160
Babbitt (Lewis), 94
Babener, Liahna, 111
Babitz, Eve, 245
ballrooms. *See* dancehalls
Bandini, Arturo, 1, 207; character development of, 57; living circumstances of, 187–88, 197, 278n24, 289n61; ethnic and racial anxieties of, 138–49 passim, 154, 173, 263n40
Banham, Reyner, 41–42, 186, 193
"Bartleby, The Scrivener" (Melville), 89–90
Berman, Marshall, 244
Best Years of Our Lives, The (Wyler), 202
Big Sleep, The (Chandler), 56, 98, 119; and concealment, 111, 113; military identity in, 290n78; multi-family housing in, 189, 191–92, 201; offices in, 119–20, 273n83; petrolandscape in, 157; single-family housing in, 187, 287n35; Sternwood family, 115–16, 157, 201, 287n35, 290n78. *See also* Chandler, Raymond; Marlowe, Philip

Billington, Ray Allen, 21, 254n52; *Westward Expansion*, 16, 18, 255n77
Black Cat tavern, 242, 243
Black Reconstruction in America (Du Bois), 183
Blacker the Berry, The (Thurman), 29
blackness, 177; of oil, 162–63, 165–68 passim. *See also* African Americans
Blades, Paul Harcourt: *Don Sagasto's Daughter*, 29
blight, urban, 197–98, 225. *See also* Bunker Hill
Blue Dahlia (Marshall), 190
Blue Hammer, The, (Macdonald), 229
boarding houses, 189, 200; in *What Way My Journey Lies* (Fenton), 189, 195, 206, 211–12, 215, 287n30. *See also* housing, multi-family
Bontemps, Arna, 170
Boone, Daniel, 3, 18
boosters, 116, 122; and African Americans, 169, 247; and "debunkers" 25–26, 39, 257n108, 258n142; and home ownership, 196; of office work, 93; and oil industry, 167; and real estate, 37, 120, 287. *See also* Davis, Mike; speculation
Boosters, The (Luther), 29, 258n123
Border and the Line, The (Franco), 42–3, 298nn80–81
border consciousness, 177
Boulding, Kenneth: *The Organizational Revolution*, 92
Bowron, Fletcher, 171
Boys in the Back Room (Wilson), 30
Branch, E. Douglas, 6, 24
Breu, Christopher, 205, 216
Bronzeville, 163–64, 169–70, 198. *See also* African Americans: community in Los Angeles; African Americans:

Index | 327

relationship with Japanese Americans
Brooks, Van Wyck, 234
Buaken, Manuel, 64, 267n101
Buffalo Bill. See Cody, William
bullshit jobs, 94
bungalow courts. See apartment courts; housing, multi-family
Bunker Hill, 43; "blight" in, 197–98; hotel living in, 188, 195, 287n30, 292n121; multi-family housing in, 186, 188–89 197; postwar redevelopment of, 225
Burgess, Ernest, 61
Byrnes, Delia, 162

Cabell, James Branch, 57; *Jurgen: A Comedy of Justice,* 262n36
Cain, James M.: biographical circumstances of, 100, 257n122; critical responses to, 96, 102; position in Los Angeles canon 31–33, 230; recurrent themes, 96, 100, 102–3; women's roles in, 107–8, 143, 242
Cain, James M., works of *Double Indemnity,* 45, 89, 95–108, 216, 258n125; *Mildred Pierce,* 103; "Paradise" 102–3; *The Postman Always Rings Twice,* 102, 103, 143. See also *Double Indemnity* (Cain)
Cain, Paul: *Fast One,* 32
California: ambiguous relationship with broader American West 70, 267–68n112; climate of, 37–38, 120–22, 230, 275n120; Edenic image of, 37–39, 121–22, 214, 232, 258–59n142, 259n152; etymology of, 38, 259n150; as "last frontier," 35–39, 121, 193, 206, 226, 230–239 passim, 295–296; natural disaster and hazard in, 37, 120–2, 167, 231–32, 236–37, 258–59n142; as racial frontier, 27, 116 151–52, 160, 268n113. See also Los Angeles; Pacific; West Coast
California Eagle, 164
canneries. See fish canneries
capitalism, 8–9, 16, 36, 167, 212, 253n37; and race, 71, 149, 152, 171–72. See also industry; labor; *Protestant Ethic and the Spirit of Capitalism, The* (Weber)
Carpio, Genevieve: *Collisions at the Crossroads How Place and Mobility Make Race,* 43
Carr, Harry: *Los Angeles: City of Dreams,* 25–27, 42, 258n13
"Cat, The" (Fante), 188
Census Office, 5, 12, 35
Chandler, Harry, 27
Chandler, Raymond: biographical circumstances of, 191, 257n122, 290n78; comments on fiction, 2, 108, 111; critical responses to, 36, 37, 39, 111–12, 114, 116, 119, 124–25, 224, 230, 290n78; domestic space in, 115–16, 187–92 passim, 200, 201, 224, 287n33; masculinity in; 127–28, 201, 293n34; military identity in, 202, 205, 290n78; offices in 89, 93, 95, 116–22, 125–32, 273n83, 275n120; position in Los Angeles canon, 31–33, 36; racism in, 154, 157–58, 247; as screenwriter, 96, 190. See also detectives; Marlowe, Philip
Chandler, Raymond, works of: *The Big Sleep,* 56, 98, 111–19 passim, 157, 187, 191–92, 201, 273n83, 287n35, 290n78; *Farewell, My Lovely,* 111, 119, 187; *The High*

Chandler, Raymond, works of (*continued*)
  Window, 117–19, 275n120; "The King in Yellow," 190–91; *The Lady in the Lake*, 113, 122, 124–131, 188; *The Long Goodbye*, 95, 113, 117–18, 202, 224 290n78; *Playback*, 224, "The Poodle Springs Story," 224, "Red Wind," 121, 230. See also *The Big Sleep* (Chandler)
Chavez, Cesar, 242
Chavez Ravine, 242–3
Chicago, 62, 124, 186
Chicanx movement, 245
Chinese Americans, 62, 152, 238–39, 243; prejudice against, 28, 152
Chinese Exclusion Act (1882), 152
Chinese Massacre (1871), 152
cinemagoing, 132, 148
citizenship: in John Fante's fiction, 73, 81–87 passim, 142–43; for Filipinos, 70, 86, 265–66n87, 73; and Italian ancestry, 142–43, 281–82n80; and Mexican Americans, 80–87 passim
City of Quartz (Davis), 25, 40, 257n108, 259n159
class, 19, 42, 48, 57–60, 259n159; clerking 90–91, 269n7; and detective fiction, 110–11; intersection with race, 62, 87, 133, 138–39, 146–149, 180
climate. See California: climate of
Climie, Margaret, 29–30
"closed frontier" literary criticism, 34–40, 49–50, 230–31, 259n159
The Closed Frontier: Studies in American Literary Tragedy (Simonson), 35
code-switching, 141, 179–182
Cody, William (pseud. Buffalo Bill), 4
Coleman, Wanda, 245; *Mambo Hips and Make Believe*, 246–47

Collins, Richard, 64
Collisions at the Crossroads: How Place and Mobility Make Race (Carpio), 43
colonialism, 64, 68–69, 116, 153, 265n76, 295–96n31
color bar. See African Americans; admission to wartime industrial work
color line, 153, 155, 159. See also African Americans; Japanese Americans
Cooper, James Fenimore, 3
cops. See police
corporate culture, 92–95, 98, 102–6 passim, 125, 129, 131
cowboy: as frontier archetype, 21, 114, 238; as proto-detective, 274n92
Cressey, Paul, 48, 61–62, 66, 77, 267n108
Crèvecœur, J. Hector St. John de, 3, 291n82
crime fiction: conventions of, 89, 104–5, 112, 114, 120, 247; Los Angeles as archetypal site of, 32, 45. See also Cain, James M., Chandler, Raymond; detectives
criminality, 3, 96, 113–141 passim, 190, 209–220 passim. See also Chandler, Raymond; crime fiction; detectives; *Double Indemnity* (Cain); *In a Lonely Place* (Hughes)
Crockett, Davy, 3, 18
Cronon, William, 4–5, 12–15 passim
Crossfire (Dmytryk), 202
Crowd, The (Vidor), 94
Cuff, Dana, 194–96 passim

Dance Marathon (Evergood), 51
dance: commodification of, 48, 63, 77; moral panic induced by, 50,

62–63, 264n61; popularity as social activity, 47–48, 51, 55
dance marathons: as frontier metaphor, 50, 53–55; historical, 48, 50–51, 55, 77–78, 87, 261n16; spatial practice of, 51, 53–54; in *They Shoot Horses, Don't They?*, 49–51 53–55, 77–79, 261n16
dance palaces, 48, 51, 62. See also dancehalls
dancehalls: John Fante's recurrent depictions of, 56; as frontier spaces, 47–48, 53–56, 59–61, 72, 78–81, 86–87; in "Helen, Thy Beauty is to Me—" (Fante), 65–74, 77–79; historical examples of, 51, 61, 63, 80, 262n23; in *A Letter from the President* (Fante and Leonard), 84–86; physical characteristics of, 51–53, 57–58, 61–62; spatial practice of, 49, 51, 53–54, 60, 71; in *They Shoot Horses, Don't They* (McCoy), 50–53; in "To Be a Monstrous Clever Fellow,' 57–60; types of, 48. See also taxi-dancing
Davis, Floyd, 65–72 passim, 76, 144
Davis, Mike, 119, 231–32, 243–44, 297n67; "boosters and debunkers" division, 25–26, 39, 257n108, 258–59n142; *City of Quartz*, 25, 40, 257n108, 259n159; "sunshine" versus "*noir*" paradigm, 39, 42, 238
Day of the Locust, The (West), 32, 56; "The Burning of Los Angeles," 37, 230–31; as "closed frontier" text, 37, 49, 230–31; housing in, 188, 195
Death in a Bowl (Whitfield), 32
decay, urban. See blight, urban
Deleuze, Gilles, 203
democracy: and frontier ideals, 3, 17, 90, 111, 167; and World War II, 171–72, 175

detectives: corporate, 95, 105–6; extrajudicial quality of, 110, 129–30, 235; as frontiersmen 36, 109–113, 120, 131, 225, 229, 235, 274n92; historical 131, 274n92; masculinity of, 127–28, 201, 225; social role of, 110–12, 114, 124, 224–25; and space, 110, 113–116, 117–119, 125–32; racialization of, 132, 247–48. See also crime fiction; Marlowe, Philip
detective fiction. See Chandler, Raymond; crime fiction; detectives
Detroit, 187
Devil in a Blue Dress (Mosley), 146, 181
Dewey, John: *Individualism: Old and New*, 8–9
DeWitt, John, 160
diaspora. See immigrants; Filipino Americans; Italian Americans; Japanese Americans
Didion, Joan, 101, 232, 236, 239, 245; *Play It as It Lays*, 41
Dimendberg, Ed, 41, 53; "centrifugal" versus "centripetal" model, 124, 186, 190
domesticity: feared feminizing effects of, 46, 199–201, 204, 221–22, 226; in *In a Lonely Place* (Hughes), 222–23; inimicality to frontier values, 199–200, 213–15, 221, 223; significance in postwar Los Angeles fiction, 223–226; in *What Way My Journey Lies* (Fenton) 206, 212–15. See also housing, single-family
Don Sagasto's Daughter (Blades), 29
"Do Re Mi" (Guthrie), 38
Double Indemnity (Cain), 45; as anticorporate novel, 95–96, 98, 101–2, 104–5; frontier values in, 96–104, 107–8, 216; gender

Double Indemnity (Cain) *(continued)* in, 107–8; insurance in, 98–102; investigatory mechanics of, 105–7; office culture in, 89, 96–98, 104–8; publication context of 258n125
Double Indemnity (Wilder), 96–98
downtown (Los Angeles), 80, 122, 188, 190–91, 225; concentration of ethnic minorities in, 149, 197–98. *See also* Bunker Hill
"Dreamer, The" (Fante), 188, 195, 266n98, 292n121
Dreams from Bunker Hill (Fante), 34, 187, 207, 292n121
Du Bois, W. E. B.: *Black Reconstruction in America,* 183
Duff, Robert, 61
Durham, Philip, 109
Dyer, Richard, 18, 163, 174

Earhart, Amelia, 50
earthquakes, 121, 123, 232. *See also* environment, natural: disaster and risk
Edmonds, Jefferson, 169
Ellison, Ralph: *Invisible Man,* 132, 181
Ellroy, James, 248
Emerson, Ralph Waldo, 234
environment, natural: disaster and risk 37, 120–2, 167, 231–32, 236–37, 258–59n142; and the frontier 14–15, 115–16, 127–28, 213, 231, 254n41; gendering of, 18–19, 236
España-Maram, Linda, 63–64, 74, 267n101
Espiritu, Augusto, 64
Etting, Ruth, 61
Evergood, Philip: *Dance Marathon,* 51
Exiles, The (Mackenzie), 225

"Facing West from California's Shores" (Whitman), 35, 240

Fair Employment Practices Committee (FEPC), 170
Fall into Eden, The (Wyatt), 37
Fante, John, 1; attempts to write about California Filipinos, 64, 74, 81; biographical circumstances of, 188, 190, 196, 257n122, 262n35, 294n158; critical reception of, 31, 64–65, 258n123; Italian American identity as recurring theme, 57, 263n37
Fante, John, works of: *1933 Was a Bad Year,* 137–38, 278n25; *Ask the Dust,* 2, 31, 42, 56, 146, 188, 263n40, 287n30, 292n121; "The Cat," 188; "The Dreamer," 188, 195, 266n98, 292n121, *Dreams from Bunker Hill,* 34, 187, 207, 292n121; "Fish Cannery," 138, 143, 146; *Full of Life,* 30, 224, 226, 243; "Helen, Thy Beauty is to Me—," 60–82, 87, 137, 263–64n53; *A Letter from the President,* 48, 63, 81–87; *The Little Brown Brothers,* 64, 294n158; "Mary Osaka, I Love You," 188; *The Road to Los Angeles,* 45–46, 57, 134, 138–149, 154, 278n24; "To Be a Monstrous Clever Fellow," 48, 56–61, 87, 139, 218, 262nn35–36. See also *Ask the Dust* (Fante); Helen, Thy Beauty is to Me—" (Fante); *Road to Los Angeles, The* (Fante)
Far West, 21, 100, 231, 238, 240. *See also* West Coast
Farewell, My Lovely (Chandler), 111, 119, 187
farming. *See* agrarianism; Japanese Americans: and agriculture
Fast One (Cain), 32
Feminist Studio Workshop, 242
Fenton, Frank: biographical circumstances of, 188, 257n122,

287n30; critical reputation of, 31; *What Way My Journey Lies*, 46, 185, 189, 195, 200, 202, 204–215, 224–226. See also *What Way My Journey Lies* (Fenton)
Filipino Americans: as "little brown brothers," 64, 265n76; community in Los Angeles, 61, 63, 70, 80, 243, 278n24; cultural life of, 267n101, 63–64, 74; ethnic identity of, 68–70, 265n85; John Fante's representations of, 64–81; height of, 72, 266n94; intermarriage and, 73, 77, 267n108; legal status of, 68–70, 85, 265–6n87, 268n118; perceptions of, 64, 66, 70, 87; prejudice against, 77, 144–45, 266–67n99, 267n105. *See also* taxi-dancing; "Helen, Thy Beauty is to Me—" (Fante)
film industry, 9, 24–25, 30, 32, 50, 78, 87. See also *They Shoot Horses, Don't They* (McCoy)
Fine, David, 35, 37, 49, 230–31, 259n159
fish canneries: John Fante's recurrent depictions of, 137–38, 278n18, 278n21; in historical Los Angeles, 154, 278n25; as multiethnic space, 140–143; in *The Road to Los Angeles* (Fante), 140, 142–49; sensory qualities of, 148
"Fish Cannery" (Fante), 138, 143, 146
Fisher, Philip, 5, 11, 23
Fitzgerald, F. Scott, 30, 150–51
Fogelson, Robert, 42, 243
Franco, Dean: *The Border and the Line*, 42–3, 298nn80–81
Frank, Waldo, 253n31; *Our America*, 7–8
free land, 13–15, 56, 94, 205, 211, 255n62. *See also* Turner, Frederick Jackson

freedom: as American value, 92, 136, 167; and capitalism, 95, 136; and democracy, 17, 172; and frontierism, 17, 167, 183, 193, 195, 238; and race, 74, 172, 175; social, 50, 74, 175; spatial, 175, 204; through technology, 95. *See also* democracy
freeways. *See* automobility
Freud, Sigmund, 159
frontier: character, 9, 10, 17, 21, 135; closure of, 5, 6, 23, 24, 35, 46, 100, 196; debate about impact of closure, 6–11, 35, 96, 135–37; and democracy, 3, 17, 90, 111, 167; dynamics, 2, 17, 22, 53–6, 65, 86, 117, 134, 185, 241; economic, 93–95, 136; environmental hostility of, 14–15, 115–16, 127–28, 213, 231, 254n41; industrial, 8, 135, 135–37, 140, 158, 253n37; and justice, 17, 39, 109–110, 235; and labor, 9, 16; as literary-critical methodology, 2, 6, 14–24 passim, 39–40; morality of, 101–2; as myth, 2, 10–12, 27, 38–39, 92, 114, 136, 231–239 passim, 249, 298n85; "new," possibility of, 6–11, 23–27, 29; as "safety valve," 55; scientific and technological, 8, 35, 93–95, 101, 135–36, 158, 270–71n36; social, 8–9, 87, 152, 172; spatiotemporal qualities of, 5, 12–14, 23, 36; violence of, 7, 14–15, 36, 109, 235; and whiteness, 12, 18–19, 27–28, 132, 174, 242, 249; and women, 12, 18–19. *See also* frontiersman; "savage" versus "civilized" dichotomy; Turner, Frederick Jackson
"Frontier Gone at Last, The" (Norris), 6–7, 248

Frontier in American History, The (Turner), 4
frontier thesis. *See* frontier; Turner, Frederick Jackson
frontiersman: as archetype, 19, 22; ambivalence toward "civilization," 7, 16–17, 45, 116; and democratic values, 17; everyman quality of, 21–22; as heroic figure, 8, 19, 21, 87, 109; individualism of, 16–17, 20; intellectual capacities of, 8; ruggedness of, 20–21, 109, 201, 209; self-erasing quality of, 35–45; and space, 13, 112–13; transferability of traits, 21–22; types of, 20–21; vulnerability of, 113–14, 201; whiteness of, 18, 27. *See also* frontier; labor: frontiersmanship as; Turner, Frederick Jackson
Full of Life (Fante), 30, 224, 226, 243
Fusco, Coco, 160, 163

gangsters, 114, 119
Gardner, Ella, 62
Gebhard, David, 226
generation gap (1960s), 233, 236
Ghosh, Amitav, 159
Giordano, Ralph, 55, 61
Glendale, 103
Goggans, Jan, 49
"Golondrina, La," (Serradell) 84–85
Goodbye Coast, The (Ide), 248
Goodyear Tire Company, 196, 200
Gothic, 114–15, 275n107
Graeber, David, 94
Grandin, Greg, 248–49
Grapes of Wrath, The (Steinbeck), 38–39
Great Depression, 8–9, 29, 49, 51, 54, 136–37, 259
Great Frontier, The (Webb), 11, 252n9
Grund, Francis, 4

Guattari, Félix, 203
Guglielmo, Thomas, 140–41
Guthrie, Woody: "Do Re Mi," 38

Hamilton, Hamish, 2
hardboiled fiction. *See* crime fiction
Hare, William, 50
Harrington, Alan: *Life in the Crystal Palace*, 92
Hawaii, 234–35, 295–96n31
"Helen, Thy Beauty is to Me—" (Fante), 60–82; publication context of, 60, 65; racialization of Filipinos in, 66, 68–70; spatiality in, 65, 71–72; taxi-dancing in, 65–74, 77–79; whiteness in, 73, 75–76
High Window, The (Chandler), 117–19, 275n120
Himes, Chester, 33; biographical circumstances of, 171–72; critical responses to, 176, 178, 179; *If He Hollers Let Him Go*, 32, 39, 45–46, 135, 163–64, 171–84; political thought of, 164, 172, 175. *See also If He Hollers Let Him Go* (Himes)
Hirahara, Naomi, 247
Hollywood (locality), 30, 187, 188
Hollywood (metonym). *See* film industry
Hollywood novel, 29, 32, 258n
Home of the Brave (Robson), 202
homosexuality, 111, 113, 293n134. *See also* masculinity
Hong, Lawrence, 61
hooks, bell, 181
Hoover, Herbert, 8, 62, 135–37, 158
horizontal city. *See* Dimendberg, Ed: "centrifugal" versus "centripetal" model; Los Angeles: as decentralized city; skyscrapers
Horkheimer, Max 193–94
Horsley, Lee, 109

Index | 333

hotels, residential, 189, 190. 195, 197, 216, 287n30, 288n50, 290n68. *See also* housing, multi-family
housing, multi-family, 185-6; fictional examples of, 188-91; as frontier, 191-197, 199-201, 208-211, 217-18, 220-21; as gendered space, 199-201, 209-12, 218, 221; in historical Los Angeles, 187-88, 196, 197-98, 208-9; immigrants and racial minorities in, 189, 198-9; in *In a Lonely Place* (Hughes), 216-221; social critique of, 193, 194, 197; spatial contestation within, 194-95, 200, 217-18; structural repetition in, 191-94; subtypes of, 188-90; in *What Way My Journey Lies* (Fenton), 189, 200, 195, 208-12, 287n30. *See also* apartments; apartment courts; boarding houses; hotels, residential; rooming houses
housing, single-family: fictional examples of, 187-188; and frontier values, 193-94, 195-97, 213, 215, 221-23; as gendered space, 186, 200, 206-7, 213, 215, 221-24; in historical Los Angeles, 186-87, 190, 193-94, 288-89n51; and social cohesion, 196, 220. *See also* domesticity
Houston, James. 35, 37, 259n150
Hughes, Dorothy B.: *In a Lonely Place*, 46, 185, 190, 202, 204-5, 215-227, 290n77. See also *In a Lonely Place* (Hughes)
Huxley, Aldous 39; *After Many a Summer*, 188

Ide, Joe, 245-6; *The Goodbye Coast*, 248
If He Hollers Let Him Go (Himes), 32, 45-46; Atlas Shipyard, 135, 171-183; bodily strength in, 173-75, 182; frontier spatiality in, 171-73, 183; gender relations in, 181-82; interracial solidarities in, 163-64; jargon in, 178-79; language use in, 177-80; racial geographies in, 39, 171-77, 179, 182; social mobility in, 172, 180-81, 183-84; wartime racial tension in, 163-64, 175-76
immigrants: Chinese, 152; Filipino, 61, 63, 265-66n87, 268n118; Italian, 138; Japanese, 152-155; living circumstances of, 80, 189, 194; Mexican, 81, 83-84; prejudice against, 63, 189; social position of, 79, 85, 87, 137; transformation of contemporary Los Angeles by, 243; and whiteness, 63, 140, 142, 168. *See also* Chinese Americans; Filipino Americans; Italian Americans; Japanese Americans; Immigration Act (1924), 155
In a Lonely Place (Hughes), 190, 200, 290n77; apartment court spatiality in 216-221; crisis of masculinity in 204-5, 225-26; domesticity in, 222-23; frontier psychology in, 215, 221, 223; gendering of space in, 216-19, 222-23; queer reading of, 293n134; surveillance in, 216, 218, 219; as "veterans problem" novel, 46. 185, 202; violence against women in, 204-5, 215, 221
Indian wars. *See* Native Americans
indigenous peoples. *See* Native Americans
individualism. *See* frontiersman: individualism of
Individualism: Old and New (Dewey), 8-9
industry: as anti-frontierist force, 9; "new frontier" potential of, 8,

industry *(continued)*
  135–37; and war work, 170–72, 180, 183. *See also* fish canneries; *If He Hollers Let Him Go* (Himes); "Life Among the Oil Fields: A Memoir" (Yamamoto); Los Angeles: industrialization of; oil; *Road to Los Angeles, The* (Fante)
insurance, 96–102, 108–9, 234–35. See also *Double Indemnity* (Cain)
Invasion of the Body Snatchers (Siegel), 226
Invisible Man (Ellison), 132, 181
Irish Americans, 173, 284n160
Irwin, John, 96, 102
Italian Americans, 28, 45; Americanness of, 141–42, 143, 146; community in Los Angeles, 149; ethnic identity of, 28, 57, 140–42, 263n37; internment in World War II, 280–1n80; and whiteness, 57, 140–1, 143, 146, 154. *See also* Fante, John; *Road to Los Angeles, The* (Fante)

Jackson, Andrew, 15, 18, 22
Jackson, Helen Hunt: *Ramona*, 29
Jackson, Kenneth T., 185
James Oviatt Building, 122–24
Jameson, Fredric, 110, 112, 114, 119, 124
Japanese Americans: and agriculture, 149, 153, 154, 155, 163; assimilative efforts of, 153, 154, 163; community in Los Angeles, 28, 149, 154, 160, 163, 246; economic position of, 153, 154, 155, 162, 169; frontiersmanship of, 28, 45–46, 152–157 passim, 160, 169; incarceration of, 151, 160–61, 165, 166; *Issei* generation, 153; migration to California, 152–53; *Nisei* generation, 153–54, 165; prejudice against, 150–155, 160–64, 169, 280n63; and racial hierarchy, 153–157, 162–64, 165–66; relationship with African Americans, 153, 163–65, 166, 245–46, 169; stereotypes of, 153, 157–58, 169
Jews: 62, 164, 197, 239
Jurgen: A Comedy of Justice (Cabell), 262n36
justice system, 83–84, 85

Kennedy, John F.: "New Frontier" speech, 35
Keynes, John Maynard, 95
Kim, Claire Jean, 153, 161, 162, 165
"King in Yellow, The" (Chandler), 190–91
Kinney, Abbot, 27
Kirk, Grayson, 86, 87, 265–66n87
Klein, Kerwin Lee, 4, 13, 15, 19, 21, 256n98
Klein, Marcus, 131, 274n92
Klein, Norman, 248–49
Knight, Eric: *You Play the Black and the Red Comes Up*, 32
Kurashige, Scott, 163, 164, 170

labor: domestic; 211, 213–214, 292n124 (*see also* domesticity); frontiersmanship as, 46, 48, 55, 57, 81–86, 133–34, 149, 183–84; migratory, 63, 70, 81, 137; physical; 59, 80, 90–91, 139, 142; as Turnerian virtue, 9, 16
Lady in the Lake, The (Chandler), 113, 122, 124–131, 188
Las Aventuras de Don Chipote (Venegas), 29, 33
Las Sergas de Esplandián (Montalvo), 38
Laslett, John, 195, 297n64

Latinx literature, 33, 245, 248, 298n80
Lears, T. J. Jackson, 91, 253n27
Leatherstocking tales (Cooper), 3–4
Lee, A. Robert, 179
Lefebvre, Henri, 51, 246: production of space, 48, 54, 71, 275n107; triadic model of space, 48–49, 54, 97, 118, 173, 261n5
Left-Handed Virgin, The (Fante), see *1933 Was a Bad Year*
Lehan, Richard, 109
LeMenager, Stephanie, 157
Leonard, Jack: *A Letter from the President*, 47–48, 63, 81–87
Letter from the President, A (Fante and Leonard), 47–48, 63, 81–87. See also Fante, John
Lewis, Sinclair: *Babbitt*, 94
Liberator, 169
"Life Among the Oil Fields: A Memoir" (Yamamoto), 45; blackness in, 162–63, 165, 166; foreshadowing of incarceration in, 151–52, 161, 166; formal ambiguity of, 150, 168; frontier resonances in, 155–58, 166, 168–69; uncanniness in, 159, 161, 162; petrolandscape in, 149, 155–159; racial position of Japanese community in, 155–157, 166, 169; temporality of 29, 34, 135; whiteness in, 159, 162, 167–68. See also Japanese Americans
Life Illustrated, 90
Life in the Crystal Palace (Harrington), 92
Limerick, Patricia Nelson, 242, 254n53. See also New Western History
Lincoln, Abraham, 18, 21–22
Lindbergh, Charles, 50
linguistic hybridity, 177–180
Little Brown Brothers, The (Fante), 64, 294n158

Little Tokyo, 163, 164, 169, 170, 198
lodging houses. See boarding houses
Lonely Crowd, The (Riesman, Denney, and Glazer), 92
Long Beach, 34, 48, 167
Long Goodbye, The (Chandler), 95, 113, 117–18, 202, 224 290n78
López-Calvo, Ignacio 33, 246, 298n80
Los Angeles: apocalyptic imagination of, 36, 230–32, 236; boundaries of, 34; cultural superficiality of 30, 32, 188, 193–94; as decentralized city, 41–42, 124, 186–87, 225–27 (*see also* suburbanization); demographic change in, 24, 27–28, 152–154, 169–70, 242–4, 256n105, 268n118; as desert, 26, 121, 258–59n142; ethnic and racial diversity of, 27–28, 33, 46, 63, 242–44 (*see also* African Americans; Chinese Americans; Filipino Americans; Italian Americans; Japanese Americans; Mexican Americans); exceptionality of, 25, 26–27, 44; frontier symbolism of, 2, 24, 34–36, 39, 44, 49, 238; as frontier town, 24, 28, 152, 209, 292n118; growth of, 24–27, 89, 135, 243; industrialization of, 134–135, 156–57, 161, 167, 170, 277n7; literary-critical approaches to, 29–30, 34–41 passim, 42–43, 49–50, 230–31, 245–46; as Pacific Rim city, 79–80, 268n113; perpetual newness in, 25, 26–27, 53; racial violence in, 28, 152, 171, 175, 232, 242–43; self-mythologizing of, 40–41, 259n159; whiteness of, 27–28, 226, 243, 247–48
Los Angeles (Mayo), 25–26, 27–28, 37–38 120–21
Los Angeles: City of Dreams (Carr), 25–27, 42, 238n13

Los Angeles: The Development, Life, and Structure of the City of Two Million in Southern California (Wagner), 25, 26–27, 28, 41, 53, 187

Los Angeles: A Guide to the City and Its Environs (Works Progress Administration) 25-6

Los Angeles Times, 27, 124, 161, 270–271n36

Los Angeles Uprising, 262

Lothrop, Gloria, 140–41

Lowe, Lisa, 152, 165, 168

Lundquist, James, 176, 178

Lurie, Alison: *The Nowhere City*, 92, 231–32, 237–239, 245

Luther, Mark Lee: *The Boosters*, 29, 258n123

Macdonald, Ross, 109, 248; *The Blue Hammer*, 229; *The Moving Target*; 229; *The Underground Man*; 229–37, 243, 249–50

Mackenzie, Kent: *The Exiles*, 225

Maclay, Charles, 37

Mad Men, 239–241

Mambo Hips and Make Believe (Coleman), 246-7

Man in the Gray Flannel Suit, The (Wilson), 92

manifest destiny, 38, 116

Marcuse, Herbert, 95

Marlowe, Philip: frontiersmanlike social role of, 109–117; in literary criticism, 109; living circumstances of, 189, 201, 224–25; masculinity of, 128–29, 201, 293n134; office of, 119–122, 275n120; racism of, 154, 157–58, 247; spatial analysis of, 117–119, 123–132, 191, 287n35; as veteran, 290n78. *See also* Chandler, Raymond; crime fiction; detectives

Martin, Carol, 50, 51

Marx, Leo, 137

"Mary Osaka, I Love You" (Fante), 188

masculinity: crisis of, 185, 208–11, 213–215, 222–226, 238; hetero-, 19, 20, 204, 208–10, 212; as individualism, 19, 201, 204–225 passim, 234–235, 249; and multi-family housing, 199–201, 210–12, 221; and office work, 90–92; physical expression of, 90, 139–40, 174, 208–10; racialized, 174, 182, 238–39; violent assertion of, 204–5, 208–9, 215, 221; and whiteness, 7, 19–20, 33, 174, 227, 241–248 passim. *See also* homosexuality; patriarchy

Mason, Gregory, 61

Mayo, Morrow: *Los Angeles*, 25–26, 27–28, 37–38, 120–21

McCann, Sean, 95, 109, 124, 195

McClung, William, 36

McCoy, Horace: *They Shoot Horses, Don't They*, 45, 49–55, 78–79, 86

McWilliams, Carey, 287n30; on the frontier, 10–11; and race, 64, 151, 280n63; on Southern California, 31, 42, 258n123; *Southern California: An Island on the Land*, 26

Melling, Philip, 49

Melville, Herman: "Bartleby, The Scrivener," 89–90

Men, The (Zinnemann), 202

Mencken, H. L., 138, 141

Merwin, Henry Childs, 111, 116, 140; "On Being Civilized Too Much," 91–92

Mexican Americans, 28, 164, 168; community in Los Angeles, 33, 63, 149 190, 242, 248, 297n64; contributions to literature of Los

Angeles, 33, 245, 248, 298n80; in John Fante's fiction, 81–87 passim, 140–147 passim, 197, 263n40, 266n98, 268n118; prejudice against, 28, 82, 140, 154, 171, 242, 248
Mexico, 83–84, 85, 113
migrant labor. *See* labor: migratory
migration: internal, 36, 37–38 79, 135, 196; international (*see* immigrants)
Mildred Pierce (Cain), 103
Military Area No. 1, 160
Mills, C. Wright: *White Collar*, 92
Modell, John, 152, 157, 162
modernity, 9, 92 102–6, passim, 116–124 passim, 136, 152, 230, 270–71n36
Molina, Natalia, 153, 164
Mosley, Walter, 245, 247; *Devil in a Blue Dress* 146, 181
Moving Target, The, (Macdonald), 229
multiethnicity, 7, 198, 243, 245, 256n105. *See also* Los Angeles: ethnic and racial diversity of
Mumford, Lewis, 217, 293n141
Murphet, Julian, 40, 122, 244

Nash, Roderick, 91, 253n27
Nash Smith, Henry, 12
Native Americans: and the frontier, 14–15, 18, 19, 114, 140, 235; in Los Angeles, 151, 225
Native Sons of the Golden West, 27
natural disaster. *See* environment, natural: disaster and risk
"New Frontier" speech (Kennedy), 35
New Western History, 12, 254n53, 255n77, 256n98
New York City, 61, 90, 124, 187, 239, 243
New York Star, 91
Nietzsche, Friedrich, 57

noir: fiction, 32, 159n259; film, 32, 190. *See also* Cain, James M.; Chandler, Raymond; crime fiction; Davis, Mike: "sunshine" versus "*noir*" paradigm
Norris, Frank, 142; "The Frontier Gone at Last," 6–7, 248
Novarro, Ramon, 66
Nowhere City, The (Lurie), 92, 231–32, 237–39, 245
Nye, Russel, 47–48

offices: anti-frontierism of, 90–93, 98, 106–8, 119, 122, 125–32; cultural critique of, 90–93; in *Double Indemnity* (Cain) and *Double Indemnity* (Wilder), 96–98, 104–8; enthusiasm for, 93–95; in *The High Window* (Chandler), 117–119; in *The Lady in the Lake* (Chandler), 125–32; rise and development of, 89, 93–95; spatial characteristics of, 93, 97–8, 116–19, 122, 125–129; surveillance culture in, 104–6, 129; as systems, 94, 105–6
oil: discovery in Los Angeles, 135, 277n7, 157; "Encounter," 159; extractive apparatus of, 150, 156–59; frontier qualities of, 158, 167; impact on landscape, 156–57, 161–62; industry 134, 155, 161, 166; as racial metaphor, 151, 158–160, 161–163, 165–66, 169. *See also* "Life Among the Oil Fields: A Memoir" (Yamamoto)
Oil! (Sinclair), 166–69
oilfield. *See* oil
"On Being Civilized Too Much" (Merwin), 91–92
organization culture, 92, 95, 98, 107, 125. *See also* offices
Organization Man, The (Whyte), 92

organization man. *See* organization culture; offices
Organizational Revolution, The (Boulding), 92
Orr, Stanley, 112, 114, 116
Our America (Frank), 7–8
overcivilization, 7, 16, 45, 91, 111, 253n27. *See also* antimodernism; Merwin, Henry Childs
Oviatt, James, 122–25

Pacific: coast (*see* West Coast); military theater, 233; Ocean, 1, 49, 50, 121, 240; as region, 80, 136, 268n113, 295–96n31, 233. *See also* Los Angeles: as Pacific Rim city
"Paradise" (Cain), 102–3
Parreñas, Rhacel Salazar, 77, 266–67n99
patriarchy, 213–15, 222, 224, 238. *See also* masculinity
Pavey, Alex, 43
Paxson, Frederick, 4, 252n10
Pearl Harbor, bombing of, 163, 164, 175
petrofiction (genre classifier), 159
petrolandscape. *See* oil: impact on landscape
petromodernity, 162. *See also* oil; modernity
Pettegrew, John, 4, 5, 14–15
piers, 49, 51, 262n23
pioneer. *See* frontier; frontiersman
Pisk, George, 230
Play It as It Lays (Didion), 41
Playback (Chandler), 224
police, 63, 84–85, 104, 113, 222, 242
"Poodle Springs Story, The" (Chandler), 224
Porter, Dennis, 125
Porter, Joseph, 36, 38

Postman Always Rings Twice, The (Cain), 102, 103, 143
privacy, 61, 195, 197, 216–219, 244
private detective. *See* detective
private eye. *See* detective
prohibition, 50
property covenants, 27, 163–64, 169–70, 198. *See also* African Americans
Protestant Ethic and the Spirit of Capitalism, The (Weber), 9, 26, 239, 254n41, 270n28
Puritanism, 9, 18, 26
Putnam's Monthly, 91
Pynchon, Thomas, 248

race: hierarchies of, 74, 142–46, 153–54, 163, 165; as industrial product, 134, 137, 169; intersection with class, 62, 87, 133, 138–39, 146–149, 180; mutability of, 66–71, 76, 144–45, 146; and "purity" 27, 143; "triangulation," of 153, 156, 161–66 passim. *See also* African Americans; Filipino Americans; Italian Americans; Japanese Americans; Mexican Americans; whiteness
racial capitalism. *See* capitalism: and race
racism: towards African Americans, 146, 169, 170–72, 175, 180–82; towards Filipino Americans, 77, 144–45, 266–67n99, 267n105; of frontier ideology 12, 18–19, 242, 249; internalized, 77, 141, 146–46, 263n40; towards Italian Americans; 140–41, 142, 145–6; towards Japanese Americans 150–155, 160–64, 169, 280n63; towards Mexican Americans, 28, 82, 140, 154, 171, 242, 248. *See also* race; whiteness

railroads, 10, 37, 152, 100–101, 273n63
Ramona (Jackson), 29
Redondo Beach, 156
"Red Wind" (Chandler), 121, 230
Revolutionary Road (Yates), 92
Revoyr, Nina: *Southland*, 245, 248
Ride the Pink Horse (Montgomery), 202
Ridge, Martin: *Westward Expansion*, 16, 18, 255n77
Riesman, David, Reuel Denney, and Nathan Glazer: *The Lonely Crowd* 92
risk, 98–99, 101, 103–8 passim. See also *Double Indemnity* (Cain)
Road to Los Angeles, The (Fante): American identity in, 138, 140, 141–42; cannery labor in, 140, 142–49; class in, 138–39, 147, 149; frontiersmanship in, 45–46, 134, 143–44, 149; geography of, 138, 149, 278n24; production and publication context of, 57, 138; race in, 138, 142–149, 154, 278n24
Rodgers, Jimmie, 9–10
Roediger, David 141, 142, 147, 177, 183, 284n160
rooming houses 188–89, 194–200 passim, 216, 225. See also housing, multi-family
Roosevelt, Franklin, 8, 135–37, 171, 184; Executive Order 8802, 170; Executive Order 9066, 160–61
Roosevelt, Theodore, 14, 18, 189, 267–68n112; *The Winning of the West*, 4, 251n5
Rose, Stanley, 30, 257n122
Roseland (Mack), 61
Ryan, Don: *Angel's Flight*, 29

San Fernando Valley, 37, 186, 230

San Francisco, 61, 104, 135
San Pedro, 138, 206, 262n35
Sanchez, George, 33
Santa Ana winds, 37, 121, 230, 231
Santa Barbara, 230
Santa Monica, 34, 48, 51, 53, 222, 262n33
Saroyan, William, 64, 154, 257n122, 265n76
Saturday Evening Post, 60, 265n77
"savage" versus "civilized" dichotomy: application as literary method; 16, 22; Turnerian theorization of, 12–13, 91; in crime fiction, 45, 107–116 passim, 131, 215–16; and social marginality, 56, 59–60, 86–87, 141; inversion of, 28, 56, 86–87, 246; spatialization of, 59–60, 115, 118–119, 131, 143, 215–16; and race, 86, 164, 165, 246
Saval, Nikil, 93
Scaggs, John, 37, 39, 109
Schelling, Friedrich, 159
Schlesinger, Arthur, Jr., 92, 135–36
scientific management, 93–95
Sedgwick, Eve Kosofsky, 115, 275n107
Seiberling, Frank, 200
Seventeen Syllables and Other Stories (Yamamoto), 150
Sevilla, Narciso Serradell: "La Golondrina," 84–85
Shinozuka, Jeannie, 163
shipyards. See *If He Hollers Let Him Go* (Himes); industry: and war work
Sides, Josh, 170
Siegfried, André, 90
Signal Hill, 167
Silver Lake, 242
Simonson, Harold, 22; *The Closed Frontier: Studies in American Literary Tragedy*, 35

Sinclair, Upton: *Oil!*, 166–69
Sklar, Robert, 9
skyscrapers, 123–24, 270–1n36
Sleepy Lagoon murder trial, 242, 248, 297n62
Slotkin, Richard, 12–16 passim, 21, 35, 254n52
So, Richard Jean, 246
Soja, Ed, 187
Sorkin, Michael, 40
South Central, 232, 246
Southern California: An Island on the Land (McWilliams), 26
Southland (Revoyr), 245, 248
space, production of. See Lefebvre, Henri
space planning, 93, 94, 105. See also scientific management
speculation, 37, 120, 167. See also boosters
sprawl, urban. See Los Angeles: as decentralized city
Stanfield, Peter, 9
Stanwyck, Barbara, 61
Starr, Kevin, 161, 257n122, 288n51
Steinbeck, John: *The Grapes of Wrath*, 38–39
Steiner, Jesse, 62
Steiner, Michael, 13
Stevenson, Adlai, 92
suburbanization, 186–87, 193–195, 224, 226, 243, 246
surveillance: corporate, 95–98 passim, 104–6; domestic, 195, 216–219
Suzuki, Masao, 163
Swanson, Gloria, 72

taxi-dancehalls. See dancehalls; taxi-dancing
taxi-dancers. See taxi-dancing
taxi-dancing: development of, 61; role in Filipino community, 63–64, 66, 74, 77, 266–67n99; in "Helen, Thy Beauty is to Me—" (Fante), 65–74, 77–79; illusory quality of, 75–77, 81; in *A Letter from the President* (Fante and Leonard), 84–86; public fascination with, 61; and racist anxieties, 63, 266–67n99, 268n118; sociospatial dynamics of, 71–72; "undesirable" clientele 268n118; 61–62; and vice, 62–63. See also dancehalls
Taylor, Frederick Winslow, 93–95, 102
Taylorism. See Taylor, Frederick Winslow
Ten Cents a Dance (miscellaneous artworks), 61
Their Dogs Came with Them (Viramontes), 248, 298n80
They Shoot Horses, Don't They? (McCoy), 45, 49–55, 78–79, 86
Thompson, Graham, 92, 105, 126, 129
Thoreau, Henry David, 234
Thurman, Wallace: *The Blacker the Berry*, 29
Tobar, Héctor, 44, 245, 260n179
"To Be a Monstrous Clever Fellow" (Fante), 48, 56–61, 87, 139, 218, 262nn35–36
Todorov, Tzvetan, 112, 114
traffic, 41, 176, 177, 207. See also automobility
trains. See railroads
Tribune, 164–65
Tropic of Orange (Yamashita), 41, 231–32, 245
Truman, Harry, 81
Trump, Donald, 249
Turner, Frederick Jackson: American Historical Association address (1893), 4; *The Frontier in American History*, 4; academic challenges to, 12, 242, 252n11, 254n52; frontier

thesis, 3–5, 8–12, 22, 46, 251; impact and reputation of, 4–6, 10, 11–12, 251n5; problematic ideas of, 12, 18–19. *See also* frontier; frontiersman
Tydings-McDuffie Act. *See* Filipino Americans: legal status of

uncanny, 159, 161–62, 166
Underground Man, The (Macdonald), 229–37, 243, 249–50
urbanization, 24, 91, 111. *See also* Los Angeles: growth of

Valdes, Luis: *Zoot Suit*, 248
Valentino, Rudolph, 66
Vanity Fair (magazine), 91
Vedder, Clyde, 62, 268n118
Venegas, Daniel: *Las Aventuras de Don Chipote*, 29, 33
Venice (California), 27, 262n23
Verdicchio, Pasquale, 64
Vermont Watchman and State Journal, 91
veterans: in Raymond Chandler's fiction, 202, 205, 290n278; frontiersmanlike qualities of, 203–5, 207, 210–11, 215; in *In a Lonely Place* (Hughes), 204–5, 215–223; in postwar popular culture, 202; psychological trauma of, 204–5, 207, 213, 225; as social problem, 202–3, 205; as "war machines," 203; in *What Way My Journey Lies* (Fenton), 204–5, 206–215
Vidal, Gore, 232, 295n15
Vidor, King: *The Crowd*, 94
violence: and criminality, 96, 102, 108, 115, 131; as frontier quality, 7, 14–15, 36, 109, 235; and masculinity, 204–5, 208–9, 213, 226; racial, 28, 152, 162, 171–177 passim, 183; as spatial gesture, 14, 173; against women, 182, 204–5, 215
Viramontes, Helena María, 245; *Their Dogs Came with Them*, 248, 298n80
von Breton, Harriette, 226

Wagner, Anton: *Los Angeles: The Development, Life, and Structure of the City of Two Million in Southern California*, 25, 26–27, 28, 41, 53, 187
Waldinger, Roger, 243
Wall Street Crash, 94. *See also* Great Depression
Waller, Willard, 202–3
Watts, 242; Rebellion, 232, 245; Writers' Workshop, 245
weather. *See* California: climate of
Webb, Walter Prescott, 4–10 passim, 16, 21, 96; *The Great Frontier*, 11, 252n9
Weber, Max: *The Protestant Ethic and the Spirit of Capitalism*, 9, 26, 239, 254n41, 270n28
Weisenburger, Steven, 230
West Coast, 134–136, 151, 153, 160, 206, 280–81n80. *See also* Far West
West, Nathanael: *The Day of the Locust*, 32, 37, 49, 56, 188, 195, 230–31. *See also* Day of the Locust, The (West)
Western (genre), 9, 10, 274n92, 298n85
westward expansion, 2–3, 14, 23, 36, 116, 167. *See also* free land; frontier; frontiersman
Westward Expansion (Billington and Ridge), 16, 18, 255n77
What Way My Journey Lies (Fenton): crisis of masculinity in, 204–5, 208–10, 213–14, 224–26;

What Way My Journey Lies (Fenton) (continued)
  domesticity in, 206, 212–15;
  frontier simulacra in, 213, 214;
  homosocial dynamics in, 207,
  208–10, 214; multi-family housing
  in, 189, 200, 195, 208–12, 287n30;
  patriarchal values in, 213, 215;
  queer reading of, 293n134; as
  "veterans problem" novel, 46, 185,
  202, 204–211, 213
White Collar (Mills), 92
White, Richard, 242, 254n53
white flight, 224, 243–4
white masculinity. *See* whiteness: and masculinity
whiteness: and American identity,
  18, 57, 140–43, 147–48, 160; as
  "everywhere and nowhere," 160,
  162, 165; and the frontier 12,
  18–19, 27–28, 132, 174, 242, 249;
  of Los Angeles, 27–28, 226, 243,
  247–48; and masculinity 7, 19–20,
  33, 174, 227, 241–248 passim. *See also* race; racism
Whitfield, Raoul: *Death in a Bowl*, 32
Whitman, Walt, 21, 90–91, 234;
  "Facing West from California's Shores," 35, 240
Whyte, William, H., 9; *The Organization Man*, 92
Wild West, 4, 94
Wilder, Billy: *Double Indemnity*, 96, 98
wilderness. *See* frontier; "savage" versus "civilized" dichotomy
wildfires, 121, 230–232, 236–37. *See also* environment, natural: disaster and risk
Williams, Hank, 10
Wilmington, 48, 80
Wilson, Edmund: *Boys in the Back Room*, 30
Wilson, Sloan, 92: *The Man in the Gray Flannel Suit*, 92
Winning of the West, The (Roosevelt), 4, 251n5
Woman's Building, 242
women: as frontier "conquests," 19,
  57–59, 219–20, 242; in frontier
  history, 12, 18–19; frontier
  masculinity threatened by, 19,
  107–08, 201, 207, 212–18, 222–23,
  242; frontier values expressed
  by, 107–08, 221, 236–238, 242;
  and whiteness, 19, 63, 63–74, 80,
  181–82; in the workplace, 95,
  103, 127–28, 181–82; writers of
  contemporary Los Angeles, 245
work, blue-collar, 44, 133, 147,
  259n159. *See also* labor; working class
work, white-collar. *See* class; offices
working class, 60, 62, 87, 138, 140,
  147, 180. *See also* class; labor; work, blue-collar
Works Progress Administration: *Los Angeles: A Guide to the City and Its Environs*, 25–6
World War II, 151; in historical Los
  Angeles, 135, 160–61, 226, 169–71;
  veterans of, 46, 185, 202–4, 208–10,
  223, 234–35. *See also* veterans
World's Columbian Exposition (1893), 4
World's Fair (1933), 62
Wyatt, David, 170, 174, 179; *The Fall into Eden*, 36–39

Yamamoto, Hisaye, biographical
  circumstances of, 150, 165; "Life
  Among the Oil Fields: A Memoir,"
  29, 34, 45, 149–50, 155–59,
  161–69; *Seventeen Syllables and*

Other Stories, 150. *See also* "Life Among the Oil Fields: A Memoir" (Yamamoto)
Yamashita, Karen Tei: *Tropic of Orange*, 41, 231–32, 245
Yates, Richard: *Revolutionary Road*, 92

You Play the Black and the Red Comes Up (Knight), 32

Zoot Suit (Valdes), 248
Zoot Suit Riots, 171, 173, 242, 243, 248, 297n62

www.ingramcontent.com/pod-product-compliance
Lightning Source LLC
Chambersburg PA
CBHW031704230426
43668CB00006B/103